EUROPEAN UNION INTERNAL MARKET LAW

This is the market's most student-friendly textbook on EU internal market law, covering everything students need to know about the legal and regulatory framework of the internal market and eliminating the need for a full EU law text. Concise and focused, chapters explore the underlying socio-economic and historical contexts of EU law, and offer a thorough examination of the law's technical aspects, ensuring that students gain a rich understanding of the way that legal rules and structures have developed from key political and social debates. Key concepts are illustrated by excerpts, summaries and discussions of classic and modern cases. Numerous features include text boxes, illustrative cases, legal interpretations, tables, and suggestions for further reading, which support students with little background knowledge of the subject, leading them to total mastery of the material.

Friedl Weiss is Professor at the Department of European, International Law and Comparative Law, University of Vienna.

Clemens Kaupa is Assistant Professor at the Department of Transnational Legal Studies, VU University Amsterdam.

D0166117

European Union Internal Market Law

Friedl Weiss and **Clemens Kaupa**

CAMBRIDGE
UNIVERSITY PRESS

University Printing House, Cambridge CB2 8BS, United Kingdom

Cambridge University Press is part of the University of Cambridge.

It furthers the University's mission by disseminating knowledge in the pursuit of education, learning and research at the highest international levels of excellence.

www.cambridge.org
Information on this title: www.cambridge.org/9781107636002

© Friedl Weiss and Clemens Kaupa 2014

First published 2014

Printed in the United Kingdom by Clays, St Ives plc.

A catalogue record for this publication is available from the British Library

ISBN 978-1-107-03535-5 Hardback
ISBN 978-1-107-63600-2 Paperback

Contents

Tables

Table of cases

3 Glocken, Case 407/85, [1988] ECR 4233 60

A and B see Skatteverket v. A and B

A-Punkt Schmuckhandel, Case C-441/04, [2006]
ECR I-2093 63–64

Abatay (Eran) and Others (C-317/01) and Nadi Sahin
(C-369/01) v. Bundesanstalt für Arbeit, Joined Cases,
[2003] ECR I-12301 27, 28–29, 199

Acoset SpA v. Conferenza Sindaci e Presidenza Prov Reg
ATO Idrico Ragusa and Others, Case C-196/08,
[2009] ECR I-9913 285–286

Air Liquide Industries, Joined Cases C-393/04 and
C-41/05, [2006] ECR I-5293 86–87

Åklagaren v. Percy Mickelsson and Joakim Roos,
Case C-142/05, [2009] ECR I-4273 66, 74

Aladzhov (Petar) v. Zamestnik director na Stolichna
direktsia na vatreshnite raboti kam Ministerstvo na
vatreshnite raboti, Case C-434/10, [2011]
ECR I-11659 118, 123

Alarape (Olaitan Ajoke) and Olukayode Azeez Tijani
v. Secretary of State for the Home Department,
Case C-529/11, [2013] ECR I-00000 171

Albore (Alfredo), Case C-423/98, [2000] ECR I-5965
296–297, 298

Alfa Vita, Joined Cases C-158/04 and C-159/04, [2006]
ECR I-8135 66, 74–75

Alliance for Natural Health, Joined Cases C-154/04 and
C-155/04, [2005] ECR I-6451 44

Allué, Joined Cases C-259/91, C-331/91 and C-332/91,
[1993] ECR I-4309 175–176

Almelo, Case C-393/92, [1994] ECR I-1477 41–42

Alpine Investments BV v. Minister Van Financiën, Case
C-384/93, [1995] ECR I-1141 21, 251

Altmark Trans GmbH and Regierungspräsidium
Magdeburg v. Nahverkehrsgesellschaft Altmark
GmbH, Case C-280/00, [2003] ECR I-7747 281,
283–284

Amministrazione delle Finanze dello Stato v.
Simmenthal SpA, Case 106/77, [1978] ECR 629 19–20

ANAV see Associazione Nazionale Autotrasporto
Viaggiatori (ANAV) v. Comune di Bari and AMTAB
Servizio SpA

André Marchandise, Case C-332/89, [1991] ECR I-1027
60–61

Angonese (Roman) v. Cassa di Risparmio di Bolzano
SpA, Case C-281/98, [2000] ECR I-4139 31, 158–159,
160–161

Anker, Case C-47/02, [2003] ECR I-10447 166–167

Anton Las see Las (Anton) v. PSA Antwerp NV

Antonissen, Case C-292/89, [1991] ECR I-745 153–154,
171

Apothekerkammer des Saarlandes (DocMorris II),
Case C-171/07, [2009] ECR I-4171 74–75

Apple and Pear Development Council, Case 222/82,
[1983] ECR 4083 46–47

Aragonesa de Publicidad Exterior, Joined Cases C-1/90
and C-176/90, [1991] ECR I-4151 43–44

Arblade see Criminal proceedings against Jean-Claude
Arblade

ASM Brescia SpA v. Comune di Rodengo Saiano,
Case C-347/06, [2008] ECR I-5641 201

Association of Pharmaceutical Importers see R v. Royal
Pharmaceutical Society of Great Britain

Associazione Nazionale Autotrasporto Viaggiatori
(ANAV) v. Comune di Bari and AMTAB Servizio SpA,
Case C-410/04, [2006] ECR I-3303 285–286

Attanasio Group Srl v. Comune di Carbognano,
Case C-384/08, [2010] ECR I-2055 208, 211

Ayuntamiento de Ceuta, Case C-45/94, [1995]
ECR I-4385 86–87, 170–171

Bachmann, Case C-204/90, [1992] ECR I-00249 188,
270–271, 312

Bâtiments et Ponts Construction SA and WISAG
Produktionsservice GmbH v. Berlaymont 2000 SA,
Case C-74/09, [2010] ECR I-7271 285

Baumbast, Case C-413/99, [2002] ECR I-7091
95, 100

Belgian State v. René Humbel and Marie-Thérèse Edel,
Case 263/86, [1988] ECR 5365 249, 282–283

Belgian State–SPF Finances v. Truck Center SA,
Case C-282/07, [2008] ECR I-10767 205

Bergström see Försäkringskassan v. Elisabeth
Bergström

Bernini, Case C-3/90, [1992] ECR I-1071 151–152, 189

Bettray, Case 344/87, [1989] ECR 1621 151–152

Bidar, Case C-209/03, [2005] ECR I-2119 110, 111, 115,
120–121, 134–136, 183

xv

Table of legislation

1 The internal market

The European Union (EU) was founded in 1957 as an economic organization, as is indicated by its original name – the European Economic Community (EEC). The creation of an internal market among the European countries has been its central endeavor, and remains so to this day. According to Article 26(2) of the Treaty on the Functioning of the European Union (TFEU), "the internal market shall comprise an area without internal frontiers in which the free movement of goods, persons, services and capital is ensured in accordance with the provisions of the Treaties." Since the Union's inception, however, its economic objectives were considered to be part of a broader, political mission. In the Union's early days, this mission was to foster general rapprochement between the Western European countries and to enable reconciliation of Germany with its former enemies in the Second World War (as well as to ensure the long-term containment of Germany's re-emerging economic power).[1] While the political environment has changed in significant ways since then, the political ambition to promote increased openness of the European countries toward each other has remained unchanged. Article 1(2) TEU holds: "This Treaty marks a new stage in the process of creating an ever closer union among the peoples of Europe, in which decisions are taken as openly as possible and as closely as possible to the citizen." The creation of such an ever-closer union among the European peoples appears as the EU's central project, which the internal market is intended to support. The internal market must therefore be understood within the context of the Union's broader, political goals. This is most clearly expressed in Article 3(3) TEU, which defines the tasks of the European Union:

The Union shall establish an internal market. It shall work for the sustainable development of Europe based on balanced economic growth and price stability, a highly competitive social market economy, aiming at full employment and social progress, and a high level of protection and improvement of the quality of the environment. It shall promote scientific and technological advance. It shall combat social exclusion and discrimination, and shall promote social justice and protection, equality between women and men, solidarity between generations and protection of the rights of the child. It shall promote economic, social and territorial cohesion,

---

1 Alan Milward, *The European Rescue of the Nation State*, London: Routledge, 2000, p. 104.

and solidarity among Member States. It shall respect its rich cultural and linguistic diversity, and shall ensure that Europe's cultural heritage is safeguarded and enhanced.

This provision expresses the expectation that the internal market can help achieve such diverse goals as balanced economic growth, social progress and an improvement of the quality of the environment. The internal market, as an economic instrument, is therefore designed to serve societal goals. At the same time, it is clear that the values espoused by Article 3(3) TEU are connected to very different political-economic programs: whereas issues such as "full employment," "social progress" and "social justice" appear to be connected to social-democratic or christian-democratic thinking, goals like "price stability" and the "highly competitive social market economy" tend to be of central importance for conservative, liberal and neoliberal thought. Finally, themes like "balanced economic growth" and the "protection ... of the environment" may be seen as connected to green political and economic thinking. Internal market law therefore is placed within this context of different, partly conflicting socio-economic visions. This can lead to competing interpretations of the Treaty freedom provisions, none of which necessarily representing a single "correct" understanding.

The central doctrinal feature of internal market law in its current state is that the obligations the Treaty defines with regard to the internal market – to create an area without borders for goods, persons, services and capital – are interpreted as individual rights, i.e. as the right to move goods and capital freely across borders, to freely provide and receive services and to access employment or self-employment in another Member State. These rights can be invoked by persons against conflicting national law in national legal proceedings. This characteristic quality of internal market law has been developed by the Court of Justice of the European Communities ("the Court") in some of its most fundamental decisions, in particular in such cases as *Van Gend en Loos* (1963) and *Costa* v. *ENEL* (1964).[2] Since then, the individual-rights perspective has developed into the dominant analytical framework in European law scholarship. The present textbook largely follows this approach. It should be emphasized, however, that this analytical framework – like any analytical framework – provides only a partial perspective: it reveals some important aspects of its object, while leaving others obscure.

While the Union citizenship provisions are not as such part of internal market law proper, they share, as interpreted by the Court, a common doctrinal framework with the economic freedoms. Most notably, the Court interprets the Union citizenship provisions as individual rights comparable to the economic freedoms. It is for this reason that the Union citizenship provisions are analyzed in conjunction with internal market law in this book. We will refer to the rights established by the

---

2 Case 26/62, *NV Algemene Transport- en Expeditie Onderneming van Gend en Loos* v. *Netherlands Inland Revenue Administration* [1963] ECR 3; Case 6/64, *Costa* v. *ENEL* [1964] ECR 1141.

Table 1.1 Overview of the Treaty freedom provisions	
Treaty freedom	**Provisions**
Union citizenship	Arts. 18–25 TFEU
Free movement of goods	Arts. 28–37 TFEU
Free movement of workers	Arts. 45–48 TFEU
Freedom of establishment	Arts. 49–55 TFEU
Freedom to provide and receive services	Arts. 56–62 TFEU
Free movement of capital and payments	Arts. 63–66 TFEU

Union citizenship and the internal market law provisions under the common term "Treaty freedoms." Table 1.1 sets out an overview of the Treaty freedom provisions.

SHORT HISTORY OF THE INTERNAL MARKET

The EEC was created by the Treaty of Rome (1957), with the goal of establishing a "common" (now "internal") market. Early Treaty reforms of the 1960s and 1970s mainly altered the institutional setup and the budgetary system of the EEC. The central Treaty changes that shaped internal market law as we see it today were set in motion by the White Paper on the completion of the internal market (1985), a strategic plan drafted by the Commission upon request by the European Council.[3] The strategy mapped out by the White Paper was subsequently implemented by the Single European Act (SEA, 1986) and the Treaty of Maastricht (1992). In this section, we will look at some of the important historical developments that shaped the system of internal market law as it exists today. Table 1.2 sets out an overview of the major Treaty reforms.

The historical context of the Treaty of Rome

Trade liberalization had already been in full swing for a decade when the Treaty of Rome was signed, at both the European and the global level.[4] Immediately after the Second World War, the European countries had established numerous bilateral trade agreements.[5] The signing of the Convention for European

3 See European Commission, Completing the Internal Market, White Paper from the Commission to the European Council (Milan, 28–29 June 1985), COM(85) 310 final, http://europa.eu/documents/comm/white_papers/pdf/com1985_0310_f_en.pdf (accessed February 18, 2014), p. 4.
4 The following section is based on Clemens Kaupa, "Dealing with Competing Socio-Economic Paradigms in Internal Market Law," dissertation, Vienna, 2013, pp. 139–142.
5 Jan Tumlir and Laura La Haye, "The Two Attempts at European Economic Reconstruction After 1945" (1981) 137 *Zeitschrift für die gesamte Staatswissenschaft/Journal of Institutional and Theoretical Economics* 367, 382.

	Treaty	Important aspects from internal market perspective	Other important reform elements
	Treaty of Paris, establishing the European Coal and Steel Community (ECSC, 1951)	Establishes common market for coal and steel; free movement of workers in coal and steel industries	Establishes European institutional framework: High Authority (now Commission), Council, Assembly (now European Parliament) and Court
EEC Treaty	Rome Treaties establishing the European Economic Community (EEC, 1957) and EURATOM	Establishes customs union and common (now "internal") market	Introduces common agricultural policy, common transport policy and common rules on competition
	Treaty of Brussels ("Merger Treaty", 1965)		Institutions of the EEC, ECSC and EURATOM are merged
	Treaty amending Certain Financial Provisions (1975)		European Parliament can reject budget; European Court of Auditors created
	Single European Act (1986)	Expansion of majority voting in Council	European Parliament is involved in legislative process; new EEC competences, e.g. environment and research
EC Treaty	Treaty of Maastricht (1992, now "EC Treaty")	Alters provisions on free movement of capital; introduces Union citizenship provisions	Creation of EU: three pillar structure; creation of European Economic and Monetary Union; new competences (education, culture)
	Treaty of Amsterdam (1997)[b]		Expansion of European Parliament competences; incorporation of Schengen Agreement
	Treaty of Nice (2001)		Institutional reforms to enable Eastern enlargement; double majority requirement in Council
TFEU	Treaty of Lisbon (2007, now "Treaty on the Functioning of the European Union")	Charter of Fundamental Rights	Abolition of pillar structure; expansion of role of European Parliament

Table 1.2 Overview of the major Treaty reforms[a]

a   Excluding Accession Treaties and the Treaty on Greenland (1984).
b   See Philippe Manin, "The Treaty of Amsterdam" (1998) 4 *Columbia Journal of European Law* 1.

Economic Cooperation in April 1948, which founded the Organization for European Economic Co-operation (OEEC) (now the Organization for Economic Co-operation and Development, OECD), constituted the first postwar multilateral attempt to abolish restrictions on trade and payments in Europe. The liberalization process begun under the auspices of the OEEC was successful: in the years that followed, intra-European trade quickly expanded, surpassing even the optimistic projections of the OEEC secretariat.[6] At the same time, trade liberalization progressed with similar high speed at the global level. Although the Havana Charter for the envisaged International Trade Organization was aborted, having failed to pass the US Congress,[7] the General Agreement on Tariffs and Trade (GATT, 1947) nonetheless came into force in 1948, having been signed by twenty-three countries (which together already accounted for 80 percent of world trade).[8] By 1956, four (of the GATT's total of eight) multilateral trade negotiating rounds – Geneva, Annecy, Torquay and Geneva II – had been successfully concluded. It was in such general climate of European and global trade liberalization that the EEC was conceived.

The EEC was a continuation and intensification of this process of trade liberalization, but it was also a qualitatively new step. European policymakers, undeniably inspired by the United States, the most productive, technologically advanced and socially progressive economy in the world, concluded that the size and structure of the US market was among the crucial factors that made this success possible.[9] "The modern world is a world of continents, of markets and economies on the grand scale," Commission president Walter Hallstein remarked in a speech at Harvard University in May 1961. "Divided economies and divided markets mean small-scale efforts, which in turn mean waste and relative poverty."[10] The European Economic Community attempted to combine the expected benefits from trade liberalization with the dynamic effects they believed would follow the formation of a single, common market of Member States.

The Treaty of Rome

The Treaty of Rome, which established the European Economic Community (EEC), was signed in 1957 and came into effect on January 1, 1958. Its signatories were Belgium, the Netherlands and Luxembourg as well as France, Germany and Italy. The same six countries had already formed the European Coal and Steel Community (ECSC) in 1951, creating a common market for coal and steel. The central elements of the EEC were the establishment of a customs union and of an internal market (then termed the "common market"). The Member States committed to provide for the free movement of goods, services and persons by 1970, after a transitional period of twelve years.[11]

In both the ECSC and the EEC, "the six members chose economic means to reach political objectives," as political scientist Stanley Hoffmann put it.[12] Most notably,

---

6 *Ibid.*, 385.
7 Douglas Irwin, "The GATT in Historical Perspective" (1995) 85 *American Economic Review* 323, 325.
8 *Ibid.*, 325.
9 See e.g. Tibor Scitovsky, *Economic Theory and Western European Integration*, London: Allen & Unwin, 1958, p. 9.
10 Rudolf Ganz, "Hallstein Notes Political Goals of Common Market," *Harvard Crimson*, 23 May 1961, www.thecrimson.com/article/1961/5/23/hallstein-notes-political-goals-of-common (accessed February 9, 2013).
11 Art. 8(1) EEC.   12 Stanley Hoffmann, "The European Community and 1992" (1989) 68 *Foreign Affairs* 27, 32.

Table 1.3 Various preferences regarding European integration, according to Leon Lindberg	
Preferred nature of European integration	**Proponents**
Integration as political unification	"This group consists of a relatively small number of strategically placed 'Europeans' in all walks of life and in all countries, mostly in Christian-Democratic parties, but some of them in Socialist parties, particularly in Belgium and the Netherlands; a majority of EPA [European Parliamentary Assembly] members; the Commission; [German chancellor Konrad] Adenauer, [French foreign minister Robert] Schuman, [Italian prime minister Giuseppe] Pella, [Belgian foreign minister Pierre] Wigny, [Dutch politician Carl] Romme, and [Belgian prime minister Paul Henri] Spaak; and [French politician Jean] Monnet and various 'federalists'."
Integration as economic unification	"This group is composed of Socialist and Christian-Democratic parties and trade unions in all countries; other groups which consider themselves in a marginal position at the national level, or which have come to the conclusion that comprehensive welfare or planning programs cannot be achieved at the national level; Belgian industry; and Dutch agriculture."
Integration as economic and political cooperation	"This head covers [French president Charles] de Gaulle and the UNR [Union pour la Nouvelle République [the Gaullist party]; center parties in France; agricultural groups in France, Belgium, Italy, and Luxembourg; and high-cost industry in all countries."
Integration as free trade	"Here we have free-trade-oriented parties; Liberals in Italy, Belgium, and the Netherlands; the [German liberal] FDP, the [German national-conservative] DP, and the Erhard wing of the [German Christian-Democratic] CDU; low-cost and highly efficient industry in all countries, especially in Germany and the Netherlands; and commerce in all countries."

economic integration served as a means to contain Germany's economic power; but it would also give the Member States greater voice on the international level. The motivations to support the foundation of the EEC of the various governments and the groups within the Member States varied, however: political scientist Leon Lindberg emphasized in 1963 that support for European integration in the various countries came from very different political parties and interest groups, and for very different reasons (see Table 1.3). In particular, he distinguished four broad viewpoints, which in turn all shaped the EEC.[13] Whereas some hoped that the EEC would mainly become a free trade project on the basis of a traditional, liberal model, others – among them the main social-democratic and christian-democratic parties – expected increased economic unification of the national economies. Other players, such as the De Gaulle government, believed that European integration would be a means to strengthen their respective nation-states, whereas the European-oriented political elites believed that the EEC could be a vehicle for eventual political integration.

13 Leon Lindberg, "The Political Dynamics of European Economic Integration" [1963] in Mette Eilstrup-Sangiovanni (ed.), *Debates on European Integration*, New York: Palgrave, 2006, p. 131.

The Treaty of Rome reflects the political compromise between the different governments and different groups within the Member States in various ways. A notable example is the Common Agricultural Policy, which created a special regime of trade and subsidies for the agricultural sector, where the general rules on the internal market applied only in part. The institutional setup of the EEC equally reflects the political compromise. The EEC was a mix between federalist (or "supra-national") and intergovernmental characteristics: the relatively strong role of the Commission as an executive authority and the independence of the Court were outweighed by the strong influence of the Member States exercised through the Council. Historian Alan Milward described this compromise as follows:

> [T]he rejection of the extreme protectionism of the 1930s and the cautious moves towards trade liberalization in the pursuit of the economic goals of the post-war consensus inevitably also endangered the position of some elements of that consensus, and it was this which gave the commercial policies of the period their peculiar mixture of liberalism and protectionism. The transition was not, as so many commentators suggest, a transition from pre-war protectionism towards classical free trade, but towards a new form of neo-mercantilism appropriate to the changed political conditions.[14]

The historical context of the White Paper

The 1970s brought Europe's largest economic downturn since the Second World War, with a recession following both the 1973 and the 1979 oil crises.[15] These downturns were accompanied by growing unemployment and rising inflation, phenomena which proved unresponsive to the set of macroeconomic interventions that had been successful in managing business cycle downturns in previous decades. Today, many economists therefore argue that the crises – while sparked by rising energy prices – were in fact triggered by deeper, structural causes that exacerbated and prolonged the downturn.[16] Economist Barry Eichengreen, for example, argued that in the early 1970s a shift in the structure of economic development took place, evident in the declining productivity growth in Europe.[17] The period after the War was a period of "catch-up" growth: Europe had experienced an innovation gap during the war in comparison to the US. Europe could follow this development by mobilizing capital on a large scale to adopt technologies that had already been developed in the US. This period of "extensive growth" ended in the 1970s, when Europe had finally "caught up" technologically with the US. It was replaced by a phase of "intensive growth," which required innovation and increased flexibility to invest in new technologies.[18] This new growth phase, Eichengreen argued, required a different institutional struc-ture: whereas the corporatist, big-industry approach was adequate for "catch-up"

---

14 Milward, *The European Rescue of the Nation State*, p. 113.
15 Barry Eichengreen, *The European Economy Since 1945: Coordinated Capitalism and Beyond*, Princeton University Press, 2007, p. 252; The following section is based on Kaupa, "Dealing with Competing Socio-Economic Paradigms," pp. 163–166.
16 See e.g. *ibid.*, 252 *et seq.*   17 *Ibid.*, 252.   18 *Ibid.*, 5–6.

growth, it failed to create an environment that sufficiently fostered innovation. The postwar economic boom had ended, and the old growth models no longer seemed to work.

Macroeconomic instability was exacerbated by the unraveling of the Bretton Woods system in the early 1970s. The Bretton Woods system was conceived in 1944 to establish a system of global macroeconomic governance, with the International Monetary Fund (IMF) and the World Bank as its main institutions. Within the system, currency exchange rates were fixed to the US dollar, which in turn was linked to gold, and thereby provided relative exchange-rate stability. When the system broke down, currencies floated freely against each other, which increased macroeconomic instability.

According to the Treaty of Rome, the main competences for instruments of macroeconomic regulation – monetary policy (including currency policy) and fiscal policy (including social policy and capital controls) – were to remain with the Member States. When the impact of the 1973 oil crisis on the European economies as well as the breakdown of the Bretton Woods system became clear, the Member States responded nationally, but increasingly turned to the European level as well. The phase between 1974 and 1985 was characterized by a period of "social activism" at the European level.[19] This included the first "Social Policy Action Programme" of 1974 and a number of Directives on labor-market-related issues. Moreover, in the 1970s the Member States attempted for the first time to coordinate their monetary policies on a European level (the so-called "European Monetary System"). And, finally, there was an increasing push toward a resumption of efforts to further integrate the European common market.

A central factor in this decision was Europe's global competition with the US, and even more so with Japan.[20] In the 1980s, the Japanese economy was on the rise, and seemed to disrupt the hitherto existing global economic balance. European policymakers and commentators were particularly concerned about Europe's growing lag in technological development, above all in the IT and telecommunication sectors.[21] The fragmented nature of the European market was believed to have had negative effects impacting adversely on the ability of companies to innovate. European businesses were, above all, interested in creating a home market large enough to sustain global corporations, which in turn could compete with the US and Japanese companies. An influential text titled *Europe 1990* that was published by the Philips corporation in the early 1980s held:

There is really no choice ... and the only option left for the Community is to achieve the goals laid down in the Treaty of Rome. Only in this way can industry compete globally, by exploiting

19 Hugh Mosley, "The Social Dimension of European Integration" (1990) 129 *International Labour Review* 147, 149.
20 See e.g. Wayne Sandholtz and John Zysman, "1992: Recasting the European Bargain" (1989) 42 *World Politics* 95, 95; Hoffmann, "The European Community and 1992," 29.
21 Eichengreen, *The European Economy Since 1945*, p. 335.

economies of scale, for what will then be the biggest home market in the world today: the European Community home market.[22]

And Fiat CEO Clemente Signoroni explained in 1989: "The final goal of the European 'dream' is to transform Europe into an integrated economic continent with its specific role, weight and responsibility on the international scenario *vis-à-vis* the US and Japan."[23] It was in this political and economic context that the Commission developed its White Paper, which led to the adoption of the SEA and ultimately to the Treaty of Maastricht.

The White Paper and the Single European Act

Because of these global economic developments, the 1980s brought an increased push to reinvigorate the integration process at the very core of the Community, the internal market. The European Council called for steps to be taken "to complete the Internal Market,"[24] and the new Commission under its president Jacques Delors was mandated to draw up a strategy to this effect. The result was the White Paper "Completing the Internal Market" of June 1985.[25] It established a roadmap that should lead to the completion of the internal market by 1992. It aimed at three central goals: (1) the removal of physical barriers (i.e. customs posts at frontiers and corresponding formalities); (2) the removal of technical barriers (i.e. different regulatory product standards in the Member States); and (3) the removal of fiscal barriers (i.e. differences in indirect taxation, such as excise taxes). Moreover, the White Paper set out a timetable for the enactment of over 320 measures by 1992, ranging from a proposal for the abolition of "customs presentation charges" to a Directive "on eradication of classical swine fever."[26]

The White Paper initiated major reforms, which were facilitated in particular by three changes in regulatory strategy. The first strategy was a rollback of the unanimity requirement for harmonizing measures, which was implemented by the Single European Act (1986). Under the voting system of the Treaty of Rome, secondary legislation had often required unanimity among the Member States in the Council. With the expansion of qualified majority voting, harmonization would become easier, as measures could no longer be blocked by individual Member States. The second strategy was the increased focus on what has become known as the principle of mutual recognition. According to the White Paper, the general principle should be that, "if a product is lawfully manufactured and marketed in one Member State, there is no reason why it should not be sold freely throughout

22 Wisse Dekker, *Europe 1990: An Agenda for Change* (1985), quoted in Sandholtz and Zysman, "1992: Recasting the European Bargain," 117.
23 Quoted in Sandholtz and Zysman, "1992: Recasting the European Bargain," 95.
24 Quoted in European Commission, Completing the Internal Market, p. 5.
25 European Commission, Completing the Internal Market.   26 See *ibid.*, Annex.

the Community."[27] This principle implied that product standards would not necessarily have to be harmonized before products could be traded in Europe. The third strategy consisted of the "new approach in harmonization": harmonization measures prior to the 1980s laid down product standards in detail, which could make the legislative process long and difficult. According to the Commission's new approach, harmonization measures would focus on essential requirements only, such as health and safety concerns.

While most of the measures proposed by the White Paper were of a mainly technical nature, the Commission nonetheless succeeded in making "1992" a project that raised broader political hopes and altered expectations on the future of European integration. This change in expectations was particularly noticeable in the business sphere, where companies merged in increased numbers and expanded to prepare for the changed requirements of a fully integrated European market.[28]

The Single European Act (1986), the first major reform of the Treaty of Rome, brought the institutional reforms envisaged by the White Paper. From the perspective of the internal market, its most important element was the expansion of majority voting in the Council. This included, most notably, the introduction of Article 100a EEC (now Article 114 TFEU), which allowed for harmonization measures based on a qualified majority in the Council. Moreover, the SEA made the European Parliament part of the legislative process, though at that time with rather limited competences.

Maastricht, Amsterdam, Nice and Lisbon

The Treaty of Maastricht, which established the European Union, brought numerous new fields of activity into the European realm. From a perspective of economic policy, the most important and far-reaching reform may well have been the adoption of the European Monetary Union (EMU), which introduced the euro as a common currency. Also of central importance was the introduction of the concept of Union citizenship. With regard to the internal market, the most significant reform concerned changes made to the free movement of capital provisions, which subsequently were found to have direct effect by the Court.

The subsequent Treaty reforms – the Treaties of Amsterdam, Nice and Lisbon – have again significantly altered the institutional and political shape of the Union. Most notably, they expanded the competences of the European Parliament, which significantly altered the political dynamics on the European level. From the perspective of this book, the most important reform may well have been the introduction of the Charter of Fundamental Rights, first as a nonbinding document (2000), and then with full legal force in 2009.

---

27 *Ibid.*, para. 58, p. 17.   28 See e.g. Hoffmann, "The European Community and 1992," 37.

THE TREATY FREEDOMS IN THEIR REGULATORY CONTEXT

The Treaty freedom provisions are laid down in Articles 18–25 TFEU (Union citizenship), 28–37 (goods) and Articles 45–66 (workers, establishment, services, capital). Many additional provisions of the TFEU also play a significant role in internal market law, providing the regulatory context within which the Treaty freedoms are applied. In this section, we briefly look at this regulatory context. Table 1.4 sets out an overview of the TFEU provisions.

Table 1.4 Overview of TFEU provisions (fields that are the subject of this book are shown in bold)		
Treaty provisions	**Subject**	**Relevant aspects from Treaty freedom perspective**
Arts. 1–6 TFEU	Competences	Defines the internal market as a shared competence between the Member States and the EU
Arts. 7–17 TFEU	Provisions having general application	Regulatory objectives that the Union institutions must take into account
Arts. 18–25 TFEU	**Non-discrimination and Union citizenship**	
Arts. 26–37, 45–66 TFEU	**Customs union and internal market provisions**	
Arts. 38–44 TFEU	Agriculture	In the absence of specific rules, internal market law applies to agricultural products (Art. 38(2) TFEU)
Arts. 67–89 TFEU	Area of freedom, security and justice	No controls on persons when crossing internal borders within the Schengen area
Arts. 90–100 TFEU	Transport	Transport services are subject to internal market rules, but exceptions can apply, for example, in regard to state aid for public transport (Art. 93 TFEU)
Arts. 101–109 TFEU	Competition law	Applies to activities of undertakings on the market, whereas internal market law applies to the collective regulation (usually by the Member States) of the exercise of the Treaty freedoms
Arts. 110–113 TFEU	**Tax provisions**	**Art. 110 TFEU (the prohibition of discriminatory taxation) complements Art. 34 TFEU**
Arts. 114–118 TFEU	**Approximation of laws (harmonization)**	
Arts. 119–144 TFEU	Economic and monetary policy	

Table 1.4 (*cont.*)		
Treaty provisions	Subject	Relevant aspects from Treaty freedom perspective
Arts. 145–197 TFEU	Other Union policies: employment; social policy; European Social Fund; educational, vocational training, youth and sport; culture; public health; consumer protection; trans-European networks; industry; economic, social and territorial cohesion; research and technological development and space; environment; energy; tourism; civil protection; administrative cooperation	
Arts. 198–204 TFEU	Association of overseas countries and territories (OCTs)	Single market rules apply partially to OCTs[a]
Arts. 205–222 TFEU	External action by the Union	Common commercial policy: tariff rates, conclusion of tariff and trade agreements, export policy (Art. 207 TFEU); conclusion of international and association agreements (Arts. 216–217 TFEU)
Arts. 223–309 TFEU	Institutional provisions	Central actors in regard to Treaty freedoms: Council, European Parliament, Commission
Arts. 310–325 TFEU	Financial provisions	
Arts. 326–334 TFEU	Enhanced cooperation	
Arts. 335–358 TFEU	General and final provisions	

a   Council Decision 2001/822/EC on the association of the overseas countries and territories with the European Community ("Overseas Association Decision") [2001] OJ L314/1, amended by Council Decision 2007/249/EC amending Decision 2001/822/EC on the association of the overseas countries and territories with the European Community, [2007] OJ L109/33.

Articles 1–6 TFEU define the competences of the Union in general terms. These are further fleshed out in other parts of the Treaty. The Union's competences encompass the Treaty freedom provisions as well as internal policies such as agriculture, transport, competition, employment, energy and external action (Articles 205–222 TFEU). This framework of competences defines the scope within which the Union's institutions can act. The Treaty provides numerous specific authorizations for legislative Union action (e.g. Article 53 TFEU, which authorizes the European legislators to issue Directives for the mutual recognition of diplomas). Articles 114–115 TFEU additionally provide for a general competence to enact secondary law if necessary for the functioning of the internal market. The distribution of competences between the Union and the Member States is further discussed below. When questions of demarcation arise between the different regulatory fields, these are resolved by a variety of doctrinal methods. The field of agriculture, for example, is considered *lex specialis* in relation to internal market law. Article 38(2) TFEU provides:

> Save as otherwise provided in Articles 39 to 44, the rules laid down for the establishment and functioning of the internal market shall apply to agricultural products.

Articles 7–17 TFEU define general political objectives such as equality between women and men (Article 8 TFEU), the promotion of a high level of employment (Article 9 TFEU), environmental protection (Article 11 TFEU) and consumer protection (Article 12 TFEU). These provisions do not create subjective rights of individuals, but define objectives that the institutions of the Union must take into account in their activities. They can therefore become relevant from an internal market law perspective, for example with regard to secondary legislation. The institutional provisions (Articles 223–309 TFEU) establish the institutions that act, and the procedures according to which they act. The role of the institutions relevant in internal market law are discussed below.

Competences

Most provisions of the TFEU up to Article 197 deal with the regulatory competences of the EU. The Treaty distinguishes between three types of competences: (1) exclusive competence of the Union; (2) shared competence between the Union and the Member States; and (3) competences that remain with the Member States.

(1) Exclusive competences: Article 2(1) TFEU provides: "When the Treaties confer on the Union exclusive competence in a specific area, only the Union may legislate and adopt legally binding acts, the Member States being able to do so themselves only if so empowered by the Union or for the implementation of Union acts." Issues relating to the customs union fall under the exclusive competence of the Union. Member States cannot pass any measure affecting the customs union unless they are empowered by the Union to do so.

(2) Shared competences: Article 2(2) TFEU provides: "When the Treaties confer on the Union a competence shared with the Member States in a specific area, the Union and the Member States may legislate and adopt legally binding acts in that area. The Member States shall exercise their competence to the extent that the Union has not exercised its competence. The Member States shall again exercise their competence to the extent that the Union has decided to cease exercising its competence." The internal market falls within the shared competence of the Union and the Member States. Member States retain the right to legislate in areas concerning the internal market, but only to the extent that the Union has not yet exercised its competence.

(3) Member State competences: competences that have not been granted to the Union remain with the Member States. Article 5(2) TEU holds: "Under the principle of

conferral, the Union shall act only within the limits of the competences conferred upon it by the Member States in the Treaties to attain the objectives set out therein. Competences not conferred upon the Union in the Treaties remain with the Member States." In these fields, the Union may be granted certain coordination tasks. Article 2(5) TFEU provides: "In certain areas and under the conditions laid down in the Treaties, the Union shall have competence to carry out actions to support, coordinate or supplement the actions of the Member States, without thereby superseding their competence in these areas." Table 1.5 sets out the exclusive and shared competences, according to Articles 3 and 4 TFEU.

Table 1.5 Exclusive and shared competences, according to Articles 3 and 4 TFEU	
Exclusive Union competence (Art. 3 TFEU)	**Shared competence (Art. 4 TFEU)**
Customs union	Internal market
The establishment of the competition rules necessary for the functioning of the internal market	Social policy, for the aspects defined in this Treaty
Monetary policy for the Member States whose currency is the euro	Economic, social and territorial cohesion
The conservation of marine biological resources under the Common Fisheries Policy	Agriculture and fisheries, excluding the conservation of marine biological resources
Common commercial policy	Environment Consumer protection Transport Trans-European networks Energy Area of freedom, security and justice Common safety concerns in public health matters

Secondary law measures

The European Union can pass secondary law measures within the limits set by the Treaty. With regard to the Treaty freedoms, the TFEU contains specific provisions authorizing secondary law measures (see Table 1.6). Moreover, Articles 114 and 115 TFEU provide general competences to pass secondary law measures to approx-imate (i.e. harmonize) national law. According to Article 115 TFEU, the Council can "issue Directives for the approximation of such laws, regulations or administrative provisions of the Member States as directly affect the establishment or functioning of the internal market." Article 115 TFEU, which goes back to the Treaty of Rome, requires unanimity in the Council, i.e. all Member States have to consent. Article 114 TFEU was introduced by the SEA to facilitate necessary harmonization. Measures passed under Article 114 TFEU only require a qualified majority. Accordingly, the European Parliament and the Council can "adopt the measures

Table 1.6 Central provisions authorizing secondary law in regard to the Treaty freedoms	
Treaty provision	**Treaty freedom**
Art. 21(2) TFEU	Union citizenship
Art. 33 TFEU	Customs cooperation
Art. 46 TFEU	Workers
Art. 48 TFEU	Workers (social security)
Arts. 50–52 TFEU	Establishment
Art. 53 TFEU	Establishment (recognition of diploma)
Art. 59 TFEU	Services (liberalization of specific services)
Arts. 114–115 TFEU	General harmonization competence

for the approximation of the provisions laid down by law, regulation or administrative action in Member States which have as their object the establishment and functioning of the internal market."

As the functioning of such a complex phenomenon as the European internal market arguably depends on a myriad of factors, the provision can – at least potentially – serve as the basis for a broad range of legal measures. However, the Court has defined certain limitations on the regulatory objectives that can legitimately be pursued by measures under Article 114 TFEU. Thus, a Directive banning advertising of and sponsorship by tobacco products[29] was challenged by Germany on the ground that the Union could not rely on Article 114 TFEU for such a Directive (*Germany* v. *Parliament and Council – Tobacco Advertising I*, 2000).[30] Germany argued that advertisements and sponsorship for tobacco products essentially constituted national markets involving only very limited cross-border trade. Differences in national regulation, therefore, do not constitute obstacles to trade that would justify a European harmonization measure. Accordingly, Article 114 TFEU does not constitute an appropriate legal basis for the measure. The Court agreed, arguing that the full-scale prohibition of advertisements went beyond what was necessary to ensure the functioning of the internal market. The Court emphasized that measures passed under the provision "must genuinely have as its object the improvement of the conditions for the establishment and functioning of the internal market" (*Germany* v. *Parliament and Council – Tobacco Advertising I*, 2000).[31] The European legislator subsequently passed a scaled-down version of the initial Directive, which

29 Directive 98/43/EC on the approximation of the laws, regulations and administrative provisions of the Member
    States relating to the advertising and sponsorship of tobacco products, [2000] OJ L213/9.
30 Case C-376/98, *Germany* v. *Parliament and Council – Tobacco Advertising I* [2000] ECR I-8419.
31 *Ibid.*, para. 84.

prohibited advertisements in print and radio as well as event sponsorship, but only if the event took place in several Member States or had "cross-border effects."[32] This second version of the Directive was again challenged by Germany (*Commission* v. *Germany – Tobacco Advertising II*, 2006).[33] This time, however, the Court found that the focus of the measure on the harmonization of national tobacco advertisement restrictions liable to specifically affect cross-border trade (print, radio, sponsoring of events with cross-border relevance) was specific enough for Article 114 TFEU to be the appropriate legal basis.

According to its paragraph (2), Article 114 TFEU "shall not apply to fiscal provisions, to those relating to the free movement of persons nor to those relating to the rights and interests of employed persons." Harmonization in these areas can therefore be based only on Article 115 TFEU, which makes harmonization less likely because of its unanimity requirement.

The role of the European institutions in internal market law

European Parliament and Council

The European Parliament and the Council can enact secondary law measures. These measures implement the Treaty freedoms, but also define and clarify their content. The standard procedure to enact secondary law in the field of internal market law is the ordinary legislative procedure (Article 294 TFEU), whereby the European Parliament and the Council adopt legislation conjointly based on a proposal by the Commission.

Commission

The Commission has the sole right of initiative to propose legislation (Article 17(2) TEU), and thereby plays an important role in the development of secondary law measures regarding the Treaty freedoms. Moreover, the Commission ensures the application of the Treaties and oversees the application of Union law (Article 17(1) TEU). When it suspects a breach of EU law by a Member State, the Commission can initiate an infringement procedure before the Court against that Member State (Article 258 TFEU).

Court of Justice of the European Communities

The Court plays a significant role in internal market law. Its interpretations of the Treaty freedom provisions in particular and of European law in general have been of central importance in the development of internal market law. The Court is called

---

32 Directive 2003/33/EC of the European Parliament and of the Council on the approximation of the laws, regulations and administrative provisions of the Member States relating to the advertising and sponsorship of tobacco products, [2003] OJ L152/16.

33 Case C-380/03, *Commission* v. *Germany – Tobacco Advertising II* [2006] ECR I-11573.

upon to provide such interpretations in essentially two types of procedures: first, in the infringement procedure brought by the Commission under Article 258 TFEU (Article 259 TFEU if a Member State brings the action); and, second, in the preliminary rulings procedure under Article 267 TFEU by which national courts request the Court to interpret provisions of primary and secondary EU law.

Further reading

EICHENGREEN, BARRY, *The European Economy Since 1945: Coordinated Capitalism and Beyond*, Princeton University Press, 2007 (an economic history of Europe after the Second World War from an American perspective that focuses on developments in both Western and Eastern Europe)

GILLINGHAM, JOHN, *European Integration, 1950–2003: Superstate or New Market Economy?*, Cambridge University Press, 2003 (a critical account by a libertarian American historian who chastises the EU for its "superstate" tendencies)

JUDT, TONY, *Postwar: A History of Europe Since 1945*, Harmondsworth: Penguin, 2006 (Judt, a British historian, describes the phase from 1945 to the fall of the Berlin Wall as a consequence of the outcomes of the Second World War)

MILWARD, ALAN, *The European Rescue of the Nation State*, London: Routledge, 2000 (a British historian who argues that the EU is not an antithesis to the nation-state, but "an integral part of the reassertion of the nation-state as an organizational concept"[34])

---

34 Milward, *The European Rescue of the Nation State*, p. 2.

2 Common framework of the Treaty freedoms

In this chapter, we attempt to outline characteristics and structures common to all Treaty freedoms. Though placed at the beginning of this book for systematic reasons, it is best consulted during and after reading the other chapters. We will discuss each Treaty freedom within the common structure shown in Table 2.1.

Subchapter	Guiding question
Table 2.1 Common structure	
Subchapter	**Guiding question**
Addressees	Who has obligations under the Treaty freedoms?
Personal scope	Who has rights under the Treaty freedoms?
Material scope	Which conditions must be fulfilled for the Treaty freedoms to apply?
Applying the Treaty freedoms	Which general rights and duties are encapsulated in the Treaty freedoms?
Rights and case groups	Which specific rights are granted by the Treaty freedoms? What are typical cases?
Justifications	Under which conditions can restrictions of the Treaty freedoms be justified?
Secondary law	Which are the most important instruments of secondary law that substantiate or clarify the Treaty freedoms?

CONVERGENCE AND CONTINUED DIVERGENCE OF THE TREATY FREEDOMS

Today, the Court applies a common analytical framework to all Treaty freedoms.[1] The Treaty freedoms therefore have largely "converged." According to Oliver/Roth, convergence means that "the same principles should apply in the absence of

---

1 On convergence, see e.g. Susanne Schmidt, "Who Cares About Nationality? The Path-Dependent Case Law of the CJEU from Goods to Citizens" (2012) **19** *Journal of European Public Policy* 8; Alina Tryfonidou, "Further Steps on the Road to Convergence Among the Market Freedoms" (2010) **35** *European Law Review* 36.

any objective reason to make a distinction."[2] As we will see, however, important doctrinal differences remain. Whereas, for example, provisions on the free movement of workers, services and the freedom of establishment have been found to have horizontal direct effect (i.e. they can be employed against non-state actors), the provisions on the free movement of goods and of capital and the provisions on Union citizenship have not.

Additionally to those doctrinal differences, it should be noted that there are also numerous factual differences. It is clear that the Treaty freedoms regulate the mobility of very different subjects, as mobility means something different for goods, capital and legal persons than it means for natural persons. In the absence of uniform EU standards, the free movement of goods usually depends on Member States allowing the marketing of products on their territory that have been produced according to the standards of another Member State. In contrast, individuals who move to another Member State require protection from economic, social and political disadvantages and face concerns such as whether they can bring their family along and whether their cross-border activities will negatively affect their social benefits, including pensions. This kind of mobility is again something quite different from the mobility of legal persons. Unlike individuals, legal persons are creations of a particular legal system which determines their legal status: mobility therefore requires legal recognition of the entity in the host state. Accordingly, while convergence between the Treaty freedoms can be observed as regards the analytical framework that the Court applies, important substantive differences between the Treaty freedoms remain and should be accounted for.

DIRECT EFFECT OF THE TREATY FREEDOMS

The Treaty freedom provisions have direct effect. The concept of "direct effect" means that certain provisions of EU law create individual rights that national authorities must protect.[3] This was first recognized by the Court in the seminal case of *Van Gend en Loos* (1963). The Court held:

Independently of the legislation of Member States, Community law ... not only imposes obligations on individuals but is also intended to confer upon them rights which become part of their legal heritage. These rights arise not only where they are expressly granted by the Treaty, but also by reason of obligations which the Treaty imposes in a clearly defined way upon individuals as well as upon the Member States and upon the institutions of the Community.[4]

According to the Court, provisions have direct effect under the following conditions: (1) the provision "contains a clear and unconditional prohibition"; and (2) the "obligation ... is not qualified by any reservation on the part of states which would

---

2 Oliver and Roth, "The Internal Market and the Four Freedoms" (2004) 41 *Common Market Law Review* 407, 441.
3 *Van Gend en Loos*, p. 13.   4 *Ibid.*, 12.

make its implementation conditional upon a positive legislative measure enacted under national law."[5] If the Treaty freedoms conflict with national law, the latter is rendered inapplicable (*Simmenthal*, 1978).[6] Table 2.2 sets out the internal market provisions having direct effect.

Table 2.2 Internal market provisions having direct effect (according to the Court's case law)	
Treaty provision	**Right granted by the provision**
Arts. 18, 20 and 21 TFEU	Freedom of movement and residence of Union citizens
Art. 30 TFEU	Prohibition of customs duties
Art. 34 TFEU	Free movement of goods
Art. 45 TFEU	Free movement of workers
Art. 49 TFEU	Freedom of establishment
Art. 56 TFEU	Freedom to provide and receive services
Art. 63 TFEU	Free movement of capital and payments
Art. 110 TFEU	Prohibition of discriminatory taxation

THE ADDRESSEES OF THE TREATY FREEDOM PROVISIONS

The primary addressees of the Treaty freedom provisions are the Member States. They need to devise national law in a way to give full effect to the Treaty freedoms. Moreover, some of the Treaty freedoms have also been found to have "horizontal" direct effect. This means that non-state actors are addressees of the Treaty freedom provisions as well.

Host state

The "host state" (or "country of destination") is the Member State to which goods are exported, where operators provide their services, where workers and self-employed persons from other Member States establish themselves and in which or to which capital is invested or transferred. The host state is prohibited from discriminating on the ground of nationality and from hindering mobility or making it less attractive. This obligation not to discriminate applies to the institutions of the central government as well as to the institutions of regional or local public authorities (*Stopover Tax*, 2009).[7]

5 *Ibid.*, 13.   6 Case 106/77, *Simmenthal II* [1978] ECR 629.
7 Case C-169/08, *Presidente del Consiglio dei Ministri* v. *Regione Sardegna – Stopover Tax* [2009] ECR I-10821, para. 29.

Home state

The "home state" (or "country of origin") is the Member State from which goods, service providers, workers, self-employed persons or capital originate. The Treaty freedoms prohibit the home state from restricting the exercise of the Treaty freedoms by either their own nationals or nationals from other Member States. With regard to the free movement of goods, this prohibition is separately stipulated in Article 35 TFEU, whereas with regard to the other Treaty freedoms the same provision applies to restrictions of both the host and the home state. The Treaty freedom provisions differ in the way they treat restrictions by the home state. According to the Court, Article 35 TFEU prohibits discriminatory provisions alone (though the decision in *Gysbrechts* might indicate change in this regard, as we will discuss below). It therefore merely prohibits rules that specifically disadvantage exports. With regard to the other Treaty freedoms, however, the Court has ruled that they also prohibit rules that are non-discriminatory and nonetheless restrict the access to the markets of other Member States. Maybe the most prominent case in this regard is *Alpine Investments* (1995).[8] The case dealt with a Dutch consumer law that prohibited the cold-calling of customers to sell risky financial products, regardless of the country in which the consumer was residing. The Court ruled that this constituted a restriction of the freedom to provide services, as the Dutch company could not even conduct calls to countries where cold-calling was legal (although the national rule was then found to be justified on the ground of consumer protection).

Non-state actors

Whereas some Treaty provisions are directly addressed to non-state actors (e.g. competition law, which is addressed to undertakings), the Treaty freedoms are usually conceptualized as creating obligations mainly for the Member States. As a general rule, private actors do not have obligations under the Treaty freedoms, unless secondary law holds otherwise.[9] However, there are significant exceptions. According to the Court, the Treaty freedoms can be applied to non-state actors in the following situations:

(1) The Treaty freedoms apply to non-state entities if they exercise regulatory competences conferred by public authorities (*Association of Pharmaceutical Importers*, 1989).[10] The Treaty freedoms also apply to entities that are otherwise attributable to the state, for example if they have been created, financed or staffed by the government.[11] The Court has ruled, for example, that the German CMA, an organization marketing German agricultural products, was attributable to the state

---

8 Case C-384/93, *Alpine Investments* [1995] ECR I-1141.
9 See e.g. Art. 7(4) Regulation 492/2011 (ex-Regulation 1612/68).
10 Joined Cases 266/87 and 267/87, *The Queen v. Royal Pharmaceutical Society of Great Britain, ex parte Association of Pharmaceutical Importers and Others* [1989] ECR 1295.
11 Oliver and Roth, "The Internal Market and the Four Freedoms," 425.

(*Commission* v. *Germany – CMA*, 2002). Although it was set up as a private company, the Court found the Treaty freedoms applicable because CMA was established by law, was bound to observe rules set by a public body and was financed by compulsory contributions laid down in law.[12]

(2) The Court has found that the Treaty freedoms on the free movement of persons (workers, establishment, services) apply to entities that regulate employment, self-employment or the provision of services in a collective manner. For example, the Court held in *Viking* (2007): "[A]ccording to settled case law, [Articles 45, 49 and 56 TFEU] do not apply only to the actions of public authorities but extend also to rules of any other nature aimed at regulating in a collective manner gainful employment, self-employment and the provision of services ... Since working conditions in the different Member States are governed sometimes by provisions laid down by law or regulation and sometimes by collective agreements and other acts concluded or adopted by private persons, limiting application of the prohibitions laid down by these articles to acts of a public authority would risk creating inequality in its application."[13] This approach has not been extended to Union citizenship or to the free movement of goods and capital. Organizations that have frequently been found to regulate employment, self-employment and the provision of services in a collective manner are sporting associations (*Walrave and Koch*, 1974) and professional associations such as bar associations (*Wouters*, 2002).

(3) If a person exercising its right under the Treaty freedoms is aggrieved by another private party, a Member State may nonetheless be found responsible if it has failed to sufficiently protect the rights of that person guaranteed by the Treaty freedoms. In *Commission* v. *France – Spanish Strawberries* (1997), the transport of Spanish agricultural products in France had been obstructed and damaged by protestors.[14] The Court found that France had not taken sufficient precautionary measures to prevent private individuals from obstructing the free movement of goods.

PERSONAL SCOPE (BENEFICIARIES)

The provisions on the free movement of persons (Articles 45, 49 and 56 TFEU) can be invoked by Union citizens, i.e. nationals of a Member State. Companies must have been formed in accordance with the law of a Member State and have their registered office, central administration or principal place of business within the Union (Article 54 TFEU). By contrast, Article 34 TFEU applies regardless of the nationality of the traders involved. The nationality of the capital owner is likewise irrelevant with regard to the free movement of capital (Article 63 TFEU).

12 Case C-325/00, *Commission* v. *Germany – CMA* [2002] ECR I-9977, paras. 17–21.
13 Case C-438/05, *International Transport Workers' Federation and The Finnish Seamen's Union* [2007] ECR I-10779, paras. 33–34.
14 Case C-265/95, *Commission* v. *France – Spanish Strawberries* [1997] ECR I-6959.

Non-EU citizens with equal or comparable rights

It is not only Union citizens who have rights under the Treaty freedom provisions: third-country nationals also do. Additionally, some groups of third-country nationals are granted comparable rights under international agreements, such as the EEA Agreement and the Association Agreement between the EU and Turkey.

Family members

Union citizens who exercise their rights under the Treaty freedoms by moving to another Member State can bring their families along. This right applies regardless of whether the family members themselves are Union citizens or third-country nationals. Family members are granted mobility and residence rights comparable to those enjoyed by Union citizens, including the right to equal treatment and to access employment and self-employment. The rights of family members are codified in the Citizenship Directive.

Citizens of EEA countries

The EU and the EEA

The Agreement on the European Economic Area (EEA) was signed in 1992 by the EU and its Member States on the one side and the EFTA states on the other.[15] As Switzerland ultimately did not ratify the Agreement, the EEA currently encompasses the EU Member States as well as Norway, Iceland and Liechtenstein. The EEA Agreement essentially replicates the EU's internal market regime,[16] so that the EU and the other EEA states form a single market. The EEA Agreement establishes the free movement of goods, persons, services and capital between its Member States. Moreover, it includes certain "flanking" policies, such as competition law, consumer protection and research and development. The EEA is a free trade area, which means that there are no customs duties between the Member States. However, it is not a customs union, which means that no common customs tariff is in place. Norway, Iceland and Liechtenstein must adopt large parts of EU law with the exception of certain areas such as the Common Agricultural Policy, fisheries, tax harmonization, external trade relations and monetary union.[17] A joint committee formally adopts new Union legislation into the law of the EEA. The Court, the Commission, the EFTA Surveillance Authority and the EFTA Court are responsible for monitoring and ensuring compliance with the obligations under the EEA Agreement.

---

15 See Friedl Weiss, "The Oporto Agreement on the European Economic Area – A Legal Still Life" (1992) 12 *Yearbook of European Law* 385.
16 See e.g. Case E-1/03, *EFTA Surveillance Authority* v. *Republic of Iceland* [2003] EFTA CR 143, para. 27; see also Elvira Méndez-Pinedo, *EC and EEA Law: A Comparative Study of the Effectiveness of European Law*, Groningen: European Law Publishing, 2009, pp. 28 and 34.
17 Bechev and Nicolaïdis, "From Policy to Polity: Can the EU's Special Relations with Its 'Neighborhood' Be Decentred?" (2010) 48 *Journal of Common Market Studies* 487.

The EEA Agreement replicates the Treaty freedoms, and secondary Union legislation is regularly incorporated into the EEA framework.[18] This means that goods from within the EEA can circulate freely in the EU and that "citizens of the EU states and the EFTA states" (EEA citizens) and companies generally have the same rights under the Treaty freedoms as Union citizens do. This does not, however, apply to the rights under the Union citizenship provisions as they have no equivalence in the EEA Agreement. The free movement rights under the EEA do not have direct effect in the EFTA countries.[19] In contrast, EEA law can have direct effect in the EU (*Opel Austria*, 1997).[20] If an EFTA state breaks its obligations under the EEA agreement, it must pay damages to the individual concerned.

The free movement provisions under the EEA Agreement are to be interpreted as generally having the same scope and meaning as the equivalent provisions under the Treaty. The Court has held:

> [O]ne of the main objectives of the EEA Agreement is to realise as completely as possible the free movement of goods, persons, services and capital throughout the whole of the EEA, so that the internal market realised in the territory of the Community is extended to the EFTA States. In that regard, many provisions of the said agreement are designed to ensure as uniform an interpretation as possible of the latter over the whole of the EEA. It is for the Court in that context to ensure that the rules of the EEA Agreement which are identical in substance with those of the Treaty are interpreted in a uniform manner within the Member States.[21]

However, the free movement rights under the EEA Agreement may have to be interpreted differently from those of the Treaty if the legal or factual situation differs. In *Commission* v. *Italy – Taxation of Dividends* (2009), the Court had to deal with an Italian rule subjecting, for reasons regarding the fight against tax evasion, dividends distributed to companies in other countries to a less favorable tax regime than those distributed to resident companies.[22] The Court found that the Italian provision was in breach of Article 63 TFEU for companies resident in an EU Member State, as the Directive on mutual cooperation between the national tax authorities in place between the EU Member States rendered differential treatment of domestic and non-domestic companies disproportionate. However, as no comparable measure existed with regard to the EEA countries, the measure was found to be in conformity with the EEA Agreement as regards companies resident in an EEA country.

Swiss citizens

Switzerland is an EFTA member, but is not a member of the EEA. The EU and Switzerland have concluded numerous bilateral agreements, which grant far-reaching rights with regard to the free movement of goods and of natural persons.

---

18 See e.g. incorporation with adaptations of the Citizenship Directive 2004/38/EC by EEA Joint Committee Decision 158/2007 of 7 December 2007; Méndez-Pinedo, *EC and EEA Law*, p. 28.

19 Case E-1/07, *Criminal proceedings against A* [2007] EFTA CR 246, para. 40.

20 Case T-115/94, *Opel Austria GmbH* v. *Council of the European Union* [1997] ECR II-39, paras. 101–102.

21 Case C-540/07, *Commission* v. *Italy – Taxation of Dividends* [2009] ECR I-10983, para. 65.   22 *Ibid.*

Switzerland and the EU

Although Swiss citizens voted against joining the EEA in 1992 and against taking up accession talks with the EU in 2001, Switzerland and the EU are cooperating in a large number of areas. There are currently around 100 bilateral agreements between the EU and Switzerland regulating numerous aspects of cooperation. Most notably, Switzerland is part of the Schengen area[23] and a signatory to the Dublin Regulation,[24] and participates in the EU's research programs.[25] From an internal market perspective, the central treaties are the free trade agreement of 1972[26] and the agreement on the free movement of persons of 1999, though in a referendum of February 2014, the Swiss citizens narrowly voted for its suspension within three years.

The objective of the agreement on the free movement of persons is, *inter alia*, "to accord a right of entry, residence, access to work as employed persons, establishment on a self-employed basis and the right to stay in the territory of the Contracting Parties" and to "facilitate the provision of services in the territory of the Contracting Parties" (Article 1). Article 2 stipulates that lawful residents shall not be subject to any discrimination on the ground of nationality. The agreement also applies to family members and persons who are not economically active, including retirees and students. Additionally, it sets out provisions on the mutual recognition of diplomas and on the coordination of social security systems. According to the agreement's Preamble, the free movement of persons between Switzerland and the EU is based on "the rules applying in the European Community." The provisions that establish rights for individuals have direct effect in the EU if the provision is clear and precise and does not require implementing measures.[27]

The agreement establishes rights of workers and self-employed (natural) persons that are essentially identical to those of Union citizens under the TFEU internal market provisions. However, the Court has emphasized that the scope of the agreement is narrower than that of the TFEU. The reason for this is that

---

23 Agreement between the European Union, the European Community and the Swiss Confederation on the Swiss Confederation's association with the implementation, application and development of the Schengen acquis, [2008] OJ L53/52.

24 Agreement between the European Community and the Swiss Confederation concerning the criteria and mechanisms for establishing the state responsible for examining a request for asylum lodged in a Member State or in Switzerland, [2008] OJ L53/5.

25 Agreement on scientific and technological cooperation between the European Community and the European Atomic Energy Community, of the one part, and the Swiss Confederation, of the other part, [2007] OJ L189/26.

26 Agreement between the European Economic Community and the Swiss Confederation, [1972] OJ L300/189.

27 See e.g. Case C-339/05, *Zentralbetriebsrat der Landeskrankenhäuser Tirols* v. *Land Tirol* [2006] ECR I-7097, Opinion of Advocate General Ruiz-Jarabo Colomer, para. 45.

"the Swiss Confederation did not join the internal market of the [Union], the aim of which is the removal of all obstacles to create an area of total freedom of movement analogous to that provided by a national market, which includes *inter alia* the freedom to provide services and the freedom of establishment" (*Grimme*, 2009).[28] Accordingly, "the interpretation given to the provisions of European Union law concerning the internal market cannot be applied by analogy to the interpretation of the Agreement, unless there are express provisions to that effect laid down by the Agreement itself" (*Fokus Invest*, 2010).[29] In *Hengartner* (2010), for example, the Court held that the Agreement does not prohibit differential treatment with regard to a tax payable for the provision of services. As the agreement does not contain any specific rule in that regard, the principle of nondiscrimination remains inapplicable.[30] Moreover, companies established in Switzerland cannot be assumed to have rights analogous to those of companies established in the EU, as the Court held for example in *Fokus Invest*. With the exception of certain provisions on the free movement of services, the Agreement grants rights to natural persons alone.[31]

Case C-541/08, Fokus Invest (2010)

A Swiss company owned the Austrian company, FIAG. FIAG bought a house in Vienna, and requested registration of its right of ownership in the land register and the removal of various entries in that register. Fokus Invest, which had a title to the same property recorded in the register and which did not want it to be removed challenged the request. According to a Viennese law, foreign natural or legal persons or Austrian companies owned by foreign persons must apply for authorization prior to the acquisition of property in Vienna. FIAG contended, however, that the measure infringed the agreement between Switzerland and the EU.

Does the agreement between Switzerland and the EU grant Swiss companies establishment rights similar to those of companies established in the EU?

No.

The agreement between Switzerland and the EU confers (almost) no rights to legal persons. Therefore, FIAG's assertion that the agreement would grant a right comparable to Articles 49–55 TFEU is incorrect.

---

28 Case C-351/08, *Grimme* [2009] ECR I-10777, para. 27.
29 Case C-541/08, *Fokus Invest AG* v. *Finanzierungsberatung-Immobilientreuhand und Anlageberatung GmbH (FIAG)* [2010] ECR I-1025, para. 28.
30 Case C-70/09, *Hengartner and Gasser* [2010] ECR I-7233, para. 43.
31 Only Art. 5(1) of the Agreement and Art. 18 of its Annex I apply to companies. See *Fokus Invest*, para. 30.

Turkish citizens

Turkey and the EU

The EEC–Turkey Association Agreement (or Ankara Agreement)[32] was signed in 1963 and aimed, according to its Preamble, to "facilitate the accession of Turkey to the Community at a later date." The Ankara Agreement has since then been substantiated by the Additional Protocol of 1970[33] and by numerous decisions of the Association Council, the joint decision-making body of the EU and Turkey established pursuant to the Agreement. As the Ankara Agreement aims at creating a common economic union, it shares many characteristics with the TFEU. In particular, a customs union between Turkey and the EU was established in the 1990s.[34] Concerning the mobility of persons, Articles 12–14 of the Ankara Agreement aim at abolishing restrictions to the free movement of workers, to the freedom of establishment and to the freedom to provide services, guided by the corresponding provisions of the TFEU. The provisions on the free movement of persons between Turkey and the EU are closely linked to the Treaty freedoms. According to the Court, the corresponding provisions of the Ankara Agreement should be interpreted "as far as possible" by analogy with Union law (*Abatay*, 2003).[35] Article 9 contains a prohibition on discrimination on the ground of nationality similar to that in Article 18 TFEU. In principle, international agreements between the EU and third countries such as the Ankara Agreement may confer rights directly upon individuals. In *Demirel* (1987), the Court held that "[a] provision in an agreement concluded by the Community with non-member countries must be regarded as being directly applicable when, regard being had to its wording and the purpose and nature of the agreement itself, the provision contains a clear and precise obligation which is not subject, in its implementation or effects, to the adoption of any subsequent measure."[36] However, the Court found the provisions on free movement in the Ankara Agreement programmatic in nature and "not sufficiently precise and unconditional to be capable of governing directly the movement of workers" (*Demirel*).[37] Since then, however, the Court has found a significant number of provisions of the Additional Protocol as well as of decisions by the Association Council to have direct effect, granting Turkish citizens significant free movement rights. Table 2.3 sets out an overview of the principal measures governing the movement rights of Turkish citizens in the EU.

---

32 Agreement establishing an Association between the European Economic Community and Turkey of 12 September 1963, [1973] OJ C113/1.

33 Additional Protocol to the Agreement establishing an Association between the European Economic Community and Turkey, of 23 November 1970, [1972] OJ L293/4.

34 Decision No. 1/95 of the EC–Turkey Association Council on implementing the final phase of the Customs Union, [1996] OJ L35/1.

35 Joined Cases C-317/01 and C-369/01, *Abatay* [2003] ECR I-12301, para. 112.

36 Case C-12/86, *Meryem Demirel* v. *Stadt Schwäbisch Gmünd* [1987] ECR 3719, para. 14.

37 *Demirel*, para. 23. *Demirel* addressed Art. 12 Ankara Agreement, which deals with the free movement of workers. The Court found in *Savas* that Art. 13 Ankara Agreement likewise does not have direct effect. See Case C-37/98, *The Queen* v. *Secretary of State for the Home Department, ex parte Abdulnasir Savas* [2000] ECR I-2927, para. 45.

Table 2.3 Overview of the principal measures governing the movement rights of Turkish citizens in the EU	
Legal acts	**Provisions with implications on free movement**
Ankara Agreement (1963)	Art. 4: Agreement aims at progressively establishing a customs union; Arts. 12–14 aim at establishing free movement of workers, freedom of establishment and freedom to provide services, guided by the relevant Treaty provisions
Additional Protocol (1970)	Art. 41(1): standstill clause in regard to establishment/services (direct effect)
Decision 1/80	Art. 6(1): rights in regard to access to employment (direct effect); Art. 7: rights of family members (direct effect); Art. 10/1: prohibition of discrimination (direct effect); Art. 13: standstill clause in regard to workers (direct effect)[a]
Decision 1/95	Arts. 5–6 prohibit quantitative import and export restrictions and measures having equivalent effect (direct effect)[b]

a   On both, see Case C-192/89, *S. Z. Sevince* v. *Staatssecretaris van Justitie* [1990] ECR I-3461, para. 26.
b   See Article 66 of Decision 1/95.

The rights of Turkish citizens who are workers and those who are self-employed differ to a considerable degree. While Member States control the initial access to their labor market by Turkish workers, the latter enjoy unrestricted access to any employment in a Member State once they have been legally employed there for four years (Article 6(1) of Decision 1/80). Once legally admitted to the EU, Turkish workers can rely on Article 10/1 of Decision 1/80, which prohibits discrimination on the basis of nationality as regards remuneration and other conditions of work. The provision has direct effect, as the Court held in *Wählergruppe Gemeinsam* (2003).[38] While Turkish workers do not have a right to move between Member States under the Ankara Agreement,[39] the Long-Term Residents Directive is applicable (see below). Article 13 of Decision 1/80 establishes a standstill clause, which prohibits the Member States from introducing new restrictions on the conditions of access to employment applicable to Turkish workers and their family members.

An analogous standstill clause applies to Turkish citizens who are service providers or who wish to establish themselves in the Union.[40] Article 41(1) of the Additional Protocol, another standstill clause, prohibits entry requirements – for example, visa requirements – for self-employed persons that are stricter than those applicable on the date the Additional Protocol entered into force with regard to the relevant Member State (this is either the date the Additional Protocol came into

38 Case C-171/01, *Wählergruppe "Gemeinsam Zajedno/Birlikte Alternative und Grüne GewerkschafterInnen/UG,"* and *Bundesminister für Wirtschaft und Arbeit and Others* [2003] ECR I-4301, para. 94.
39 Case C-171/95, *Recep Tetik* v. *Land Berlin* [1997] ECR I-329, para. 29.
40 According to the Court, the standstill clauses of Art. 13 Decision 1/80 and of Art. 41(1) Additional Protocol converge: see Case C-256/11, *Dereci* [2011] ECR I-11315, para. 93.

force, or the date when the Member State became a member of the EU).[41] According to the Court, the standstill clause does not grant substantive rights, but "specifies, *ratione temporis*, the provisions of a Member State's legislation that must be referred to for the purposes of assessing the position of a Turkish national who wishes to exercise freedom of establishment in a Member State" (*Dereci*, 2011).[42] The Court has found the standstill clause to have direct effect (*Savas*, 2000).[43] The standstill clause prohibits, for example, requiring a Turkish company to apply for work permits for its employees if this requirement was not in place when the Additional Protocol came into force (*Abatay*, 2003).[44] In *Soysal* (2009), the Court held that Article 41(1) prohibits a requirement that Turkish nationals must have a visa to enter the territory of a Member State in order to provide services there on behalf of an undertaking established in Turkey if such visa requirement was not in place on the date the Additional Protocol came into force.[45] Member States cannot revoke measures that improved the situation of Turkish citizens even if the situation thereby created is not worse than at the time the standstill clause entered into force (*Dereci*, 2011).[46]

Third-country nationals who are long-term residents

Third-country nationals having legally resided in a Member State for more than five years have the right to obtain long-term residence status, according to Article 4 of the Long-Term Residents Directive (LTRD).[47] This status provides that long-term residents must be treated equally to nationals (Article 11 LTRD) in particular in relation to access to employment and self-employed activity, education and vocational training, recognition of professional qualifications and free movement and residence (Article 14 LTRD). However, the rights of long-term residents are subject to more limitations than those of Union citizens.

MATERIAL SCOPE

Cross-border element

The Treaty freedoms apply only to situations that feature a cross-border element. The Court has ruled that the Treaty freedom provisions are not applicable to "situations which are purely internal to a Member State."[48] Paradigmatic examples of cross-border situations are:

---

41 Case C-16/05, *The Queen, Veli Tum and Mehmet Dari* v. *Secretary of State for the Home Department* [2007] ECR I-7415, para. 47.
42 *Dereci*, para. 89.   43 *Savas*, para. 54.   44 *Abatay*, para. 117.
45 Case C-228/06, *Mehmet Soysal and Ibrahim Savatli* v. *Bundesrepublik Deutschland* [2009] ECR I-1031, para. 62.
46 *Dereci*, paras. 93–94; see also Joined Cases C-300/09 and C-301/09, *Staatssecretaris van Justitie* v. *F. Toprak and I. Oguz* [2010] ECR I-12845, para. 62.
47 Council Directive 2003/109/EC concerning the status of third-country nationals who are long-term residents, [2004] OJ L16/44.
48 Case 115/78, *J. Knoors* v. *Staatssecretaris van Economische Zaken* [1979] ECR 399, para. 24.

- *Goods* cross the border from one Member State to another.
- *Service* providers temporarily enter another Member State to provide a service, or provide it long distance (e.g. via the Internet).
- *Workers* take up a job in another country. If they continue to reside in one Member State and are employed in another, they are referred to as "frontier workers."
- *Self-employed persons* establish themselves or set up a company or a branch in another Member State.
- *Union citizens* enter and reside in another Member State.
- *Capital and payments* are transferred from one Member State to another or to third countries.

APPLYING THE TREATY FREEDOM PROVISIONS: PROHIBITION OF DISCRIMINATION AND OF RESTRICTIONS

The Treaty freedoms prohibit direct and indirect discrimination on the ground of nationality. Additionally, the Treaty freedoms also prohibit indistinctly applicable measures, which are not discriminatory but nonetheless liable to hinder or make less attractive intra-Union trade or mobility (such measures are referred to as "restrictions" or "obstacles").

Direct discrimination

Laws, rules or practices are directly discriminatory if they explicitly put nationals or products of other Member States at a disadvantage on the ground of their nationality or origin. The Court routinely holds that the principle of equal treatment, which is inherent in all Treaty freedoms, requires that comparable situations should not be treated differently and that different situations should not be treated in the same way, unless such treatment is objectively justified.[49] An example for a directly discriminatory measure is dealt with in the *Delay* case:

Case C-276/07, Delay (2008)

Nancy Delay, a Belgian citizen, was employed as a French-language exchange assistant at the University of Florence under fixed-term contracts successively renewed from 1986 to 1994. Subsequently, she was employed for an indefinite period, but with less pay. By contrast, a national-language assistant was entitled by law to have

---

49 Case C-276/07, *Nancy Delay v. Università degli studi di Firenze, Istituto nazionale della previdenza sociale (INPS) and Repubblica italiana* [2008] ECR I-3635, para. 19.

his or her fixed-term employment contract converted into one for an indefinite period, and all the acquired rights (including salary and seniority rights) are guaranteed from the date of his or her original recruitment. The university denied the same right to Ms. Delay, arguing that it applied only to language assistants, but not to "exchange assistants."

Does Article 45 TFEU prohibit discrimination of "exchange assistants" if they fulfill a similar task as domestic language assistants?
Yes.

A national law is discriminatory if an "Italian worker placed in a situation comparable to that of the applicant in the main proceedings would have been entitled to recognition of his or her rights acquired since the date of his first recruitment."[50]

In some cases, the Court had to deal with measures that granted advantages exclusively to residents of a certain region of a Member State. In these situations, inhabitants of other regions of that same Member State and nationals of other Member States are equally put at a disadvantage. The Court has nonetheless found that such measures may constitute discrimination on the ground of nationality, as "[i]t is enough that the measure should benefit ... certain categories of persons pursuing occupational activity in the Member State in question" (*Government of Communauté Française*, 2008).[51]

Indirect discrimination

National laws, rules or practices are indirectly discriminatory if they apply indistinctly to nationals and non-nationals alike but create detrimental effects mainly for non-nationals. According to the Court, a provision of national law must be regarded as indirectly discriminatory "if it is intrinsically liable to affect migrant workers more than national workers and if there is a consequent risk that it will place the former at a particular disadvantage" (*Hartmann*, 2007).[52] Residence requirements are usually held to constitute indirect discrimination. Although they do not differentiate on the ground of nationality, they nevertheless put non-nationals at a disadvantage because nationals of a Member State are far more likely to be also resident in that state than are non-nationals (e.g. *Bressol*, 2010).[53]

---

50 *Ibid.*, para. 20.
51 Case C-212/06, *Government of Communauté française and Gouvernement wallon v. Gouvernement flamand* [2008] ECR I-1683, para. 50; see also Case C-281/98, *Roman Angonese v. Cassa di Risparmio di Bolzano SpA* [2000] ECR I-4139, para. 41.
52 Case C-212/05, *Gertraud Hartmann v. Freistaat Bayern* [2007] ECR I-6303, para. 30.
53 Case C-73/08, *Nicolas Bressol and Others and Céline Chaverot and Others v. Gouvernement de la Communauté française* [2010] ECR I-2735, para. 45.

Prohibition of restrictions

The Treaty freedoms prohibit national measures that are indistinctly applicable to both domestic and non-domestic persons or products alike, but nonetheless constitute a barrier to cross-border trade or mobility. This broad understanding of the Treaty freedoms originates in the leading case of *Dassonville*. The Court held that Article 34 TFEU prohibits "all trading rules enacted by Member States which are capable of hindering, directly or indirectly, actually or potentially, intra-community trade."[54] In the following decades, the Court transferred this concept to the other Treaty freedoms as well: the cases usually identified with this policy change are *Säger* (1991) for services, *Bosman* (1995) for workers and *Gebhard* (1995) for establishment. It should be emphasized that the distinction between indirectly discriminatory measures on the one hand and indistinctly applicable, but restrictive measures on the other is blurred. As the current doctrinal system treats both kinds of measures the same way, the distinction is of little factual relevance.

JUSTIFICATIONS

While the Treaty freedoms generally prohibit discriminatory and restrictive measures of the Member States, it is likewise recognized that there are instances where such measures may serve important regulatory purposes, and should therefore be justifiable. The Treaty explicitly recognizes certain justificatory grounds, such as public policy, public security and public health. Moreover, the Court has also acknowledged that both indirectly discriminatory[55] and restrictive national measures can be justified on other important grounds in the public interest as well. All such national measures must in any case be proportionate in order to be justifiable. The burden of proof is upon the Member State to provide evidence in that regard.

Treaty-based justifications

According to the Treaty, discriminatory or restrictive measures can be justified on certain important considerations in the public interest. These grounds are different for the various Treaty freedoms. Article 36 TFEU provides that such national measures applicable to goods can be justified on the grounds of public morality, public policy or public security, the protection of health and life of humans, animals or plants, the protection of national treasures possessing artistic, historic or archaeological value, and the protection of industrial and commercial property. With regard to workers, establishment and services, the Treaty recognizes justifications on the grounds of

---

54 Case 8/74, *Procureur du Roi* v. *Benoît and Gustave Dassonville* [1974] ECR 837, para. 5.
55 See e.g. Case C-20/12, *Giersch* [2013] ECR I-00000, para. 46.

public policy, public security and public health as well as those concerning activities connected with the exercise of official authority (Article 51 TFEU for establishment) and employment in the public service (Article 45(4) TFEU for workers). For Union citizenship, exceptions are laid down in Article 27 of the Citizenship Directive (2004/38/EC). With regard to the free movement of capital, the Treaty acknowledges restrictions on grounds of public policy or public security, as well as certain restrictions with regard to taxation and to capital movements to and from third countries.

According to settled case law, measures that are directly discriminatory – i.e. measures that differentiate on the ground of nationality of persons or the origin of goods or capital – can only be justified by the Treaty-based exceptions.[56] As the prohibition of direct discrimination on the ground of nationality is a central concern of the EU's internal market system, national laws that breach this principle should be severely limited.

Justifications on overriding grounds in the public interest

As mentioned above, the so-called *Dassonville* formula holds that national measures may infringe Union law even though they apply indistinctly to nationals and non-nationals alike. Because the *Dassonville* formula has a very broad scope, the Court had to ensure that legitimate national regulatory measures are not inhibited by the Treaty freedoms. Thus, it first ruled in *Cassis de Dijon* that national measures that constitute restrictions could be justified also on grounds other than those explicitly mentioned in the Treaty. Since then, the Court has accepted a broad range of potential justifications for indirectly discriminatory and indistinctly applicable measures.

Justifications accepted by the Court include:

- environmental protection (*Commission* v. *Denmark – Beer Bottles*, 1988);[57]
- consumer protection (*Cassis de Dijon*, 1979);[58]
- protection of fundamental rights (*Schmidberger*, 2003);[59]
- protection of workers (*Arblade*, 1999);[60]
- protection of media plurality (*United Pan-Europe Communications*, 2007);[61]
- road safety (*Commission* v. *Italy – Italian Trailers*, 2009);[62]
- defending and promoting one or several of the official languages of a Member State (*UTECA*, 2009).[63]

56 See e.g. Case C-388/01, *Commission* v. *Italy – Access to Museums* [2003] ECR I-721, para. 19; see also Case C-490/04, *Commission* v. *Germany – Temp Work Agencies* [2007] ECR I-6095, para. 86.
57 Case 302/86, *Commission* v. *Denmark – Beer Bottles* [1988] ECR 4607, para. 9.
58 Case 120/78, *Rewe-Zentral AG* v. *Bundesmonopolverwaltung für Branntwein* [1979] ECR 649, para. 8.
59 Case C-112/00, *Schmidberger* v. *Republic of Austria* [2003] ECR I-5659, para. 74.
60 Joined Cases C-369/96 and C-376/96, *Arblade* [1999] ECR I-8453, para. 60.
61 Case C-250/06, *United Pan-Europe Communications Belgium SA and Others* v. *Belgian State* [2007] ECR I-11135, para. 44.
62 Case C-110/05, *Commission* v. *Italy – Italian Trailers* [2009] ECR I-519, para. 60.
63 Case C-222/07, *Unión de Televisiones Comerciales Asociadas (UTECA)* v. *Administración General del Estado* [2009] ECR I-1407, para. 27.

The list of public interests that can justify indirectly discriminatory or restrictive measures is non-exhaustive. In the absence of common Union standards, it is up to the Member States to decide on the level of protection they wish to grant. This right, however, is subject to certain limitations. Member States cannot apply a protective standard that exceeds the standard set by EU law if the area is fully harmonized. If the field is subject only to minimum harmonization, on the other hand, Member States are allowed to enforce a higher standard. The Court does not accept justifications that serve purely economic goals (*Campus Oil*, 1984),[64] such as the protection of domestic businesses.[65]

Proportionality

National measures that infringe the Treaty freedoms must be proportionate in order to be justified. This holds true for both types of justifications. In legal scholarship, the proportionality requirement is usually presented as having three prongs (however, the Court expressly employs only the first two).

- *Appropriateness.*[66] A national measure must be appropriate to achieve the purported regulatory goal. In *Stopover Tax* (2009),[67] a Sardinian law provided that companies without a tax domicile in Sardinia must pay an extra tax for aircraft and boats making a stopover in Sardinia. The Court rejected the argument that this tax was justified as a measure to fight pollution, as the differential treatment of resident and nonresident companies was not an appropriate tool to reduce pollution. The national legislation must pursue the objective in a consistent and systematic manner.[68]
- *Necessity.* A national measure must not go beyond what is necessary in order to attain the objective sought. If a less restrictive measure is available to achieve the same end, a national measure fails the proportionality test. The Court held, for example, that a requirement to provide sufficient product information on a product's label may be a less restrictive alternative for the protection of public health than an outright prohibition of the product and still achieve a similar result (*Solgar Vitamins*, 2010).[69]
- *Proportionality (in the narrow sense).* In this step, the Court is assumed to perform a balancing test, comparing the projected positive effects of a national measure with its negative impact. If the negative impact outweighs the positive effects, the measure fails the proportionality test.

---

64 Case 72/83, *Campus Oil* [1984] ECR 2727, para. 7.
65 Joined Cases C-49/98, C-50/98, C-52/98 to C-54/98 and C-68/98 to C-71/98, *Finalarte* [2001] ECR I-7831, para. 39.
66 The Court also employs the term "suitability." See e.g. Case C-55/94, *Gebhard* [1995] ECR I-4165, para. 39.
67 Case C-169/08, *Presidente del Consiglio dei Ministri* v. *Regione Sardegna – Stopover Tax* [2009] ECR I-10821.
68 Case C-169/07, *Hartlauer* [2009] ECR I-1721, para. 55.
69 Case C-446/08, *Solgar Vitamins* [2010] ECR I-3973, para. 57.

When assessing whether the principle of proportionality has been observed, account must be taken of the fact that a Member State has the power to determine the degree of protection which it wishes to afford to a public interest goal and the way in which that degree of protection is to be achieved (*Blanco Pérez*, 2010).[70] Since that degree of protection may vary from one Member State to another, Member States must be granted a certain margin of discretion. Consequently, the fact that one Member State imposes less strict rules than another does not mean that the latter's rules are disproportionate.[71] In any event, it is for a Member State to show that its measures conform to the proportionality requirement. However, the Court held that "[w]hilst it is true that it is for a Member State which invokes an imperative requirement as justification for the hindrance to free movement of goods to demonstrate that its rules are appropriate and necessary to attain the legitimate objective being pursued, that burden of proof cannot be so extensive as to require the Member State to prove, positively, that no other conceivable measure could enable that objective to be attained under the same conditions" (*Commission v. Italy – Italian Trailers*, 2009).[72]

Further reading

BARNARD, CATHERINE, "Derogations, Justifications and the Four Freedoms: Is State Interest Really Protected?," in Catherine Barnard, and Okeoghene Odudu (eds.), *The Outer Limits of European Union Law*, Oxford: Hart Publishing, 2009

BARNARD, CATHERINE "Restricting Restrictions: Lessons for the EU from the US?" (2009) 68 *Cambridge Law Journal* 575

DAVIES, GARETH, "Understanding Market Access: Exploring the Economic Rationality of Different Conceptions of Free Movement Law" (2010) 11 *German Law Journal* 671

NIC SHUIBHNE, NIAMH, *The Coherence of EU Free Movement Law: Constitutional Responsibility and the Court of Justice*, Oxford University Press, 2013

NIC SHUIBHNE, NIAMH, and MACI, MARSELA, "Proving Public Interest: The Growing Impact of Evidence in Free Movement Case Law" (2013) 50 *Common Market Law Review* 965

OLIVER, PETER, and ROTH, WULF-HENNING, "The Internal Market and the Four Freedoms" (2004) 41 *Common Market Law Review* 407

SCHMIDT, SUSANNE, "Who Cares About Nationality? The Path-Dependent Case Law of the CJEU from Goods to Citizens" (2012) 19 *Journal of European Public Policy* 8

STONE SWEET, ALEC, and MATHEWS, JUD, "Proportionality Balancing and Global Constitutionalism" (2008–2009) 47 *Columbia Journal of Transnational Law* 72

SYRPIS, PHIL (ed.), *The Judiciary, the Legislature and the EU Internal Market*, Cambridge University Press, 2012

TRYFONIDOU, ALINA, "Further Steps on the Road to Convergence Among the Market Freedoms" (2010) 35 *European Law Review* 36

---

70 Joined Cases C-570/07 and C-571/07, *Blanco Pérez* [2010] ECR I-4629, para. 44.
71 Case C-110/05, *Commission* v. *Italy – Italian Trailers* [2009] ECR I-519, para. 65.   72 *Ibid.*, para. 65.

Free movement of goods

3 (Articles 28–37 TFEU)

INTRODUCTION

Many Western countries reacted to the Great Depression of the 1930s with massive protectionism. After the Second World War, Western industrialized countries attempted to quickly establish a modicum of global free trade. Trade liberalization in Europe took place under the auspices of the Organization for European Economic Co-operation (OEEC) (now the OECD), an organization that had been created in 1948 to administer the postwar Marshall Plan. At the same time, the General Agreement on Tariffs and Trade (GATT) was conceived to liberalize trade on a global level. The European Economic Community (EEC) was therefore created by the Treaty of Rome in 1957 in a climate of trade liberalization.

In the 1950s, trade in goods was at the core of all trade liberalization efforts (in contrast, cross-border trade in services became a significant phenomenon only in the 1980s and 1990s). This is reflected in the legal structure of the EEC: its core was constituted by a customs union, which provided for the free movement of goods among the Member States unrestrained by tariffs, quantitative restrictions or measures having equivalent effect. However, the EEC was more than just a customs union: it aimed at a relatively far-reaching integration of the economies of the Member States, which provided not only for factor mobility (i.e. mobility of labor and capital), but also for a partial harmonization of the relevant national legislation. According to a well-known scheme of regional integration developed by economist Bela Balassa in the early 1960s, European economic integration as envisaged by the Treaty of Rome was considered already well-advanced (see Table 3.1).

In this chapter, we will look at the main provisions of the TFEU with regard to the free movement of goods. This includes the provisions relating to the customs union and the prohibition of quantitative restrictions as well as the prohibition of discriminatory taxation. First, however, we will look at relevant trade theory underlying these provisions.

Table 3.1 Schematic overview of the steps of economic integration according to Bela Balassa[a]	
Integrative step	**Central characteristics**
Free trade area	Abolition of tariffs and quantitative restrictions between member states. However, each member state retains its own tariffs on imports from third countries.
Customs union	Abolition of tariffs and quantitative restrictions between member states and adoption of a common customs tariff on imports from third countries.
Common market	Restrictions on factor mobility are abolished.
Economic union	Harmonization of national measures to a certain extent in order to remove obstacles on mobility of factors of production resulting from regulatory disparities between member states.
Economic and monetary union	Complete integration of common monetary, fiscal, social and macroeconomic policies managed by a supranational authority.

a   Bela Balassa, *The Theory of Economic Integration*, London: George Allen, 1961, p. 2.

The economics of trade

Paul Samuelson stated in his 1939 article, "The Gains from International Trade," what is essentially the core assumption of trade economics: "[S]ome trade is better than no trade."[1] The idea that trade has the potential to raise the net welfare of all countries lies at the heart of international trade theory.[2] The assumption is essentially uncontested by economists of all persuasions. What is contested, however, is why and under which conditions trade is beneficial.[3]

Classical trade theory developed in the eighteenth century.[4] It was conceived as a refutation of mercantilist theory and policy, which had been the dominant conceptual framework in the preceding centuries.[5] Adam Smith conceptualized gains from trade in terms of "absolute advantage": countries benefit if they specialize in what they do best and then trade.[6] If England was more efficient in producing cloth than Portugal, and Portugal was more efficient in producing wine than England, under conditions of perfectly free trade and no transportation (and other transaction) costs, England

1 Paul A. Samuelson, "The Gains from International Trade" (1939) 5 *Canadian Journal of Economics and Political Science/Revue canadienne d'Economique et de Science politique* 195.

2 Helpman shows, for example, that since the beginning of the industrial revolution, the expansion of trade correlates with higher growth of the world economy. Elhanan Helpman, *The Mystery of Economic Growth*, Cambridge, MA: Harvard University Press, 2010, p. 56.

3 Bertil Ohlin put the issue as follows: "The immediate cause of trade is always that goods can be bought cheaper from outside in terms of money than they can be produced at home, and *vice versa*. It remains to be shown why some goods can be more cheaply produced in one region than in another." Bertil Ohlin, *Interregional and International Trade*, Cambridge, MA: Harvard University Press, 1967, p. 7.

4 It is based, most importantly, on the writings of David Hume, Adam Smith, David Ricardo and John Stuart Mill. See e.g. David Ricardo, *Principles of Political Economy and Taxation*, Amherst, NY: Prometheus Books, 1996.

5 Ernesto Screpanti and Stefano Zamagni, *An Outline of the History of Economic Thought*, Oxford University Press, 2005, p. 55. See e.g. Adam Smith, *The Wealth of Nations*, Amherst, NY: Prometheus Books, 1991, p. 328.

6 Smith, *The Wealth of Nations*, p. 342.

would produce all the cloth and Portugal all the wine.[7] Thus, Smith assumed that, under free trade, products are produced where production costs are lowest.[8]

In 1817, David Ricardo brought forward the model of "comparative" (or relative) advantage. It shows trade to be beneficial for all participants even if no country enjoys absolute advantage in the production of any product. In his well-known example of bilateral trade between Portugal and England, Portugal had absolute advantage in the production of both wine and cloth, but produced wine relatively more efficiently than cloth. England had no absolute advantage in the production of either product. However, with trade, both countries may nonetheless benefit:[9] If England specializes in the production of cloth (which it produces relatively more efficiently than it produces wine) while Portugal focuses on wine production (which it produces relatively more efficiently than it produces cloth), then more goods can be produced in total with the same input of labor. In effect, trade raises the real incomes of all trade partners in comparison to autarky.[10] Whereas Smith's model was about each country specializing in producing the product where it enjoys an absolute advantage over the trading partner, in Ricardo's model trade is beneficial even if a country has no absolute advantage whatsoever.[11]

Neoclassical theory started to develop into a consistent body of thought in the late nineteenth century. The exponents of classical theory – Smith, Ricardo, Mill and Marx – had defined the value of a product by the amount of labor that went into the production of the good. Accordingly, Smith, Ricardo and Mill explained the advantages of trade in terms of labor value: trade is beneficial because on an aggregate level more units of cloth and wine are produced with the same input of labor. Neoclassical theory, however, saw prices solely as a function of supply and demand, and not as a function of some absolute, intrinsic value. Therefore, neoclassical scholars attempted to reformulate the benefits of trade on the basis of the supply/demand function. The best-known neoclassical trade model is Heckscher–Ohlin, which held that countries "will tend to specialise (either partially or wholly) in the production of the commodity using much of its most abundant factor."[12] Whereas the classical model assumes that it is beneficial for countries to trade because of differences in labor productivity, the Heckscher–Ohlin model holds that countries trade because of their different factor endowment (e.g. a vast landmass in one country, and vast labor supply in another). Eli Heckscher argued that "[t]he prerequisites of initiating trade

---

7 Paul A. Samuelson, "A Ricardo–Sraffa Paradigm Comparing Gains from Trade in Inputs and Finished Goods" (2001) 39 *Journal of Economic Literature* 1205.

8 Joseph Schumpeter, *History of Economic Analysis*, Oxford University Press, 1996, p. 607.

9 Schumpeter, *History of Economic Analysis*, p. 614.

10 In Ricardo's model, the differences between the countries are based on labor productivity, i.e. differences in technology, skills, soil, weather, etc., that affect the productivity of labor.

11 John Stuart Mill, *Principles of Political Economy with Some of Their Application to Social Philosophy*, Book III, Exchange, in William Allen (ed.), *International Trade Theory: Hume to Ohlin*, New York: Random House, 1967, p. 74).

12 Paul A. Samuelson, "International Trade and the Equalization of Factor Prices" (1948) 58 *Economic Journal* 165. See also Ohlin, *Interregional and International Trade*, p. 7.

may thus be summarised as different relative scarcity, i.e. different relative prices of the factors of production in the exchanging countries, as well as different proportions between the factors of production in different commodities."[13]

In the 1970s, the classical and neoclassical trade models came under scrutiny and criticism by adherents of the "New Trade Theory" (NTT). NTT scholars such as Paul Krugman found that these models lacked plausibility in particular when it came to trade between industrialized countries, and in understanding intra-industry trade, both of which dominate contemporary world trade.[14] The industrialized countries of the world do not differ radically in either productivity levels (Ricardo) or factor endowment (Heckscher–Ohlin). Elhanan Helpman, another NTT scholar argued: "The factor proportions theory contributes very little to our understanding of the determination of the volume of trade in the world economy, or the volume of trade within groups of countries. The Ricardian view of comparative advantage is also of little help in this respect."[15] For NTT scholars, the reason why industrialized countries traded was to be found in two phenomena: increasing returns to scale and network effects.

Neoclassical theory assumed constant returns to scale (the output rises in the same proportion as the input). This would mean two things: (1) company size does not matter, and (2) the only factor that influences the location of production are production costs. NTT scholars, however, argued that the contemporary reality of international trade disproves this assumption: not only is global trade dominated by large multinational corporations, but certain industries also tend to cluster together in certain regions (e.g. Hollywood for movies, Silicon Valley for computers, Basel for pharmaceuticals or the City of London for banking).[16] Both phenomena of international trade are inexplicable from a neoclassical perspective, as the assumption of constant returns to scale allows for no benefit of size.[17] In contrast to the Ricardo and Heckscher–Ohlin models, the NTT models hold that the reason for trade mainly lies in the structure of the industries, not factor endowment or general labor productivity.[18] A specific industrial organization (of a company or of an industry) creates specialization and network effects, which cause increasing returns to scale. Beneficial structures are, inter alia, geographic proximity: if all specialists, skilled workers and companies of a certain industry are located in one region, this region will both be better in producing these things, and remain better because no other region can catch up. As economic models are simplifications of reality, it is likely that none of the above-mentioned theories is completely accurate. Rather, it seems more plausible that each of the models describes different aspects of international trade.

13 Eli Heckscher, "The Effect of Foreign Trade and the Distribution of Income," in William Allen (ed.), *International Trade Theory: Hume to Ohlin*, New York: Random House, 1967, p. 28.
14 Elhanan Helpman, "Imperfect Competition and International Trade: Evidence from Fourteen Industrial Countries" (1987) 1 *Journal of the Japanese and International Economies* 63.
15 *Ibid.*, 63.   16 R. Baldwin, "The Growth Effects of 1992," NBER Working Paper No. 3119 (1989), pp. 18–19.
17 Elhanan Helpman and Paul Krugman, *Market Structure and Foreign Trade*, Brighton: Harvester Wheatsheaf, 1985, p. 3.
18 *Ibid.*, 1.

Main Treaty provisions at a glance

The Treaty aims at eliminating all restrictions on the cross-border trade of goods. In particular, it provides three instruments to realize the free movement of goods in the EU:

- A customs union in which all customs duties between the Member States are prohibited and a common customs tariff in relation to third countries is established (Articles 28–32 TFEU). The key provision is Article 30 TFEU, which prohibits customs duties and charges having equivalent effect between Member States.
- A prohibition of discriminatory taxation on goods from other Member States (Article 110 TFEU).[19]
- The abolition of all quantitative restrictions on imports and exports between Member States and of measures having equivalent effect (Articles 34–36 TFEU).

Whereas Articles 30 and 110 TFEU deal with fiscal measures, Articles 34–36 TFEU deal with non-fiscal measures. Table 3.2 sets out an overview of the main Treaty provisions with regard to the free movement of goods.

Table 3.2 Overview of the main Treaty provisions with regard to the free movement of goods		
Treaty provision	**Fiscal or non-fiscal?**	**Subject matter**
Art. 30 TFEU	Fiscal measures	Money duties on market access
Art. 110 TFEU	Fiscal measures	Taxation of goods which have entered the market of a Member State
Arts. 34–36 TFEU	Non-fiscal measures	Non-fiscal regulation of goods, in regard to both market access and national market regulation

Direct effect

As discussed in the previous chapter, the Court first found a Treaty provision to have direct effect in *Van Gend en Loos* (1963). According to the Court, Article 12 EEC, which was a standstill clause that prohibited Member States from establishing any new customs duties on imports or exports, could be directly invoked. After the end of the transitional period, the Court extended direct effect to what is now Article 30 TFEU, which generally prohibits customs duties on imports or exports or any charges having equivalent effect (*Capolongo*, 1973).[20] Articles 34 and 35 TFEU have also been found to have direct effect, as the Court first accepted in *Dassonville*

---

19 Case C-206/06, *Essent Netwerk* [2008] ECR I-5497, para. 40.
20 Case 77/72, *Capolongo* [1973] ECR 611, para. 11.

$(1974)^{21}$ and *Redmond* (1978), respectively.[22] And, finally, Article 110 TFEU has direct effect as well, as the Court first held in *Fink-Frucht* (1968).[23]

SCOPE

Personal scope (beneficiaries)

Articles 30, 34–36 and 110 TFEU apply irrespective of the nationality of the traders involved (*Diamantarbeiders*,1969).[24]

Material scope

Articles 30, 34–36 and 110 TFEU apply to the movement of goods across national borders. These goods must either originate in the Member States or come from third countries and be in free circulation in the Union (Article 28(2) TFEU).

Goods

The Court has defined goods as products that "can be valued in money and which are capable, as such, of forming the subject of commercial transactions"[25] (*Commission* v. *Italy – Art Works*, 1968) and "possess tangible physical characteristics."[26] Generally, the definition of goods poses few problems. Products like computers or shoes clearly are goods within the meaning of Articles 30, 34–36 and 110 TFEU. Some products, however, are more difficult to classify. The following products have been classified as "goods" by the Court: artwork (*Commission* v. *Italy – Art Works*, 1968), collectors' gold and silver coins, provided they are not coins in circulation as legal tender (*R* v. *Thompson*, 1978)[27] and waste (*Commission* v. *Belgium – Walloon Waste*, 1992).[28] Waste is a "good" within the scope of Article 34 TFEU because "objects which are shipped across a frontier for the purposes of commercial transactions are subject to [Article 34 TFEU], whatever the nature of those transactions,"[29] as the Court held in *Commission* v. *Belgium – Walloon Waste*. The Court has also found that electricity, an "intangible" product, falls within the concept of goods (*Almelo*, 1994).[30] However, most other

---

21 Case 8/74, *Dassonville* [1974] ECR 837.   22 Case 83/78, *Redmond* [1978] ECR 2347, paras. 66 and 67.
23 Case 27/67, *Fink-Frucht* [1968] ECR 223, 232.
24 Case 2/69, *Diamantarbeiders* [1969] ECR 211, paras. 24–26.
25 Case 7/68 *Commission* v. *Italy – Art Works* [1968] ECR 424, 428.
26 Case C-97/98, *Jägerskiöld* [1999] ECR I-7319, Opinion of Advocate General Fennelly, para. 20.
27 Case 7/78 *Thompson* [1978] ECR 2247, para. 26.
28 Case 2/90, *Commission* v. *Belgium – Walloon Waste* [1992] ECR I-4431, para. 28; see also Case C-221/06, *Stadtgemeinde Frohnleiten* [2007] ECR I-9643, para. 37.
29 *Commission* v. *Belgium – Walloon Waste*, para. 26.
30 Case C-393/92, *Almelo* [1994] ECR I-1477, para. 28; see also Case 158/94, *Commission* v. *Italy* [1997] ECR I-5789, para. 17.

Table 3.3 Delineating the free movement of goods from the other Treaty freedoms	
Goods or . . .	
. . . workers	Restrictions on the movement of personal belongings of workers are covered by Art. 45 TFEU (*Weigel,* 2004)[a]
. . . services	If the service is manifested in a product (films on DVDs, music on CDs, computer programs on discs), it is a good (*Commission/Greece – Computer Games,* 2006).[b] If the physical object only helps to carry out the service, it does not constitute a good (lottery tickets are merely ancillary to the organization of a lottery).[c]
. . . capital and payments	Old silver alloy coins which are no longer legal tender are goods.[d] Valid coins and money bills, on the other hand, fall under Art. 63 TFEU.

a   Case C-387/01, *Weigel* [2004] ECR I-4981, paras. 54–55.
b   Case C-65/05, *Commission* v. *Greece – Computer Games* [2006] ECR I-10341, para. 24.
c   Case C-275/92, *Schindler* [1994] ECR I-01039, para. 22.
d   *R* v. *Thompson* [1978] ECR 2247, para. 31.

intangible products fall outside the scope of goods. This includes television advertisements (*Sacchi,* 1974), intellectual property rights and fishing permits (*Jägerskiöld,* 1999).

Origin of goods

Article 28(2) TFEU provides that the provisions on the free movement of goods apply "to products originating in Member States and to products coming from third countries which are in free circulation in Member States." It is presumed that goods within the EU fulfill this criterion, unless proven otherwise: Article 101(1) of the EU Customs Code holds that "all goods in the customs territory of the Community shall be presumed to have the customs status of Community goods, unless it is established that they are not Community goods."[31] The first criterion of Article 28(2) TFEU ("originating in Member States") is fulfilled by all products produced within the EU, with a few exceptions that do not concern us here. Third-country products are considered to be in free circulation in the Member States if they have been imported legally. Article 29 TFEU provides that "[p]roducts coming from a third country shall be considered to be in free circulation in a Member State if the import formalities have been complied with and any customs duties or charges having equivalent effect which are payable have been levied in that Member State." Once goods from third countries are in "free circulation," they are treated equally with goods originating in the Member States (*Criel,* 1976).[32]

31   Regulation 450/2008 of the European Parliament and of the Council of 23 April 2008 laying down the Community Customs Code (Modernized Customs Code), [2008] OJ L145/1.
32   Case 41/76, *Criel* [1976] ECR 1921, para. 43.

Cross-border element

Generally, Articles 30, 34 and 110 TFEU apply only to situations that feature a cross-border element. The Court has repeatedly held that Articles 30 and 34 TFEU do not apply to transactions which are purely internal to a Member State (*Oosthoek*, 1982).[33] There are, however, a few decisions that arguably dealt with situations purely internal to a Member State, where the Court still found Article 30 or 34 TFEU to be applicable. As concerns Article 34 TFEU, this is usually the case when the Court finds that, even though the specific facts of the case may be confined to a Member State, the measure in question nonetheless has the potential to hinder intra-Union trade (e.g. *Pistre*, 1997). A characteristic example are national rules that require a producer to purchase domestic products. In *PreussenElektra* (2001), a German rule required an energy company to purchase electricity from renewable sources produced within its area of supply. Even though the facts of the case are confined to Germany (the law, the company and the product), the measure nonetheless came within the scope of Article 34 TFEU because the requirement to purchase energy from domestic producers prevented the company from obtaining supplies from traders in other Member States[34] (the Court then found the requirement justified on grounds of environmental protection[35]). As regards Article 30 TFEU, the judgments in question deal with charges imposed when goods cross a territorial boundary within a Member State. In *Simitzi* (1995), a tax was levied on all products that entered the Dodecanese islands, regardless of whether they came from the Greek mainland or other Member States.[36] And, in *Carbonati Apuani* (2004), a tax was imposed on all marble from Carrara that crossed the municipality's territorial boundaries, no distinction being made between marble destined for Italy and marble destined for other Member States. The Court held in all such cases "that a charge imposed when goods cross a territorial boundary within a Member State constitutes a charge having effect equivalent to a customs duty."[37]

ADDRESSEES

States

The main addressees of Articles 30, 34–36 and 110 TFEU are the Member States, even though they are explicitly addressed only by Article 110 TFEU. These provisions bind the national governments as well as all administrative sub-units and other institutions, including local and regional authorities and the different branches of government

---

33 Case 286/81, *Oosthoek* [1982] ECR 4575, para. 9.
34 Case C-379/98, *PreussenElektra* [2001] ECR I–2099, para. 70.   35 *Ibid.*, paras. 73–75.
36 Joined Cases C-485/93 and C-486/93, *Simitzi* [1995] ECR I-2655.
37 Case C-72/03, *Carbonati Apuani* [2004] ECR I-08027, para. 25.

(legislative, executive, judicial).[38] In *Commission* v. *Belgium – Public Warehouses* (1983), the Court found that storage charges levied by the municipalities in connection with customs formalities may constitute a charge having equivalent effect to customs duties within the meaning of Article 30 TFEU.[39] In *Aragonesa de Publicidad* (1991), the Court held that Article 34 TFEU "may apply to measures adopted by all the authorities of the Member States, be they the central authorities, the authorities of a federal State, or other territorial authorities."[40] And, in *Essent Netwerk* (2008) – a case that dealt with the levy of a surcharge on the price for electricity transmission by a company designated by law – the Court held that, "for the purposes of the application of [Articles 30 and 110 TFEU], it is of little account that the financial charge is not levied by the State. The fact that the price surcharge is levied by the net operators is, therefore, irrelevant."[41]

Union institutions

The Treaty freedoms bind not only the Member States, but also the institutions of the EU. Secondary EU law – i.e. law enacted by the Union institutions – must comply with primary law, including the Treaty freedoms. In *Ramel* (1978), the Court first found an EU measure invalid in light of Article 30 TFEU.[42] The case concerned a Regulation that authorized Member States to raise a levy in intra-Union trade which effectively constituted a charge having equivalent effect to customs duties. And, in *Meyhui* (1994), the Court held that a Directive that prohibits affixing to crystal glass products their description in a language other than that of the Member State in which those goods are marketed constitutes a barrier to intra-Union trade and may, therefore, violate Articles 34–36 TFEU (however, the Court found the measure justified on grounds of consumer protection).[43] And, with regard to discriminatory taxation, the Court held in *Gaston Schul* (1982):[44] "The requirements of [Article 110 TFEU] are of a mandatory nature and do not allow derogation by any measure adopted by an institution of the Community."[45] The Court has routinely acknowledged the "broad discretion" of the Union legislature, ruling only against measures that are "manifestly inappropriate having regard to the objective which the competent institution is seeking to pursue" (*Alliance for Natural Health*, 2005).[46] Persons can inform the Commission about national practices that violate EU law, but the Commission is under no legal obligation to commence infringement proceedings against the Member State in question, as the Court has held, for example, in *Star Fruit Company* (1989).[47]

---

38 On the application of Arts. 34–36 TFEU to judicial authorities, see Case 58/80, *Dansk Supermarked* [1981] ECR 181, para. 12.
39 Case 132/82, *Commission* v. *Belgium* [1983] ECR 1649, para. 14.
40 Joined Cases C-1/90 and C-176/90, *Aragonesa de Publicidad Exterior* [1991] ECR I-4151, para. 8.
41 *Essent Netwerk*, para. 46.   42 Joined Cases 80/77 and 81/77, *Ramel* [1978] ECR 927, para. 38.
43 Case C-51/93, *Meyhui* [1994] ECR I-3879; see also Joined Cases C-154/04 and C-155/04, *Alliance for Natural Health* [2005] ECR I-6451.
44 Case 15/81, *Gaston Schul* [1982] ECR 1409.   45 *Ibid.*, para. 42.
46 Joined Cases C-154/04 and C-155/04, *Alliance for Natural Health* [2005] ECR I-6451, para. 52.
47 Case 247/87, *Star Fruit Company* [1989] ECR 291.

Non-state actors

Article 34 TFEU applies to non-state actors only if their activities can be attributed to the state. In *Buy Irish* (1982), an "Irish Goods Council" conducted an advertising campaign to promote buying domestic products with such slogans as "Tip just a few purchases over to Irish products and tip jobs in Ireland's favour."[48] Although the "Council" was founded as a private limited company, its management committee was partly appointed and its operations mostly funded by the Irish government, which also had established the broad conceptual outline of the campaign. Under these circumstances, the Court found Article 34 TFEU to be applicable to the "Council." Activities of non-state actors can also be attributed to the state if they perform delegated sovereign functions. This is the case, for example, with associations that have been granted the power to regulate a specific trade or profession, as the Court decided in *Association of Pharmaceutical Importers* (1989).

Cases 266 and 267/87, Association of Pharmaceutical Importers (1989)

The Pharmaceutical Society of Great Britain was the regulatory and professional body of pharmacists. The Pharmaceutical Society adopted a Code of Ethics, which prohibited a pharmacist from substituting any other product for a product specifically named in the prescription, even if he or she believes the quality of the other product to be identical. This rule applied even when the same product – produced by the same company – was imported from another Member State where it was sold under a different name (i.e. a parallel import). After the adoption of the Code of Ethics, parallel imports to the United Kingdom practically ceased.

Can a measure adopted by a professional body – even though it is not a state entity – come within the scope of Article 34 TFEU?
Yes.

The Court found that Article 34 TFEU applies to the Pharmaceutical Society because the power to govern the professional activities of pharmacists had been conferred upon it by the State. Enrolment in the society was obligatory to carry on this business, and the Society's disciplinary committee had the power to impose disciplinary sanctions, including removal from the registers.[49] The Court held that the Code of Ethics violated Article 34 TFEU; however, it found that the measure may be justified on the ground of public health (Article 36 TFEU).[50]

---

48 Case 249/81, *Commission v. Ireland – Buy Irish* [1982] ECR 4005, 4010.   49 *Ibid.*, para. 14.   50 *Ibid.*, para. 24.

In *Fra.bo* (2012), the Court found that the standardization and certification activities of an institution established under private law are subject to Article 34 TFEU if "the national legislation considers the products certified by that body to be compliant with national law and that has the effect of restricting the marketing of products which are not certified by that body."[51] The case concerned the refusal by DVGW, a German certification body, to issue its certification for the copper fittings used for water piping produced by Fra.bo on the ground that the company had failed to comply with its testing requirements. Certification by the DVGW is not a precondition for introducing a product for drinking water use to the German market. While the relevant regulation, the *AVBWasserV*, requires the mark of a recognized inspection body and specifically mentions the DVGW mark in that regard, the parties are free to depart from the requirements set out in the regulation.[52] Moreover, compliance with the *AVBWasserV* can also be established through an alternative procedure carried out by an independent expert.[53] Despite this, the Court found that "the lack of certification by the DVGW places a considerable restriction on the marketing of the products concerned on the German market. Although the *AVBWasserV* merely lays down the general sales conditions as between water supply undertakings and their customers, from which the parties are free to depart, it is apparent from the case-file that, in practice, almost all German consumers purchase copper fittings certified by the DVGW."[54] Accordingly, by virtue of its authority granted by national legislation to certify the products, the DVGW "in reality holds the power to regulate the entry into the German market of products such as the copper fittings at issue in the main proceedings."[55] Therefore, Article 34 TFEU applied to the activities of the DVGW.

The free movement of goods provisions therefore apply to non-state actors if the latter fulfill certain sovereign functions or if their activities are otherwise attributable to the state.[56] Unless such connection exists, the Court does not apply the provisions to private actors (i.e. does not accord them horizontal direct effect). This was not always the case: in its early case law, the Court had held that it is impossible in any circumstances for agreements between individuals to derogate from the mandatory provisions of the Treaty on the free movement of goods (e.g. *Dansk Supermarked*, 1981),[57] thereby suggesting that a violation of Article 34 TFEU by private actors is possible. In its more recent case law, however, the Court has rejected any horizontal direct effect of Article 34 TFEU (*Sapod Audic*, 2002).[58] Instead, as the Court had previously held, private actors are subject to competition law only. In *Van de Haar*

---

51 Case C-171/11, *Fra.bo* [2012] ECR I-00000, para. 32.   52 *Ibid.*, paras. 3 and 30.   53 *Ibid.*, para. 29.
54 *Ibid.*, para. 30.   55 *Ibid.*, para. 31.
56 See e.g. Case 222/82, *Apple and Pear Development Council* [1983] ECR 4083, para. 33; Case C-265/95, *Commission v. France – Spanish Strawberries* [1997] ECR I-6959, para. 52; Case C-112/00, *Schmidberger* [2003] ECR I-5659.
57 Case 58/80, *Dansk Supermarked* [1981] ECR 181, para. 17.
58 Case C-159/00, *Sapod Audic* [2002] ECR I-5031, para. 74.

(1984),[59] the Court argued that Article 101 TFEU "belongs to the rules on competition which are addressed to undertakings and associations of undertakings and which are intended to maintain effective competition in the common market," whereas Article 34 TFEU "belongs to the rules which seek to ensure the free movement of goods and, to that end, to eliminate measures taken by Member States which might in any way impede such free movement."[60]

Only with regard to the exercise of intellectual property rights has the Court suggested that it would scrutinize the exercise of such rights by the rights-holders for its compliance with Article 34 TFEU (e.g. *Deutsche Grammophon*, 1971). This effectively constitutes horizontal direct effect.[61] This issue is relevant, for example, with regard to parallel imports of pharmaceutical products (e.g. *Orifarm*, 2011, see below).

Even though Article 34 TFEU generally does not have direct effect, Member States may be held responsible for the actions of private actors under certain circumstances (this is sometimes called "indirect" horizontal effect). In *Commission* v. *France – Spanish Strawberries* (1997), the Court found that France was in breach of Article 34 TFEU because it had not made sufficient efforts to prevent protestors from systematically attacking and damaging transports of Spanish fruit and vegetables. In *Schmidberger* (2003), the Court similarly ruled that the failure of the Austrian authorities to ban an environmental protest that shut down a major transit route for thirty hours constituted a restriction of the free movement of goods. However, the Court found the measure to be justified on the ground that the Austrian authorities had also to respect the protestors' fundamental right to freedom of expression, and had done so in a proportionate way by limiting the disruption to road traffic as far as possible.[62]

CUSTOMS UNION (ARTICLES 28–32 TFEU)

Introduction

The customs union provisions were at the core of the Treaty of Rome, pursuing the goal of reducing and ultimately abolishing customs duties. According to the Treaty of Rome, customs duties were subject to a so-called standstill clause: no new and no higher customs duties could be introduced; existing duties were to be progressively abolished within twelve years (Article 8 EEC). The Member States successfully accomplished this requirement ahead of the target date as they completed the customs union in July 1968.[63]

---

59 Joined Cases 177/82 and 178/82, *Van de Haar* [1984] ECR 1797, paras. 11–14.   60 *Ibid.*, paras. 11–12.
61 Case 78/70, *Deutsche Grammophon* [1971] ECR 487, para. 13.   62 *Schmidberger*, para. 87.
63 Décision du Conseil du 26 juillet 1966, relative à la suppression des droits de douane et à l'interdiction des restrictions quantitatives entre les Etats membres et à la mise en application des droits du Tarif douanier commun pour les produits autres que ceux énumérés à l'annexe II du Traité, [1966] JO 165/2971.

The EU and the GATT

The General Agreement on Tariffs and Trade (GATT) came into force on January 1, 1948. According to its Preamble, it is "directed to the substantial reduction of tariffs and other barriers to trade and to the elimination of discriminatory treatment in international commerce." The agreement had been signed "with a view to raising standards of living, ensuring full employment and a large and steadily growing volume of real income and effective demand, developing the full use of the resources of the world and expanding the production and exchange of goods." Today, the GATT is part of the framework of the World Trade Organization (WTO), which also encompasses the agreement establishing the WTO providing the common institutional framework, the General Agreement on Trade in Services (GATS) and the Agreement on Trade-Related Aspects of Intellectual Property Rights (TRIPS), among numerous other texts.[64]

The reduction of tariffs on goods is achieved in multilateral trade negotiating rounds, in the course of which states offer tariff reductions in return for equivalent tariff reductions by others. So far, eight trade rounds have been successfully concluded (the ninth – the Doha Round – began in 2001 and made only marginal progress in 2013). The GATT is based on the principle of the most-favored-nation (MFN) treatment (Article I GATT) according to which any contracting party must extend, immediately and unconditionally, any advantage it grants to any product originating in or destined for any other country to all other GATT contracting parties. Article III GATT establishes the principle of national treatment, which holds that states cannot subject goods from other states to any less favorable treatment in regard to internal taxation, other internal charges and regulations. The GATT's regulatory system is essentially reproduced in the provisions of the TFEU on the free movement of goods and the customs union. The prohibition of quantitative restrictions in Article 34 TFEU, for example, corresponds to Article XI GATT, which requires a "general elimination of quantitative restrictions."

Since customs unions and free trade areas abolish tariffs among their members, but retain them *vis-à-vis* other states, they would in principle violate the MFN principle of Article I GATT. However, for customs unions and free trade areas, Article XXIV GATT provides an exception from the MFN obligation. The EEC was formed as a regional trade agreement in accordance with Article XXIV GATT. The establishment of the EEC was observed with suspicion by some commentators, who believed that the open trade system under the GATT might be undermined by a regional trade organization. The UN Economic Commission for Europe held in 1956 that "there is fairly widespread apprehension that the new departure in Western

---

64 See WTO, "The Results of the Uruguay Round of Multilateral Trade Negotiations: The Legal Texts", Cambridge University Press, 2000.

European trading policies may represent the start of a retreat to a more protection-ist attitude towards imports from the outside world, in contrast with the efforts to reduce trade restrictions and discrimination affecting imports from outside Western Europe which have been pursued so far."[65] Similar charges were again levelled against the Union in the 1980s, when – especially American – commentators cau-tioned that the "1992" project to complete the single market might create what was called "fortress Europe."[66]

Today, the EU has exclusive competence in respect to trade relations with third countries as part of the Common Commercial Policy (Articles 206–207 TFEU). This includes relations with the WTO, of which the EU is a full member.[67]

Prohibition of customs duties on imports and exports and of charges having equivalent effect (Article 30 TFEU)

Article 30 TFEU reads: "Customs duties on imports and exports and charges having equivalent effect shall be prohibited between Member States. This prohibition shall also apply to customs duties of a fiscal nature." In the following sections, we will have a closer look at the prohibition of customs duties and of charges having equivalent effect.

Prohibition of customs duties on imports and exports

Article 30 TFEU prohibits the levying of customs duties on both imports from and exports to other Member States. As the Court explained, "any pecuniary charge – however small – imposed on goods by reason of the fact that they cross a frontier constitutes an obstacle to the movement of such goods" (*Diamantarbeiders*, 1969).[68] It is irrelevant for the application of Article 30 TFEU whether the financial charge is levied by the state or by another entity.[69] A charge enacted by law levied by the operator of an electricity network, for example, is subject to Article 30 TFEU (*Essent Netwerk*, 2008).[70]

---

65 UNECE, "Economic Survey of Europe" (1956), 21–22, quoted in Robert Looper, "The Significance of Regional Market Arrangements" (1959) *University of Illinois Law Forum* 364, 380.

66 While the term is still in use today, it is now used to refer to the restrictive immigration and asylum system that the European countries have established. See e.g. John Conybeare, "1992, The Community, and the World – Free Trade or Fortress Europe?" in Dale Smith and James Lee Ray (eds.), *The 1992 Project and the Future of Integration in Europe*, Armonk, NY: M. E. Sharpe, 1993.

67 The EU has been involved in a number of high-profile trade disputes with other WTO members, most notably on growth hormones used in beef production, on genetically modified organisms (GMOs) and on bananas: *EC – Bananas III*, Panel Report, WT/DS27/R/USA, May 22, 1997, and Appellate Body Report, WT/DS27/AB/R, September 9, 1997; *EC – Hormones*, Panel Report, WT/DS26/R/USA, August 18, 1997, and Appellate Body Report, WT/DS26/AB/R, WT/DS48/AB/R, January 16, 1998; *EC – Approval and Marketing of Biotech Products*, Panel Report, WT/DS291/R, WT/DS292/R, WT/DS293/R, September 29, 2006.

68 *Diamantarbeiders*, paras. 11 and 14.   69 Case 132/82, *Commission* v. *Belgium* [1983] ECR 1649, para. 8.

70 *Essent Netwerk*, para. 46.

Prohibition of charges having equivalent effect to customs duties

Article 30 TFEU also covers measures that do not constitute customs duties but have the similar effect of levying pecuniary charges on goods upon crossing a border. The Court defined as "any pecuniary charge, however small and whatever its designation and mode of application, which is imposed unilaterally on domestic or foreign goods when they cross a frontier, and which is not a customs duty in the strict sense, constitutes a charge having equivalent effect ... even if it is not imposed for the benefit of the state, is not discriminatory or protective in effect or if the product on which the charge is imposed is not in competition with any domestic product" (*Diamantarbeiders*, 1969).[71] The prohibition prevents Member States from overtly or covertly introducing protectionist measures. In the *Gingerbread* case of 1962, for example, Belgium argued that a charge on imported gingerbread was necessary to "equate the price of the foreign product with the price of the Belgian product."[72] The Court rejected this explicit case of protectionism.

However, Article 30 TFEU also prohibits measures that are free of any protectionist intention. The Court has, for example, ruled that a pecuniary charge levied for the purposes of a compulsory public health inspection of raw hides crossing the frontier constitutes a charge having an effect equivalent to customs duties (*Bresciani*, 1976).[73] In *Diamantarbeiders* (1969), the Court ruled that a charge of 0.3 percent on imported diamonds which was used to finance the social benefits of diamond workers constituted a charge having equivalent effect and was therefore prohibited by the Treaty. Article 30 TFEU also prohibits charges on the export of goods. In *Commission* v. *Italy – Art Works* (1968), the Court had to deal with an Italian tax levied on the export of art works from Italy.[74] The Court held that "[t]he disputed tax falls within [Article 30 TFEU] by reason of the fact that export trade in the goods in question is hindered by the pecuniary burden which it imposes on the price of the exported articles."[75]

Measures that the Court found to be charges having equivalent effect include:

- Statistical levies on imports and exports, financing statistics on the actual movement of goods (*Commission* v. *Italy – Statistical Levy*, 1969).[76]
- A health check of poultry meat upon entering the Belgian territory (*Commission* v. *Belgium*, 1984).[77]

---

71 *Diamantarbeiders*, paras. 11 and 14.
72 Joined Cases 2/62 and 3/62, *Commission* v. *Luxembourg and Belgium – Gingerbread Case* [1962] ECR 813, 434.
73 Case 87/75, *Bresciani* [1976] ECR 129, para. 9.
74 Case 7/68, *Commission* v. *Italy – Art Works* [1968] ECR 424.   75 *Ibid.*, 429.
76 Case 24/68, *Commission* v. *Italy – Statistical Levy* [1969] ECR 193.
77 Case 314/82, *Commission* v. *Belgium* [1984] ECR 1543.

- Storage charges on imported goods waiting for the completion of customs formalities (*Commission* v. *Belgium – Customs Warehouses*, 1983).[78]
- A charge on goods unloaded in an Italian port solely for imported goods (*Variola*, 1973).[79]

Fees charged by reason of the fact that goods cross a border are not classified as charges having equivalent effect to a customs duty where, "if the charge in question is the consideration for a service actually rendered to the importer and is of an amount commensurate with that service" (*Commission* v. *Belgium – Customs Warehouses*, 1983).[80]

Common Customs Tariff

While customs duties between Member States have been abolished, the EU has a common tariff – the Common Customs Tariff (CCT) – for goods entering from third countries. Goods are charged the same tariff, regardless of whether they first enter the EU in Portugal or, say, Estonia. The revenue from the CCT goes to the EU budget, and therefore is an autonomous source of revenue for the Union.[81] There are three possible ways to determine the tariff rates of the CCT. First, these can be fixed by the Council with a qualified majority on a proposal from the Commission (Article 31 TFEU). Second, tariffs may be established by "tariff and trade agreements" with third countries (Article 207 TFEU). Here, the Council – acting upon a recommendation by the Commission – authorizes the Commission by qualified majority to negotiate trade agreements with third countries or international organizations. Third, tariffs may also be fixed pursuant to association agreements (Article 217 TFEU). The effective tariffs are published annually by the Commission. Once goods from third countries have entered the EU and duties have been paid on them, they can circulate freely in all Member States (Article 28(2) and 29 TFEU).

Important secondary law

Combined nomenclature
There are thousands of different types of products that are traded across the globe. In order to facilitate trade and to make international agreements on tariffs possible, these products have been classified. The World Customs Organization has developed a system of tariff nomenclature (the so-called "Harmonized System") to classify goods traded internationally. For the EU, the nomenclature is laid down

---

78 Case 132/82, *Commission* v. *Belgium – Customs Warehouses* [1983] ECR 1649.
79 Case 34/73, *Variola* [1973] ECR 981.
80 Case 132/82, *Commission* v. *Belgium – Customs Warehouses* [1983] ECR 1649, para. 8.
81 Commission, *European Union Public Finance*, Luxembourg, 2008, p. 238.

in Council Regulation 2658/87.[82] As tariffs on rather similar products sometimes vary widely, the Court frequently has to deal with the issue of the classification of goods. This can be seen in the following case, where the Court had to deal with the classification of imported frozen camel meat.

Case C-559/10, Deli Ostrich NV (2011)

The Antwerp Customs and Excise Office and Deli Ostrich NV disagreed over the classification of frozen camel meat from animals that were not farm-raised (see the excerpt from Council Regulation 2658/87 below). Camel meat falls under Section I ("Live animals; animal products"), Chapter 2 ("Meat and edible meat offal"), heading 0208 ("Other meat and edible meat offal, fresh, chilled or frozen"), subheading 0208 90 ("Other"). The parties disagreed whether frozen camel meat was to be classified as 0208 90 40 ("Of game, other than of rabbits or hares: other") or 0208 90 95 ("other"). The difference between these two classifications essentially was whether the camels were to be considered "game" or not. The factual difference is that the latter is charged customs duties at a rate of 9 percent, whereas the former is free of customs duties.

Table 3.4 Excerpt from Annex I to Council Regulation 2658/87 on the tariff and statistical nomenclature and on the Common Customs Tariff (the classifications relevant to the decision *Deli Ostrich* case are shown in bold).

CN Code	Description	Conventional rate of duty
0208	Other meat and edible meat offal, fresh, chilled or frozen:	
0208 10	– Of rabbits or hares: – – Of domestic rabbits:	
0208 10 11	– – – Fresh or chilled	6.4%
0208 10 19	– – – Frozen	6.4%
0208 10 90	– – Other	Free
0208 30 00	– Of primates	9%
0208 40	– Of whales, dolphins and tortoises (mammals of the order *Cetacea*); of manatees and dugongs (mammals of the order *Sirenia*):	
0208 40 10	– – Whale meat	6.4%
0208 40 90	– – Other	9%

82 Council Regulation 2658/87 on the tariff and statistical nomenclature and on the Common Customs Tariff [1987] OJ L256/1; amended by Commission Regulation 1549/2006 of 17 October 2006 amending Annex I to Council Regulation 2658/87 on the tariff and statistical nomenclature and on the Common Customs Tariff [2006] OJ L301/1.

Table 3.4 (*cont.*)		
CN Code	Description	Conventional rate of duty
0208 50 00	– Of reptiles (including snakes and turtles)	9%
0208 90	– Other:	
0208 90 10	– – Of domestic pigeons – – Of game, other than of rabbits or hares:	6.4%
0208 90 20	– – – Of quails	Free
0208 90 40	**– – – Other**	Free
0208 90 55	– – Seal meat	6.4%
0208 90 60	– – Of reindeer	9%
0208 90 70	– – Frogs' legs	6.4%
0208 90 95	**– – Other**	9%

The Court held:

In the present case, it is apparent from the decision of the referring court that the parties to the main proceedings do not dispute that the meat at issue comes from camels which are not farm-raised. Furthermore, the Commission provided, in its written observations, factual details which confirm that a large proportion of the camel population in Australia has returned to the wild and that those wild camels are indeed regularly harvested, in particular for processing into food and feed, facts from which it can, if appropriate, be inferred that the meat at issue comes from camels which were hunted.[83]

The Court therefore found that the meat in question was to be classified as game under 0208 90 40 (resulting in a lower tariff for the importer).

Modernized Customs Code

The Modernized Customs Code lays down the customs rules and procedures applicable to the import to and export from the European Union.[84] It specifies rules of origin (Articles 35–39), the calculation of the value of goods for customs purposes (Articles 40–43), procedures regarding the entry of goods, their presentation to customs, their unloading, temporary storage (Articles 91–100), the customs declaration (Articles 108–116), etc. The Code provides for a right of appeal against decisions taken by the customs authorities (Article 23).

83 Case C-559/10, *Deli Ostrich* [2011] ECR I-10873, para. 30.
84 Council Regulation 2913/92 of 12 October 1992 establishing the Community Customs Code, [1992] OJ L302/1; to be replaced by the Modernized Customs Code by June 2013 by the latest; see Regulation 450/2008 of the European Parliament and of the Council of 23 April 2008 laying down the Community Customs Code (Modernized Customs Code), [2008] OJ L145/1.

QUANTITATIVE RESTRICTIONS ON IMPORTS AND MEASURES HAVING EQUIVALENT EFFECT (ARTICLE 34 TFEU)

Introduction

Quantitative restrictions (QRs) are limitations on the quantity of products that can be imported (e.g. an import quota on cars). They distort trade to a far greater extent than tariffs; the latter merely make trade more costly. QRs, on the other hand, prompt its cessation altogether once a quota is exhausted. QRs are prohibited under both the GATT (Article XI) and the TFEU (Article 34 TFEU). After the Second World War, most European countries had pre-war QRs on imports in place. However, under the stewardship of the OEEC (now OECD), they were quickly reduced in the late 1940s and early 1950s. According to the Treaty of Rome, QRs had to be abolished according to a timetable until the transitional period ended in 1970.

The 1950s and 1960s were a time of economic boom and of international economic stability. The Bretton Woods system ensured international economic stability and thereby facilitated trade. However, the Bretton Woods system fell apart in the early 1970s, coinciding with the first oil crisis in 1973, which triggered a worldwide recession. The EC Member States, facing the first major economic downturn for a quarter of a century, experienced pressure from domestic constituencies to grant protection from these international economic dynamics. As the Member States were barred from reintroducing customs duties and QRs by the EEC Treaty, they introduced other limitations to trade, a phenomenon which was later described as the rise of nontariff barriers.[85] The prohibition of measures having equivalent effect to QRs subsequently became an important instrument to combat such nontariff obstacles. Starting with the decision in *Dassonville* in 1974, the Court interpreted Article 34 TFEU as a general prohibition of nontariff barriers.

Prohibitions of Article 34 TFEU: quantitative restrictions and measures having equivalent effect

Article 34 TFEU provides:

Quantitative restrictions on imports and all measures having equivalent effect shall be prohibited between Member States.

These two prohibitions will be considered in turn.

---

85 European Commission, Completing the Internal Market, White Paper from the Commission to the European Council (Milan, 28–29 June 1985), COM(85) 310 final, http://europa.eu/documents/comm/white_papers/pdf/com1985_0310_f_en.pdf, p. 5.

Quantitative restrictions

Article 34 TFEU prohibits all QRs on imports. This covers measures such as import quotas, but also full bans (i.e. zero quotas). Examples of QRs include: a ban on the import of pornographic material (*Henn and Darby*, 1979),[86] an import ban on crayfish to prevent crayfish plague (*Commission* v. *Germany*, 1994)[87] or a prohibition of the importation of pasteurized milk and unfrozen pasteurized cream (*Commission* v. *United Kingdom*, 1988).[88] The distinction between QRs and measures having equivalent effect is sometimes unclear, but as both are prohibited, this has no practical consequence.

Measures having equivalent effect to quantitative restrictions

The concept of measures having equivalent effect to quantitative restrictions (MEQRs) was first defined in Commission Directive 70/50/EEC, which the Commission was authorized to issue according to Article 33(7) EEC (now abolished). The Directive – issued shortly before the end of the transitional period on December 31, 1969 – held that MEQRs are "measures, other than those applicable equally to domestic or imported products, which hinder imports which could otherwise take place, including measures which make importation more difficult or costly than the disposal of domestic production."[89] In *Dassonville* (1974), one of the earliest judgments dealing with the concept of MEQRs, the Court adopted an even broader understanding of MEQRs. Its definition of MEQRs – which is still valid today – is know as the "*Dassonville* formula."

Case 8/74, Dassonville (1974)

According to Belgian law, spirits imported for sale bearing a designation of origin must be accompanied by an official document certifying such designation to be lawful. "Scotch whisky" is a designation of origin recognized by the Belgian government for whisky produced in Scotland. The traders Benoît and Gustave Dassonville bought a consignment of Scotch whisky in France which had been legally imported to France. But as French law did not require a certificate of origin for imported Scotch whisky, the consignment was not accompanied by such documentation. Upon import, the Belgian authorities instituted criminal proceedings against the Dassonvilles for not possessing the required certificate of origin.

---

86 Case 34/79, *Henn and Darby* [1979] ECR 3795.
87 Case C-131/93, *Commission* v. *Germany* [1994] ECR I-3303.
88 Case 261/85, *Commission* v. *United Kingdom* [1988] ECR 547.
89 Art. 2(1) Commission Directive 70/50/EEC of 22 December 1969 based on the provisions of Article 33(7), on the abolition of measures which have an effect equivalent to quantitative restrictions on imports and are not covered by other provisions adopted in pursuance of the EEC Treaty, [1970] OJ L13/29.

Does the Belgian law requiring spirits bearing a designation of origin to be accompanied by an official certificate constitute an MEQR prohibited by Article 34 TFEU? Yes.

The Court found that "a trader, wishing to import into Belgium Scotch whisky which is already in free circulation in France, can obtain such a certificate only with great difficulty, unlike the importer who imports directly from the producer country."[90] It went on to define MEQRs in the following way: "All trading rules enacted by Member States which are capable of hindering, directly or indirectly, actually or potentially, intra-community trade are to be considered as measures having an effect equivalent to quantitative restrictions" (the "Dassonville formula").[91] The Court emphasized that Member States have the right to uphold measures to prevent product counterfeiting and unfair practices in the interest of consumers. However, such measures must not constitute a means of arbitrary discrimination or a disguised restriction on trade (Article 36 TFEU). Formalities "which only direct importers are really in a position to satisfy without facing serious difficulties" do not pass this test, and therefore constitute unjustifiable MEQRs.

According to the first prong of the *Dassonville* formula, all measures that affect the way goods are traded or sold constitute MEQRs. In the Preamble to Directive 70/50/EEC, the Commission had argued that "'measures' means laws, regulations, administrative provisions, administrative practices, and all instruments issuing from a public authority, including recommendations." The Court adopted this broad understanding, as can be seen in its case law. The Court has held, for example, that favorable credit terms by the Agricultural Bank of Greece for the purchase of Greek agricultural machinery that are not available for the purchase of imported agricultural machinery constitute an MEQR (*Commission* v. *Greece*, 1985).[92] In *Buy Irish* (1982), the Court contended that even measures that do not have a binding effect may be capable of influencing the conduct of traders and consumers, and therefore constitute MEQRs. Bilateral agreements concluded by a Member State can also constitute an MEQR (*Exportur*, 1992).[93]

We have already seen that the second prong of the *Dassonville* formula ("enacted by Member States") is held to include measures by non-state actors that have either been authorized (*Association of Pharmaceutical Importers*, 1989) or are in some other form attributable to the state (*Buy Irish*, 1982). The third prong – "capable of hindering, directly or indirectly, actually or potentially, intra-community trade" – defines the broad material scope of Article 34 TFEU. Under the formula, it is not

---

90 *Dassonville*, para. 4.   91 *Ibid.*, para. 5.   92 Case 192/84, *Commission* v. *Greece* [1985] ECR 3973.
93 Case C-3/91, *Exportur* [1992] ECR I-5529, para. 8.

necessary to demonstrate (for example, with the help of statistics) that a measure in fact hinders cross-border trade, it merely must have the potential to do so. The Court has held that no minimum impact on trade is necessary to trigger the applicability of Article 34 TFEU, i.e. no *de minimis* rule applies (*Van de Haar*, 1984).[94] As the *Dassonville* formula is effect-oriented, it is irrelevant whether the national authorities did in fact have a protectionist intention or not. It has consequently been argued by many scholars that virtually any national measure can fall under the *Dassonville* formula.[95] Only situations that are completely internal to a Member State remain outside of the scope of Article 34 TFEU.

Applying Article 34 TFEU: MEQRs and the prohibition of distinctly and indistinctly applicable measures

In this section, we will explore how the Court applies the *Dassonville* formula in practice. We will employ the important distinction between distinctly and indistinctly applicable measures, categories which had originally been introduced by the above-mentioned Directive 70/50/EEC. Pursuant to the Directive, only measures that apply distinctly to domestic and imported products were included in the concept of MEQRs. However, the Court has taken a different approach. According to the *Dassonville* formula, it is irrelevant whether a national measure is distinctly or indistinctly applicable. Consequently, the *Dassonville* formula covers both types of measures. First, it covers measures that explicitly differentiate between domestic goods and imported goods but impose heavier burdens on the latter. These discriminatory measures are "distinctly applicable." Second, it covers "indistinctly applicable measures" that do not differentiate on the face of it between domestic and imported goods (with regard to the other Treaty freedoms, such rules are either "indirectly discriminatory" or are said to create obstacles to trade). Although the Court has taken the view that both distinctly and indistinctly applicable measures alike are covered by the *Dassonville* formula, the distinction is relevant with regard to justifications, as we will see below.

Distinctly applicable measures

National measures that are "distinctly applicable" treat imported and domestic goods differently. Thus, the concept of "distinctly applicable measures" is mostly synonymous with the concept of (directly and indirectly) "discriminatory measures" that is employed with regard to the other Treaty freedoms. Generally, distinctly applicable measures are

---

94 See also Case C-166/03, *Commission* v. *France – Gold* [2004] ECR I-6535, para. 15.
95 See e.g. Eleanor Spaventa, "The Outer Limit of the Treaty Free Movement Provisions: Some Reflections on the Significance of Keck, Remoteness and Deliège," in Catherine Barnard and Okeoghene Odudu (eds.), *The Outer Limits of European Union Law*, Oxford: Hart Publishing, 2009, p. 246.

easy to identify. Distinctly applicable measures may, for example, impose additional requirements only on imported products but not on domestic products, prefer domestic over imported goods or limit their distribution. The Court had to deal with a distinctly applicable measure in *Commission* v. *Ireland – Irish Souvenirs*.

Case 113/80, Commission v. Ireland – Irish Souvenirs (1981)

An Irish measure prohibited the sale of imported articles of jewelry depicting motifs or possessing characteristics which suggest that they are souvenirs of Ireland unless they bear an indication of their country of origin or the word "foreign." This includes, for example, the depiction of Irish personalities, the Irish clover ("Shamrock"), Irish events or landscapes.

Does the measure constitute a breach of Article 34 TFEU?

Yes.

The measure is distinctly applicable, as it differentiates between products made in Ireland and those made in other countries (it is "overtly discriminatory," as the Court put it). The Irish government did not dispute the fact that the measure has restrictive effects on the free movement of goods, but argued that it would be justified in the interest of consumer protection and of fairness in commercial transactions between producers. However, the Court did not accept these justifications.

Other examples of distinctly applicable measures include the following:

- Animal feeding-stuffs of animal origin imported to Germany were subject to a systematic inspection at the border with regard to salmonella infection. Additionally, importers had to produce a certificate from the competent authority of the exporting country that those feeding-stuffs had undergone a process to destroy salmonella bacteria. The Court found that such a double-check (which domestic products were not subject to) violated Article 34 TFEU (*Denkavit Futtermittel*, 1979).[96]
- A rule prescribing that fish imports to Belgium must be notified twenty-four hours in advance and in writing by the importer in order for a public health inspection to take place. According to the Court, these conditions constitute an infringement of Article 34 TFEU unless they are based on objective requirements (*United Foods*, 1981).[97]

Indistinctly applicable measures

Indistinctly applicable measures apply to domestic and imported goods in the same way. While indistinctly applicable measures do not discriminate against imported goods by prescribing additional or more burdensome requirements, they can under

---

96 Case 251/78, *Denkavit Futtermittel* [1979] ECR 3369.   97 Case 132/80, *United Foods* [1981] ECR 995.

certain circumstances nonetheless impede intra-Union trade. The Court ruled for the first time on an indistinctly applicable measure in *Cassis de Dijon* (1979).[98] In this case, which will be discussed further below, the Court had to deal with a German rule that prohibited the sale of fruit liqueurs with an alcohol content below 25 percent. While this rule applied indistinctly to domestic and imported goods alike, it still made the sale of certain imported liqueurs with a lower alcohol content, such as Cassis de Dijon, impossible. Since then, the Court has in numerous decisions confirmed that the *Dassonville* formula encompasses distinctly and indistinctly applicable measures alike, for example in the German beer case.

Case 178/84, Commission v. Germany – Beer Case (1987)

According to a German law (the so-called *Reinheitsgebot*, or purity law), top-fermented beer must be made exclusively from malted barley, hops, yeast and water. More relaxed rules apply to bottom-fermented beer, so that certain other cereals can replace barley. This does not apply, however, to maize or rice. Fermented beverages could be sold under the designation "*Bier*" only if they conformed to these manufacturing rules.

Does a national rule that limits the use of the designation "*Bier*" to beverages produced according to the national manufacturing standard breach Article 34 TFEU?

Yes.

The manufacturing rule itself does not violate Article 34 TFEU, as it applies only to producers in Germany. However, the marketing rules prohibit the sale of beverages under the designation "Bier" which are not made in conformity with the German rules. This constitutes an obstacle to importation. Germany argued that the measure is justified on the ground of consumer protection, as German consumers associate the designation with specific ingredients. The Court found, however, that such a goal can be achieved by less restrictive means. A requirement to list the ingredients on the label of the product would serve the interest of consumer protection, while restricting Article 34 TFEU to a lesser extent than a sales ban.

The trade-impeding effect of indistinctly applicable measures often stems from the fact that a good is regulated twice – once in the country of origin and once in the country of destination. While neither the country of origin's nor the country of destination's regulatory measures by themselves are discriminatory, taken together they may severely impede intra-Union trade by imposing a double regulatory burden.

---

98 Case 120/78, *Rewe-Zentral AG* v. *Bundesmonopolverwaltung für Branntwein (Cassis de Dijon)* [1979] ECR 649.

Examples of indistinctly applicable measures include the following:

- An Italian law on pasta products required that only durum wheat be used for the industrial manufacture of dry pasta. A German manufacturer, 3 Glocken, received an administrative penalty for selling pasta made from a mixture of durum and common wheat. Even though the measure applies to domestic and imported products alike, it puts imported goods that are produced from different ingredients at a disadvantage (*3 Glocken*, 1988).[99]

- A French law limited the use of the name "Edam" to cheese with a fat content of more than 40 percent, thus prohibiting the sale of German Edamer cheese, which had a fat content of only 35 percent. Even though the measure applies to domestic and imported cheese alike, it nonetheless affects imported cheese more if it traditionally has a lower fat content (*Deserbais*, 1988).[100]

- An Austrian rule required that animal transports for slaughter must go to the nearest suitable slaughterhouse (*Monsees*, 1999). The Court found that the measure makes "all international transit by road of animals for slaughter almost impossible in Austria," and therefore unduly restricted the free movement of goods.[101]

Limiting the scope of Article 34 TFEU: the Keck formula

Measures that are found to be MEQRs do not necessarily violate Article 34 TFEU if they can be justified on the ground of public interest (see below). However, the broad scope of the *Dassonville* formula means that virtually any national measure can be challenged, and would then have to be scrutinized on an individual basis. This effect has been criticized by a number of scholars over the years.[102] The dilemma was that a narrow understanding of the *Dassonville* formula – i.e. one that would only apply to distinctly applicable measures – seemed to catch too few of the problematic national measures, whereas a broad understanding that encompassed both distinctly and indistinctly applicable measures would catch too many. Moreover, whereas distinctly applicable measures were relatively easy to identify on formal grounds, indistinctly applicable measures require a more complex examination and bolder, substantive assessments by the national courts. This reduces the operability of the Treaty rules and legal certainty. A prominent example for this dilemma were the Sunday trading cases (sometimes referred to by scholars as the "Sunday trading saga"): here, rules on opening hours were challenged by retailers from all around Europe. In *Torfaen Borough Council* (1989), B&Q, a chain of hardware stores, challenged the United Kingdom's prohibition of Sunday trading.[103] It argued that the prohibition reduces "in absolute terms the sales of goods in those premises, including goods imported

99 Case 407/85, *3 Glocken* [1988] ECR 4233.   100 Case 286/86, *Deserbais* [1988] ECR 4907.

101 Case C-350/97, *Monsees* [1999] ECR I-2921, paras. 29–31.

102 See e.g. Eric White, "In Search of the Limits to Article 30 of the EEC Treaty" (1989) 26 *Common Market Law Review* 235; Kamiel Mortelmans, "Article 30 of the EEC Treaty and Legislation Relating to Market Circumstances: Time to Consider a New Definition?" (1991) 28 *Common Market Law Review* 115.

103 Case 145/88, *Torfaen Borough Council* [1989] ECR 3851; Case C-312/89, *SIDEF* [1991] ECR I-997; Case C-332/89, *André Marchandise* [1991] ECR I-1027; Case C-306/88, *Rochdale Borough Council* [1992] ECR I-6457;

from other Member States."[104] The Court held that, even though Sunday trading rules would not make the marketing of imported goods more difficult than of domestic goods, the national measure would still have to be justified on objective grounds and fulfill the proportionality requirement. The Court then found the measure to be justified because "[s]uch rules reflect certain political and economic choices in so far as their purpose is to ensure that working and non-working hours are so arranged as to accord with national or regional socio-cultural characteristics." However, this solution was apparently too ambiguous, as national courts continued to submit references relating to opening hours. The Court therefore attempted to clarify its position in its subsequent decisions, arguing that "Article [34] of the Treaty must be interpreted as meaning that the prohibition which it lays down does not apply to national legislation prohibiting the employment of staff on Sundays."[105]

The Court subsequently looked for a more general doctrinal solution to the difficulties arising from the broad scope of the *Dassonville* formula. In *Keck and Mithouard* (1993), it found the solution – proposed a few years earlier by Commission staff member Eric White[106] – in a distinction between product requirements and selling arrangements (White had proposed to distinguish between rules "relating to the *characteristics* of a product," and those related to "the *circumstances* in which goods may be sold and used on the territory of the Member State"[107]). Whereas Article 34 TFEU should fully apply to the former, the latter should be exempted *prima facie*. The decision was designed to reduce legal uncertainty about national rules by altogether excluding from the scope of Article 34 TFEU certain rules that were typically of little concern from a perspective of intra-Union trade.

Cases C-267/91 and C-268/91, Keck and Mithouard (1993)

A French law prohibited the resale of products in an unaltered state at prices lower than their actual purchase price, i.e. resale at a loss. Two supermarket owners, Bernard Keck and Daniel Mithouard, were prosecuted for infringing the law. They contended that the rule was incompatible with Article 34 TFEU.

Does the French prohibition of reselling at a loss violate Article 34 TFEU?
No.

In a rare move, the Court explicitly altered its previous case law and explained that rules on the sale of products, as long as they affect all foreign and domestic traders and goods in the same legal and factual manner do not fall under Article 34 TFEU, as they "by nature" do not prevent market access for non-domestic goods any more

---

Case C-304/90, *Reading Borough Council* [1992] ECR I-6493; Case C-169/91, *Council of the City of Stoke-on-Trent* [1992] ECR I-6635; Joined Cases C-401/92 and C-402/92, *Tankstation 't Heukske* [1994] ECR I-2199; Joined Cases C-69/93 and C-258/93, *Punto Casa* [1994] ECR I-2355.
104 *Torfaen Borough Council*, para. 10.   105 *Rochdale Borough Council*, para. 7.
106 White, "In Search of the Limits to Article 30," 235.   107 *Ibid.*, 280 (emphasis in the original).

than for domestic products. The French prohibition of reselling at a loss therefore does not constitute a breach of Article 34 TFEU. In particular, the Court held:

[C]ontrary to what has previously been decided, the application to products from other Member States of national provisions restricting or prohibiting certain selling arrangements is not such as to hinder directly or indirectly, actually or potentially, trade between Member States within the meaning of the *Dassonville* judgment ... so long as those provisions apply to all relevant traders operating within the national territory and so long as they affect in the same manner, in law and in fact, the marketing of domestic products and of those from other Member States. Provided that those conditions are fulfilled, the application of such rules to the sale of products from another Member State meeting the requirements laid down by that State is not by nature such as to prevent their access to the market or to impede access any more than it impedes the access of domestic products. Such rules therefore fall outside the scope of [Article 34 TFEU] of the Treaty.

The Court therefore established a distinction between product requirements ("relating to designation, form, size, weight, composition, presentation, labelling, packaging") and selling arrangements which fall outside the scope of Article 34 TFEU if they affect domestic and non-domestic traders in the same legal and factual manner. The reason for this distinction is that selling arrangements – although they may restrict the volume of sales from another Member State by limiting specific ways of promotion – neither aim at limiting imports nor usually have the effect of doing so. Keep in mind that, following the Court's logic in *Cassis de Dijon*, measures may impede trade even though they are indistinctly applicable because traders have to face a double regulatory burden, one in the state of exportation and one in the state of importation. Selling arrangements, on the other hand, do not impede the trader but the retailer, who only has to fulfill one set of rules (of the Member State where he or she sells the product). The Court has declared that "the need in certain cases to adapt the products in question to the rules in force in the Member State in which they are marketed prevents ... requirements from being treated as selling arrangements."[108]

Examples of product requirements include the following:

- Mars ice-cream bars were presented in wrappers marked "+10%" on a band of a different color.[109] The band, however, covered more than 10 percent of the wrapper, giving the (wrong) impression that a larger part of the ice-cream bar was added for free than was actually the case. This could be seen as misleading consumers and was therefore prohibited under German law. The measure constituted a product requirement, as it regulated the packaging of a product. The

108 Case C-390/99, *Canal Satéllite Digital* [2002] ECR I-607, para. 30.
109 Case C-470/93, *Mars* [1995] ECR I-1923.

Table 3.5 Selling arrangements	
Product requirements	**Selling arrangements**
Market access rules (which products are allowed to access the market of a Member State?)	Rules on market circumstances (on the "behavior" of traders once they have entered the market)
Relating to designation, form, size, weight, composition, presentation, labeling, packaging	– Rules concerning "who (pharmacist, door-to-door sales-man, employee) sells the product, and when (Sundays, at night), where (shop, door-to-door) and how (with a gift) does he go about it?"[a] – if they apply to both domestic and non-domestic traders in the same manner, in law and in fact

a   Kamiel Mortelmans, "Article 30 of the EEC Treaty and Legislation Relating to Market Circumstances: Time to Consider a New Definition?" (1991) 28 *Common Market Law Review* 115, 116.

Court did not accept the justifications brought forward by Germany, and therefore found the measure to violate Article 34 TFEU (*Mars*, 1995).

- A German rule restricted the expiry dates which may be indicated on the packaging of medicinal products to two specified dates per year (30 June and 31 December).[110] The provision was a product requirement because it regulated the labeling of a product. It was hindering intra-Union trade because it forced importers to alter the packaging in order to make it conform to the German provision. Thus, the measure infringed Article 34 TFEU (*Commission* v. *Germany*, 1994).
- A Spanish law prohibited the marketing under the name "chocolate" of cocoa and chocolate products which are lawfully manufactured and marketed in other Member States, when they contain vegetable fats other than cocoa butter (*Commission* v. *Spain* – *Spanish Chocolate*, 2003).[111]

Examples of selling arrangements include the following:

- *Punto Casa* (1994) was an early case where the Court applied the *Keck* formula to a national rule on Sunday trading. An Italian law required shops to be closed on Sundays.[112] As it applied to all traders operating within the national territory and affected them all in the same manner, in law and in fact, the measure was a selling arrangement and therefore did not breach Article 34 TFEU.
- In *Commission* v. *Greece* (1995), a Greek law that prescribed that processed milk for infants must be sold exclusively in pharmacies[113] did not breach Article 34 TFEU.
- An Austrian law prohibited the sale of specific products – among them gold and silver jewelry, medical accessories, cosmetic products and food supplements – at

110 Case C-317/92, *Commission* v. *Germany* [1994] ECR I-2039.
111 Case C-12/00, *Commission* v. *Spain* – *Spanish Chocolate* [2003] ECR I-459.
112 Joined Cases C-69/93 and C-258/93, *Punto Casa* [1994] ECR I-2355, para. 12.
113 Case C-391/92, *Commission* v. *Greece* [1995] ECR I-1621.

private homes.[114] A trader, organizing "jewellery parties" at private homes, was charged with infringement of the law. The Court ruled that the provision in question was a selling arrangement as it applied to all relevant traders and affected them in the same manner. Therefore, it did not breach Article 34 TFEU (*A-Punkt Schmuckhandel*, 2006).

As mentioned, not every selling arrangement is *per se* excluded from the scope of Article 34 TFEU. Rather, the rules must affect in the same way, in law and in fact, the sale or marketing of domestic products and those of other Member States. Some selling arrangements may still bar non-domestic goods from accessing the market. In particular, this is the case when the prohibition of certain selling arrangements makes it difficult or impossible for imported products to enter a Member State's market. For example, in *De Agostini* (1997), the Court established that selling arrangements capable of hindering market access of imported goods are not exempted from Article 34 TFEU and must be justified on overriding grounds of the public interest.

Cases C-34/95, C-35/95 and C-36/95, De Agostini (1997)

De Agostini was an Italian producer of magazines, which were printed in Italy. It started to sell a line of magazines in Sweden named "Everything About Dinosaurs!" and broadcasted commercials on Swedish television. However, because a Swedish law prohibited television commercials designed to attract the attention of children of less than twelve years of age, the Consumer Ombudsman pressed charges against the company.[115]

Does the prohibition of television ads targeting children under twelve years of age conflict with Article 34 TFEU?

No.

Prohibitions of television ads for products of a specific sector or of certain promotion methods are selling arrangements.[116] Applying the *Keck* conditions, the Court held that the rule obviously affects domestic products and those from other Member States in the same way in law. However, it cannot be excluded that an outright ban of a type of promotion for a product which is sold legally might in fact have a greater impact on products from other Member States. The Court held that, "[a]lthough the efficacy of the various types of promotion is a question of fact to be determined in principle by the referring court, it is to be noted that in its observations De Agostini

---

114 Case C-441/04, *A-Punkt Schmuckhandel* [2006] ECR I-2093.
115 Joined Cases C-34/95, C-35/95 and C-36/95, *De Agostini* [1997] ECR I-3843.
116 Case C-412/93, *Leclerc-Siplec* [1995] ECR I-179.

stated that television advertising was *the only effective form of promotion enabling it to penetrate the Swedish market* since it had no other advertising methods for reaching children and their parents."[117] If the national measure does not have the same impact, in law and in fact, on domestic and non-domestic products, it cannot be exempted from the scope of Article 34 TFEU and must therefore be justified on grounds of overriding requirements of general public importance or the grounds listed in Article 36 TFEU.

In *De Agostini*, the key emphasis of the Court lies on the issue of market access.[118] Selling arrangements do not put extra burdens on the way a good has to be produced or packaged and thus do not *per se* put importers at a disadvantage. However, they may in some instances have the effect of preventing or hindering imported products from successfully entering the market. The Court found this to be the case in *Gourmet International* (2001), a judgment relating to restrictions on advertisements. Sweden has a relatively strict policy on alcohol, having a government monopoly on the sale of alcohol (with certain exceptions). A Swedish law prohibited advertising in periodicals for spirits, wines or strong beers. Gourmet International published a magazine targeting traders (such as restaurants), which featured ads for wine and whisky. The authorities applied for an injunction, arguing that such ads violate Swedish law. The Court found that a general prohibition of advertisements affected imported products more than domestic ones. The consumption of alcoholic beverages "is linked to traditional social practices and to local habits and customs, a prohibition of all advertising directed at consumers ... is liable to impede access to the market by products from other Member States more than it impedes access by domestic products, with which consumers are instantly more familiar."[119] For this reason, the measure is not a selling arrangement within the meaning of the *Keck* formula.

Justifications

National measures that are QRs or MEQRs are prohibited, unless they can be justified on important grounds in the public interest. There are two types of justifications: first, the Treaty-based justifications of Article 36 TFEU; and, second, other justificatory grounds based on the Court's case law. In the context of the

---

117 *De Agostini*, para. 43.
118 Case C-405/98, *Gourmet International* [2001] ECR I-1795, para. 18: "It should be pointed out that, according to paragraph 17 of its judgment in *Keck and Mithouard*, if national provisions restricting or prohibiting certain selling arrangements are to avoid being caught by Article 30 of the Treaty, they must not be of such a kind as to prevent access to the market by products from another Member State or to impede access any more than they impede the access of domestic products."
119 *Gourmet International*, para. 21.

Keck's critics

The *Keck* decision has been intensely debated ever since it was issued.[120] Some early critics found the concepts of the formula unclear (what exactly are "certain selling arrangements"?). This initial criticism decreased, however, as the Court further shaped and defined the formula in its subsequent case law. Others argued that selling arrangements may have a significantly restrictive effect as well, so that the blanket exemption of such measures by the *Keck* formula may be unwarranted. Advocate General Jacobs argued in his influential opinion in *Leclerc-Siplec* (1995) that restrictions on advertisement in particular may have a detrimental effect on imported goods even though they undoubtedly are selling arrangements. As we have seen, the Court incorporated this argument in its subsequent decisions on advertising rules (e.g. in *De Agostini*). A number of commentators (including Advocate General Poiares Maduro) have made the criticism that the *Keck* formula applies to the provisions on the free movement of goods only. These critics prefer a unified approach applicable to all freedoms alike.[121] More recently, the Court has been confronted with national rules that limited not the sale, but the use of certain products, such as jet-skis (*Mickelsson*, 2009). Although such rules undoubtedly do not constitute product requirements, the Court held that they should not be treated analogously to selling arrangements either (we will discuss these cases below). Some commentators have seen these decisions as a possible sign of the Court reforming its approach.[122] The Court, however, has continued to apply the *Keck* formula despite all the criticism it faced over the years. Even though it showed willingness to follow suggestions for improvement, it nonetheless upheld the core of *Keck*. The likely reason is that the rule provides a functional rule of thumb to distinguish between national measures with and without a restrictive effect, even though the formula may not be accurate in every single case. By contrast, the general system of Article 34 TFEU requires an individual, case-based evaluation of both the restrictive effects and the justificatory grounds, which makes it more difficult for national courts to apply, and reduces predictability, thereby limiting legal certainty. Thus, while the *Keck* formula continues to have its critics, its simplicity and usability seem to justify its continued application.

120 See e.g. Norbert Reich, "The 'November Revolution' of the European Court of Justice: Keck, Meng and Audi Revisited" (1994) 31 *Common Market Law Review* 459; Peter Oliver, "Some Further Reflections on the Scope of Articles 28–30 (Ex 30–36) EC" (1999) 36 *Common Market Law Review* 783; Gormley, "Silver Threads Among the Gold. 50 Years of the Free Movement of Goods" (2008) 31 *Fordham International Law Journal* 1637.
121 Joined Cases C-158/04 and C-159/04, *Alfa Vita* [2006] ECR I-8135, Opinion of Advocate General Poiares Maduro, paras. 50–51.
122 Peter Oliver, *Free Movement of Goods in the European Union*, Oxford: Hart Publishing, 2010, p. 130.

free movement of goods, the latter are called "mandatory requirements." Both are subject to the proportionality requirement.

Treaty-based justifications

Article 36 TFEU provides:

The provisions of Articles 34 and 35 shall not preclude prohibitions or restrictions on imports, exports or goods in transit justified on grounds of public morality, public policy or public security; the protection of health and life of humans, animals or plants; the protection of national treasures possessing artistic, historic or archaeological value; or the protection of industrial and commercial property. Such prohibitions or restrictions shall not, however, constitute a means of arbitrary discrimination or a disguised restriction on trade between Member States.

QRs and MEQRs therefore do not necessarily violate EU law; however, Member States must have good reasons to uphold such measures. Furthermore, according to Article 36 TFEU, such restrictions on grounds of public interest must not "constitute a means of arbitrary discrimination or a disguised restriction on trade." The first prong of this formula is an objective requirement: the differentiation between domestic and imported goods must be based on objective grounds. The second prong essentially is a prohibition of protectionism. The Treaty recognizes that there are certain circumstances and certain public regulatory goals that justify import or export restrictions; however, these restrictions must be devised in such a way that their negative effects on trade are as limited as possible, and are incidental effects and not the main purpose of the national measure. Over the years, the Court has systematized these requirements in the three-pronged proportionality test (see below). Article 36 TFEU applies both to import and export restrictions (Articles 34 and 35 TFEU), and to both QRs and MEQRs. It justifies both distinctly and indistinctly applicable measures.

Mandatory requirements

Article 36 TFEU contains an exhaustive list: the Court has routinely ruled that, as an exception to the rule, it must be interpreted narrowly so that the list of justifications cannot be expanded. At the same time, we have seen that the *Dassonville* formula is so broad that virtually any national measure can potentially fall within its scope: this can include national measures that serve a variety of reasonable regulatory goals. The Court never intended to make national regulation more difficult *per se*; it accepted that in the absence of harmonizing measures it was up to the Member States to find plausible regulatory solutions. In *Dassonville*, for example, the Court agreed that it was up to Belgium to take measures to prevent unfair practices in connection with the designation of a product's origin;[123] however, it also held that such "measures should be reasonable and that the means of proof required should not act as a hindrance to trade between Member States and

---

123 *Dassonville*, para. 6.

should, in consequence, be accessible to all Community nationals" (a requirement that the Belgian measure did not fulfil).[124] A few years after *Dassonville*, the Court systematized this approach and developed a unified doctrinal system for justifications of indistinctly applicable measures in the case *Rewe-Zentral AG*, usually known as "*Cassis de Dijon*" after the product that led to the dispute. In *Cassis de Dijon*, the Court found that indistinctly applicable measures can be justified if they serve mandatory requirements of public policy.

Case 120/78, Rewe-Zentral AG (Cassis de Dijon) (1979)

Rewe, a German trading company, imported French "Cassis de Dijon" (known for its use in cocktails like Kir Royal), a liquor containing 15–20 percent alcohol. According to German law, only fruit liqueurs with a minimum alcohol content of 25 percent could be marketed.

Does a prohibition of marketing beverages with an alcohol content below a fixed limit constitute an MEQR?

Yes.

The Court found that rules fixing a minimum alcohol content for alcoholic beverages constitute MEQRs. Germany countered that the measure served the goal of public health protection and the protection of the consumer against unfair commercial practices. The Court conceded that in the absence of harmonization measures it is for the Member States to regulate the marketing of alcohol on their own territory. It argued that obstacles resulting from disparities between the laws of the Member States must therefore be accepted "in so far as those provisions may be recognized as being necessary in order to satisfy mandatory requirements relating in particular to the effectiveness of fiscal supervision, the protection of public health, the fairness of commercial transactions and the defence of the consumer."[125] However, the Court rejected the assertion that a minimum alcohol content could serve as a protection of public health, and held that the goal of consumer protection could equally be achieved with a labeling requirement. It concluded that "[t]here is therefore no valid reason why, provided that they have been lawfully produced and marketed in one of the Member States, alcoholic beverages should not be introduced into any other Member State."[126] This statement has been the starting-point of the subsequent development of the principle of mutual recognition in the free movement of goods (see below).

The Court gave a non-exhaustive list of examples for these mandatory requirements. In the following decades, the Member States brought forward a large number of mandatory requirements, many of which the Court has accepted. Also

---

124 *Ibid.*, para. 6.   125 *Cassis de Dijon*, para. 8.   126 *Ibid.*, para. 14.

note that the Court puts the mandatory requirements under the condition of proportionality.[127]

The following mandatory requirements have for example been recognized by the Court:

- the effectiveness of fiscal supervision (*Cassis de Dijon*);
- the protection of public health (*Cassis de Dijon*);
- the fairness of commercial transactions (*Cassis de Dijon*);
- consumer protection (*Cassis de Dijon*);
- environmental protection (*Commission* v. *Belgium – Walloon Waste*, 1992);[128]
- protection of fundamental rights (*Schmidberger*, 2003).

Proportionality

National measures that are justifiable either under Article 36 TFEU or as mandatory requirements must be proportionate. The proportionality requirement is conceptualized as a three-pronged test:

- The national measure must be "suitable" (or "appropriate") to achieve the purported goal.[129] It must be conceivable that the measure can in principle lead to the desired outcome. This is not the case if a measure is unsystematic or irrational. The Court has ruled for example in *Hartlauer* (2009) that "national legislation is appropriate for ensuring attainment of the objective pursued only if it genuinely reflects a concern to attain it in a consistent and systematic manner."[130]
- The measure must be "necessary." The measure must not go beyond what is necessary to achieve the intended outcomes. The Court often (but not always) deploys this criterion as a less restrictive means test. It held for example in *De Peijper* (1976) that a measure aimed at protecting the health and life of humans is not justified if it can be "as effectively protected by measures which do not restrict intra-Community trade so much."[131] The necessity requirement clearly implies an element of (political) choice by the Court.[132] The Court sometimes evades the difficulty of deciding whether a measure is necessary to reach a certain goal by scrutinizing solely the legislative process, but not the regulatory choice *per se*. In *Commission* v. *Austria – Brenner Motorway* (2005), the Court argued that an environmentally motivated ban on the use by heavy vehicles of a certain section of the Brenner, a major transit route, was disproportionate because Austria had failed to "examine carefully the possibility of using measures less restrictive of freedom of movement."[133]

---

127   Case 261/81, *Rau* [1981] ECR 3961, para. 12.
128   Case C-2/90, *Commission* v. *Belgium – Walloon Waste* [1992] ECR I-4431, para. 32.
129   Case 331/88, *Fedesa* [1990] ECR I-4023, para. 14.
130   Case C-169/07, *Hartlauer* [2009] ECR I-1721, para. 55.
131   Case 104/75, *De Peijper* [1976] ECR 613, para. 17.
132   Alec Stone Sweet and Jud Mathews, "Proportionality Balancing and Global Constitutionalism" (2008–2009) 47 *Columbia Journal of Transnational Law* 72, pp. 89 and 143.
133   Case C-320/03, *Commission* v. *Austria – Brenner Motorway* [2005] ECR I-9871, para. 87.

- The measure must be proportionate *stricto sensu*: this means that the positive effects of the measure must outweigh its negative effects.

It must be noted that this three-pronged proportionality test is a product of legal scholarship rather than an accurate depiction of the Court's practice. The Court sometimes considers the first prong only in passing, and often leaves out the third prong entirely. Instead, it usually focuses on the second prong, the necessity requirement. It is up to the national authorities to demonstrate that their measures fulfill the proportionality requirement; they bear the burden of proof.[134] The proportionality test scrutinizes the effects of the national measures in light of the Treaty freedom provisions, but it does not judge the regulatory goals of the Member States. The Court has repeatedly held that the Member States themselves have the right to choose the level of protection. In other words, the Court scrutinizes the means, but not the end; it does not question the legitimacy of the policy goals. The Court argued for example in *Commission* v. *Germany – Hospital Pharmacies*:

[I]n the field of public health, account must be taken of the fact that a Member State has the power to determine the degree of protection which it wishes to afford to public health and the way in which that degree of protection is to be achieved. Since that degree of protection may vary from one Member State to the other, Member States must be allowed discretion and, consequently, the fact that one Member State imposes less strict rules than another Member State does not mean that the latter's rules are disproportionate.[135]

Mutual recognition

The principle of mutual recognition – first acknowledged by the Court in *Cassis de Dijon* – limits a Member State's ability to require goods imported from other Member States to conform to its own product standards. It holds as a general rule that Member States must allow the sale of products lawfully produced or marketed in another Member State. Member States can require products to conform to its own technical standards only if such requirement can be justified under Article 36 TFEU or by mandatory requirements.

We have already seen that the Court acknowledged in *Cassis de Dijon* that Member States have plausible regulatory concerns ("mandatory requirements") that may justify upholding national standards, even though they constitute obstacles to the free movement of goods. In particular, such rules often relate to safety, health, environmental concerns and consumer protection. In the absence of harmonized measures, the Member States are not obliged to forego their intended level of protection. However, often enough, products have been produced according to standards that are essentially similar to that of the importing Member State. In such a case, requiring a product to conform to standards and controls that it has

---

134 Case C-141/07, *Commission* v. *Germany – Hospital Pharmacies* [2008] ECR I-6935, para. 50.
135 *Ibid.*, para. 51.

already fulfilled in another Member State would be disproportionate. The Court argued in *Cassis de Dijon* that "[t]here is therefore no valid reason why, provided that they have been lawfully produced and marketed in one of the Member States, alcoholic beverages should not be introduced into any other Member State."[136] Even though, strictly speaking, this finding constituted an *obiter dictum* in the decision[137] (i.e. a statement that is not essential to explain the outcome of the case), it quickly became one of the most important principles of internal market law.[138] The Commission – according to its own accounts motivated by "growing numbers of restrictive measures" by the Member States – seized the opportunity and issued a communication to emphasize the importance of the principle, later to be known as the principle of mutual recognition.[139]

According to the principle of mutual recognition, double regulation or duplicate controls go beyond what is necessary to attain the objectives pursued if the rules to which the product has been subjected are equivalent to those in the importing country. The Court held in *Canal Satéllite Digital* (2002) that "a measure introduced by a Member State cannot be regarded as necessary to achieve the aim pursued if it essentially duplicates controls which have already been carried out in the context of other procedures, either in the same State or in another Member State."[140] The principle of mutual recognition therefore limits the ability of Member States to invoke derogations from the principle of free movement. Only in cases where the regulation of the country of origin is found not to be equivalent to its own standards can it invoke mandatory requirements to justify measures that are obstacles to the free movement of goods. It has been argued that the equivalence requirement prevents a potential regulatory race to the bottom, as countries are not required to admit products that only comply with significantly lower regulatory standards.[141]

The principle of mutual recognition requires an active approach on the part of the national authorities of the importing country (*Commission* v. *Portugal – Polyethylene Pipes*, 2005).[142] They must recognize regulation and certificates from other Member States, scrutinize their own rules, and facilitate procedures to obtain access to the national market of the importing Member State.[143] To ease the procedural burden and reduce legal uncertainty for importers, Regulation 764/2008 lays down a procedure that national authorities must follow if they

---

136 *Cassis de Dijon*, para. 14.
137 Karen Alter and Sophie Meunier-Aitsahalia, "Judicial Politics in the European Community: European Integration and the Pathbreaking Cassis de Dijon Decision" (1994) 26 *Comparative Political Studies* 535, 539.
138 A recent case where the Court explicitly referred to the principle of mutual recognition is Case C-110/05, *Commission* v. *Italy – Italian Trailers* [2009] ECR I-519, para. 34.
139 Communication from the Commission concerning the consequences of the judgment given by the Court of Justice on 20 February 1979 in Case 120/78 ("Cassis de Dijon"), [1980] OJ C256/2.
140 *Canal Satéllite Digital*, para. 36.
141 Jacques Pelkmans, "Mutual Recognition in Goods. On Promises and Disillusions" (2007) 14 *Journal of European Public Policy* 609, 708.
142 Case C-432/03, *Commission* v. *Portugal – Polyethylene Pipes* [2005] ECR I-9665, para. 47.   143 *Ibid.*, para. 47.

intend to take a decision which would hinder the free movement of a product lawfully marketed in another Member State.[144] The Regulation applies to all administrative decisions addressed to economic operators that have the effect of prohibiting the product from being placed on the market or requiring its modification or additional testing on the basis of any national technical rule. Technical rules within the meaning of the Regulation are measures that lay down required characteristics of the product (e.g. levels of quality, performance or safety) or other requirements imposed on the product (e.g. conditions of use, recycling, reuse or disposal). The Regulation lays down rules and principles that national authorities must follow, including the obligation to issue certain information to the economic operator and time limits within which decisions must be made. Most importantly, the national authorities bear the burden of proof: they must produce evidence that their decision is justified and proportionate (Article 6). Therefore, the three-pronged test of proportionality would seem equally applicable to the principle of mutual recognition.

The principle of mutual recognition applies only if no harmonization measure is in place. In practice, mutual recognition and harmonization are often intertwined. For example, the principle of mutual recognition is often reiterated and substantiated in harmonization measures (regulatory mutual recognition) and thereby complements the general principle of mutual recognition that is enforceable in national courts (judicial mutual recognition).[145] The complex relationship between mutual recognition and harmonization can be seen in the following case.

Case C-432/03, Commission v. Portugal – Polyethylene Pipes (2005)

A Portuguese undertaking had imported polyethylene pipes from Italy for installation in a building. An Italian institute, IIP, had certified the pipes, and the undertaking requested the Portuguese technical authority, the LNEC, to attest the equivalence of the certificate. However, the LNEC rejected the attestation on the ground that the IIP was not a member of the European Union of Agrément (UEAtc), a European network of institutes engaged in technical approvals for construction products.[146]

Does the refusal to attest equivalence conflict with Article 34 TFEU?

Yes.

---

144 Regulation 764/2008 of the European Parliament and of the Council of 9 July 2008 laying down procedures relating to the application of certain national technical rules to products lawfully marketed in another Member State and repealing Decision No. 3052/95/EC, [2008] OJ L218/21.

145 Pelkmans, "Mutual Recognition in Goods. on Promises and Disillusions" (2007) 14 *Journal of European Public Policy* 699.

146 Case C-432/03, *Commission* v. *Portugal – Polyethylene Pipes* [2005] ECR I-9665.

The Court's analysis of the legal question proceeded in four distinct steps.

(1) *Is there a harmonization measure in place?* Directive 89/106 approximates national provisions relating to construction products.[147] However, the Directive does not lay down a harmonized standard for polyethylene pipes.[148]

(2) *Are there other technical specifications recognized at Union level?* No.

(3) *Does a regulatory mutual recognition principle apply?* The Directive provides that Member States must generally allow products to be placed on their market if they satisfy the national provisions of another Member State that are consistent with the Treaty. The Directive provides for a specialized procedure according to which Member States must permit products that have satisfied tests and inspections carried out by an approved body in the producing Member State (Article 16).[149] Member States must exchange information on such institutions. However, Article 16 does not provide for a situation – like the one in the present case – where Italy has not informed Portugal about an approving body such as the IIP. Accordingly, the regulatory principle of mutual recognition as laid down in the Directive remains inapplicable.

(4) *Does the judicial principle of mutual recognition apply?* In the absence of harmonizing rules, Member States are free to decide on whether to require prior authorization for the marketing of the products concerned.[150] However, such a measure must be proportionate; it must not duplicate controls which have already been carried out (principle of mutual recognition).[151] As the Portuguese authorities had not taken the certificate issued by an approval body in another Member State into account, they failed in their duty of cooperation which arises from Article 34 TFEU.

Case groups

In this section, we look at some examples of how the Court has applied Article 34 TFEU in practice.

Import licenses and import controls

Import licenses constitute distinctly applicable MEQRs. Commission Directive 70/50/ EEC – the instrument with which the Commission first defined the concept of MEQRs – provided that measures which subject imports to a condition constitute MEQRs, unless they are pure formalities (Article 2(2)). The Court, however, applied a stricter standard right from the start. In *International Fruit Company* (1971), it held that "Articles 30 and 34 [now Articles 34 and 35 TFEU] preclude the application to

---

147 Council Directive 89/106/EEC on the approximation of laws, regulations and administrative provisions of the Member States relating to construction products, [1989] OJ L40/12.
148 *Commission* v. *Portugal – Polyethylene Pipes*, para. 33.   149 *Ibid.*, para. 36.   150 *Ibid.*, para. 44.
151 *Ibid.*, para. 45.

intra-Community trade of a national provision which requires, even as a pure formality, import or export licences or any other similar procedure."[152] More recently, the Court has characterized as an MEQR the requirement of a transfer license for putting vehicles into circulation which had been lawfully registered and used in another Member State (*Commission* v. *Finland – Car Transfer Licence*, 2007).[153] The Court has long held that controls of imported goods, including veterinary or sanitary inspections, also constitute MEQRs. Thus, it found early on in *Simmenthal I* (1976) that veterinary and public health inspections of imported animals and animal products constitute MEQRs, though potentially justifiable under Article 36 TFEU.[154] In a recent case, the Court characterized a requirement subjecting used cars imported into the Netherlands to a test of their general condition prior to registration as an MEQR (*Commission* v. *Netherlands – Used Cars*, 2007).[155]

Restrictions on the use of certain products

In two recent cases, the Court had to decide whether the prohibition of the use of certain types of vehicles falls under Article 34 TFEU. *Mickelsson* (2009) dealt with restrictions on the use of jet-skis, and *Commission* v. *Italy* (2009) with one on motorcycle trailers. In both cases, the Member States concerned did not restrict relevant imports in any form, but legally restricted the use of the products. In *Mickelsson*, jet-skis could be used only on a limited number of Swedish waterways, and the Italian highway code prohibited motorcycles towing trailers. The Advocates General involved in these cases disagreed on the doctrinal nature of these national provisions. In *Mickelsson*, Advocate General Kokott believed that restrictions on use should be treated analogously to selling arrangements in *Keck* and should therefore be exempted from the application of Article 34 TFEU (except when the national rule made the use of the product factually impossible). On the other hand, in *Commission* v. *Italy* Advocate General Bot argued that the exemption did not apply in such cases. The Court followed the latter view, and held that restrictions on use may greatly reduce consumer demand for such products, which limits demand in a Member State's market and consequently hinders market access.[156] In both cases, however, the Court found the measure to be potentially justifiable: the Italian prohibition could be justified on the ground of road safety, and the Swedish measure on the ground of environmental protection.

Infrastructure requirements

As we saw in *Keck*, the Court has held that national measures on "selling arrangements" are generally assumed not to constitute a restriction within the meaning of

---

152 Joined Cases 51 to 54/71, *International Fruit Company* [1971] ECR 1107, 1108.
153 Case C-54/05, *Commission* v. *Finland – Car Transfer Licence* [2007] ECR I-2473.
154 Case 35/76, *Simmenthal I* [1976] ECR 1871, para. 8.
155 Case C-297/05, *Commission* v. *Netherlands – Used Cars* [2007] ECR I-7467.
156 Case C-142/05, *Mickelsson* [2009] ECR I-4273, para. 27; Case C-110/05, *Commission* v. *Italy – Italian Trailers* [2009] ECR I-519, para. 57.

the *Dassonville* formula as long as they affect the marketing of domestic and imported products in the same manner in law and in fact. Since *Keck*, the Court has sometimes had to deal with the question whether certain national rules governing selling arrangements would affect domestic and imported goods differently. The Court has found certain infrastructure requirements to affect domestic and imported goods differently. In *Alfa Vita* (2006), the Court was faced with a Greek law that required bakeries to fulfill certain infrastructural requirements.[157] The bakeries had to have areas for kneading equipment, a solid-fuel store and a flour store. According to a ministerial notification, even shops (like Alfa Vita, a supermarket) that used ovens merely to bake frozen bread (using the "bake-off method") had to fulfill all of these infrastructural requirements. The Court found that the national measures did not sufficiently take the specific situation of "bake-off" products into account: the products are usually pre-prepared and then delivered to sales outlets where only a brief thawing or final baking are carried out. Subjecting such sales outlets to the full requirements of traditional bakeries makes the marketing of such products more difficult. As such "bake-off" bread can be more easily imported than freshly made bread, the measure constitutes a barrier to imports and therefore cannot constitute selling arrangements within the meaning of *Keck*. In *Ker-Optika* (2010), a Hungarian rule required contact lenses to be sold exclusively in shops with a minimum area of 18 square meters where the services of an optometrist or an ophthalmologist qualified in the field of contact lenses are employed. Ker-Optika was prohibited from selling contact lenses via the Internet by a decision of the Hungarian authorities. The Court held that "the prohibition on selling contact lenses by mail order deprives traders from other Member States of a particularly effective means of selling those products and thus significantly impedes access of those traders to the market of the Member State concerned."[158] Therefore, the "legislation does not affect in the same manner the selling of contact lenses by Hungarian traders and such selling as carried out by traders from other Member States."[159] As the *Keck* formula consequently does not apply, the measure is a restriction within the meaning of the *Dassonville* formula. While the Court accepted that such measures may in principle be justified on the ground of public health, it found that there are less restrictive measures that could serve the same purpose in practice, including individualized information and advice through the website. By contrast, the Court has proved to be far more deferential to special rules governing pharmacies in Germany. In *DocMorris I* (2003),[160] the Court found a German prohibition of Internet sales of prescription drugs justifiable on grounds of public health; and in *DocMorris II* (2009) the Court held that the Treaty freedoms "do not preclude national legislation ... which prevents persons not having the status of pharmacist from owning and operating pharmacies."[161]

---

157 Joined Cases C-158/04 and C-159/04, *Alfa Vita* [2006] ECR I-8135.
158 Case C-108/09, *Ker-Optika* [2010] ECR I-12213, para. 54.   159 *Ibid.*, para. 55.
160 Case C-322/01, *DocMorris I* [2003] ECR I-14887.   161 Case C-171/07, *DocMorris II* [2009] ECR I-4171.

Indications of origin

We have already encountered *Commission* v. *Ireland – Irish Souvenirs,* in which an Irish measure required that jewelry not produced in Ireland depicting motifs or possessing characteristics which suggest that they are souvenirs of Ireland needed to bear an indication of their country of origin or the word "foreign." This included, for example, the depiction of Irish personalities, the Irish clover ("Shamrock"), Irish events or landscapes. The Court found the measure to be restrictive and not justifiable on the ground of consumer protection. In a similar case, the United Kingdom (*Commission* v. *United Kingdom,* 1985)[162] prohibited the retail of certain goods unless they are marked with or accompanied by an indication of origin. The UK measures required the indication of origin to be clear and legible, and not to be hidden or obscured. The Commission argued that the obligation of retailers to indicate the origin even if the product itself does not carry marks of origin would create an implicit bias toward products that do, as they would cause less effort to the retailer. Producers, who wish to retain their customers, would ultimately feel obliged to origin-mark their products. The Court held that, as the real goal of the measure was to distinguish between domestic and imported products, it would enable consumers to "assert any prejudices which they may have against foreign products."[163] Origin-marking is therefore liable to make the marketing of imported products more difficult. The Court then rejected the attempt of the United Kingdom to justify such a restriction on the basis of consumer protection.

While the obligation to origin-mark domestic and imported products was prohibited by the Court, it found the indication of regional origin to be a justifiable interest under certain conditions. Since the late 1970s, the EU has issued measures according to which regional indications could be reserved for products that were in fact produced in a certain region. The protection of indications of regional origin aimed at ensuring the diversification of agricultural production and improvements in quality.[164] Designations of origin could be registered for agricultural products and foodstuffs originating in a certain region and having a specific quality or reputation. There are three distinct schemes of registration established by European law (see Table 3.6).[165] So far, over 1,000 products have been registered under these schemes.[166]

In *Exportur* (1992), the Court confirmed that measures which protect regional indications can be justified on grounds of the protection of industrial and commercial property within the meaning of Article 36 TFEU, as they aim at preventing

---

162 Case 207/83, *Commission* v. *United Kingdom* [1985] ECR 1201.   163 *Ibid.,* para. 17.

164 Council Regulation 510/2006 of 20 March 2006 on the protection of geographical indications and designations of origin for agricultural products and foodstuffs [2006] OJ L93/12, Preamble, recital 2.

165 Council Regulation 510/2006 of 20 March 2006 on the protection of geographical indications and designations of origin for agricultural products and foodstuffs; Council Regulation 509/2006 of 20 March 2006 on agricultural products and foodstuffs as traditional specialties guaranteed [2006] OJ L93/1.

166 MEMO/11/84, February 15, 2011, "Background Note: 1000th Quality Food Name Registered."

Table 3.6 Schemes of geographical indications

Scheme	Legal characteristics	Examples
Protected designation of origin (PDO)	Products from a specific region that have qualities that are "due to a particular geographical environment with its inherent natural and human factors." The production, processing and preparation take place in that region.	Camembert de Normandie (cheese, France) Roquefort (cheese, France) Prosciutto di Parma (meat products, Italy)
Protected geographical indication (PGI)	Products from a specific region "which possess a specific quality, reputation or other characteristics attributable to that geographical origin." Either production, processing or preparation has taken place in that region.	Kölsch (beer, Germany) Limone di Siracusa (fruits, Italy) Budějovické pivo (beer, CZ)
Traditional specialty guaranteed (TSG)	Products of traditional character, based either on their composition or on the means of production.	Kabanosy (meat products, Poland) Pizza Napoletana (Italy) Jamón Serrano (meat, Spain)

producers from "taking advantage of the reputation attaching to the products of the undertakings established in the regions or places indicated by those names."[167] However, such arguments cannot justify geographical indications that encompass the whole or significant parts of the territory of a Member State. The Court found, for example, that the "Quality from Germany" label and the "Walloon label of quality" could not be justified on overriding grounds in the public interest.[168]

Parallel imports

The issue of parallel imports arises when products are sold at different prices in different Member States as a result of either the manufacturer's business strategy or national legislation. The same pharmaceutical product may cost less in country B than in country A. Traders who wish to take advantage of this price difference will buy the product in B and export it to A. However, this may run parallel to the manufacturer's own distributive channels. The Court generally found parallel imports to be desirable to counter the fragmentation of the internal market. It argued in *Hartlauer* (2003) that, "in completing the internal market as an area without internal frontiers in which free competition is to be ensured, parallel imports play an important role in preventing the compartmentalisation of national markets."[169] The case dealt with the issue of comparative advertising. Directive 84/450/EEC on misleading advertising allowed comparative advertising under certain conditions. Hartlauer had bought brand-name spectacle frames

---

167 *Exportur*, para. 37.
168 Case C-325/00, *Commission* v. *Germany – Markenqualität aus deutschen Landen* [2002] ECR I-9977; Case C-255/03, *Commission* v. *Belgium – Walloon Label of Quality* [2004], unreported.
169 Case C-44/01, *Hartlauer* [2003] ECR I-3095, para. 63.

from a parallel importer and not from the official distributor. A competing company, which had bought its frames from the official distributor and was targeted by Hartlauer with comparative advertising, argued that these different distribution channels made comparative advertising misleading. The Court found, however, that products acquired from the official distributor and through parallel import are comparable.

Most cases of parallel imports concern pharmaceutical products. Producers have traditionally attempted to employ their trade mark rights to undermine parallel importers (most recently in *Orifarm*, 2011). In *Upjohn* (1999), a company of the same name sold an antibiotic as "Dalacine" in France and "Dalacin" in Denmark. Paranova, a parallel importer, bought "Dalacine" in France and sold it under the trade mark "Dalacin" in Denmark. Upjohn applied for an injunction against Paranova. The Court referred to Article 7(1) of the trade mark Directive,[170] which stated that "[T]he trade mark shall not entitle the proprietor to prohibit its use in relation to goods which have been put on the market in the Community under that trade mark by the proprietor or with his consent." The Court explained that "[w]ith regard to the right in a trade mark, its specific purpose is in particular to guarantee the proprietor the exclusive right to use that trade mark for the purpose of putting a product on the market for the first time and therefore to protect him against competitors wishing to take advantage of the status and reputation of the trade mark by selling products which bear it unlawfully."[171] Conversely, a trader does not require the consent of the trade mark proprietor to export and market a product that the proprietor has already put on the market.[172]

Under certain conditions, parallel importers are also allowed to re-package pharmaceutical products and affix the trade mark of that product (*Hoffmann-La Roche*, 1978).[173] Consumers in country A may be hesitant to buy pharmaceutical products that had been originally packaged for sale in country B and were subsequently merely relabeled for sale in country A. Even though the trade mark proprietors can in principle rely on its rights to prevent a parallel importer from repackaging pharmaceutical products and using that trade mark, this may constitute a derogation from the free movement of goods, which is prohibited if the exercise of those rights contributes to artificial partitioning of the markets between Member States (*Hoffmann-La Roche*).[174]

Medicinal products are generally subject to authorization. However, parallel importers must be granted a simplified authorization procedure either if the same

---

170 First Council Directive 89/104/EEC of 21 December 1988 to approximate the laws of the Member States relating to trade marks, [1989] OJ L40/1, now Directive 2008/95/EC of the European Parliament and of the Council of 22 October 2008 to approximate the laws of the Member States relating to trade marks, [2008] OJ L299/25. Art. 7(1) remains unchanged.
171 Case C-379/97, *Upjohn* [1999] ECR I-6927, para. 15.
172 Joined Cases C-427/93, C-429/93 and C-436/93, *Bristol-Myers Squibb* [1996] ECR I-3457, para. 31.
173 Case 102/77, *Hoffmann-La Roche* [1978] ECR 1139, para. 14.
174 *Ibid.*, para 14; see also Case C-143/00, *Boehringer Ingelheim* [2002] ECR I-3759, para. 14.

(*De Peijper*, 1976)[175] or a largely similar product (*Smith & Nephew*, 1996)[176] has already received a marketing authorization in the Member State of destination.[177]

Important secondary law

In this section, we look at some of the secondary legislation in the field of the free movement of goods. Many legislative acts harmonize, partly or fully, the conditions according to which products can be produced and sold within the EU.

Harmonization of technical standards

Harmonized standards (i.e. rules that relate to the physical properties and the performance of a product) across the Union make the free movement of goods easier: if a product has to conform to the same technical standards in every Member State, cross-border trade is greatly facilitated. It has been estimated that goods covered by harmonized measures account for at least half of intra-Union trade.[178] Until the 1980s, harmonization in the field of the free movement of goods took the form of detailed, exhaustive determination of product requirements. This detailed harmonization approach still exists, usually in areas that had been successfully harmonized before the reforms of the 1980s. It is employed in such areas as foodstuffs, pharmaceutical products and motor vehicles. The downside of the detailed harmonization approach is that the legislative process tends to be complex and therefore relatively slow. Since the mid 1980s, the EU has followed a strategy it terms the "new approach" to harmonization.[179] According to the new approach, first announced in the Commission's White Paper on the completion of the internal market (1985), the harmonization measure is supposed to lay down in general terms only the most important public regulatory interests in the field of health and safety. Technical specifications, on the other hand, are not laid down in a legislative act, but in European standards. These standards, the elaboration of which is mandated by the Commission to one of the three European standards organizations, are published in the EU's *Official Journal*.[180] The standards provide detailed solutions to the general requirements laid down in harmonization legislation. Products that comply with these standards are presumed to be in conformity with the EU's harmonized acts. However, the European standards are voluntary: manufacturers may opt for a different solution to achieve the required health and safety standards. The "new approach" based on harmonized standards has so far been employed in over thirty areas. In the field of machinery, for example, the

---

175 *De Peijper*, paras. 21 and 36.   176 Case C-201/94, *Smith & Nephew* [1996] ECR I-5819, para. 32.
177 See Commission, Communication on parallel imports of proprietary medicinal products for which marketing authorizations have already been granted, COM(2003) 839 final, December 30, 2003, p. 8.
178 Pelkmans, "Mutual Recognition in Goods," p. 704.
179 Council Resolution of 7 May 1985 on a new approach to technical harmonization and standards, [1985] OJ C136/1.
180 The three organizations are the European Committee for Standardization (CEN), the European Committee for Electrotechnical Standardization (CENELEC) and the European Telecommunications Standards Institute (ETSI).

Table 3.7 Examples of harmonized measures

Field	Measure
Chemical substances	Regulation No. 1907/2006 (REACH)
General product safety	Directive 2001/95/EC
Medical devices	Directive 93/42/EEC
Machinery	Directive 2006/42/EC
Packaging and packaging waste	Directive 94/62/EC

Commission has recognized about 700 standards. Table 3.7 and Table 3.8 set out examples of harmonized measures.

The fast pace of innovation, a characteristic feature of modern, industrialized states, entails a constantly increasing volume of new regulation, concerning both technical standards and other requirements, for example in the field of health, safety or environmental protection. While the demand for new regulation is often owed to the complexity and high performance levels of modern economies, there is a risk of a refragmentation of the internal market if national authorities fail to take European considerations sufficiently into account. Neither legislative harmonization on the European level nor the judicial enforcement of the principle of mutual recognition constitute ideal remedies against the risk of refragmentation by national regulation. In practice, Directive 98/34/EC (ex-Directive 83/189/EEC) provides a very important mechanism to ensure the continued unity of the internal market, namely, the obligation on Member States to inform the Commission about any planned new Regulation.[181] Member States are obliged to communicate plans to introduce new or to change existing standards, and have to postpone adoption of

Table 3.8 Examples of harmonized standards in the field of machinery

Title of harmonized standard	Reference
Safety rules for the construction and installation of lifts – Part 3: Electric and hydraulic service lifts	EN 81-3:2000+A1:2008
Safety of machinery – Minimum gaps to avoid crushing of parts of the human body	EN 349:1993+A1:2008
Food processing machinery – Dough mixers – Safety and hygiene requirements	EN 453:2000+A1:2009
Agricultural machinery – Vine shoot tipping machines – Safety	EN 706:1996+A1:2009
Drilling rigs – Safety	EN 791:1995+A1:2009

---

181 Directive 98/34/EC of the European Parliament and of the Council of 22 June 1998, laying down a procedure for the provision of information in the field of technical standards and regulations and of rules on Information Society services, [1998] OJ L204/37, as amended by Directive 98/48/EC, [1998] OJ L217/18.

the Regulation for at least three months. At the request of the Commission, this standstill period can be extended to a year, within which consultations take place.

Rights and duties of manufacturers in the EU

(1) The manufacturer has to comply with the requirements laid down in the relevant harmonizing legislation. For a toy maker, this would be the Toy Safety Directive.[182]

(2) This can be achieved by complying with the harmonized standards (if they exist for the relevant aspect), or in other ways. Producers who choose not to follow harmonized standards carry the burden of proof that their products nonetheless conform to the requirements of the harmonized legislation.

(3) If no harmonized standard exists, the product has to be submitted to a "notified body," organizations denoted by a Member State that carry out conformity assessments. In the case of toys, the TÜV Nord in Germany would be an option. Not all harmonization measures require third party assessment (e.g. smaller boats); others require it even if the manufacturer has complied with all harmonized standards (e.g. elevators).

(4) If the product complies with the requirements, then it must affix a CE marking on the product. A product bearing a CE marking is presumed to fulfill all the necessary requirements and can be marketed throughout the EU (and the EEA).

Consumer protection

Consumer protection has been only partly harmonized; the earliest measures stem from the mid 1980s. The harmonization measures on consumer protection are based on Article 114 TFEU. Four Directives form the core of the European legislation on consumer protection: the doorstep selling Directive,[183] the distance selling Directive,[184] the Directive on unfair terms in consumer contracts[185] and the Directive on the sale of consumer goods and associated guarantees.[186] The new Directive on consumer rights (2011/83/EU) replaces the first two measures, and will apply to contracts concluded after June 13, 2014.[187] The measures covers contracts

---

182 Directive 2009/48/EC of the European Parliament and of the Council of 18 June 2009 on the safety of toys, [2009] OJ L170/1.

183 Council Directive 85/577/EEC of 20 December 1985 to protect the consumer in respect of contracts negotiated away from business premises, [1985] OJ L372/31.

184 Directive 97/7/EC of the European Parliament and of the Council of 20 May 1997 on the protection of consumers in respect of distance contracts, [1997] OJ L144/19.

185 Council Directive 93/13/EEC of 5 April 1993 on unfair terms in consumer contracts, [1993] OJ L95/29.

186 Directive 1999/44/EC of the European Parliament and of the Council of 25 May 1999 on certain aspects of the sale of consumer goods and associated guarantees, [1999] OJ L171/12.

187 Directive 2011/83/EU of the European Parliament and of the Council of 25 October 2011 on consumer rights, amending Council Directive 93/13/EEC and Directive 1999/44/EC of the European Parliament and of the Council and repealing Council Directive 85/577/EEC and Directive 97/7/EC of the European Parliament and of the Council, [2011] OJ L304/64, Art. 28(2).

Table 3.9 Important secondary law on consumer protection		
Directive	**No.**	**Important provisions**
Doorstep selling Directive (replaced by consumer rights Directive)	85/577/EEC	Right of withdrawal from off-premises contract within seven days without giving any reason (Art. 5; fourteen days in new consumer rights Directive)
Distance selling Directive (replaced by consumer rights Directive)	97/7/EC	Right of withdrawal from a distance contract of seven days without giving any reason (Art. 6; fourteen days in new consumer rights Directive)
Directive on unfair terms in consumer contracts	1993/13/EC	Directive defines unfair contract terms in standard contract terms of consumer contracts. Unfair terms do not bind the consumer (Art. 6)
Directive on the sale of consumer goods and associated guarantees	1999/44/EC	Legal warranty of two years (Art. 5)

relating to goods as well as services. Table 3.9 sets out a list of important secondary law on consumer protection.

The older measures follow the minimum harmonization principle. This means that they lay down minimum standards of protection that can be exceeded by the Member States if they prefer a higher level of protection. By contrast, the newer Directives adopted during the past decade, including the new consumer rights Directive,[188] follow the full harmonization principle.[189] This means that Member States can no longer depart from the common standard laid down in the harmonization measures. The Commission justified the change to the full harmonization approach with the argument that disparities in the levels of protection between the Member States create costly barriers for traders and undermine consumer confidence.[190] However, the full harmonization approach has been criticized as a watering-down of consumer protection.[191]

QUANTITATIVE RESTRICTIONS ON EXPORTS AND MEASURES HAVING EQUIVALENT EFFECT (ARTICLE 35 TFEU)

While Article 34 TFEU deals with imports, Article 35 TFEU is applicable to situations where Member States attempt to prohibit or disadvantage the export of goods to other Member States. Article 35 TFEU does not apply to exports to third

---

188 Preamble, recital 5.
189 See e.g. Directive 2002/65/EC of the European Parliament and of the Council of 23 September 2002 concerning the distance marketing of consumer financial services and amending Council Directive 90/619/EEC and Directives 97/7/EC and 98/27/EC, [2002] OJ L271/16; Directive 2005/29/EC of the European Parliament and the Council of 11 May 2001 on unfair commercial practices, [2005] OJ L149/22.
190 Preamble, recital 6.
191 Hans-W. Micklitz and Norbert Reich, "Crónica de una Muerte Anunciada: The Commission Proposal for a 'Directive on Consumer Rights,'" (2009) 46 *Common Market Law Review* 471, 519.

countries. Similar to import restrictions, Article 35 TFEU prohibits both quantitative restrictions (QRs) on exports and measures having equivalent effect.

Quantitative restrictions

QRs on exports are either quotas or total export prohibitions for certain goods. In *Hedley Lomas* (1996),[192] a company was refused a license to export live sheep to Spain, as the UK ministry argued that Spanish slaughterhouses did not fulfill EU standards. This – being a zero-quota – constituted a breach of Article 35 TFEU. In *Delhaize* (1992), the Court dealt with a Spanish rule that prohibited the sale of Rioja wine in bulk except within the region itself. The measure was part of a general attempt by the Spanish government to achieve quality improvement, and aimed at ensuring that the bottling of Rioja wine took place solely within the region itself. We have already seen that the Court has found the protection of regional indications of origin to be a justifiable objective under certain circumstances. However, the Court found that a prohibition of exports, as was the case in *Delhaize*, constituted an unjustifiable QR.

Measures having equivalent effect

Article 35 TFEU prohibits not only QRs on exports, but also measures that have equivalent effect (MEQRs). The provision is thus similarly structured to Article 34 TFEU, but with an important difference: while MEQRs under Article 34 TFEU prohibit both discriminatory (distinctly applicable) and indistinctly applicable measures that constitute a restriction on intra-Union trade (the *Dassonville* formula), Article 35 TFEU solely prohibits (directly and indirectly) discriminatory measures, but not indistinctly applicable measures. After its decision in *Dassonville*, the Court at first applied the *Dassonville* formula (prohibition of restrictions) also in the field of exports (*Bouhelier*, 1977).[193] However, two years later in *Groenveld* (1979),[194] the Court reversed its ruling in *Bouhelier* and decided that Article 35 TFEU – contrary to Article 34 TFEU – solely prohibited discrimination, but did not contain a prohibition of restrictive, indistinctly applicable measures. Since *Groenveld*, the Court has employed a three-tier test to establish a possible breach of Article 35 TFEU:[195] (1) the national measure must have as its specific object or effect the restriction of patterns of exports; and thereby (2) the establishment of a difference in treatment between the domestic trade of a Member State and its export trade; (3) in such a way as to provide a particular advantage for national production or for the domestic market of the state in question at the expense of the production or trade of other Member States.

---

192 Case C-5/94, *Hedley Lomas* [1996] ECR I-2553.   193 Case 53/76, *Bouhelier* [1977] ECR 3151, para. 16.
194 Case 15/79, *Groenveld* [1979] ECR 3409.   195 *Ibid.*, para. 7.

The *Groenveld*-test, therefore, is much more limited than the *Dassonville* formula, as it is conditional upon differential treatment and the existence of a protectionist effect (both of which are not required under the *Dassonville* formula, as we have already seen).[196] The only exception is agricultural products, where the Court always applies the *Dassonville* formula (*Kakavetsos-Fragkopoulos*, 2011).[197] The *Groenveld*-test was confirmed in the Court's subsequent case law, though the Court does not always accurately scrutinize all prongs of its test. Generally, national rules conform to Article 35 TFEU if they apply without distinction. In *Oebel* (1981), the Court found that the prohibition of night-work in bakeries did not violate Article 35 TFEU, as the measures were not caught by the *Groenveld*-test. The Court held it applies "by virtue of objective criteria to all the undertakings in a particular industry which are established within the national territory, without leading to any difference in treatment whatsoever on the ground of the nationality of traders and without distinguishing between the domestic trade of the State in question and the export trade."[198] Minimum standards for enclosures for fattening calves that apply without distinction as to whether the animals are or are not intended for export do not violate Article 35 TFEU, as the Court held in *Holdijk* (1982). In *Jongeneel Kaas* (1984), the Court held that Dutch minimum standards in cheese production, the obligation to affix a compliance control stamp on the cheese, and obligatory testing by an inspection agency, did not violate Article 35 TFEU, "provided that such requirement applies without distinction to domestic production marketed in the Member State concerned and production intended for export."[199]

However, from time to time, national measures have been successfully challenged for their restrictive effects on exports. Some cases, for example, concern the export of waste. In *Sydhavnens Sten & Grus* (2000), the Court found a municipal system of waste management in Copenhagen to violate Article 35 TFEU, as it required undertakings to process waste within the confines of the municipality, thereby restricting export.[200] In *Grilli* (2003), an Italian citizen bought a second-hand car in Hamburg and wanted to drive it to Italy. He attached temporary number plates that had been issued to him beforehand by the Italian authorities. He was fined by the German police, as German law required him to use German – not Italian – temporary number plates for exporting cars from Germany. The Court found this rule to be a restriction contrary to Article 35 TFEU.

Over the years, the different treatment of MEQRs under Article 34 and Article 35 TFEU by the Court has been criticized by a number of Advocates General.[201] It

---

196 Case C-12/02, *Grilli* [2003] ECR I-11585, para. 42.
197 Case C-161/09, *Kakavetsos-Fragkopoulos* [2011] ECR I-915; see also Case 94/79, *Vriend* [1980] ECR 327, para. 8; Case C-272/95, *Deutsches Milch-Kontor* [1997] ECR I-1905, para. 24.
198 Case 155/80, *Oebel* [1981] ECR 1993, para. 16.   199 Case 237/82, *Jongeneel Kaas* [1984] ECR 483, para. 6.
200 Case C-209/98, *Sydhavnens Sten & Grus* [2000] ECR I-3743; see also Case C-203/96, *Dusseldorp* [1998] ECR I-4075.
201 For a summary, see Peter Oliver, "Some Further Reflections on the Scope of Articles 28–30 (Ex 30–36) EC" (1999) 36 *Common Market Law Review* 783, 800.

seems that – while paying lip service to it – the Court may in fact have abandoned the *Groenveld*-test in its decision in *Gysbrechts*:

Case C-205/07, Gysbrechts (2008)

Mr. Gysbrechts' company sold food supplements over the Internet. Whereas Belgian customers could use any means of payment, customers in other Member States had to pay by credit card, and thereby had to state the number and expiry date of their card. The company was charged by the Belgian authorities with violating a provision of the consumer protection law, which prohibited the seller from requiring that the consumer provide a deposit or any form of payment before expiry of the period of seven working days within which withdrawal from the contract is permitted. According to the Belgian authorities, providing the credit card number on the order form for goods enables the company to collect the price of those goods before expiry of the period for withdrawal, which contravenes the requirements laid down by law.

Does a rule prohibiting sellers to request credit card information before the expiry of the withdrawal period in cross-border distance selling conflict with Article 35 TFEU?

Yes.

The measure deprives traders of an efficient tool against the risk of nonpayment, which is more acute with regard to customers residing in another Member State considering difficulties in instigating legal proceedings. Although the rule is indistinctly applicable, "its actual effect is none the less greater on goods leaving the market of the exporting Member State than on the marketing of goods in the domestic market of that Member State."[202] The measure thus constitutes an MEQR, but can, in principle, be justified by the overriding reasons of public interest, namely, consumer protection. However, the Court found the measure to be disproportionate.

By contrast to the Court, Advocate General Trstenjak found that none of the three prongs of the *Groenveld* test were fulfilled: neither does the measure have as its object or effect a restriction of export patterns, nor is there differential treatment in law or in fact, nor does it, consequently, provide an advantage for the domestic market.[203] The decision has also been criticized from the perspective of consumer protection. Micklitz and Reich argued: "In *Gysbrechts*, the CJEU, for the first time, set aside national consumer protection rules prohibiting the Internet trader from requesting the number of the consumer's payment card – thus reaching beyond

---

202 Case C-205/07, *Gysbrechts* [2008] ECR I-9947, para. 43.
203 *Gysbrechts*, Opinion of Advocate General Trstenjak, paras. 34–40.

the minimum protection clause of Directive 97/7/EC – as a violation of the proportionality requirement inherent in the free movement regime."[204] It remains to be seen whether *Gysbrechts* is the beginning of a change in the case law on Article 35 TFEU or a single irregularity.

Justifications

Measures falling under Article 35 TFEU may – similar to Article 34 TFEU – be justified by Member States either by invocation of the explicit derogations listed in Article 36 TFEU (e.g. *Grilli*)[205] or because of overriding reasons in the public interest (e.g. *Kakavetsos-Fragkopoulos*).

INTERNAL TAXATION (ARTICLE 110 TFEU)

Article 110 TFEU prohibits discriminatory taxation by the Member States. The provision holds: "No Member State shall impose, directly or indirectly, on the products of other Member States any internal taxation of any kind in excess of that imposed directly or indirectly on similar domestic products. Furthermore, no Member State shall impose on the products of other Member States any internal taxation of such a nature as to afford indirect protection to other products." According to the Court, Article 110 TFEU "seeks to guarantee the complete neutrality of internal taxation as regards competition between products already on the domestic market and imported products" (*Tatu*, 2011).[206]

Systematically, Article 110 TFEU complements the provisions on the free movement of goods:[207] While Article 30 TFEU ensures that goods from other Member States are not charged upon entry into the country, Article 110 TFEU ensures that – once the good has entered the country – it is not taxed differently from similar domestic goods.

Article 110 TFEU covers pecuniary charges resulting from a general system of internal taxation applied systematically, in accordance with the same objective criteria, to categories of products irrespective of their origin or destination.[208] Article 110 TFEU must be interpreted widely so as to cover all taxation procedures which, directly or indirectly, undermine the equal treatment of domestic products and imported products. The prohibition laid down in that article must therefore apply whenever a fiscal charge is likely to discourage imports of goods originating in other Member States to the benefit of domestic production.[209] Although the

---

204 Hans-W. Micklitz and Norbert Reich, "Crónica de una Muerte Anunciada: The Commission Proposal for a 'Directive on Consumer Rights,'" (2009) 46 *Common Market Law Review* 471, 476.
205 *Grilli*, para. 84.   206 Case C-402/09, *Tatu* [2011] ECR I-2711, para. 35.
207 Case 24/68, *Commission* v. *Italy* [1969] ECR 193, para. 5.
208 Joined Cases C-393/04 and C-41/05, *Air Liquide Industries* [2006] ECR I-5293, para. 56.
209 Case C-45/94, *Ayuntamiento de Ceuta* [1995] ECR I-4385, para. 29.

wording of Article 110 TFEU solely refers to "products of other Member States," the Court has held regularly that the provision also prohibits any tax discrimination against domestic products intended for export to other Member States (*Freskot*, 2003).[210] According to the Court, the provisions "relating to charges having equivalent effect and those relating to discriminatory internal taxation cannot be applied together, so that under the system of the Treaty the same measure cannot belong to both categories at the same time."[211] Table 3.10 sets out the differences between Article 30 TFEU and Article 110 TFEU.

Table 3.10 Differentiating between Article 30 TFEU and Article 110 TFEU	
Article 30 TFEU	**Article 110 TFEU**
Customs duties or charges having equivalent effect	Taxation
Charged on occasion of the product crossing the border	Charges resulting from a general system of internal taxation applied systematically, in accordance with the same objective criteria, to categories of products irrespective of their origin or destination.[a]
No charge whatsoever is allowed	Only (directly or indirectly) discriminatory measures are prohibited.

a   Case C-158/82, *Commission* v. *Denmark* [1983] ECR 3572, para. 19.

Article 110 TFEU covers all taxes, charges or fees on goods or which affect goods. Taxes on capital[212] or services are not covered. Article 110 TFEU encompasses two

Harmonized and non-harmonized fields in taxation

The area of taxation is considered to be one of the core elements of national sovereignty, as it is directly connected with the capability of the Member States to pay for its policies and activities. Thus, many areas of taxation – direct taxes such as corporate tax, income tax or property tax – remain in the competence of the Member States. Unanimity among the Member States is necessary for harmonizing direct taxes (Articles 114(2) and 115 TFEU). Until today, efforts to harmonize direct taxes have been unsuccessful. Only very few secondary acts harmonizing direct taxes have been passed so far. Indirect taxes, on the other hand, have been (partly) harmonized since the 1960s. Article 113 TFEU allows the harmonization of "turnover taxes, excise duties and other forms of indirect taxation." Most notably, value added tax (VAT) has been harmonized.[213] Other harmonizing legislation has been passed for certain other consumer taxes, such as tobacco, alcohol and petroleum products.

---

210 Case C-355/00, *Freskot* [2003] I-5263, para. 45.   211 *Stadtgemeinde Frohnleiten*, para. 26.
212 Case 267/86, *Van Eycke* [1988] ECR 4769, para. 25.
213 See Council Directive 2006/112/EC of 28 November 2006 on the common system of value added tax, [2006] OJ L347/1.

prohibitions: the prohibition of discriminatory taxes on similar products in paragraph 1 and the prohibition of protectionist measures on products that are in competition in paragraph 2.

Similar goods (Article 110(1) TFEU)

Article 110(1) TFEU prohibits taxes that are imposed on non-domestic products if "similar" domestic products are taxed less. Originally, the Court held goods to be similar if they "are normally to be considered as coming within the same fiscal, customs or statistical classification."[214] Subsequently, the Court started to consider the similarity from a substantive perspective, asking if they are used similarly and comparably.[215] The Court held that products are similar if they "have similar characteristics and meet the same need from the point of view of consumers."[216] According to settled case law, Article 110(1) TFEU is infringed where the tax charged on the imported product and that charged on the similar domestic product are calculated in a different manner on the basis of different criteria which lead, if only in certain cases, to higher taxation being imposed on the imported product.[217] This includes situations where the rate of taxation on domestic and imported products is the same, but the basis of assessment for levying the tax differs (*Kalinchev*, 2010).

The following non-domestic and domestic products have been found to be similar by the Court:

- Fruit wines and wines made of grapes are similar because they are both made from "the same kind of basic product," undergo the same process of natural fermentation, have roughly similar taste and smell and "can meet the same needs from the point of view of consumers, as they can be consumed in the same way, namely to quench thirst, as refreshments and at meal times."[218]
- Used cars sold in a Member State are similar to imported used cars. If a tax levied upon an imported used car is as high as the excise tax once paid for a similar new car, the former is put at a disadvantage if the tax was calculated without taking the vehicle's actual depreciation into account, making the import of a used car relatively more expensive (*Kalinchev*, 2010).[219]

An example for products that were held not to be similar can be found in the case *Johnnie Walker* (1986).[220] Here, the Court ruled that whisky and fruit liquor wines

214 Case 27/67, *Fink-Frucht* [1968] ECR 223, 232.
215 Case C-101/00, *Tulliasiamies* [2002] ECR I-7487, para. 56.
216 Case 168/78, *Commission* v. *France – Spirits* [1980] ECR 347, para. 5.
217 Case C-2/09, *Kalinchev* [2010] ECR I-4939, para. 39.
218 Case 106/84, *Commission* v. *Denmark – Fruit Wines* [1986] ECR 833, paras. 14–15.
219 See also Case C-345/93, *Nunes Tadeu* [1995] ECR I-479, para. 20; Case C-393/98, *Gomes Valente* [2001] ECR I-1327, para. 44.
220 Case 243/84, *Johnnie Walker* [1986] ECR 875.

are not similar. They are based on different agricultural products, the chemical production process is different (fermentation v. distillation), as is the alcohol content. Article 110(1) TFEU prohibits both direct and indirect discrimination. Directly discriminatory measures tax goods differently depending on the origin of the good. Indirectly discriminatory measures do not expressly differentiate on the ground of origin of the product, but in effect tax non-domestic goods higher than domestic goods.

Examples of directly discriminatory tax measures include the following:

- Germany taxed milk powder imported from Luxembourg higher than milk powder from Germany (*Lütticke*, 1966).[221]
- Germany offered a tax rebate for spirits made from fruits, whereas it did not offer the same rebate for similar non-domestic spirits (*Hansen & Balle*, 1978).[222]
- A Polish regulation levies a charge on imported second-hand cars, but not on second-hand cars already registered in Poland (*Kawala*, 2007).[223]
- An Austrian law imposed a levy on the long-term depositing of waste (*Stadtgemeinde Frohnleiten*, 2007).[224] It exempted waste derived from the rehabilitation of disused hazardous sites in Austria, without exempting the same kind of waste from sites located in other Member States.

A number of cases provide examples for indirectly discriminatory taxation. The decision in *Humblot* (1985) dealt with a French tax on cars. In the 1980s, French carmakers did not produce cars with an engine performance higher than 16 CV (*chevaux-vapeur*, an older measurement unit for car power). A French tax provided for two different tax systems: cars below 16 CV had to pay a maximum of 1,100 francs, whereas cars above it had to pay 5,000 francs. The Court decided that the tax measure was indirectly discriminatory, as the 5,000 franc tax in practice only applied to non-domestic cars.[225] In *Essent Netwerk* (2008), a Dutch law charged a surcharge on both imported and domestic electricity. The surcharge paid for so-called "stranded costs," i.e. investments made by the electricity companies prior to the market liberalization that are no longer profitable under market conditions. The Court found that this system – although the tax was charged on imported and domestic energy alike – was in fact particularly beneficial for domestic producers, as they did not have to pay for their past (unprofitable) investments. The Court held that a charge that is imposed on domestic and imported products alike may still be prohibited if the revenue from that charge supports activities which specifically benefit the taxed domestic products. The case *Tatu* (2011) dealt with a pollution tax on cars:

---

221 Case 57/65, *Lütticke* [1966] ECR 3159.   222 Case 148/77, *Hansen & Balle* [1978] ECR 1787, para. 20.
223 Case C-134/07, *Kawala* [2007] ECR I-10703.
224 Case C-221/06, *Stadtgemeinde Frohnleiten* [2007] ECR I-9643.   225 Case 112/84, *Humblot* [1985] ECR 1367.

Case C-402/09, Tatu (2011)

Mr. Tatu, a Romanian national residing in Romania, bought a used car in Germany and registered it in Romania. For this purpose he was charged an amount of approximately 30 percent of the car's market value as pollution tax. The tax was charged on all cars registered for the first time in Romania after 2008. This means that used cars bought in Romania that were registered before 2008 are not charged this tax on their resale.

Does a tax on the first registration of a used car in a Member State violate Article 110 TFEU if used cars bought in Romania are not charged the same tax?

Yes.

The measure is not directly discriminatory as it does not distinguish between the origin of the cars or the nationality of their owners. However, the tax is indirectly discriminatory because it "discourages the placing in circulation in that Member State of second-hand vehicles purchased in other Member States without discouraging the purchase of second-hand vehicles of the same age and condition on the domestic market."[226]

Competing goods (Article 110(2) TFEU)

Article 110(2) prohibits measures that protect domestic goods if these goods compete with non-domestic goods, even if they are not "similar" within the meaning of paragraph 1. Even products which are not similar may still compete with each other because they serve related purposes. Paragraph 2 applies if three conditions are fulfilled. First, there must be a competitive relationship between the two goods. It is sufficient that competition is possible, it does not need to be established for the individual case.[227] Second, the non-domestic product must be a substitute for the domestic product in a specific aspect. It is not necessary, however, that the function of the product is a complete substitute for that of the domestic product. Third, the measure must have a protective effect. The protectionist function of the measure in question is evident if non-domestic goods are subject to higher taxation than the domestic product.[228] This is the case, for example, when the higher-taxed goods are mostly imported (*COGIS*, 1982).[229] Table 3.11 sets out a comparison between Article 110(1) and Article 110(2) TFEU.

A case that exemplifies the application of paragraph 2 is the British *Wine and Beer* case.

---

226 *Tatu*, para. 61.
227 Case 184/85, *Commission* v. *Italy – Banana Consumption Tax* [1987] ECR 2013, paras. 12–13.

Table 3.11 Comparison between Article 110(1) and Article 110(2) TFEU	
Article 110(1) TFEU	**Article 110(2) TFEU**
Similar products	Goods that are not similar, but compete with each other
Similarity is established by the similar formal classification of the goods and their similar material function	Products in a competitive situation, are (at least partly) substitutable and the measure has protectionist effects

Case 170/78, Commission v. United Kingdom – Wine and Beer (1983)

The UK taxed wine five times higher than beer.

Does the tax violate Article 110(2) TFEU?

Yes.

As the tax on beer is significantly lower than the tax on wine (mostly produced abroad), the measure reinforces the competitive advantage of beer on the market. Although wine and beer are produced in different ways and are consumed in different social settings and by different social groups, the Court nonetheless found that beer is in a competitive relationship with the "lightest and cheapest varieties" of wines.[230] The tax has a protective effect: "the effect of the UK tax system is to stamp wine with the hallmarks of a luxury product which, in view of the tax burden which it bears, can scarcely constitute in the eyes of the consumer a genuine alternative to the typical domestically produced beverage."[231] Thus, the tax constituted a violation of Article 110(2) TFEU.

It is not necessary, however, that competing products must be taxed at exactly the same rate. In a Swedish case, (imported) wine was taxed higher than (often domestically produced) strong beer (*Commission* v. *Sweden – Wine and Beer*, 2008).[232] The Court found that the difference in the excise duty applicable to those products is so slight that it is not likely to influence consumer behavior. The national rule, therefore, did not have a relevant protectionist effect.

228 *Commission* v. *Italy – Banana Consumption Tax*, para. 13.
229 Case 216/81, *COGIS* [1982] ECR 2701, para. 11.
230 Case 170/78, *Commission* v. *United Kingdom – Wine and Beer Cases* [1983] ECR 2265, para. 12.
231 *Ibid.*, para. 27.   232 Case C-167/05, *Commission* v. *Sweden* [2008] ECR I-2127.

Further reading

ALTER, KAREN, and MEUNIER-AITSAHALIA, SOPHIE, "Judicial Politics in the European Community: European Integration and the Pathbreaking Cassis de Dijon Decision" (1994) 26 *Comparative Political Studies* 535

GORMLEY, LAURENCE, "Free Movement of Goods and Their Use – What Is the Use of It?" (2009) 33 *Fordham International Law Journal* 1589

"Silver Threads Among the Gold . . . 50 Years of the Free Movement of Goods" (2007) 31 *International Law Journal* 1637

MORTELMANS, KAMIEL, "Article 30 of the EEC Treaty and Legislation Relating to Market Circumstances: Time to Consider a New Definition?" (1991) 28 *Common Market Law Review* 115

OLIVER, PETER, *Free Movement of Goods in the European Union*, Oxford: Hart Publishing, 2010

"Of Trailers and Jet Skis: Is the Case Law on Article 34 TFEU Hurtling in a New Direction?" (2009) 33 *Fordham International Law Journal* 1423

"Some Further Reflections on the Scope of Articles 28–30 (Ex 30–36) EC" (1999) 36 *Common Market Law Review* 783

PELKMANS, JACQUES, "Mutual Recognition in Goods: On Promises and Disillusions" (2007) 14 *Journal of European Public Policy* 609

REICH, NORBERT, "The 'November Revolution' of the European Court of Justice: Keck, Meng and Audi Revisited" (1994) 31 *Common Market Law Review* 459

SPAVENTA, ELEANOR, "Leaving Keck Behind?" (2009) 35 *European Law Review* 914

VAN GESTEL, ROB, and MICKLITZ, HANS-W., "European Integration Through Standardization: How Judicial Review Is Breaking Down the Club House of Private Standardization Bodies" (2013) 50 *Common Market Law Review* 145

WHITE, ERIC, "In Search of the Limits to Article 30 of the EEC Treaty" (1989) 26 *Common Market Law Review* 235

4 Union citizenship (Articles 18–25 TFEU)

INTRODUCTION

Union citizenship was introduced in 1992 by the Treaty of Maastricht. In the course of the two decades since then, Union citizenship has become one of the Union's most ambitious legal projects. Union citizenship is, in the words of the Court, "destined to be the fundamental status of nationals of the Member States."[1]

Today, Union citizenship is considered not only an emblematic showpiece of evolutionary progress in European integration, but also tangible proof that the Union has transcended its original confines as a regional trade organization. Yet it is noteworthy that there have been important initiatives predating the Maastricht Treaty that created rights for individuals beyond a narrow economic scope. As early as 1951, Walter Hallstein, the Commission's first President, described the freedom of movement of workers in the European Coal and Steel Community as coming close to what he called a European citizenship; and, in 1968, the Commission's Vice-President, Lionello Levi-Sandri, declared that the free movement of economically active persons "represents something more important and more exacting than the free movement of a factor of production. It represents rather an incipient form – still embryonic and imperfect – of European citizenship."[2] And, indeed, the Union's early legislation on worker mobility has moved beyond the narrow framework of mere economic mobility. Regulation 1612/68 (1968), for example, granted broad equal treatment rights not only for workers but also for their families in areas such as social and tax advantages and access to the education system. The underlying assumption was that workers would not exercise their mobility rights if they were treated like second-class citizens. Advocate General Jacobs took the view in *Konstantinidis* (1993) that:

[A] Community national who goes to another Member State as a worker or self-employed person . . . is entitled not just to pursue his trade or profession and to enjoy the same living and working conditions as nationals of the host State; he is in addition entitled to assume that,

---

1 Case C-184/99, *Grzelczyk* [2001] ECR I-6193, para. 31.
2 Both quoted in Wollenschläger, "A New Fundamental Freedom beyond Market Integration: Union Citizenship and its Dynamics for Shifting the Economic Paradigm of European Integration" (2010) 17 *European Law Journal* 1, 31–32.

wherever he goes to earn his living in the European Community, he will be treated in accordance with a common code of fundamental values ... In other words, he is entitled to say "*civis europeus sum*" and to invoke that status in order to oppose any violation of his fundamental rights.[3]

In the first years after the signing of the Maastricht Treaty, it was argued that the new provisions would not and could not create any significantly new entitlements other than those already granted by the Treaties. Some scholars opined that Union citizenship was merely a marketing gag by the governments to promote an idea of the EU capable of arousing emotions – at least more than people were willing to invest into a "mere" economic union. In 1996, renowned scholar Joseph Weiler famously called Union citizenship "little more than a cynical exercise in public relations on the part of the High Contracting Parties."[4] And Advocate General Colomer argued retrospectively in *Petersen* (2008): "At the outset, the concept of citizenship of the Union ... provided a basis for the provisions guaranteeing freedom of movement which was more symbolic than real."[5] In 1998, however, the Court surprised most commentators when it ruled in *Martínez Sala* (1998) that

Case C-85/96, Martínez Sala v. Freistaat Bayern (1998)

Ms. Martínez Sala, a Spanish national, lived in Germany, at some point without a residence permit. In 1993, she gave birth to a child and applied for a child-raising allowance. The application was dismissed by the authorities on the grounds that she had neither German nationality nor a residence permit at the time of her application.

Does a benefit such as a child-raising allowance, which is automatically granted to persons fulfilling certain objective criteria, without any individual and discretionary assessment of personal needs, fall within the scope of Union law as a social advantage?

Yes.

Can a Member State require nationals from other Member States to produce a formal residence permit – which German nationals are not obliged to have – in order to receive a child-raising allowance?

No.

The child-raising allowance is a social advantage within Article 7 of Regulation 492/2011, and is thus within the scope of the EU Treaty. Therefore, Ms. Martínez Sala

---

3 Case C-168/91, *Konstantinidis* [1992] ECR I-1191, Opinion of Advocate General Jacobs, para. 46.

4 Weiler, "Citizenship and Human Rights," in Winter, Curtin, Kellermann and de Witte (eds.), *Reforming the Treaty on European Union*, The Hague: Kluwer Law International, 1996, p. 66; quoted in Wollenschläger, "A New Fundamental Freedom," pp. 31–32.

5 Case C-228/07, *Petersen* [2008] ECR I-6989, Opinion of Advocate General Colomer, para. 26.

may base a claim for the allowance on the principle of nondiscrimination. The Court found that Union law precludes a Member State from requiring nationals of other Member States authorized to reside in its territory to produce a formal residence permit issued by the national authorities in order to receive a child-raising allowance, whereas that Member State's own nationals are merely required to be permanently or ordinarily resident in that Member State.

the Union citizenship provisions are an autonomous source of rights, creating entitlements for individuals regardless of economic activity.

Union citizenship has become an important focal point for those who envision the European Union as moving not only beyond its initial role as an economic organization, but also beyond the political limitations of traditional nation-states, nationality and nationalisms. For Advocate General Colomer, for example, the introduction of Union citizenship in 1992 has been a political sea change, which allowed the Court "to interpret the will of the legislature, affording individuals who exercise freedom of movement greater status than that attributed to economic operators."[6] According to Advocate General Colomer, "the Court has transformed the paradigm of *homo economicus* into that of *homo civitatis*."[7] Colomer believes that the Court's jurisdiction has developed from a purely formalist and limited understanding of the rights under Union citizenship – focused on barriers to mobility and on discrimination – toward a substantial understanding. According to Colomer, the citizenship provisions do not merely establish a right to equal treatment, but aim at creating a new form of European solidarity.[8] Colomer stated:

It is, therefore, the notion of *belonging* in a material sense, aside from any administrative requirements, which justifies the inclusion of citizens of the Union in the political community. When the ties of identity with a single State are broken so that they may be shared with others, a connection is woven in a wider sphere. As a result, the notion of *European belonging* is created, which the Treaties seek to strengthen.[9]

While Union citizenship may indeed strengthen a new – European – sense of belonging, it also alters the existing understanding of national community. While Union citizenship does not replace, but rather adds to, national citizenship, the latter is still likely to change in the process. The right of Union citizens to vote in local and European elections of their host state is a telling example: the idea of a political community cannot remain the same if individuals can take part in elections (and get elected) without a nationality requirement, on the sole ground that they are resident in the state. Another example is access to the welfare system: access to the national welfare system has been an important benefit of national citizenship. Through the Union's legislation on the access of migrant workers to significant parts of the host state's welfare system and the subsequent expansion of

6 *Ibid.*, para. 15.   7 *Ibid.*, para. 15.   8 *Ibid.*, para. 27.   9 *Ibid.*, para. 31 (emphasis in the original).

this right to Union citizens in general, national citizenship is no longer considered the exclusive gate-keeper to the services of the welfare state. This, however, changes the idea of what citizenship is. Many commentators understand this as an advantage: they see the dawn of a cosmopolitan idea of European citizenship that creates solidarity which does not end at the borders of the Member States.[10] Such hopes of what European citizenship could become clearly transcend the classical concept of nationality that originated in the nineteenth century, which equated nationality with absolute allegiance to the state, and with "blood ties" to some imagined native ethnicity.[11]

Critics warn, however, that, if this process is based solely on claims of individual rights, it risks tearing apart existing systems of solidarity, without creating new ones in their place.[12] In this sense, the process of European unification could create a two-class system: whereas the relatively wealthy and well-educated middle and upper classes benefit from increased mobility, the rest of the population might suffer from the disruptions of national solidarity-based welfare systems. Other commentators point to yet another, darker, phenomenon that has accompanied European integration: they argue that, at the same pace as the EU abolishes internal obstacles to migration, it creates new ones at its external borders.[13] This phenomenon is poignantly described as "fortress Europe," and calls one-sided cosmopolitan and post-national hopes about the European Union into question. The political debate about European integration can be touched on only briefly in this book; however, it seems important to note that the integration process – like every political development – creates opportunities as well as perils.

Main Treaty provisions at a glance

Part Two TFEU is titled "Non-Discrimination and Citizenship of the Union," and assembles the following provisions: Article 20 TFEU which establishes Union citizenship; Article 21 TFEU which assigns the right to Union citizens to move and reside freely within the territory of the Member States, and Article 18 TFEU which stipulates a general prohibition of discrimination on the grounds of nationality. Articles 22–25 TFEU establish a number of political and civil rights for European citizens. These include political rights *vis-à-vis* the Union's institutions, independently of the citizen's residence, such as the right to petition the European Parliament; and political rights *vis-à-vis* Member States of which the Union citizen

10 E.g. Dimitry Kochenov, "Double Nationality in the EU: An Argument for Tolerance" (2011) 17 *European Law Journal* 323.
11 Benedict Anderson, *Imagined Communities. Reflections on the Origin and Spread of Nationalism*, London: Verso, 2002.
12 Christopher Newdick, "Citizenship, Free Movement and Healthcare: Cementing Individual Rights by Corroding Social Solidarity" (2006) 43 *Common Market Law Review* 1645.
13 Sonja Buckel and Jens Wissel, "The Transformation of the European Border Regime and the Production of Bare Life" (2010) 4 *International Political Sociology* 33.

Provision	Content	Introduced
Table 4.1 Overview of Union citizenship provisions		
Art. 18 TFEU	General prohibition of discrimination on grounds of nationality	Treaty of Rome (1957)
Art. 19 TFEU	Authorization for legislation combating discrimination on other grounds (sex, race, religion, disability, age, sexual orientation)	Treaty of Amsterdam (1997)
Art. 20 TFEU	Establishment of Union citizenship	Treaty of Maastricht (1993)
Art. 21 TFEU	Right to move and reside freely within the territory of the Member States	Treaty of Maastricht (1993)
Art. 22 TFEU	Right to vote and to stand as a candidate for European and municipal elections	Treaty of Maastricht (1993)
Art. 23 TFEU	Right to diplomatic or consular protection in third countries	Treaty of Maastricht (1993)
Art. 24 TFEU	Citizen's initiative; right to petition European Parliament and to apply to the Ombudsman; right to write to European institutions in any European language	Treaty of Maastricht (1993)
Art. 25 TFEU	Authorization to adopt legislation to strengthen or add to these rights	Treaty of Maastricht (1993)

is not a national, including the right to vote in European and municipal elections and the right to diplomatic or consular protection. Finally, Article 19 TFEU authorizes the European legislators to pass Directives to fight discrimination on grounds, *inter alia*, of sex, race and age. Articles 18, 20 and 21 TFEU are the central provisions for our concerns; however, we will briefly look at Articles 19 and 22–25 TFEU as well. It is on the basis of Articles 18, 20 and 21 TFEU that the Court has developed its main case law on Union citizenship. We will first look at each of these three provisions independently, and then see how the Court applies them to create a general prohibition of discrimination of Union citizens and a prohibition on restricting their rights to move and reside freely in the EU. Table 4.1 provides an overview of Union citizenship provisions.

Article 18 TFEU
Article 18 TFEU provides:

Within the scope of application of the Treaties, and without prejudice to any special provisions contained therein, any discrimination on grounds of nationality shall be prohibited.

It sets out the prohibition of discrimination on grounds of nationality and the obligation to treat nationals and EU citizens equally within the scope of the Treaties. Article 18 TFEU was first included in the Treaty of Rome, and thus precedes the other Union citizenship provisions by almost four decades.[14] However, before the introduction of Union citizenship, the provision played only a minor role in the Court's adjudication. The reason is that Article 18 TFEU has a residual character; it applies only if no other European legal measures (such as the Treaty freedoms) provide for more specific rights of nondiscrimination. Although Article 18 TFEU did not play a prominent role in the Court's earlier decisions, one important line of cases was in fact based on it. Indeed, since the 1980s the Court has held that access to vocational training in other Member States, including access to university education, falls under Article 18 TFEU. This means that Member States must provide equal access to vocational training for nationals and non-nationals alike. Additional fees for non-nationals are prohibited (*Gravier*, 1985).[15] Article 18 TFEU applies only "within the scope of application of the Treaties." In *Gravier*, the Court had held that even though educational organization and policy were not as such within the scope of the Treaty,[16] provisions in secondary law and the Union competence for a "vocational training policy" intended to support the Member States in Article 166 TFEU were sufficient to bring access to vocational training within the scope of the Treaties. This, then, allowed the Court to apply Article 18 TFEU to prohibit differential treatment with regard to university tuition fees.[17]

The role of Article 18 TFEU has changed significantly since the introduction of Union citizenship. In the Court's current case law, the application of Article 18 TFEU is usually triggered when Union citizens (personal scope) exercise their right to move and reside freely in another Member State (material scope) laid down in Article 21 TFEU. When Union citizens move to another Member State, the non-discrimination provision of Article 18 TFEU applies. Conversely, Union citizens who do not exercise this right cannot invoke Article 18 TFEU. Article 18 TFEU applies only to situations that are objectively comparable. If the situation of the citizen and the noncitizen are not objectively comparable, the equal treatment requirement does not apply. The Court routinely holds that "the principle of equal treatment or non-discrimination, which is one of the general principles of Community law, requires that comparable situations must not be treated differently and that different situations must not be treated in the same way unless such treatment is objectively justified."[18]

Article 20 TFEU

Article 20(1) TFEU provides:

Citizenship of the Union is hereby established. Every person holding the nationality of a Member State shall be a citizen of the Union. Citizenship of the Union shall be additional to and not replace national citizenship.

---

14 Art. 7 EEC Treaty.   15 Case 293/83, *Gravier* [1985] ECR 593.   16 *Ibid.*, para. 19.   17 *Ibid.*, para. 25.
18 Case C-300/04, *Eman and Sevinger* [2006] ECR I-8055, para. 57.

The status of a Union citizen is dependent on national citizenship. The criteria to acquire national citizenship remain in the discretion of the Member States. In recent years, however, the Court (and in particular some of the Advocates General) have advanced the notion that Union citizenship may in fact be an autonomous source of rights, which can potentially limit the discretion of Member States. This issue has been particularly present in *Rottmann* (2010). Even though Article 20 TFEU nominally constitutes Union citizenship, the Court has relied on Article 20 TFEU only in relatively few cases. First, in early cases it has employed Article 20 TFEU where Union citizens invoke rights against their home state (e.g. *Morgan*, 2007). This practice has subsequently been discontinued. In its more recent case law, the Court usually employs Article 21 TFEU for claims of mobile citizens against their home state. Second, and more importantly, the Court employs Article 20 TFEU in cases where the very right of individuals to exercise rights under the Union citizenship provisions in the future seems to be at risk (*Rottmann*, 2010; *Ruiz Zambrano*, 2011). We will discuss this issue and the relevant decisions further below.

Article 21 TFEU

Article 21(1) TFEU provides:

Every citizen of the Union shall have the right to move and reside freely within the territory of the Member States, subject to the limitations and conditions laid down in the Treaties and by the measures adopted to give them effect.

Under the Treaty of Rome, the right to move to and reside freely in another Member State was a corollary of the economic freedoms. The movement and residence rights were subsequently expanded by secondary law to include economically inactive persons such as students or retired persons. Article 21 TFEU finally created an explicit foundation for this development in primary law.

The rights granted by Article 21 TFEU are subject to limitations in primary and secondary law, as the provision explicitly states.[19] The Citizenship Directive 2004/38 provides that movement and residence rights may be restricted on grounds of public policy, security and health. Additionally, the rights granted by Article 21 TFEU may be subject to limitations in the public interest. We will discuss these limitations below. As we have seen, the Court often uses Article 21 TFEU in conjunction with Article 18 TFEU: if an individual moves to or resides in another Member State, it triggers the application of Article 18 TFEU. The Court, however, has ruled that Article 21 TFEU also holds an independent prohibition of discrimination and restrictions. This is the case if states do not discriminate on grounds of nationality, but on grounds of mobility (making Article 18 TFEU inapplicable). The right to move and reside in another Member State granted by the other Treaty freedoms is *lex specialis* to Article 21 TFEU (just like the prohibition of discrimination under the Treaty freedoms is *lex*

---

19 See to that effect Case C-356/98, *Kaba* [2000] ECR I-2623, para. 30; Case C-33/07, *Jipa* [2008] ECR I-5157, para. 21.

specialis to Article 18 TFEU, as we have already seen). This means that workers, self-employed persons and service providers rely on the mobility rights granted by Articles 45, 49 and 56 TFEU, respectively, and not on those granted by Article 21 TFEU.

Direct effect of Articles 18, 20 and 21 TFEU

Articles 18, 20 and 21 TFEU have direct effect.[20] This means that they apply directly in national law. National rules that conflict with Articles 18, 20 and 21 TFEU must not be applied by national authorities, and individuals can invoke these provisions in national courts. The Court has first found Article 21 TFEU to have direct effect in the decision *Baumbast* (2002).

Case C-413/99, Baumbast (2002)

In 1990, Mr. Baumbast and his family, all German citizens, were granted residence permits in the United Kingdom for five years. Mr. Baumbast was employed, then self-employed, in the United Kingdom, and later worked for a German company in China and Lesotho. He and his family enjoyed comprehensive health coverage in Germany. In 1996, the United Kingdom refused to renew their residence permits, claiming that Mr. Baumbast was no longer a worker within the meaning of Article 45 TFEU, nor did he have a general right of residence.

Does an EU citizen who no longer enjoys a right of residence as a migrant worker in the host Member State enjoy a right of residence by direct application of Article 21 TFEU?

Yes.

A citizen of the European Union enjoys a right of residence by direct application of Article 21 TFEU in the host Member State. The exercise of that right is subject to the limitations and conditions referred to in that provision. The host Member State may require that Union citizens are fully insured and have sufficient resources so that they do not become an unreasonable burden on the public finances of the host Member State. Both conditions were met by Mr. Baumbast.

SCOPE

The citizenship provisions apply to Union citizens (personal scope) who move to another Member State or are involved in a cross-border situation (material scope) and who are economically inactive (in distinction to the other Treaty freedoms).

---

20 For the direct effect of Art. 18 TFEU, see e.g. *Gravier* (1985); for the direct effect of Art. 20 TFEU, see e.g. *Ruiz Zambrano* (2011).

Personal scope (beneficiaries)

Who is a Union citizen?

According to Article 20(1) TFEU, all citizens of the Member States are *ipso iure* Union citizens. There is no autonomous way of gaining Union citizenship. The stipulation that Union citizenship "does not replace national citizenship" was introduced by the Treaty of Amsterdam. It aimed at reducing fears that Union citizenship would erode national citizenship. The Court has regularly held that it is for each Member State, having due regard to Union law, to lay down the conditions for the acquisition and loss of nationality (*Micheletti*, 1992).[21] The rules on the acquisition and loss of nationality lie exclusively within the competence of the Member States.[22] This view conforms to traditional international law, which holds that it is exclusively up to the state to lay down the rules concerning nationality.[23] In the decision of *Rottmann* (2010), Advocate General Poiares Maduro questioned the extent of the discretion available to the Member States to determine who their nationals are. National and European citizenship, he argued, "are two concepts which are both inextricably linked and independent. Union citizenship assumes nationality of a Member State but it is also a legal and political concept independent of that of nationality."[24] And:

Access to European citizenship is gained through nationality of a Member State, which is regulated by national law, but, like any form of citizenship, it forms the basis of a new political area from which rights and duties emerge, which are laid down by Community law and do not depend on the State. This, in turn, legitimizes the autonomy and authority of the Community legal order. That is why, although it is true that nationality of a Member State is a precondition for access to Union citizenship, it is equally true that the body of rights and obligations associated with the latter cannot be limited in an unjustified manner by the former. In other words, it is not that the acquisition and loss of nationality (and, consequently, of Union citizenship) are in themselves governed by Community law, but the conditions for the acquisition and loss of nationality must be compatible with the Community rules and respect the rights of the European citizen.[25]

Consequently, the rules on the acquisition and loss of citizenship must be regulated with due regard to Union law. According to Advocate General Poiares Maduro, "state rules on nationality cannot restrict the enjoyment and exercise of the rights and freedoms constituting the status of Union citizenship without justification."[26] Thus, even though the conditions to access national citizenship lie within the Member States' competence, they are under an obligation to exercise these competences in accordance with Union law.

21 Case C-369/90, *Micheletti* [1992] ECR I-4239, para. 10.
22 Convention on the Reduction of Statelessness, New York, August 30, 1961; European Convention on Nationality, Strasbourg, November 6, 1997; International Court of Justice, *Nottebohm*, Judgment of April 6, 1955, ICJ Reports 1955, p. 4.
23 Convention on Certain Questions Relating to the Conflict of Nationality Laws, The Hague, April 12, 1930, Arts. 1 and 2.
24 Case C-135/08, *Rottmann* [2010] ECR I-01449, Opinion of Advocate General Poiares Maduro, para. 23.
25 *Ibid.*, para. 23.   26 *Ibid.*, para. 32.

Case C-135/08, Rottmann (2010)

Austrian citizen Janko Rottmann moved to Germany to evade a trial for fraud in Austria. He applied for naturalization in Germany, failing to disclose the criminal proceedings in Austria. He was subsequently naturalized in Germany and therefore lost his Austrian citizenship, in accordance with Austrian law. When the German authorities finally became aware of the trial, they initiated proceedings to withdraw the naturalization, as it had been obtained through deception. This would leave Mr. Rottmann stateless, so that he would, consequently, lose his status as a Union citizen.

Is it contrary to EU law to withdraw from a citizen the nationality acquired by naturalization and obtained by deception inasmuch as that withdrawal deprives the person of his status as a Union citizen, and renders him stateless?

No.

The fact that national citizenship falls within the competence of the Member States does not alter the fact that the national authorities must have due regard to the requirements of EU law.[27] As a decision to withdraw the naturalization would cause Mr. Rottmann to lose his status as a Union citizen, the decision falls within the ambit of EU law.[28] This does not compromise the competences of the Member States to lay down the conditions for the acquisition and loss of nationality, "but rather enshrines the principle that, in respect of citizens of the Union, the exercise of that power, in so far as it affects the rights conferred and protected by the legal order of the Union, as is in particular the case of a decision withdrawing naturalization such as that at issue in the main proceedings, is amenable to judicial review carried out in the light of European Union law."[29] The national court has to ascertain whether the decision to withdraw citizenship is proportionate with regard to the consequences for the person in light of EU law. Issues to be taken into account when evaluating the proportionality are: the consequences for the person and his or her family; the gravity of the offence; the lapse of time between the naturalization decision and the decision to withdraw it; and whether it is possible for that person to recover his original nationality.[30]

The Union citizenship provisions generally do not apply to legal persons. However, the Treaties grant a number of political and civil rights that can be invoked by legal persons as well, including the right to petition the European Parliament (Article 227 TFEU), to lodge complaints with the European Ombudsman (Article 228 TFEU) and to access documents (Article 15 TFEU). Moreover, a number of fundamental rights laid down in the Charter of Fundamental Rights can be invoked by natural and legal persons alike.[31]

---

27 *Rottmann*, para. 40.   28 *Rottmann*, para. 42.   29 *Rottmann*, para. 48.   30 *Rottmann*, paras. 55–56.
31 See e.g. Case C-279/09, *DEB* [2010] ECR I-13849.

Economically inactive persons

We have already seen that the Treaty freedoms are *lex specialis* to the citizenship provisions. This means that the citizenship provisions are applicable only to individuals who are neither employed nor self-employed, that is, they are economically inactive. The citizenship provisions are, in Advocate General Colomer's words, "provisions of last resort."[32] Generally speaking, the Court applies a similar understanding to all provisions relating to the free movement of (natural) persons, thereby moving toward a convergence of these provisions. This can be seen in cases like *Commission* v. *Germany – Tax Deductibility of School Fees* (2007), where the Court held that its ruling applies to Union citizens, employed and self-employed alike.[33] However, the differentiation remains relevant for a number of fields, most notably in the area of social advantages. While the secondary law and the Court's case law provide for virtually unlimited equal treatment of employed and self-employed individuals, it remains much more restrained with regard to the right of economically inactive individuals to equal access to social advantages.

Material scope

Cross-border element

The Court has repeatedly ruled that the Union citizenship provisions do not apply to situations that are purely internal to a Member State, and which comprise no factor linking them with any of the situations governed by European Union law. Cross-border mobility of EU citizens is therefore a precondition for the application of the citizenship provisions.[34]

The Court essentially employs the Union citizenship provisions in three types of situation:

- if a Union citizen (personal scope) moves to another Member State (Article 21 TFEU – material scope) and is subject to unequal treatment (Article 18 TFEU) or is obstructed in the exercise of his or her rights in the host state (*Bressol*, 2010);[35]
- if the home state of a Union citizen treats a cross-border situation (e.g. a student going abroad to study) worse than a comparable domestic situation (*Morgan*, 2007);[36]
- national measures are prohibited if they force the Union citizen to leave the Union, thereby "depriving citizens of the Union of the genuine enjoyment of the substance of the rights conferred by virtue of their status as citizens of the Union"[37] (*Ruiz Zambrano*, 2011; *Chen*, 2004).

---

32 *Petersen*, Opinion of Advocate General Colomer, para. 34.
33 Case C-318/05, *Commission* v. *Germany – Tax Deductibility of School Fees* [2007] ECR I-6957.
34 Case C-148/02, *Garcia Avello* [2003] ECR I-11613, para. 24.   35 Case C-73/08, *Bressol* [2010] ECR I-2735.
36 Joined Cases C-11/06 and C-12/06, *Morgan* [2007] ECR I-9161.
37 Case C-34/09, *Ruiz Zambrano* [2011] ECR I-1177, para. 42.

Situations that are purely internal to a Member State, on the other hand, do not fall within the Union citizenship provisions, as the Court has held for example in *McCarthy* (2011).

Case C-434/09, McCarthy (2011)

Shirley McCarthy, a British national living in the United Kingdom, was married to a Jamaican national who lacked leave to remain in the United Kingdom. She successfully applied for an Irish passport, and then for a residence permit in the United Kingdom as a Union citizen with her spouse, believing that her husband should now have a right of residence. The UK authority, however, denied the application.

Are the Union citizenship provisions applicable to the situation of a Union citizen who has never exercised her right of free movement, who has always resided in a Member State of which she is a national and who is also a national of another Member State?

No.

The residence rights granted under the Citizenship Directive and the Treaty provisions are conditional upon the exercise of the right of free movement. However,

no element of the situation of Mrs. McCarthy, as described by the national court, indicates that the national measure at issue in the main proceedings has the effect of depriving her of the genuine enjoyment of the substance of the rights associated with her status as a Union citizen, or of impeding the exercise of her right to move and reside freely within the territory of the Member States, in accordance with Article 21 TFEU. Indeed, the failure by the authorities of the United Kingdom to take into account the Irish nationality of Mrs. McCarthy for the purposes of granting her a right of residence in the United Kingdom in no way affects her in her right to move and reside freely within the territory of the Member States, or any other right conferred on her by virtue of her status as a Union citizen.[38]

The following cases are examples where the Court has held that the situation is not purely internal to a Member State, so that the Union citizenship provisions apply:

- In *Garcia Avello* (2003), children with dual Belgian and Spanish nationality born in Belgium to a Belgian mother (Ms. Weber) and a Spanish father (Mr. Garcia Avello) were denied the right to receive a name composed according to the Spanish rules ("Garcia Weber") by the Belgian authorities. This would have meant that the children had different names according to Spanish and to Belgian law. The situation fell within the material scope of the citizenship provisions because the children were "nationals of one Member State lawfully resident in the territory of another Member State."[39] The Court decided that this discrepancy in names would be "liable to cause serious inconvenience . . . at both professional and private levels,"[40] thereby violating Articles 18 and 20 TFEU.

---

38 Case C-434/09, *McCarthy* [2011] ECR I-3375, para. 49.   39 *Garcia Avello*, para. 27.   40 *Ibid.*, para. 36.

- In *Zhu and Chen* (2004), Catherine Chen was born to Chinese parents in Belfast (thereby acquiring Irish citizenship by Irish law, even though Belfast is situated in Northern Ireland, which is part of the United Kingdom), and then moved with her mother to Wales. The UK authorities denied long-term residence to the child and the mother, arguing that they had not exercised their mobility right because they had stayed in the United Kingdom, so that the citizenship provisions were not applicable.[41] The Court argued, however, that the situation falls under the material scope as it concerns a national of a Member State residing in another Member State. The Court subsequently held that both the child and the mother as her primary carer have a right to long-term residence. Catherine must be "entitled to be accompanied by the person who is his or her primary carer and accordingly that the carer must be in a position to reside with the child in the host Member State for the duration of such residence."[42] Otherwise, "the host Member State would deprive the child's right of residence of any useful effect."

- In *Schempp* (2005), Mr. Schempp, a German citizen residing in Munich, was prohibited by German tax law from deducting the maintenance he paid to his former wife residing in Austria, as such payments are not taxable in Austria. Payments to a former spouse residing in Germany, on the other hand, would have been deductible, as they are taxable in Germany.[43] As the former spouse had exercised her mobility right under Article 21 TFEU, the situation of Mr. Schempp cannot be purely internal, so that the Union citizenship provisions apply. The Court then decided, however, that the unfavorable tax situation was no consequence of unjustified unequal treatment of domestic and cross-border situations, and found no breach of Articles 18 and 21 TFEU.

The reasoning of the Court in these cases involving situations deemed not purely internal to a Member State can be analytically summarized as shown in Table 4.2.

Table 4.2 Schematic overview of three cases that were not considered to be "purely internal" to a Member State by the Court

It is no purely internal situation in . . .	Despite the fact that . . .	Because . . .
. . . Garcia Avello	. . . the children were born in Belgium, had Belgian nationality and had always resided in Belgium.	. . . the children also had Spanish citizenship and therefore were nationals of one Member State lawfully residing in another Member State.
. . . Schempp	. . . Mr. Schempp had not made use of his right to freedom of movement.	. . . the former spouse had moved to another Member State so that Mr. Schempp's tax situation changed.
. . . Rottmann	. . . it was about Germany revoking the German nationality of a German citizen.	. . . Mr. Rottmann had come into this situation only because he had made use of his freedom of movement from Austria to Germany.[a]

a Advocate General Poiares Maduro in *Rottmann* (2010), para. 11.

---

41 Case C-200/02, *Zhu and Chen* [2004] ECR I-9925, para. 18.   42 *Ibid.*, para. 45.
43 Case C-403/03, *Schempp* [2005] ECR I-6421.

The argument first established in *Zhu and Chen* (2004) has been further developed in the decision in *Ruiz Zambrano* (2011), where the Court argued that the residence right of the caregiving father can be based on Article 20 TFEU. The case had the potential to shake up the "purely internal" rule, as it dealt with a situation without any cross-border links. The Court argued that it was nevertheless competent to rule because "Article 20 TFEU precludes national measures which have the effect of depriving citizens of the Union of the genuine enjoyment of the substance of the rights conferred by virtue of their status as citizens of the Union."[44] This seemed to indicate that, in situations where a national measure undermines the very substance of Union citizenship, or the factual possibility to make effective use of these rights, these situations cannot be seen as purely internal to a Member State, even though the concerned individual has not made use of its right to freedom of movement.[45]

Case C-34/09, Ruiz Zambrano (2011)

Gerardo Ruiz Zambrano and his wife, both Colombian nationals, applied for asylum in Belgium. Although the Belgian authorities rejected their application in 2000, they benefited from the *non-refoulement* clause, however, which prohibited the authorities to send them back to Colombia because of the ongoing civil war. In 2004 and 2005, their children, Diego and Jessica, were born and received Belgian nationality as they would otherwise have been stateless because, according to Colombian law, children born outside its territory receive Colombian citizenship only if their parents take specific legal steps, which they did not take. The parents then applied again for residence in Belgium as the parents of a Belgian national. The application was rejected, however, as the authorities accused the parents of deliberately refraining from registering their children for Colombian nationality. The children have never left Belgium.

Do the citizenship provisions confer a right of residence and a right to take up work without having to obtain a permit on the parents of minor children, if the former are third-country nationals, and the latter are EU citizens?

Yes.

Article 20 TFEU precludes national measures which have the effect of depriving citizens of the Union of the genuine enjoyment of the substance of the rights conferred by virtue of their status as citizens of the Union.[46] The Court held:

It must be assumed that such a refusal would lead to a situation where those children, citizens of the Union, would have to leave the territory of the Union in order to accompany

---

44 *Ruiz Zambrano*, para. 42.   45 E.g. *Schempp*, para. 22.   46 *Ruiz Zambrano*, para. 42.

their parents. Similarly, if a work permit were not granted to such a person, he would risk not having sufficient resources to provide for himself and his family, which would also result in the children, citizens of the Union, having to leave the territory of the Union. In those circumstances, those citizens of the Union would, in fact, be unable to exercise the substance of the rights conferred on them by virtue of their status as citizens of the Union.[47]

Following *Ruiz Zambrano*, scholarly speculation was rife that the decision had effectively ended the "purely internal" rule.[48] The Court, however, showed in the subsequent decisions of *McCarthy* (2011) (discussed above) and *Dereci* (2011) that this was not the intention,[49] and that the decision in *Ruiz Zambrano* has to be interpreted narrowly. Indeed, in *Dereci* (2011), the Court ruled that the "criterion relating to the denial of the genuine enjoyment of the substance of the rights conferred by virtue of European Union citizen status refers to situations in which the Union citizen has, in fact, to leave not only the territory of the Member State of which he is a national but also the territory of the Union as a whole."[50]

Furthermore, in *Ymeraga* (2013) the Court has emphasized that the Charter of Fundamental Rights makes no difference in this regard.[51] The case concerned a Luxembourg citizen of Kosovan descent who was joined in Luxembourg by members of his family, who were third-country nationals. The Court reiterated that Directive 2004/38 as well as the Union citizenship provisions of the Treaty confer rights to family members of Union citizens only if the latter reside in a Member State other than that of which they are nationals. The Court held that "[a]ny rights conferred on third-country nationals by the Treaty provisions on Union citizenship are not autonomous rights of those nationals but rights derived from the exercise of freedom of movement by a Union citizen."[52] The referring court asked whether the Charter of Fundamental Rights, in particular Articles 20 (equality), 21 (nondiscrimination), 24 (rights of the child) and 33 (family life), confer a right of family reunification. The Court held that according to its Article 51(1), the Charter applies to Member States only when they are implementing Union law. As Mr. Ymeraga has not exercised his right of movement, his situation and that of his family are not governed by EU law, and the Charter remains inapplicable. The Court emphasized, however, that "[s]uch a finding does not prejudge the question whether, on the basis of an examination in the light of the provisions of the European Convention for the Protection of Human Rights and Fundamental Freedoms, to which all Member States are parties, to the third-country nationals in the main proceedings may not be refused a right of residence."[53]

---

47 *Ibid.*, para. 44.
48 See e.g. Dimitry Kochenov, "Double Nationality in the EU: An Argument for Tolerance" (2011) 17 *European Law Journal* 323.
49 Case C-256/11, *Dereci* [2011] ECR I-11315.   50 *Ibid.*, para. 66.
51 Case C-87/12, *Ymeraga* [2013] ECR I-00000. See also Case C-40/11, *Yoshikazu Iida* v. *Stadt Ulm* [2012] ECR I-00000.
52 *Ymeraga*, para. 35.   53 *Ibid.*, para. 44.

Mobility in Europe

How mobile are Europeans?

Europeans have the right to move to another country: but do they actually exercise that right?[54] "Eurobarometer" surveys show that inter-state mobility of EU citizens is very low: as of 2008, 2.3 percent of EU citizens reside in another Member State;[55] if citizens are included who have resided in the past in another Member State, the number is slightly higher, at 4 percent (compared to 3 percent who have moved at some point outside the Union). The number of European citizens who have moved to another region within their home country is much higher, amounting to 18 percent. In total, this means that about 22 percent of EU citizens have at some point lived in a region other than the one in which they were born. In comparison, about 32 percent of US citizens live outside the US state in which they were born. EU and the US mobility numbers should not, however, be compared uncritically. As the authors of the study "Mobility in Europe" argue: "[M]igration between states in the US takes place within the same linguistic, political and cultural context, unlike long-distance migration in Europe."[56]

Who is mobile, and who isn't?

There are huge differences in mobility among Europe's citizens. One of the most important factors is the educational level: well-educated individuals are much more likely to move to another region (34 percent) than individuals with average or low educational levels (20 percent and 17 percent, respectively). The study "Mobility in Europe" argues that "this difference in mobility may be because workers with a lower level of education face significantly higher employment risks: as a result, they are more dependent upon their social networks (in particular their extended families) if they should become unemployed."[57] Mobility is highest in the Nordic countries, and is lowest in the southern and the new Member States. The countries with the highest regional and inter-state mobility are Sweden, Denmark and Finland; the countries with the lowest mobility are Slovakia, Poland and Lithuania.

Mobility of Union citizens and of third-country nationals

The number of foreign-born individuals (from both EU and non-EU countries) of active working age has risen in the EU-15 from 11 percent in 1995 to 13 percent in 2006.[58] The Member States with the highest number of foreign-born individuals in relation to the working population is Luxembourg (40 percent), Austria and Sweden (both 15 percent). Greece, Italy and Portugal, on the other hand, rank at about 8 percent.

---

54 European Foundation for the Improvement of Living and Working Conditions (Eurofound), "Mobility in Europe – The Way Forward," European Foundation for the Improvement of Living and Working Conditions, 2007. See also Communication from the Commission to the Council, the European Parliament, the European Economic and Social Committee and the Committee of the Regions, Reaffirming the Free Movement of Workers: Rights and Major Developments, July 13, 2010 COM(2010) 373 final.
55 Commission, Reaffirming the Free Movement of Workers, p. 2.   56 Eurofound, "Mobility in Europe," p. 6.
57 *Ibid.*, 7.
58 Holger Bonin *et al.*, "Geographic Mobility in the European Union: Optimizing its Economic and Social Benefits," IZA Research Report No. 19, 2008, www.iza.org/en/webcontent/publications/reports/report_pdfs/iza_report_19.pdf (accessed February 20, 2014), p. 17.

When does a situation come "within the scope of application of the Treaties" (Article 18 TFEU)?

Article 18(1) TFEU prohibits discrimination on grounds of nationality "within the scope of application of the Treaties." Member States have repeatedly argued that the provision means that the Union must have competence in the regulatory field in question for the equal treatment provision to apply. The Dutch government argued for example in *Tas-Hagen* (2006) that a benefit intended to compensate civilian war victims that featured an indirectly discriminatory residence requirement cannot be challenged under the Union citizenship provisions because the EU does not have legislative competence in this area.[59] It was argued:

> [Article 21 TFEU] can be relied upon only if, over and above the mere exercise of the right to freedom of movement, the facts of the main proceedings relate to a matter covered by Community law, with the result that Community law is applicable *ratione materiae* to that case. Under this view, Mrs. Tas-Hagen and Mr. Tas cannot plead any infringement of [Article 21 TFEU] in this case because benefits for civilian war victims do not come within the scope of Community law.[60]

The Court, however, rejected this view, arguing that the Union citizenship provisions are applicable because the case falls both into their personal scope (as Ms. Tas-Hagen and Mr. Tas are Union citizens) and the material scope (as they have moved from the Netherlands to Spain). The Court held that even though benefits intended to compensate civil war victims fall within the competence of the Member States, they must nonetheless comply with the obligations deriving from Union law, in particular the equal treatment provision:

> Member States must exercise that competence in accordance with Community law, in particular with the Treaty provisions giving every citizen of the Union the right to move and reside freely within the territory of the Member States.[61]

Essentially, this simply means that Member States cannot discriminate on grounds of nationality or the exercise of mobility rights even in those areas where they retain legislative competence unless such differential treatment is objectively justified.

ADDRESSEES

Addressees of the Union citizenship provisions are the Member States. While the Union citizenship provisions were initially understood to grant rights to mobile individuals primarily against the host state, it is now clear that they can equally be invoked by Union citizens against their home states.[62] This is the case when the home state treats a cross-border situation less favorably than a comparable domestic situation. In *Morgan* (2007), Germany awarded grants for studying abroad on

---

59 Case C-192/05, *Tas-Hagen* [2006] ECR I-10451, para. 20.   60 *Ibid.*, para. 20.   61 *Ibid.*, para. 22.
62 *Petersen*, Opinion of Advocate General Colomer, para. 22.

condition that the student had already studied for at least one year in Germany, so that the study abroad constituted a continuation of the studies in Germany. The Court decided that this was contrary to Articles 20 and 21 TFEU, because the rule "is liable to discourage them from moving subsequently to another Member State in order to pursue their studies."[63] While the Treaty freedoms relating to the free movement of persons (workers, establishment and services) can be invoked not only against states, but in certain situations also against non-state actors that obstruct their freedoms, the Court has not transposed the principle to Union citizenship. This means that currently Union citizenship does not have horizontal direct effect.

APPLYING ARTICLES 18, 20 AND 21 TFEU: THE PROHIBITION OF DISCRIMINATION AND OF RESTRICTIONS

We have already looked at three of the central provisions of the TFEU's Part Two, namely, Articles 18, 20 and 21. How exactly these provisions should be applied, however, is not self-evident from their wording. In this section, we will try to show that the Court applies these provisions (usually in some combination, most often Article 21 in conjunction with Article 18) so that they create: (1) a general prohibition of discrimination of mobile Union citizens; and (2) a prohibition of restrictions on their mobility. Whereas the first group deals with national measures that differentiate overtly or covertly on the ground of nationality or of the fact that an individual has exercised his or her mobility rights, the second group deals with provisions that do not differentiate on these grounds, but nonetheless create obstacles to the mobility of Union citizens. We differentiate between these two groups for analytical purposes, even though the Court does not necessarily employ these categories.

Prohibition of discrimination

The Court generally distinguishes between direct and indirect discrimination. Direct discrimination occurs when a national measure explicitly differentiates on the basis of nationality (e.g. in *Bidar* (2005), where British students can receive maintenance grants, but non-British students cannot[64]). A measure is indirectly discriminatory if it is formally neutral, but nonetheless creates adverse effects primarily for non-nationals.[65] Residence requirements are often indirectly discriminatory: while nationals and non-nationals alike can be residents of a Member State, there are in fact usually many more nationals than non-nationals who fulfill this criterion (e.g. *Bressol*, 2010).

---

63 *Morgan*, para. 31.   64 Case C-209/03, *Bidar* [2005] ECR I-2119.   65 *Ibid.*, para. 51.

The Court's case law exhibits two main case groups:

- First, if Union citizens (personal scope) actually move to and reside in another Member State, they exercise their right under Article 21 TFEU (material scope). The Court generally holds that in such situation Union citizens have a right of equal treatment in the host state. This includes equal access to social benefits subject to certain conditions (*Grzelczyk*, 2001; *Bidar*, 2005), equal treatment with regard to tax rules (*Rüffler*, 2009) and equal access to universities (*Gravier*, 1985). From a doctrinal perspective, the Court usually holds that the exercise of the right under Article 21 TFEU triggers the equal treatment provision of Article 18 TFEU, so that the provisions are employed conjointly. This group of cases comprises by far the greatest number of the Court's decisions.
- Second, the Court rules that Member States should not put their own citizens at a disadvantage because their situation includes a cross-border element. The Court has argued in *Turpeinen* (2006), for example, that the right to move and reside freely in the Member States "could not be fully effective if a national of a Member State could be deterred from availing himself of them by obstacles placed in the way of his stay in the host Member State by legislation in his State of origin penalising the fact that he has used them."[66] In *D'Hoop* (2002), the Court decided that a Member State could not deny its own national a social allowance for school graduates solely because she had graduated in another Member State.[67] In more general terms, it could be argued that situations that exhibit a cross-border element should not be treated less favorably than comparable, purely internal situations. In this case group, the Court solely applies Article 21 TFEU (though in a few earlier cases it had applied Articles 20 and 21 TFEU conjointly), arguing that it contains a prohibition of discrimination of situations that embody a cross-border element.

In *D'Hoop* (2002), the Court described the right of returning citizens against their home state as follows:

> The situations falling within the scope of Community law include those involving the exercise of the fundamental freedoms guaranteed by the Treaty, in particular those involving the freedom to move and reside within the territory of the Member States, as conferred by [Article 21 TFEU]. In that a citizen of the Union must be granted in all Member States the same treatment in law as that accorded to the nationals of those Member States who find themselves in the same situation, it would be incompatible with the right of freedom of movement were a citizen, in the Member State of which he is a national, to receive treatment less favourable than he would enjoy if he had not availed himself of the opportunities offered by the Treaty in relation to freedom of movement.[68]

The two case groups differ for two reasons: (1) they differ with regard to the addressee, because the first is about rights of mobile citizens against the host state, whereas the second is about rights of mobile citizens against their home

---

66 Case C-520/04, *Turpeinen* [2006] ECR I-10685, para. 21.
67 Case C-224/98, *D'Hoop* [2002] ECR I-6191, para. 40.   68 *Ibid.*, paras. 29–31.

state; (2) they also differ with regard to the comparator: in the first case, the host state treats citizens differently on the grounds of their nationality; whereas in the second group the state differentiates between domestic and cross-border situations. While the first case group could be described as a prohibition of discrimination on the grounds of nationality, the second group could be described as a prohibition of discrimination on the ground of cross-border movement.

Prohibition of restrictions

The textual core of the Union citizenship provisions contains the prohibition of discrimination on the ground of nationality. We have already seen, however, that the right to move and reside freely in the Member States is also infringed by national measures that do not discriminate on the ground of nationality, but nonetheless put situations with a non-domestic connecting factor at a disadvantage (e.g. *D'Hoop*, 2002: allowance for graduates of domestic, but not of foreign schools; *Schwarz and Gootjes-Schwarz*: tax break for tuition paid for domestic, but not for foreign schools; *Tas-Hagen*: a pension is paid only to nationals who reside in the Member State). We have, therefore, argued that there are two types of discriminatory situations: one in which national measures differentiate on the grounds of nationality, and the other on the grounds of residence or location. Most of the Court's Union citizenship cases fall into one of these two groups. A few decisions, however, cannot be easily explained on these grounds. In these cases, the Court rejects national measures that put mobile citizens at a disadvantage even without a discriminatory reference to either nationality or residence/location as happened for example in the *Stewart* case.

Case C-503/09, Stewart (2011)

Lucy Stewart is a British citizen who has Down's syndrome. In 2000, she moved to Spain with her parents, both of whom were retirees. She received a disability living allowance from the United Kingdom in Spain, according to the Regulation on the coordination of social security schemes.[69] The family also applied for "short-term incapacity benefit" for Lucy, a benefit awarded for periods of incapacity for work. The benefit was conditional, however, on the requirement of the recipient to be ordinarily resident in the United Kingdom, and to having been present in the United Kingdom for at least twenty-six of the past fifty-two weeks preceding the date of the claim.

Does the ordinary residence and the requirement to have been resident for a certain length of time conflict with EU law?

Yes.

---

69 Ex-Regulation 1408/71, now Regulation 883/2004.

The short-term incapacity benefit is an invalidity benefit within the meaning of the Regulation if the claimant has a permanent or long-term disability.[70] The regulation precludes an ordinary residence requirement.[71] While the requirement to have been resident for a certain length of time does not constitute a residence clause prohibited by the Regulation, it still constitutes an infringement of Article 21 TFEU:

Legislation, such as that at issue in the main proceedings, which makes acquisition of the right to short-term incapacity benefit in youth subject to a condition of past presence is likely, by its very nature, to deter claimants such as the appellant from exercising their right to freedom of movement and residence by leaving the Member State of which they are nationals to take up residence in another Member State. Indeed, while claimants who have not made use of the opportunities offered by the Treaty in relation to freedom of movement and residence can easily satisfy the abovementioned condition, that is not the case for claimants who have taken advantage of them.[72]

While the aim to ensure a continuous effective link between that Member State and the recipient of a noncontributory benefit is justifiable in principle, it could be established with a less restrictive means in practice, for example by establishing whether the claimant has passed a significant part of her life in the United Kingdom.

Cases like *Stewart* differ (though sometimes only in degrees) from the above-mentioned discriminatory cases. While the conditions laid down in national law can be fulfilled by mobile citizens as well, they nonetheless make mobility more difficult. The Court opposes national measures that constitute obstacles to the right to move and reside freely in the Member States. Other examples include *Pusa* (2004). Here, a Finnish retiree lived in Spain and received a pension from Finland. According to the double-taxation agreement between Finland and Spain, his income was subject to income tax in Spain. A Finnish court authorized an attachment to Mr. Pusa's pension for the purpose of recovering a debt incurred by Mr. Pusa. The calculation of the amount to be withheld was based on his gross pension after all compulsory deductions. As income tax was not deducted in Finland, Mr. Pusa was considered to have a higher income, so that the amount to be withheld was higher than if his income had been taxable in Finland. According to the Court, Mr. Pusa was put at a disadvantage because the Finnish measure does not take the tax paid in Spain into account, resulting in Mr. Pusa having less disposable income than if he had resided in Finland.[73] In *Rüffler* (2009), a German retiree resided in Poland. He received an invalidity pension and an occupational pension from Germany with compulsory health insurance contributions being deducted. Under Regulation 1408/71 (now Regulation 883/2004), he had a right to healthcare benefits provided in Poland at the expense of the German health insurance.

70 Case C-503/09, *Stewart* [2011] ECR I-6497, para. 54.   71 *Ibid.*, para. 70.   72 *Ibid.*, para. 85.
73 Case C-224/02, *Pusa* [2004] ECR I-5763, paras. 29–32.

According to the double-taxation agreement between Poland and Germany, his invalidity pension was taxable in Germany, and his occupational pension was taxable in Poland. He applied to have his German health contributions deducted from his Polish income tax. The Polish authority refused this, as only contributions paid pursuant to the Polish law on publicly financed healthcare can be deducted. The Court ruled that a national tax system that allows deductions only for contributions paid in Poland violated Article 21 TFEU.

In its decisions on the other Treaty freedoms, the Court routinely holds that not only discriminatory, but also nondiscriminatory, national measures can violate Union law if they restrict the exercise of the Treaty freedoms. It has been suggested by a number of commentators that the Court has moved in this direction also in the field of Union citizenship, pointing in particular at the Court's language that resembles that used with regard to the prohibition of restrictions in the other Treaty freedom cases.[74] In *Morgan* (2007), for example, the Court held that a measure breaches Article 21 TFEU because it "is liable to discourage [students] from moving subsequently to another Member State in order to pursue their studies."[75] Some of the Advocates General in particular have pushed toward this broad understanding of Article 21 TFEU. They interpret the provision as including both a prohibition of discrimination and of nondiscriminatory barriers to mobility. Advocate General Jacobs argued in *Pusa*: "The conclusion ... must thus be that, subject to the limits set out in [Article 21 TFEU] itself, no unjustified burden may be imposed on any citizen of the European Union seeking to exercise the right to freedom of movement or residence. Provided that such a burden can be shown, it is immaterial whether the burden affects nationals of other Member States more significantly than those of the State imposing it."[76] And Advocate General Geelhoed simply held in *De Cuyper* that "(d)iscrimination need not be established for [Article 21 TFEU] to apply."[77]

JUSTIFICATIONS

National measures that differentiate on the ground of nationality or have the effect of restricting mobility are not always illegal. They can be justified under the following conditions:

- If a national and a non-national are in objectively different situations, the principle of nondiscrimination may require Member States to treat non-nationals differently from nationals (*Garcia Avello*, 2003).[78] The principle holds that comparable

---

74 See e.g. Yuri Borgmann-Prebil, "The Rule of Reason in European Citizenship" (2008) 14 *European Law Journal* 328; more cautious is Eleanor Spaventa, "Seeing the Wood Despite the Trees? On the Scope of Union Citizenship and Its Constitutional Effects" (2008) 45 *Common Market Law Review* 13.

75 *Morgan*, para. 31.   76 *Pusa*, Opinion of Advocate General Jacobs, para. 22.

77 Case C-406/04, *De Cuyper* [2006] ECR I-6947, Opinion of Advocate General Geelhoed, para. 104.

78 *Garcia Avello*, para. 34.

situations must not be treated differently and that different situations must not be treated in the same way (*Huber*, 2008).[79] The Court has ruled that, with regard to issues of taxation, residents and nonresidents are often in different situations, which justifies unequal treatment (*Schumacker*, 1995).

- If the limitation is stipulated by secondary law, Member States can restrict the right to move and reside freely. The Citizenship Directive provides, for example, that states can restrict residence of more than three months to individuals with sufficient resources and a comprehensive health insurance. Such limitations must nonetheless adhere to the proportionality principle (*Bidar*, 2005).

- Discriminatory measures can be justified on grounds of public security, public policy and public health alone. An example is the expulsion of convicted felons: whereas a Member State cannot expel its own citizens under any circumstances, it is allowed to expel convicted citizens of other Member States under certain, very limited conditions. While such a measure is directly discriminatory (as it is treating nationals and non-nationals differently), it can be justified on the ground of public security.

- Indirectly discriminatory or indistinctly applicable measures with restrictive effects can be justified on grounds of public security, public policy and public health as well as on other grounds of the public interest.[80]

Any national measures must be proportionate. The Court's proportionality test usually encompasses three distinct criteria:

- whether the national measure is appropriate for securing the attainment of the objective pursued;[81]

- whether it does not go beyond what is necessary in order to attain it (that is, whether there is no less restrictive measure that would lead to the same result);[82] and

- the public interest pursued by the measure outweighs the interest of the individual and the general public of protecting the right to move and reside freely.[83]

Limitations under the Citizenship Directive

Article 27 Citizenship Directive authorizes Member States to restrict the rights deriving from Union citizenship for reasons of public security, public policy or public health (see the next section). Moreover, Member States can limit the residence rights of Union citizens who stay for more than three months to individuals having sufficient resources and comprehensive health coverage (Article 7

---

79 Case C-524/06, *Huber* [2008] ECR I-9705, para. 75.
80 *Bressol*, Opinion of Advocate General Sharpston, para. 128.   81 *De Cuyper*, para. 42.   82 *Ibid.*, para. 42.
83 Case C-145/09, *Tsakouridis* [2010] ECR I-11979, para. 50.

Citizenship Directive, see below). From its wording, Article 7 Citizenship Directive establishes conditions, which means that, as soon as one of these conditions is no longer fulfilled, the residence right lapses. However, the Court increasingly interprets Article 7 as limitations to the residence rights of Union citizens which must conform to the proportionality principle.

From a formal to a substantive understanding of the limits of the rights conferred by Article 21 TFEU: the rising importance of the proportionality principle

The mobility and residence rights of economically inactive Union citizens have been enacted as formal conditions: only if the conditions are met, the rights are triggered. Conversely, this would mean that, when the conditions are no longer met, then the right would cease as well. Most notably, residence rights were made subject to the conditions of sufficient resources and comprehensive sickness insurance. In cases such as *Grzelczyk* (2001), however, the Court has reinterpreted these formal conditions into substantive limitations that are treated as one of a number of interests to be considered in the balancing exercise of the proportionality test.[84] The difference is important: if the resources and insurance clause is considered to be a condition of the right of residence, the fact that one of these conditions is no longer fulfilled terminates the right of residence. However, if these conditions are seen as substantive limitations of Article 21 TFEU, then the termination of the residence right is no longer a necessary consequence. Instead, the Court subjects the different interests to a proportionality test: the student's right to social benefits may outweigh the state's interest in restricting access to social benefits. The formal conditions have therefore been slowly integrated into the general balancing test under the proportionality principle.

Public policy and public security

Member States may restrict the rights granted under the Union citizenship provision on grounds of public policy and public security, but only to a very limited extent. Article 27 Citizenship Directive holds that Member States may restrict the freedom of movement and residence of Union citizens and their families on grounds of public policy, public security or public health. Public security is generally interpreted to cover both internal and external security. The Court held that a threat to the functioning of the institutions and essential public services and to the survival of the population, as well as the risk of a serious disturbance to foreign relations or to peaceful coexistence of nations, or a risk to military interests, may

---

84 Yuri Borgmann-Prebil, "The Rule of Reason in European Citizenship" (2008) 14 *European Law Journal* 328; more cautious is Eleanor Spaventa, "Seeing the Wood Despite the Trees? On the Scope of Union Citizenship and Its Constitutional Effects" (2008) 45 *Common Market Law Review* 13, 347.

affect public security.[85] Public security can justify measures only if they are "of fundamental importance for a country's existence" (*Campus Oil*, 1984).[86] Public policy is generally interpreted along the lines of preventing disturbances of the social order.[87] Member States essentially retain the freedom to determine the requirements of public policy and public security in accordance with their national needs. These can vary from one Member State to another and from one era to another (*Jipa*, 2008).[88] However, these exceptions must be interpreted strictly. Their scope cannot be determined unilaterally without any control by the institutions of the EU.[89] The public policy derogation can only be invoked if the Member State can show that action on its part would have consequences for public order with which it could not cope by using the means at its disposal.[90] Invoking the public policy or security exceptions to restrict movement and residence rights is only possible, according to the Directive, if the individual concerned represents a "genuine, present and sufficiently serious threat to one of the fundamental interests of society."[91] Such threat, the Court held in *Jipa* (2008), must go beyond "the perturbation of the social order which any infringement of the law involves."[92]

Article 27(2) Citizenship Directive specifies that measures taken on the grounds of public policy or public security shall comply with the principle of proportionality. This means that the measure must be appropriate to ensure the achievement of the objective it pursues and does not go beyond what is necessary to attain it. Article 29 Citizenship Directive holds that measures taken on grounds of public policy or public security shall comply with the principle of proportionality and shall be based exclusively on the personal conduct of the individual concerned. Previous criminal convictions shall not in themselves constitute grounds for taking such measures. Expulsion must not be a systematic and automatic consequence of a criminal conviction (*Orfanopoulos*, 2004).[93] The personal conduct of the individual concerned must represent a genuine, present and sufficiently serious threat affecting one of the fundamental interests of society. Justifications that are isolated from the particulars of the case or that rely on considerations of general prevention shall not be accepted (*Bonsignore*, 1975). Union citizens who are refused entry or who face expulsion also have broad procedural rights under EU law, most notably the right to appeal and the right to have an application for entry reassessed after a reasonable time has elapsed since the last decision prohibiting a person from entering the country (*Mann Singh Shingara*, 1997).[94]

---

85 *Tsakouridis*, para. 44.   86 Case 72/83, *Campus Oil* [1984] ECR 2727, para. 34.
87 Communication from the Commission to the European Parliament and the Council on guidance for better transposition and application of Directive 2004/38/EC on the right of citizens of the Union and their family members to move and reside freely within the territory of the Member States, COM(2009) 313 final, para. 3.1.
88 E.g. *Jipa*, para. 23.
89 *Jipa*, para. 23; see also Case C-326/07, *Commission* v. *Italy* [2009] ECR I-2291, para. 70.
90 Case C-265/95, *Commission* v. *France – Spanish Strawberries* [1997] ECR I-6959, para. 56.
91 Case 36/75, *Rutili* [1975] ECR 1219, para. 28.   92 *Jipa*, para. 23.
93 Joined Cases C-482/01 and C-493/01, *Orfanopoulos* [2004] ECR I-5257, para. 68.
94 Joined Cases C-65/95 and C-111/95, *Mann Singh Shingara* [1997] ECR I-3343, para. 44.

In *Huber* (2008), all foreigners, including Union citizens, were registered in a database in Germany. Germany argued that this was justified on the ground of public security, namely, to fight crime. Although the Court acknowledged that this is a legitimate objective in principle, "the fight against crime … necessarily involves the prosecution of crimes and offences committed, irrespective of the nationality of their perpetrators." A register solely for foreigners can therefore not be justified. In *Jipa* (2008), a Romanian citizen had been repatriated to Romania from Belgium on account of his "illegal residence," and the Romanian ministry applied to a court for a measure prohibiting Mr. Jipa from travelling to Belgium for a period of up to three years. While the expulsion from Belgium may be taken into account for the purpose of restricting a citizen's mobility right by Romania, the Court held that it can do so only to the "extent that his personal conduct constitutes a genuine, present and sufficiently serious threat to one of the fundamental interests of society."[95] By relying solely on the fact of the repatriating measure and failing to assess Mr. Jipa's personal conduct with regard to a possible threat to public policy or security, the Romanian authorities have likely not met the necessary requirements.[96] In *Aladzhov* (2011), the director of a company was prohibited from leaving Bulgaria until there had been a full settlement of the tax debts of his company.[97] While a travel ban to recover tax debts may be admissible under Article 27(1) in principle, the Court found that the measure is likely to be prohibited for two reasons. First, it probably is not proportionate, as it prevents Mr. Aladzhov from travelling abroad in his professional capacity, thereby depriving him of income necessary to repay the debts; and, second, if the travel ban is solely based on his status as a joint director of a company without specific assessment of his personal conduct and no reference to the potential threat to public policy he represents, it has failed to meet the requirements of Article 27. Similarly, the Court held in *Gaydarov* (2011) that a previous criminal conviction is not by itself sufficient to automatically assume that a person represents a genuine, present and sufficiently serious threat to one of the fundamental interests of society.[98]

A person subject to a measure restricting his or her mobility rights must have access to an effective judicial remedy.[99] The persons concerned shall have access to judicial and, where appropriate, administrative redress procedures in the host Member State to appeal against or seek review of any decision taken against them on the grounds of public policy, public security or public health (Article 31 Citizenship Directive). Article 30(1) requires that persons against whom a restrictive measure has been enacted must be informed "precisely and in full, of the public policy, public security or public health grounds on which the decision taken in their case is based." Exceptions can be made only if such disclosure would be "contrary

---

95 *Jipa*, para. 26.   96 *Ibid.*, para. 27.
97 Case C-434/10, *Aladzhov* [2011] ECR I-11659; see also Case C-249/11, *Byankov* [2012] ECR I-00000.
98 Case C-430/10, *Gaydarov* [2011] ECR I-11637, para. 38.   99 *Ibid.*, para. 41.

Table 4.3 Restrictions of mobility and residence rights	
Member States may restrict mobility and residence rights on grounds of public policy, public security or public health, but the measures must . . .	
. . . not serve economic ends.	Art. 27(1) Citizenship Directive
. . . be proportional.	Art. 27(2) Citizenship Directive
. . . be exclusively based on the personal conduct of the individual concerned.	Art. 27(2) Citizenship Directive
. . . restricted to cases where the individual represents a genuine, present and sufficiently serious threat affecting one of the fundamental interests of society.	Art. 27(2) Citizenship Directive
. . . not be solely based on considerations of general prevention.	Art. 27(2) Citizenship Directive
. . . not be a systematic and automatic consequence of a criminal conviction.	Orfanopoulos
. . . provide an effective judicial remedy.	Art. 31 Citizenship Directive

to the interests of State security." The Court has held that this exception must be interpreted narrowly (*ZZ*, 2013).[100]

Though the conduct of the person concerned may not justify the adoption of measures of public policy or public security within the meaning of Article 27 Citizenship Directive, the Member State remains entitled to impose other penalties on him that do not interfere with freedom of movement and residence, such as a fine, provided that they are proportionate.[101] Table 4.3 sets out the conditions under which Member States may restrict mobility and residence rights on grounds of public policy, public security or public health.

Public health

Member States may restrict the rights granted under the Treaty freedoms if fundamental health concerns are at stake. Article 29 Citizenship Directive holds that the only diseases which justify measures restricting freedom of movement are those diseases with epidemic potential as defined by the relevant instruments of the World Health Organization and other infectious diseases or contagious parasitic diseases if they are the subject of protection provisions applying to nationals of the host Member State. Diseases occurring after a three-month period from the date of arrival shall not constitute grounds for expulsion from the territory. In *Bressol* (2010), the Belgian authorities sought to justify quotas on the access to medical studies at Belgian universities for nonresident Union citizens on grounds of the protection of public health, arguing that nonresident students were likely to leave

---

100 Case C-300/11, *ZZ* [2013] ECR I-00000, para. 49.   101 Case C-127/08, *Metock* [2008] ECR I-6241, para. 97.

Belgium after graduation, thus seriously endangering the Belgian health system (see the case discussion below).

Overriding reasons in the public interest

Member States pursue legitimate policy goals that go beyond the very restricted scope of the fundamental interests enshrined in the public policy, public security and public health exceptions. National measures that discriminate or restrict mobility can be justified if they pursue legitimate aims and if the measure is proportionate. In principle, there are no formal restrictions on what kind of national policy goals may be invoked to justify a restriction of the Union citizenship provisions, and the Court has recognized a broad range of regulatory goals as potentially justifying restrictions of rights granted under the Union citizenship provisions.

Legitimate policy objectives so far recognized by the Court include:

- preventing a risk to the existence of a national education system and to its homogeneity (*Bressol*, 2010; *Commission* v. *Austria – University Access*, 2005);[102]
- promotion of mobility and integration of disabled persons (*Gottwald*, 2009);
- restricting social benefits to individuals who have demonstrated a certain degree of integration into the society of the host state, so that the costs of that benefit do not become an unreasonable burden that could have negative consequences for the overall level of assistance that may be granted by that state (*Bidar*, 2005; *Grzelczyk*, 2001; *D'Hoop*, 2002; *Collins*, 2004);
- the need to monitor the employment and family situation of unemployed persons (*De Cuyper*, 2006).

In *Bidar* (2005), the United Kingdom awarded loans for student maintenance costs subject to three conditions: (1) the applicant is resident in England or Wales on the first day of the first academic year; (2) the applicant has been resident in the United Kingdom for the past three years; and (3) the applicant is ordinarily resident in the United Kingdom and is not subject to restrictions as to the period for which they may remain in the United Kingdom.[103] The Court found the measure indirectly discriminatory, as it is much easier for British citizens to fulfill the residence requirements than for noncitizens. In principle, however, such measures could be justified. The Court held that:

[I]t is permissible for a Member State to ensure that the grant of assistance to cover the maintenance costs of students from other Member States does not become an unreasonable burden which could have consequences for the overall level of assistance which may be granted by that State. In the case of assistance covering the maintenance costs of students, it is thus legitimate for a Member State to grant such assistance only to students who have demonstrated a certain degree of integration into the society of that State.[104]

---

102 *Bressol*, para. 53; Case C-147/03, *Commission* v. *Austria – University Access* [2005] ECR I-5969, para. 66.
103 *Bidar*, Opinion of Advocate General Geelhoed, para. 4.   104 *Bidar*, paras. 56–57.

Residence requirements such as those in question (conditions (1) and (2)) may be a legitimate instrument to establish the degree of integration into the host state's society. Condition (3), however, cannot in practice be attained by students who are citizens from another Member State. Condition (3) is therefore not justifiable.

The decision in *Gottwald* (2009) dealt with an Austrian measure that granted a free road toll sticker ("*Autobahnvignette*") to disabled persons resident or ordinarily resident in Austria, but not to nonresident individuals. The measure is intended to foster mobility of disabled persons who cannot use public transport and are dependent on a private car. While this provision is indirectly discriminatory, it is justifiable. The residence requirement establishes a degree of connection to the Austrian society, and, "with regard to benefits that are not covered by Community law, such as that at issue in the main proceedings, Member States enjoy a wide margin of appreciation in deciding which criteria are to be used when assessing the degree of connection to society."[105] Moreover, the Austrian government is interpreting the residence condition widely; even nonresident Union citizens have a right to receive the road toll sticker if they regularly travel to Austria. According to the Court, the proportionality requirement is therefore met.

RIGHTS OF UNION CITIZENS: SECONDARY LAW AND CASE LAW

In this section, we take a closer look at the specific rights of Union citizens. These rights have been developed both in the Court's case law and in secondary law. The most important secondary legislation is the Citizenship Directive.

The Citizenship Directive

The Citizenship Directive 2004/38/EC was enacted in 2004 and consolidated existing secondary law and the Court's case law on movement and residence rights in one single comprehensive document.[106] As the Court has observed, the Citizenship Directive "aims to facilitate the exercise of the primary and individual right to move and reside freely within the territory of the Member States that is conferred directly on Union citizens by the Treaty and that it aims in particular to strengthen that right."[107] It applies not only to citizens relying on Article 21 TFEU, but also to workers and self-employed persons relying on the mobility rights of the other Treaty freedoms.

---

105 Case C-103/08, Gottwald [2009] ECR I-9117, para. 34.
106 Repealing Directives 64/221/EEC, 68/360/EEC, 72/194/EEC, 73/148/EEC, 75/34/EEC, 75/35/EEC, 90/364/EEC, 90/365/EEC and 93/96/EEC.
107 *Metock*, paras. 59–82; *McCarthy*, para. 28.

Personal scope (beneficiaries)

The Directive applies to all Union citizens exercising their right to move and reside freely in another Member State (Article 1(a) Citizenship Directive). This includes both economically active persons (exercising their right to work, establish themselves or provide services in another Member State) and persons who are not economically active (e.g. students, retired persons, etc.). It also includes family members of Union citizens who themselves are either Union citizens or citizens of third countries. The Citizenship Directive also applies to EEA citizens.

Material scope

The Directive applies to all Union citizens who move to or reside in a Member State other than that of which they are nationals (Article 3 Citizenship Directive).[108] Union citizens who have never exercised their right of free movement and have always resided in their home state do not fall under the scope of the Citizenship Directive.[109] They may, however, still have certain rights under primary law (see *Ruiz Zambrano*, 2011).

Right of entry

Union citizens have the right to enter another Member State carrying only a passport or an identity card. Family members who are not Union citizens have the right to enter a Member State carrying only a passport (Article 5 Citizenship Directive). Union citizens must not be obliged to hold an entry visa. Family members who are not Union citizens may be obliged to hold an entry visa unless they have a residence card. The Member States shall make obtaining an entry visa for family members who are third-country nationals as easy as possible, subject to an accelerated procedure and – as soon as possible – free of charge. When a Union citizen or a family member does not have the necessary travel documents or, if required, the necessary visas, the Member State concerned shall, before turning them back, give such persons every reasonable opportunity to obtain the necessary documents or have them brought to them within a reasonable period of time or to corroborate or prove by other means that they are covered by the right of free movement and residence (Article 5(4) Citizenship Directive).[110] The Member State may require the person concerned to report his or her presence within its territory within a reasonable and nondiscriminatory period of time. Failure to comply with this requirement may make the person concerned liable to proportionate and nondiscriminatory sanctions (Article 5(5) Citizenship Directive).

108 *Ruiz Zambrano*, para. 39.   109 *Dereci*, para. 54; *McCarthy*, paras. 31 and 39.
110 See also Case C-459/99, *MRAX* [2002] ECR I-6591.

Right of exit

Union citizens with a passport or identity card and family members who are third-country nationals with a passport have the right to leave another Member State (Article 4 Citizenship Directive).[111]

Right of residence and right of permanent residence

The Citizenship Directive provides for three distinct sets of requirements for residence, depending on the length of stay.

Right of residence for up to three months (Article 6 Citizenship Directive)
Union citizens and their accompanying family members who are not Union citizens have the right of residence in another Member State for a period of up to three months without any requirement other than to hold a valid passport or identity card. Member States cannot oblige Union citizens to register with them for that time period (Article 8 Citizenship Directive). The right extends for a period of three months unless the person becomes "an unreasonable burden on the social assistance system of the host Member State" (Article 14(1) Citizenship Directive).

Right of residence for more than three months (Article 7 Citizenship Directive)
Union citizens have the right of residence for a period of longer than three months if they:

- are economically active (workers or self-employed); *or*
- have sufficient resources for themselves and their family members not to become a burden on the social assistance system of the host Member State during their period of residence *and* have comprehensive sickness insurance cover in the host Member State; *or*
- are students and have comprehensive sickness insurance cover in the host Member State and assure the relevant national authority, by means of a declaration or by such equivalent means as they may choose, that they have sufficient resources for themselves and their family members not to become a burden on the social assistance system of the host Member State during their period of residence.

Union citizens retain their status as a worker or self-employed person if they:

- are temporarily unable to work because of an illness or accident;
- have become involuntarily unemployed during the first twelve months and have registered as a job-seeker; if involuntary unemployment occurs before completion of one year of work, the status of worker shall be retained for at least six months;
- embark on vocational training.

---

111 See also Case C-434/10, *Aladzhov* [2011] ECR I-11659.

Family members (being either Union citizens or third-country nationals) have the same right of residence as the Union citizen that they are accompanying. This applies, however, only to the spouse/partner and dependent children if the Union citizen is a student. Member States can require Union citizens to register for periods of residence longer than three months (Article 8 Citizenship Directive).

According to Article 8(4) Citizenship Directive, Member States may not lay down a fixed amount which they regard as "sufficient resources." Rather, they must evaluate the individual situation of the person. Member States cannot demand resources greater than the threshold that qualifies nationals of the host Member State for social assistance, or, where this criterion is not applicable, greater than the minimum social security pension paid by the host Member State. Resources from a third person must be accepted (*Zhu and Chen*, 2004).

What happens if Union citizens lose their sufficient resources?

Having sufficient resources is a prerequisite for Union citizens who are not economically active for staying legally in another Member State. However, the financial position of a person may change over time, perhaps for reasons beyond his or her control. This happened in the case of Rudy Grzelczyk, a French student in Belgium. After financing his studies over three years with part-time jobs, he applied for social aid in his final year when he could not continue to work due to time constraints imposed by his studies. The Court ruled that by applying for social aid Mr. Grzelczyk failed to fulfill the precondition of sufficient resources for continued legal residence. Thus, in principle, Belgium may withdraw the residence permit or not renew it, but not automatically: the right to residence must remain intact as long as the student does not "become an 'unreasonable' burden on the public finances of the host Member State."[112] There must be "a certain degree of financial solidarity between nationals of a host Member State and nationals of other Member States, particularly if the difficulties which a beneficiary of the right of residence encounters are temporary." Recital 16 of the Citizenship Directive provides:

As long as the beneficiaries of the right of residence do not become an unreasonable burden on the social assistance system of the host Member State they should not be expelled. Therefore, an expulsion measure should not be the automatic consequence of recourse to the social assistance system. The host Member State should examine whether it is a case of temporary difficulties and take into account the duration of residence, the personal circumstances and the amount of aid granted in order to consider whether the beneficiary has become an unreasonable burden on its social assistance system and to proceed to his expulsion.

---

112 *Grzelczyk*, para. 44.

In order to establish whether resources are no longer sufficient and whether an individual has become an "unreasonable burden," the Member State has to carry out a proportionality test. The Commission has explained the criteria of recital 16 as follows:[113]

(1) Duration
   • For how long is the benefit being granted?
   • Is it likely that the EU citizen will get out of the safety net soon?
   • How long has the residence lasted in the host Member State?
(2) Personal situation
   • What is the level of connection of the EU citizen and his or her family members with the society of the host Member State?
   • Are there any considerations pertaining to age, state of health, family and economic situation that need to be taken into account?
(3) Amount
   • What is the total amount of aid granted?
   • Does the EU citizen have a history of relying heavily on social assistance?
   • Does the EU citizen have a history of contributing to the financing of social assistance in the host Member State?

The loss of "sufficient resources" is no sufficient condition for an expulsion: instead, such a measure must also be proportionate for protecting the host state's finances in light of the person's specific circumstances. And Article 14 Citizenship Directive clarifies that "an expulsion measure shall not be the automatic consequence of a Union citizen's or his or her family member's recourse to the social assistance system of the host Member State." The Court held that the condition of "sufficient resources" is met if the individual can rely on the resources of the mother (*Zhu and Chen*, 2004) or the partner (*Commission* v. *Belgium – Sufficient Resources*, 2006).

The host Member State may verify the existence of the preconditions only when there is reasonable doubt (Article 14(2) Citizenship Directive). The host Member State is not allowed to systematically carry out such verifications (e.g. by controlling all Union citizens on their territory). In case of an application for renewal of a residence permit, Member States must not systematically examine whether economically inactive persons still fulfill the condition of possessing sufficient resources (*Commission* v. *Netherlands*, 2008).[114]

---

113 Communication from the Commission to the European Parliament and the Council on guidance for better transposition and application of Directive 2004/38/EC on the right of citizens of the Union and their family members to move and reside freely within the territory of the Member States, COM(2009) 0313 final, para. 2.3.1.
114 Case C-398/06, *Commission* v. *Netherlands* [2008] ECR I-56*.

Permanent residence: after five years of legal residence (Article 16 Citizenship Directive)

After a continuous period of five years of legal residence in the host Member State, a Union citizen acquires the right of permanent residence. This right is not subject to the conditions of economic activity, sufficient resources or comprehensive health insurance. This also applies to family members who are not Union citizens. The continuity of residence is not affected by temporary absences (Article 16(3) Citizenship Directive). Once acquired, the right of permanent residence can be lost only through absence from the host Member State for more than two consecutive years. Under certain conditions, the right of permanent residence can be gained even before the fulfillment of the period of five years (Article 17 Citizenship Directive).[115]

Right to equal treatment (Article 24 Citizenship Directive)

Union citizens and their family members residing in another Member State on the basis of the Citizenship Directive have the right to equal treatment with the nationals of that Member State. The Member States may, however, exclude them from certain social advantages: (1) Member States are not obliged to pay social assistance during the first three months of residence. (2) Nor are they obliged to grant maintenance aid for studies, including vocational training, consisting in student grants or student loans prior to the acquisition of the right of permanent residence (i.e. in the first five years). This restriction, however, does not apply to persons who retain the status of a worker or self-employed person and to their family members. Moreover, the Court has developed significant exceptions to this restriction, most notably in the decisions in *Grzelczyk* and *Bidar* (see below).

The rights of family members of Union citizens

The Citizenship Directive distinguishes between two types of family members of Union citizens. Family members listed under Article 2(2) Citizenship Directive must be granted the same equal treatment rights by the Member States as the Union citizens they accompany. According to Article 2(2) Citizenship Directive, the following persons are considered to be family members:

- the spouse;
- the partner with whom the Union citizen has contracted a registered partnership, on the basis of the legislation of a Member State, if the legislation of the host Member State treats registered partnerships as equivalent to marriage and in accordance with the conditions laid down in the relevant legislation of the host Member State;

---

115 Case C-123/08, *Wolzenburg* [2009] ECR I-9621.

- direct descendants (children, grand-children, etc.) of the Union citizen or of the spouse/partner who are under the age of twenty-one or are dependants;
- direct relatives in the ascending line (parents, grand-parents, etc.) of the Union citizen or of the spouse/partner if they are dependants.

With regard to the second type of family members – listed in Article 3(2) Citizenship Directive – Member States have the obligation to facilitate entry and residence, in accordance with its national legislation. The second group includes:

- any other family members, irrespective of their nationality, not falling under the definition of Article 2(2) who, in the country from which they have come, are dependants or members of the household of the Union citizen having the primary right of residence, or where serious health grounds strictly require the personal care of the family member by the Union citizens;
- the partner with whom the Union citizen has an enduring relationship, duly attested.

While Member States have discretion with regard to the second group of family members, Article 3(2) Citizenship Directive obliges them to undertake an extensive examination of the personal circumstances and the obligation to justify any denial of entry or residence to these individuals. The Court has emphasized that the Member States have wide discretion with regard to the criteria they apply to determine the right of entry or residence of individuals who fall under Article 3(2). However, these criteria must be laid down in legislation, and any decision must be founded on an "extensive examination of [the] personal circumstances" of the applicants (*Rahman*, 2012).[116] Applicants have a right of judicial review with regard to whether the national legislation and its application conform to the requirements of the Directive. The Court emphasized that the Member States cannot employ their discretion in a way that would "deprive that provision of its effectiveness."

Family Members may be either Union citizens themselves or third-country nationals. Essentially, the Citizenship Directive treats both groups equally in most regards. However, family members who are third-country nationals may be required to have an entry visa (Article 5(2) Citizenship Directive). A valid residence card, however, exempts them from this requirement. The Member States are obliged to facilitate access to the necessary visas, shall make the issuance free of charge and issue them on the basis of an accelerated procedure. Family members who are not Union citizens shall receive a residence card by the host Member State if their planned period of residence exceeds three months (Articles 9 and 10 Citizenship Directive). Family members share the right to equal treatment laid down in Article 24 Citizenship Directive. This includes the right to take up employment or self-employment (Article 23 Citizenship Directive). The right of family members – being

---

116 Case C-83/11, *Rahman* [2012] ECR I-00000, para. 26.

either Union citizens or third-country nationals – derive from and therefore depend on the right of the Union citizen whom they are accompanying. However, family members may under certain conditions acquire an originary right when the Union citizen dies or departs from the Member State of residence or when the marriage or registered partnership is divorced (Articles 12–13 Citizenship Directive).

Protection against expulsion (Article 28 Citizenship Directive)

The Citizenship Directive aims to restrict the expulsion of Union citizens, and to make it an instrument of last resort. The Citizenship Directive provides for two grounds for expulsion: (1) expulsion on the ground of public policy or public security; and (2) expulsion on the ground that the conditions of sufficient resources and health coverage are no longer fulfilled. The Directive's Preamble provides:

> Expulsion of Union citizens and their family members on grounds of public policy or public security is a measure that can seriously harm persons who, having availed themselves of the rights and freedoms conferred on them by the Treaty, have become genuinely integrated into the host Member State.[117]

Accordingly, Article 28 Citizenship Directive is termed "Protection against expulsion." It establishes a system that renders expulsion more difficult the greater a Union citizen's degree of integration into the host Member State.[118] An expulsion order has to be based on an individual assessment of the person's situation, based on the length of the person's residence, age, state of health, family situation, economic situation, social and cultural integration into the host Member State and links with the country of origin. Permanent residents may not be expelled except on serious grounds of public policy or public security (Article 28(2) Citizenship Directive). Union citizens who are minors or who have been resident for at least ten years in the host Member State may not be expelled except on imperative grounds of public security (Article 28(3) Citizenship Directive). This means that expulsions are restricted to "exceptional circumstances."[119] Union law "prevents the deportation of a national of a Member State if such deportation is ordered for the purpose of deterring other aliens, that is . . . on reasons of a 'general preventive nature'"[120] (*Bonsignore*, 1975) and must not automatically follow a criminal conviction (*Orfanopoulos*, 2004). The Court held in *P. I.* (2012), which dealt with an Italian citizen convicted of rape of a minor in Germany, that "it is open to the Member States to regard criminal offences such as those referred to in the second subparagraph of Article 83(1) TFEU as constituting a particularly serious threat to one of the fundamental interests of society, which might pose a direct threat to the calm and physical security of the population and thus be covered by the concept of 'imperative grounds of public security', capable of justifying an

---

117 Citizenship Directive, Preamble, recital 23.   118 *Ibid.*, recital 24.   119 *Ibid.*
120 Case 67/74, *Bonsignore* [1975] ECR 297, para. 7.

expulsion measure under Article 28(3)."[121] Article 83(1) TFEU allows the European legislator to establish minimum rules concerning the definition of criminal offenses and sanctions in the areas of particularly serious crime with a cross-border dimension, which includes "sexual exploitation of women and children." The Court cautioned, however, that the seriousness of the offense can justify expulsion only if this is not outweighed by other, countervailing considerations. The Court has discussed this question extensively in the *Tsakouridis* decision.

Case C-145/09, Tsakouridis (2010)

Panagiotis Tsakouridis, a Greek national born, raised and schooled in Germany, had a record of several criminal convictions, including for intentional and dangerous assault. While working in Rhodes, he was arrested and subsequently transferred to Germany on an international arrest warrant. He was convicted for drug dealing as part of an organized group and sentenced to six years' imprisonment. According to German law, a sentence of five or more years for an intentional criminal offense constitutes "imperative grounds of public security" which permit expulsion of residents of 10 or more years. A German court subsequently ruled that Mr. Tsakouridis had lost his right of entry and residence in Germany and was liable to be the subject of an expulsion order.

Does the goal of fighting crime in relation to organized drug-dealing constitute "imperative grounds of public security" that can in principle justify the expulsion of an individual who has been resident for the past ten years in a host state?
Yes.

The duration of the sentence, however, can only be one among a number of factors that are to be considered by the national authorities. The national court has to balance the interest of the host state and the interest of the individual:

In the application of Directive 2004/38, a balance must be struck more particularly between the exceptional nature of the threat to public security as a result of the personal conduct of the person concerned, assessed if necessary at the time when the expulsion decision is to be made ... by reference in particular to the possible penalties and the sentences imposed, the degree of involvement in the criminal activity, and, if appropriate, the risk of reoffending ... on the one hand, and, on the other hand, the risk of compromising the social rehabilitation of the Union citizen in the State in which he has become genuinely integrated, which ... is not only in his interest but also in that of the European Union in general.[122]

Table 4.4 sets out the main issues the Court proposed that the national court should consider in *Tsakouridis*.

---

121 Case C-348/09, *P.I.* [2012] ECR I-00000.   122 *Tsakouridis*, para. 50.

Table 4.4 Issues the Court proposed that the national court should consider in Tsakouridis	
Pro expulsion	**Contra expulsion**
A Member State may, in the interests of public policy, consider that the use of drugs constitutes a danger for society such as to justify special measures against foreign nationals who contravene its laws on drugs.	Right to respect for private and family life (Mr. Tsakouridis' father lives in Germany) and solidity of the social, cultural and family ties with the host Member State (he has spent all of his childhood and youth in Germany).

Article 14 Citizenship Directive stipulates that "an expulsion measure shall not be the automatic consequence of a Union citizen's or his or her family member's recourse to the social assistance system of the host Member State." This means that an individual – even though he or she might become an "unreasonable burden on the social assistance system" during his or her first three months of residence or who no longer fulfills the criterion of "having sufficient resources" – may still not be expelled solely on this ground. Recital 16 of the Preamble to the Citizenship Directive provides that: "The host Member State should examine whether it is a case of temporary difficulties and take into account the duration of residence, the personal circumstances and the amount of aid granted in order to consider whether the beneficiary has become an unreasonable burden on its social assistance system and to proceed to his expulsion." In *Commission* v. *Belgium – Sufficient Resources* (2006), the Court held that the fact that an individual does not produce the required documents for obtaining a residence permit in Belgium within the prescribed period does not indicate that the conditions laid down by Union law, such as the financial conditions, have not in fact been met.[123] Moreover, an automatic order for expulsion in a case where the administrative requirements are not met in time is disproportionate, because it does not allow an individual assessment of the facts which could establish that the individual in fact meets the conditions laid down in Union law.[124] Article 14(4) generally prohibits the expulsion of workers or self-employed persons and their families. It also prohibits the expulsion of job-seekers and their families as long as they can "provide evidence that they are continuing to seek employment and that they have a genuine chance of being engaged." In both types of expulsion – public policy/security and no sufficient resources – the Citizenship Directive demands the exercise of a proportionality analysis by the national authorities that takes into account the details of the individual case. Even though an individual may not have sufficient resources and therefore claims social assistance, this may still not be an "unreasonable burden on the social assistance system of the host Member State," taking into account the individual's duration of residence and personal circumstances. The Court argued in *Tsakouridis* (2010):

---

123 Case C-408/03, *Commission* v. *Belgium – Sufficient Resources* [2006] ECR I-2647.
124 *Commission* v. *Belgium – Sufficient Resources*, paras. 68–69.

[A]n expulsion measure must be based on an individual examination of the specific case . . . and can be justified on imperative grounds of public security within the meaning of Article 28(3) of Directive 2004/38 only if, having regard to the exceptional seriousness of the threat, such a measure is necessary for the protection of the interests it aims to secure, provided that that objective cannot be attained by less strict means, having regard to the length of residence of the Union citizen in the host Member State and in particular to the serious negative consequences such a measure may have for Union citizens who have become genuinely integrated into the host Member State.[125]

Equal access to universities and vocational training

In the early 1980s, the Court developed a right of equal treatment with regard to access to vocational training and university education. Initially, this right was a collateral right to the free movement of workers provisions. In *Forcheri* (1984), Belgium charged a tuition fee for foreign students. The wife of a Commission employee was charged for attending college classes. Drawing from different primary and secondary law provisions, the Court argued that access to higher education falls within the scope of the Treaty. Not only did Regulation 1612/68 (now Regulation 492/2011) provide a right of equal access to vocational training courses for the children of a worker, it also aimed at facilitating the integration of the worker's family in the host state's society. Moreover, the Treaty grants some coordinating authority to the Union in the field of education, namely, to create a common vocational policy (now Article 166 TFEU). Based on these provisions, the Court concluded that, "although it is true that educational and vocational training policy is not as such part of the areas which the Treaty has allotted to the competence of the Community institutions, the opportunity for such kinds of instruction falls within the scope of the Treaty."[126] The additional tuition fee for foreign students therefore violated Article 18 TFEU. In *Gravier* (1985), the Court severed the right of equal access to vocational training and university education completely from the workers' provisions and emphasized an independent right of students (regardless of whether they had worked before) to equal treatment regarding access to universities. In that case, Belgium charged foreign students an annual university enrolment fee ("Minerval"). Ms. Gravier, a French citizen, studied strip cartoon art at an art school. Referring to its decision in *Forcheri* (1984), the Court held that unequal treatment with regard to the enrolment fee constitutes a breach of Article 18 TFEU.

In these decisions, the principle of equal treatment and the Court's support of student mobility collided with the position taken by some Member States that benefits for individuals should not be seen in isolation from tax duties: the former should not be granted without the latter, as taxes fund public services. In *Forcheri* (1984), it was argued that – as EU officials did not pay taxes in Belgium – the Belgian treasury would not receive any payment from Ms. Forcheri's husband, and could therefore not grant free access to its public services.[127] The argument anticipated a conflict that has kept the Court busy ever since: creating a right of noncitizens to

125 *Tsakouridis*, para. 49.   126 Case 28/83, *Forcheri* [1984] ECR 1425, para. 17.   127 *Ibid.*, para. 4.

access public services and noncontributory social benefits (see below) potentially entails distributive conflicts. Why, it might be asked, should a French student, for example, have the right to free university education in Belgium (because students in Belgium do not pay tuition fees) if Belgian students going to France would have to pay tuition fees (because students in France do). In effect, Belgian taxpayers would pay for the education of French students, whereas Belgian students in France would pay (at least in part) for their own costs. This conflict came to the fore in the Austrian and Belgian university access cases in 2005.[128]

In the early 2000s, Belgium and Austria were in a comparable situation, both providing open (no *numerus clausus*) and free (no tuition fees) university access for their nationals; and both having large neighboring states with the same national language – France and Germany – both of which operated a system based on restricted access (*numerus clausus*) and tuition fees. Both Belgium and Austria, therefore, had mechanisms in place that aimed at restricting the influx of students from their neighboring countries. *Commission* v. *Austria – University Access* (2005) dealt with the Austrian rule that university access was granted only under the following conditions: (1) either the students graduated from an Austrian high school; or (2) they fulfilled the requirements of university access in the state where they had graduated from high school. This meant that all students from countries without a *numerus clausus* could enroll at Austrian universities without any difficulty, because these students fulfilled the requirements to enroll in their home country as well. Students from countries with a *numerus clausus*, such as Germany, on the other hand, had to prove that they had been admitted to a German university; but these were exactly those students who no longer had much inclination to move to Austria because they were already admitted to a university in their home country. Students who had failed to pass the *numerus clausus*, on the other hand, could not evade the limitations and go to Austria instead. The Court found that the measure was indirectly discriminatory: while nationals and non-nationals alike can graduate from an Austrian high school in principle, it is mostly Austrians who do so in practice. Thus, in fact the measure adversely affects non-nationals much more than nationals. Austria argued that, without that system, the number of students – especially in medicine – would be drastically higher, thereby threatening the financial equilibrium of the education system. The Court found that this claim was insufficiently substantiated, as it was based only on estimates. It further argued that nondiscriminatory entry exams could constitute less restrictive means; thereby ignoring, however, that university entry exams are themselves a politically highly contested issue at least in some countries. In the subsequent decision in *Bressol* (2010), it corrected its proposition and argued that it is up to the Member States to decide whether they want open or restricted university access. Belgium and Austria reformed their higher education access policies and introduced quotas for non-resident students. This system subsequently became the issue in *Bressol*.

---

128 Case C-65/03, *Commission* v. *Belgium – University Access* [2004] ECR I-6427; Case C-147/03, *Commission* v. *Austria – University Access* [2005] ECR I-5969.

Case C-73/08, Bressol (2010)

Because of a considerable influx of non-Belgian students, the Walloon (French-speaking) community of Belgium reserved 70 percent of study places in paramedical programs for students who fulfilled a qualified residence requirement (either by having a permanent residence right, for example, as a citizen, or having had their principle residence in Belgium for the past three years, or refugee status in Belgium, etc.). The remaining 30 percent of places were open for nonresidents.

Does the quota of 30 percent for nonresidents conflict with Articles 21 and 18 TFEU?
Yes, but the measure is justified.

Because the residence condition is more easily satisfied by Belgians, it is indirectly discriminatory. However, Belgium argued that the measure is justified to avert the risk to public health due to the pressure of students on the education system. More non-Belgian students would put pressure on the education system and would potentially limit the number of medical professionals who remain in Belgium after completing their education. The Court agreed, arguing that "it cannot be ruled out a *priori* that a reduction in the quality of training of future health professionals may ultimately impair the quality of care provided in the territory concerned, since the quality of the medical or paramedical service within a given area depends on the competence of the health professionals who carry out their activity there."[129] The quota could therefore be justified as protecting public health.[130] However, the Court instructed the national court to closely analyze the claims of the Belgian government on the basis of quantitative data.

The university access cases show that the creation of entitlements for individual mobile Union citizens may cause disruptions on the aggregate level, as these entitlements could entail significant additional costs for a Member State. This may cause distributive conflicts, which often have repercussions in domestic politics, influence national debates and sometimes even create nationalist back-lashes. We encounter a similar debate in the next section, which deals with the access to noncontributory social benefits.

Entitlement to the social benefits of the host state

Whereas migrant workers generally have the right to equal access to both contributory and noncontributory social advantages, the situation is different if the right of residence is not based on economic activity, but solely on the Union citizenship status. Most notably, under the Citizenship Directive residence rights of more than

---

129 *Bressol*, para. 67.   130 *Ibid.*, para. 70.

three months are conditional on the individual having sufficient resources and comprehensive health coverage (Article 7 Citizenship Directive). Restrictions by Member States on access to social advantages for individuals invoking their Union citizenship status as being equal to that of workers is often justified on the basis of the following political considerations. Welfare systems are assumed to have a symmetric structure: individuals contribute through social insurance contributions and taxes, whereby they acquire a right to receive social benefits. Workers from other Member States easily fit into this model, as they pay taxes and contributions in the host state. Economically inactive individuals who move to another state, however, are seen as merely drawing from the host state's resources without contributing to it. Such distributive concerns – sometimes disparagingly referred to as "social tourism," implying bad faith on the part of the migrating individuals – have resulted in differences between the rights of workers to equal access to social benefits and those of individuals relying solely on the Union citizenship provisions.

Social benefits for students

By means of Directive 93/96 regulating student mobility, Member States were able to establish limitations on students' rights to equal access to social benefits in the host state: students were required to have "sufficient resources to avoid becoming a burden on the social assistance system of the host Member State" and to be covered by sickness insurance (Article 1), but were explicitly excluded from access to student maintenance grants by the host Member State (Article 3).[131] Accordingly, the Court upheld equal treatment for students solely with regard to tuition and registration fees, but had long ruled that no equal treatment requirement applied with regard to social benefits for students (*Brown*, 1988).[132] In 2001, however, the Court changed its position and held that – under certain conditions – students should in fact have a right to social benefits as well. In *Grzelczyk* (2001), the Court ruled that a student – having studied for some years in Belgium – would have the right to apply for a noncontributory social benefit on the ground of poverty as long as he does "not become an 'unreasonable' burden on the public finances of the host Member State."[133] The Court explained that there is "a certain degree of financial solidarity between nationals of a host Member State and nationals of other Member States, particularly if the difficulties which a beneficiary of the right of residence encounters are temporary." And, in *Bidar* (2005), the Court ruled that a student has the right to receive a student loan in the United Kingdom because he could demonstrate a certain degree of integration into the society of the host state (the Court called this a "genuine link"). Such a "genuine link" can be demonstrated, for example, by the length of time an individual has resided in the host state.[134] However, the Court has also developed a general rule in *Grzelczyk* allowing

131 Council Directive 93/96/EEC of 29 October 1993 on the right of residence for students, [1993] OJ L317/29.
132 Case 197/86, *Brown* [1988] ECR 3205.   133 *Grzelczyk*, para. 44.
134 *Bidar*, para. 59; Case C-158/07, *Förster* [2008] ECR I-8507, para. 50.

Member States to limit the access of noncitizens to student benefits. The Court argued that in principle Member States must show a certain degree of financial solidarity with nationals of other Member States. Nonetheless, Member States are allowed to ensure that student maintenance costs do not become an unreasonable burden that would have adverse consequences for the general level of assistance granted by that state.

The Member States reacted in 2004 and included a provision in the Citizenship Directive providing that they would not be obliged to grant any kind of maintenance grants to students before they acquired permanent residence status after five years (Article 24(2) Citizenship Directive). In *Förster* (2008), the Court essentially adhered to this position.[135] Ms. Förster, a German student in the Netherlands, was refused a maintenance grant. The Court held that a "condition of five years' uninterrupted residence is appropriate for the purpose of guaranteeing that the applicant for the maintenance grant at issue is integrated into the society of the host Member State."[136] The decision in *Förster* is interesting from a doctrinal point of view. We have seen in Article 21 TFEU that, according to the Treaty text, the right to move and reside freely in the Member States is "subject to the limitations and conditions laid down in the Treaties and by the measures adopted to give them effect." The restrictions on maintenance grants for students laid down both in Directive 93/96 and the Citizenship Directive constitute such a limitation. The Court, however, has held that such limitations must still conform to Articles 18 and 21 TFEU.[137] It therefore subjects them to an additional test: "That requirement must also be proportionate to the legitimate objective pursued by the national law in order to be justified in the light of Community law. It may not go beyond what is necessary in order to attain that objective."[138] The right of a (well-integrated) student to receive a maintenance grant in the host state developed in *Bidar* (2005) is based directly on an interpretation of Article 21 TFEU. The Court seems to understand it as a quasi-constitutional require-ment, which may be implemented and thereby particularized, but not annulled or undermined by secondary law. In this sense, the Court assumes that its interpretation of Article 21 TFEU is higher-ranking than the secondary law. This explains why in *Bidar* (2005) the Court recognized the entitlement to a student maintenance grant, in direct conflict with secondary law: the "limitations" to Article 21 TFEU are not merely a formal requirement (i.e. if there is a limitation in secondary law then the mobility right is limited), but also a substantive requirement: any limitation to Article 21 TFEU must pursue a legitimate objective and be proportionate.

"Noncontributory" social aid

The Court first held in *Martínez Sala* (1998) that an entitlement to a noncontribu-tory social aid (in Ms. Martínez Sala's case, a child-raising allowance) can be based directly on the Union citizenship provisions. But, while economically active

---

135 *Förster*, para. 55.   136 *Ibid.*, para. 52.   137 *Ibid.*, paras. 42–43.   138 *Ibid.*, para. 53.

individuals have a very broad right of equal treatment regarding social benefits, the entitlements of economically inactive citizens is considerably weaker. We have seen in *Grzelczyk* (2001) and *Bidar* (2005) that the Court generally accepts that Member States can limit noncontributory social benefits to Union citizens with a certain degree of integration in the society of the host state. In defining the conditions of this link to the host state's society, "Member States enjoy a wide margin of appreciation in deciding which criteria are to be used when assessing the degree of connection to society."[139] A common way to establish such a link is through a minimum residence requirement, as the Court has recognized in such cases as *Bidar* (2005), *Förster* (2008) and *Gottwald* (2009): "The Court has accepted on certain conditions that national rules may require, in order to establish the existence of a certain degree of integration, that the recipient of the benefit in question has been resident or ordinarily resident in the Member State concerned for a certain period of time."[140] Article 24(2) Citizenship Directive provides that Member States are not obliged to grant social assistance for the first three months of residence or for the period during which a Union citizen first seeks employment in the host state. On the other hand, the Court has ruled that host states are obliged to achieve a minimum level of solidarity with regard to Union citizens, especially when they have resided for a longer period in that state and have become poor only temporarily. This was the case in *Grzelczyk* (2001) and *Trojani* (2004).[141]

Case C-456/02, Trojani (2004)

Michel Trojani, a French national, had moved to Belgium, living first at a campsite and a youth hostel and later at a Salvation Army hostel, where in return for board and lodging and some pocket money he did various jobs as part of a personal socio-occupational reintegration program. He has been issued a Belgian residence permit and applied for social aid, the so-called "minimex."

Is Mr. Trojani a worker within the meaning of Article 45 TFEU?
Possibly, but unlikely.[142]

Does he have mobility and residence rights under Article 21 TFEU?
No.

Does the right of equal treatment under Article 18 TFEU entitle him to receive social aid if he is in possession of a national residence permit?
Yes.

---

139 *Gottwald*, para. 34; *Tas-Hagen*, para. 36.
140 *Gottwald*, para. 35; see also *Bidar*, para. 59 and *Förster*, para. 50.
141 Case C-456/02, *Trojani* [2004] ECR I-7573.   142 *Ibid.*, para. 29.

Although M Trojani was doing various jobs, his work was probably not "real and genuine"[143] – though it is for the referring national court to decide this – as his tasks will likely not be regarded as forming part of the normal labor market. Likewise, he cannot rely on the residence right granted by Article 21 TFEU, because he does not fulfill the preconditions laid down in secondary law, as he does not have sufficient resources. However, the Court noted that Belgium had already issued a residence permit. Because he is lawfully resident in Belgium, he is entitled to equal treatment under Article 18 TFEU. He therefore is entitled to receive minimex. However, it remains open to the host Member State to take the view that a national of another Member State who has recourse to social assistance no longer fulfills the conditions of his right of residence.

Entitlement to social benefits of the home state

In a number of cases, the Court had to decide on the applicability of the Union citizenship provisions to measures implemented by the home state, most notably to their refusal to pay certain benefits to their citizens living abroad. Since 2000,[144] the Court has continuously ruled that Union citizens can invoke the Union citizenship provisions against their own home states if they are placed at a disadvantage because they have exercised their mobility rights.[145] This was the case, for example, in *D'Hoop* (2002).

Case C-224/98, D'Hoop (2002)

Belgium granted a so-called "tideover allowance" to university graduates looking for their first job. It was, however, only granted to Belgians who had completed secondary school education in Belgium. Ms. D'Hoop, a Belgian citizen, who had graduated from secondary school in France, studied in Belgium. Her application for a tideover allowance was rejected.

Can an allowance for jobseekers who have graduated from university be reserved for individuals who have completed their secondary education in Belgium?
No.

The Court held:

By linking the grant of tideover allowances to the condition of having obtained the required diploma in Belgium, the national legislation thus places at a disadvantage certain of its nationals *simply because they have exercised their freedom to move* in order to pursue education in another Member State.[146]

---

143 *Ibid.*, para. 29.   144 Case C-135/99, *Elsen* [2000] ECR I-10409.   145 *Morgan*, para. 25.
146 Case C-224/98, *D'Hoop* [2002] ECR I-6191, para. 34.

In *Morgan* (2007), Germany awarded grants for studying abroad only under the condition that the applicant had previously studied at least one year in Germany. The Court decided that this was contrary to Articles 20 and 21 TFEU, because the rule "is liable to discourage [citizens] from moving subsequently to another Member State in order to pursue their studies."[147] Interestingly and in some way different from *Morgan* (2007), the Court had previously decided in *De Cuyper* (2006) that a Member State can refuse payment of benefits – in this case, unemployment benefits – to a citizen who moves to another Member State.[148] Belgium had refused to pay unemployment benefits to Mr. De Cuyper after it was discovered that he was in fact residing in France. Belgium ceased payments even though Mr. De Cuyper was exempted from the requirement to submit to the local control procedures, i.e. to be available for employment. The Court found this refusal to constitute a restriction of Article 21 TFEU, but ruled that it was justified because the Belgian inspectors needed to regularly monitor whether the information provided by the unemployed person corresponds to their real situation.

Taxation

Direct taxation (that is, where persons are directly liable to pay taxes, such as income tax) remains in the competence of Member States, whereas indirect taxation (where a process, like a sale, is taxed) is partly harmonized. Nonetheless, national taxation rules can conflict with the Union citizenship provisions. The standard case consists of national rules under which a tax benefit is granted for a domestic, but not for a comparable non-domestic, transnational situation. In *Schwarz and Gootjes-Schwarz* (2007), Germany granted a tax deduction for fees paid for private schools, but only if they were located in Germany.[149] According to the Court, the non-deductibility of school fees paid to a private school in another Member State constituted a breach of Article 21 TFEU. The decision in *Rüffler* (2009) dealt with a retired German citizen who lived in Poland, and parts of his German pension were taxed there.[150] While individuals could deduct payments to the compulsory health insurance in Poland, Polish law did not provide the same possibility for Mr. Rüffler's payments to the German health insurance scheme. This was found to be contrary to Article 21 TFEU. In *Zanotti* (2010), the Court ruled that Italy was in breach of Article 21 TFEU when it refused to grant tax deductibility for tuition fees for a university in the Netherlands when such deduction was granted for universities established in Italy.

There are numerous reasons why countries have different taxation regimes for internal and cross-border situations, not all of them being unjustified as such. Discrimination occurs only if objectively comparable situations are treated

---

147 *Morgan*, para. 31.   148 Case C-406/04, *De Cuyper* [2006] ECR I-6947.
149 Case C-76/05, *Schwarz and Gootjes-Schwarz* [2007] ECR I-6849.
150 Case C-544/07, *Rüffler* [2009] ECR I-3389.

differently by national law. If, conversely, situations are not comparable, unequal treatment cannot constitute a violation of Union law. The Court held that unequal treatment can be justified only by objective circumstances that are "independent of the nationality of the persons concerned."[151] The Court has ruled, for example, that the situations of residents and nonresidents are usually not comparable for tax purposes (see *Schumacker*, below).[152] If, on the other hand, residents and nonresidents are in an objectively comparable situation (e.g. if they receive most of their income in the Member State in question), a different treatment constitutes a discrimination under Article 21 TFEU. In *Turpeinen* (2006), a Finnish retiree residing in Spain was subject to a higher level of income tax than retirees residing in Finland, despite the fact that the Finnish pension constituted most of Ms. Turpeinen's income. The Court found the two situations to be comparable, so that the higher taxation for Ms. Turpeinen constituted a breach of Article 21 TFEU. In *Commission* v. *Greece – Tax Breaks for Houses* (2011), a Greek law granted an exemption from the transfer tax for individuals acquiring a first home. As the tax break was granted solely to Greek nationals and residents, but not to nonresidents who intend to settle in Greece in the future, the Court found it to be in breach of Article 18 TFEU. Greece had argued that the measure was "justified ... by objectives intended *inter alia*, first, both to make it easier for Greeks who have emigrated and persons of Greek origin to purchase a home and to encourage their return, given that Greece has experienced a sharp decrease in its population because of massive emigration abroad."[153] The Court responded, however, that "such considerations do not establish that there are objective circumstances, independent of the nationality of the persons concerned, which are capable of justifying discrimination such as that resulting from the exemption ... as their very foundation is the nationality of the persons concerned."[154]

The fact that Union citizens experience disadvantageous taxation in cross-border situations is not necessarily a sign for discriminatory conduct by the Member States. As the taxation systems have not been harmonized in important parts, disadvantages (as well as advantages) often occur solely on the basis that the different Member States have different tax regimes and different tax rates. The mere fact that the exercise of mobility rights is not tax neutral is not sufficient proof for the existence of a discriminatory situation. The Court recalled in *Schempp* (2005) that "the Treaty offers no guarantee to a citizen of the Union that transferring his activities to a Member State other than that in which he previously resided will be neutral as regards taxation. Given the disparities in the tax legislation of the Member States, such a transfer may be to the citizen's advantage in terms of indirect taxation or not, according to circumstances."[155]

---

151 Case C-155/09, *Commission* v. *Greece – Tax Breaks for Houses* [2011] I-65, para. 71.
152 *Turpeinen*, paras. 26–28.   153 *Commission* v. *Greece – Tax Breaks for Houses*, para. 70.
154 *Ibid.*, para. 71.   155 *Schempp*, para. 45; see also Case C-365/02, *Lindfors* [2004] ECR I-7183.

The cases discussed in this section mostly concern retired persons, as the taxation of economically active persons falls under the market freedom provisions. However, the cases concerning the taxation of Union citizens are similar to those under the other Treaty freedoms. What has been said in this section generally applies to tax cases under the other Treaty freedoms as well.

Family names

Rights derived from European citizenship may conflict with national laws regulating surnames. Relevant cases with regard to surnames of children include *Garcia Avello* (2003, see above) and *Grunkin and Paul* (2008). The latter case dealt with Mr. Grunkin and Ms. Paul, a married couple of German nationality residing in Denmark where their child was born. As a child of German parents, the child received German nationality. The last name of the child was registered in Denmark as "Grunkin-Paul." The laws of both Germany and Denmark were applicable: German law by reason of the child's nationality, Danish law because of the child's residence. But the German authorities refused to recognize the name registered in Denmark, as German law did not allow for a double-barreled surname composed of the surnames of both the father and mother. The Court held that a discrepancy in surnames – for example, with regard to documents and diplomas – would cause a serious inconvenience for the child, which constituted an obstacle to freedom of movement.[156] The German authorities were therefore precluded from refusing to recognize a child's surname, as determined and registered in another Member State in which the child – who, like his parents, has only the nationality of the first Member State – was born and has been resident since birth.[157] In *Runevič-Vardyn* (2011), however, the Court emphasized that the inconvenience caused by name rules must in fact be "serious," i.e. the discrepancies cause doubts as to the person's identity and the authenticity of their documents. The inconvenience caused by the refusal of the Lithuanian authorities to change the spelling of the name of a Lithuanian citizen of the Polish minority on documents from the Lithuanian form ("Malgožata Runevič-Vardyn") to the Polish form ("Małgorzata Runiewicz-Wardyn") did not necessarily reach the required level of seriousness.

OTHER RIGHTS CONFERRED BY PART TWO OF THE TFEU

While the core of what is usually referred to as "Union citizenship" are the mobility and equal treatment rights based on Articles 18, 20 and 21 TFEU, Part Two of the TFEU grants a number of other rights as well. The personal and material scope of the provisions discussed in this section differ from that pertaining to those discussed above.

---

156 Case C-353/06, *Grunkin and Paul* [2008] ECR I-7639, para. 29.   157 *Ibid.*, para. 39.

Prohibition of discrimination on other grounds (Article 19 TFEU)

Article 19 TFEU enables the Union to pass measures against other forms of discrimination within the limits of the Union's legislative powers. The Council and the European Parliament have already used that grant of legislative power to enact Directives against discrimination on the following grounds: sex, racial or ethnic origin, religion or belief, disability, age and sexual orientation. The Directives prohibit direct discrimination, indirect discrimination and harassment on these grounds, and may cover the fields of employment, access to goods and services, social protection and education. Currently, not all Directives cover all areas. A proposal that passed the European Parliament in 2009 would raise the protective level with regard to religion, disability, age and sexual orientation, but the Council has not yet agreed.[158] Table 4.5 sets out an overview of the main regulatory fields covered by the anti-discrimination Directives.

Whereas Article 19 TFEU was introduced by the Treaty of Amsterdam in 1999, the prohibition of discrimination on the grounds of sex dates back to the Treaty of Rome in 1957. Article 157 TFEU provides that "[e]ach Member State shall ensure that the principle of equal pay for male and female workers for equal work or work of equal value is applied." In its judgment in *Defrenne II* (1976),[159] the Court held that the equal pay provision has horizontal direct effect in the fields of employment and industrial relations. This means that the provision can be invoked by individuals in national courts not only against Member States, but also against private employers.

Table 4.5 Overview of the main regulatory fields covered by the anti-discrimination Directives			
	Sex (2004/113/EC and 2006/54/EC – Equal Treatment Directive)	Race (2000/43/EC – Race Equality Directive)	Religion, disability, age, sexual orientation (2000/78/EC – Employment Equality Framework Directive)
In employment and occupation	Yes	Yes	Yes
Access to goods and services	Yes[a] (but not in regard to media content or advertisement)	Yes	No
Social protection	No	Yes	No
Education	No[b]	Yes	No

a   Article 3(1) Directive 2004/113/EC.
b   Article 3(3) Directive 2004/113/EC.

158 European Parliament legislative resolution of 2 April 2009 on the proposal for a Council Directive on implementing the principle of equal treatment between persons irrespective of religion or belief, disability, age or sexual orientation (COM(2008) 426 final).
159 Case 43/75, *Defrenne II* [1976] ECR 455.

The right to vote and stand as a candidate in other Member States for European and municipal elections (Article 22 TFEU)

Article 20(2)(b) TFEU grants Union citizens the right to cast a vote in the country of residence irrespective of their nationality, and also to stand as a candidate. This right covers European Parliament and municipal elections. These rights must be granted to citizens of other Member States on the same conditions as for nationals of that state.

Case C-300/04, Eman and Sevinger (2006)

The claimants were Dutch citizens residing on the Caribbean island of Aruba, which is part of the Kingdom of the Netherlands and is listed as an "Overseas Country and Territory" (OCT) in Annex II to the TFEU. These OCTs have "special relations" with EU countries, but are not part of the EU, and are instead associated (Part Four, Articles 198–204 TFEU). According to Dutch electoral law, they cannot vote in European elections. Dutch citizens who reside in a nonmember country, on the other hand, are allowed to vote. The latter rule is intended to allow Dutch citizens who still have links to Dutch society to participate in elections.

Can national electoral law exclude their own citizens from voting in a European election if they reside in an OCT even though they would be allowed to vote if they were residing in third countries?

No.

In the current state of Union law, it is still within the competence of each Member State (in compliance with EU law) to define which persons can vote and stand for elections for the European Parliament. Article 22(2) TFEU is not applicable to this situation because it does not grant a general right to participate in European elections, but a right of EU citizens to participate under the same conditions as nationals of the state of residence do. However, the measure fails to comply with the general principle of equal treatment: Dutch citizens residing in an OCT and in a non-Member State are in a comparable situation, yet are treated unequally.

The electoral procedure for the European elections has been harmonized only in part. A Council Decision provides "Common Principles" on the European election.[160] The Decision requires a system of proportionate representation, and provides that the election must be by direct universal suffrage and must be free and secret. Apart from these common principles, the electoral systems of Member States can vary.

---

160 Council Decision of 25 June and 23 September 2002 amending the Act concerning the election of the representatives of the European Parliament by direct universal suffrage, annexed to Decision 76/787/ECSC, EEC, Euratom (2002/772/EC, Euratom) [2002], L 283/1.

Right to diplomatic and consular protection (Article 23 TFEU)

Articles 20(2)(c) and 23 TFEU and Article 46 Charter of Fundamental Rights create a right of Union citizens to receive diplomatic or consular protection in third countries where their own Member State does not maintain such representation. Protection must be granted by the authorities of a Member State to citizens of other Member States under the same conditions as apply to their own nationals. The institutions of the Member States are bound by the provision, and their actions are subject to judicial review by the Court. A refusal to grant consular protection may render a Member State liable for harm caused under the principle of state liability.[161]

The Citizens' Initiative (Article 24 TFEU)

The Treaty of Lisbon introduced the European Citizens' Initiative (CI) as a new legal instrument (Article 11(4) TEU; Article 24(1) TFEU).[162] The aim is to encourage participation of citizens and to make the Union more accessible.[163] Organizers may register a CI with the Commission and must then collect (online or offline) at least 1 million signatures from at least seven Member States within the following twelve months. The organizers must collect a certain minimum number of signatures from each of these seven Member States.[164] The CI is an "invitation" to the Commission to propose legislation, and must concern an area where the Commission in fact has the power to do so (e.g. internal market, transport or the environment). A successful CI does not actually force the Commission to issue a proposal; the Commission is merely obliged to meet with the organizers of the CI, to examine the CI, to organize a public hearing at the European Parliament, and to issue a communication in which it spells out its "legal and political conclusions," and the actions it intends to take, if any.[165] Conceptualizing the CI as a mere "invitation" to the Commission to issue a proposal aims at protecting the Commission's prerogative to issue proposals in the legislative process.

Other political rights (Article 24 TFEU)

Part Two of the TFEU grants the following additional rights:

- the right to petition the European Parliament (Articles 24 and 227 TFEU);
- the right to apply to the European Ombudsman (Articles 24 and 228 TFEU);

---

161 Communication from the Commission to the European Parliament and the Council, Consular protection for EU citizens in third countries: State of play and way forward, March 23, 2011, COM(2011) 149/2, p. 4.
162 Regulation 211/2011 of the European Parliament and of the Council of 16 February 2011 on the citizens' initiative, [2011] OJ L65/1.
163 Regulation 211/2011, Preamble, recital 2.
164 Art. 7(1) Regulation 211/2011 (minimum number of signatures = seats in European Parliament x 750). See Annex I to the Regulation.
165 Arts. 10(1) and 11 Regulation 211/2011.

- the right to write to the Union's main institutions in one of the EU's (currently twenty-four: see Article 55(1) TEU) official languages and receive an answer in the same language (Article 24 TFEU);
- the right to access documents of the Union institutions, bodies, offices and agencies (Article 15(3) TFEU; Article 42 Charter of Fundamental Rights).

The Charter of Fundamental Rights codifies numerous other political, human and social rights, partly reiterating the rights discussed above in this section.

Further reading

BORGMANN-PREBIL, YURI, "The Rule of Reason in European Citizenship" (2008) 14 *European Law Journal* 328

BUCKEL, SONJA, and WISSEL, JENS, "The Transformation of the European Border Regime and the Production of Bare Life" (2010) 4 *International Political Sociology* 33

DE WITTE, FLORIS, "Who Funds the Mobile Student? Shedding Some Light on the Normative Assumptions Underlying EU Free Movement Law: Commission v. Netherlands" (2013) 50 *Common Market Law Review* 203

GOUDAPPEL, FLORA, *The Effects of EU Citizenship: Economic, Social and Political Rights in a Time of Constitutional Change*, The Hague: TMC Asser Press, 2010

KOCHENOV, DIMITRY, "Double Nationality in the EU: An Argument for Tolerance" (2011) 17 *European Law Journal* 323

"The Right to Have What Rights? EU Citizenship in Need of Clarification" (2013) 19 *European Law Journal* 502

NEWDICK, CHRISTOPHER, "Citizenship, Free Movement and Health Care: Cementing Individual Rights by Corroding Social Solidarity" (2006) 43 *Common Market Law Review* 1645

SPAVENTA, ELEANOR, "From Gebhard to Carpenter: Towards a (Non)Economic European Constitution" (2004) 41 *Common Market Law Review* 743

"Seeing the Wood Despite the Trees? On the Scope of Union Citizenship and Its Constitutional Effects" (2008) 45 *Common Market Law Review* 13

WOLLENSCHLÄGER, FERDINAND, "A New Fundamental Freedom Beyond Market Integration: Union Citizenship and Its Dynamics for Shifting the Economic Paradigm of European Integration" (2011) 17 *European Law Journal* 1

Free movement of workers
(Articles 45–48 TFEU)

INTRODUCTION

The freedom of movement for workers is a core feature of the European Union and, from its inception, distinguished it from other regional economic organizations. The European Coal and Steel Community (ECSC, 1951) established the mobility of workers in the coal and steel sectors.[1] The Treaty of Rome (1957) provided for the gradual establishment of a general freedom of movement of workers in the EEC. Article 48(1) EEC provided: "Freedom of movement for workers shall be secured within the Community by the end of the transitional period at the latest." Even before the end of the transitional period in 1969, the Community institutions began to implement the Treaty provisions governing the free movement of workers. An early example is Directive 64/221/EEC on the "co-ordination of special measures concerning the movement and residence of foreign nationals which are justified on grounds of public policy, public security or public health."[2] It limited the discretionary powers of the Member States to restrict movement of the citizens of other Member States. One of the most important acts of legislation was Regulation 1612/68, spelling out the principle of equal treatment with regard to employment.[3] Directive 68/360/EEC, furthermore, eliminated many restrictions on movement and residence,[4] creating movement and residence rights which, a few years later in the 1970s, were extended to self-employed persons (see Chapter 6 below). The early European legislative measures aimed at establishing a far-reaching principle of equal treatment which the Court then further generalized. In *Sagulo* (1977), the Court held that "community law ... is based on the freedom of movement of persons and, apart from certain exceptions, on the general application of the principle of equal treatment with nationals."[5] It extended the principle of equal treatment to areas that it held to be important

---

1 Art. 69 ECSC Treaty.   2 Now replaced by the Citizenship Directive.
3 Now replaced by Regulation 492/2011.
4 Council Directive 68/360/EEC of 15 October 1968 on the abolition of restrictions on movement and residence within the Community for workers of Member States and their families, [1968] OJ L257/13.
5 Case 8/77, *Sagulo* [1977] ECR 1495, para. 12.

to facilitate mobility and the integration of the worker and his or her family into the host society.

Migration patterns during the first decades of the EEC

In the 1950s, France absorbed most of the migrant labor, and the largest percentage of the overall number of migrant workers (30 percent) came from Italy.[6] From the late 1950s onwards, Germany became the largest recipient of migrant labor. While Italian migrants remained by far the most significant group of migrants from within the EEC until 1973, they could not sufficiently satisfy the exploding demand for labor in Europe. In the period from 1970–1973, around 750,000 migrant workers received a first work permit in the EEC, of which only one-quarter originated from EEC countries. Non-EEC migrant workers came in particular from Greece, Spain and Portugal and other Mediterranean countries, particularly Turkey and Yugoslavia. Labor migration (from both EEC and non-EEC countries) was of major importance for Europe's post-Second World War economic revival and growth. Molle and Van Mourik remark that "[i]n the period 1960–1974, foreign labour was essential to the economy of European receiving countries."[7] The absolute number of migrant workers who were nationals of EEC Member States remained relatively stable between 1958 to 1984, rising from 576,000 to a peak of 905,000 in the early 1970s, and then declining again to 636,000 in 1984.[8] Most labor migration from non-EEC countries was short-term: generally, unmarried, unskilled workers stayed for up to two years, and then returned home.[9] Molle and Van Mourik explain: "Much of the migration described here was so-called 'organised' migration through recruitment bureaus of the host countries established in the countries of origin. These bureaus often took upon themselves the organisation of transportation, medical checks and housing. That means that the size and direction of the flows was ultimately determined by policy."[10] After the oil shock of 1973 and the subsequent recession, the number of migrant workers dropped sharply, from 4.5 million to 3.3 million between 1974 and 1984. A couple of EEC countries developed schemes to facilitate return migration, for example through financial incentives.[11] But, most importantly, in the years following the oil shocks of 1973 and 1979 and the subsequent recessions, immigration policy toward third countries became much more restrictive in all Member States. Table 5.1 sets out the first work permits granted to foreign workers by six EEC Member States.

---

6 On the following, see Willem Molle and Aad Van Mourik, "International Movements of Labour Under Conditions of Economic Integration: The Case of Western Europe" (1988) 26 *Journal of Common Market Studies* 317, 322–327.
7 *Ibid.*, 322.   8 *Ibid.*, 323.   9 *Ibid.*, 323.   10 *Ibid.*, 323.   11 *Ibid.*, 325–326.

Table 5.1 First work permits granted to foreign workers by six EEC Member States[a]			
Years	**Total**	**Of which EEC**	**Of which Italy**
1958–1961	273,000	60%	49%
1962–1965	595,000	36%	32%
1966–1969	565,000	30%	26%
1970–1973	751,000	26%	21%

a   Table taken from Willem Molle and Aad Van Mourik, "International Movements of Labour Under Conditions of Economic Integration: The Case of Western Europe" (1988) 26 *Journal of Common Market Studies* 317, 322.

Main Treaty provisions at a glance

Article 45 TFEU provides for a right of workers to go to another Member State to look for a job, to accept offers of employment actually made, to move freely within the Member States for this purpose, to stay in a Member State for the purpose of employment, and to remain in the Member State after the employment has terminated. According to the Court, Article 45 TFEU provides two prohibitions: a prohibition of discrimination on the grounds of nationality, and a prohibition of (nondiscriminatory) restrictions to the free movement of workers. The rights of workers have been defined further in secondary law, most importantly in Regulation 492/2011 (ex-Regulation 1612/68) and the Citizenship Directive (discussed in Chapter 4 above), as well as the case law of the Court. Articles 46–48 TFEU contain competences for EU legislative action. Table 5.2 sets out an overview of the Treaty provisions in the field of the free movement of workers.

Table 5.2 Overview of Treaty provisions in the field of the free movement of workers	
Provision	**Subject-matter**
Art. 45 TFEU	The right to move to, to accept job offers, to reside and to work in another Member State, and to remain after employment
Art. 46 TFEU	Authority to enact certain secondary law – Directives or Regulations – for the coordination of employment services and the regulation of labor markets
Art. 47 TFEU	Joint program to encourage the exchange of young workers
Art. 48 TFEU	Authority to enact secondary legislation on social security "necessary to provide freedom of movement for workers" (Regulation No. 883/2004 on the coordination of social security systems has been passed under this provision – see below)

Direct effect of Article 45 TFEU

Article 45 TFEU has direct effect, as the Court first held in *French Sailors* (1974) and *Van Duyn* (1974).

Case 41/74, Van Duyn (1974)

Ms. Van Duyn, a Dutch citizen, wished to enter the United Kingdom to take up an offer of employment as a secretary with the Church of Scientology. The United Kingdom, however, refused her entry, as it considered the Church of Scientology to be a socially harmful organization. According to Article 3(1) Directive 64/221/EEC, Member States could restrict the free movement of workers only on the ground of public policy if the decision is based exclusively on the personal conduct of the individual, not on general considerations.[12] Van Duyn challenged the refusal of entry on the basis of Article 45 TFEU and Article 3(1) Directive 64/221.

Does Article 45 TFEU have direct effect?

Yes.

Does Article 3(1) of Directive 64/221/EEC providing that public policy and security measures must be exclusively based on personal conduct have direct effect?

Yes.

If so, can the United Kingdom nonetheless refuse entry to Ms. Van Duyn?

Yes.

The Court found that Article 45 TFEU "has a direct effect in the legal orders of the Member States and confers on individuals rights which the national courts must protect."[13] The same applies to Article 3(1) Directive 64/221, which requires Member States to base measures restricting the free movement of workers exclusively on the personal conduct of the individual concerned. However, the Court then held that a Member State "is entitled to take into account as a matter of personal conduct of the individual concerned, the fact that the individual is associated with some body or organization the activities of which the Member State considers socially harmful." Accordingly, the denial of entry is justifiable on grounds of public policy.

---

12 Directive 64/221/EEC of 25 February 1964 on the co-ordination of special measures concerning the movement and residence of foreign nationals which are justified on grounds of public policy, public security or public health, [1964] OJ 56/850.

13 Case 41/71, *Van Duyn* v. *Home Office* [1974] ECR 1337, 1352.

PERSONAL SCOPE (BENEFICIARIES)

Article 45 TFEU applies to workers who are Union citizens. Additionally, other groups – job-seekers, employers and workers who retain their status after employment – have certain rights under Article 45 TFEU as well.

Union citizens and persons having comparable rights

Article 45 TFEU applies to Union citizens. Additionally, other groups of persons enjoy analogous rights. Citizens from the EEA countries (Norway, Iceland and Liechtenstein) have equal rights under Article 28 EEA Agreement, which is practically identical to Article 45 TFEU. Swiss nationals benefit from analogous rights, laid down in the EU–Switzerland bilateral agreement on the free movement of persons.[14] Workers who are Turkish citizens have significant rights under the EU–Turkey Association Agreement.

Turkish workers

Turkey has special relations with the EU in many different ways. One particularly striking example is the rights of Turkish workers in the EU. The Association Agreement between the EEC and Turkey of 1963, which aimed at the establishment of a customs union and eventual full membership of Turkey in the EEC, provided that the EEC and Turkey would "progressively secur[e] freedom of movement for workers between them" (Article 12), guided by the corresponding provisions of the EEC Treaty. The 1970s protocol to the Agreement established a timetable to that end, and laid down a general principle of nondiscrimination with regard to conditions of work and remuneration between workers of Turkish nationality and those from a Member State (Article 37). Finally, Article 6(1) of Decision 1/80 of the Association Council laid down the following rights of Turkish workers:

- to renew their permits to work for the same employer, if a job is available, after *one year's* legal employment
- to respond to another offer of employment, with an employer of his or her choice, made under normal conditions and registered with the employment services of that state, for the same occupation, after *three years* of legal employment and subject to the priority to be given to workers of Member States of the Union

14 Agreement between the European Community and its Member States, of the one part, and the Swiss Confederation, of the other, on the free movement of persons, [2002] OJ L114/6.

- free access in that Member State to any paid employment of his choice, after *four years* of legal employment

Apprentices (*Kurz*, 2002),[15] students with part-time jobs and au pairs (*Payir*, 2008)[16] fall under Article 6(1) as well. Family members of Turkish workers have a right to work after a certain period of residence (Article 7). Article 7 has direct effect (*Kahveci*, 2012).[17] In *Dülger* (2012), the Court held that family members do not need to be Turkish citizens themselves to benefit from Article 7 Decision 1/80.[18] The Court held that "[a]s it is an essential way of making family life possible, the family reunification enjoyed by Turkish workers who belong to the labour force of the Member States contributes both to improving the quality of their stay and to their integration in those Member States and, therefore, promotes social cohesion in the society concerned" (*Dülger*, 2012).[19] Children of Turkish workers are to be admitted to courses of general education, apprenticeship and vocational training (Article 9). Decision 1/80 incorporates a standstill clause (Article 13): Member States and Turkey are prohibited from introducing new restrictions on the conditions of access to employment. In *Toprak and Oguz* (2010),[20] the Court scrutinized a Dutch law that held that a Turkish citizen whose marriage had been dissolved could receive an independent residence permit if he or she had been legally resident for at least three years. This had also been the legal situation in 1980; however, between 1983 and 2000 the measure was more beneficial, with a residence requirement of only one year. The Court found that any tightening of a provision is prohibited under the standstill clause; the one-year requirement could therefore not be rolled back by the Dutch government, even though it was enacted after 1980. The rights granted by Decision 1/80, such as the rights of family members under Article 7, have direct effect.[21] The Court held in *Bozkurt* (1995)[22] that the principles enshrined in Article 45 TFEU must be extended, as far as possible, to Turkish nationals who enjoy rights under the EEC–Turkey Association Agreement. This means that, as a general rule, a nondiscrimination principle applies to Turkish workers unless the relevant provisions under the Agreement state otherwise. However, the Court does draw certain distinctions between Turkish workers and workers who are Union citizens. In *Ziebell* (2011), the Court found that the protection against expulsion of Turkish workers (Article 14(1) Decision 1/80) does not have the same scope as that of workers who are Union citizens (Article 28(3)(a) Citizenship Directive).

---

15 Case C-188/00, *Kurz* [2002] ECR I-10691.   16 Case C-294/06, *Payir* [2008] ECR I-203.
17 Joined Cases C-7/10 and C-9/10, *Kahveci* [2012] ECR I-00000, para. 24.
18 Case C-451/11, *Dülger* [2012] ECR I-00000, para. 65.   19 *Ibid.*, para. 42.
20 Joined Cases C-300/09 and C-301/09, *Toprak and I. Oguz* [2010] ECR I-12845.
21 Case C-303/08, *Bozkurt* [2010] ECR I-13445, para. 31.
22 Case C-434/93, *Bozkurt* [1995] ECR I-1475, paras. 19–20.

Who is a worker?

A worker is an individual in an employment relationship, i.e. an individual who performs services for and under the direction of another person in return for which the individual receives remuneration (*Lawrie-Blum*, 1986).[23] This includes, for example, professional and semi-professional athletes, as they receive remuneration for their services (*Donà*, 1976).[24] The Court employs a very broad definition of "workers" which includes, for example, part-time workers as long as the work is effective and genuine, only excluding purely marginal and ancillary activities (*Levin*, 1981).

Case 53/81, Levin v. Staatssecretaris van Justitie (1982)

Ms. Levin, a British citizen, applied for a residence permit in the Netherlands which was refused on the grounds that she was not engaged in a gainful occupation in the Netherlands. For this reason, the Dutch authorities considered that she was not a worker within the meaning of Article 45 TFEU and had no right of residence under EU law. Ms. Levin appealed to the Staatssecretaris van Justitie, because she had meanwhile taken up a part-time occupation. The Staatssecretaris countered, however, that her new part-time occupation was still not covered by Article 45 TFEU, as she earned a wage lower than the national minimum required for subsistence.

Does the concept of "worker" encompass part-time jobs that do not pay a subsistence-level wage?

Yes.

The meaning of the concept of "worker" should not be fixed unilaterally by one of the Member States. This, however, would be the case if "the principle of freedom of movement for workers could be made subject to the criterion of what the legislation of the host state declares to be a minimum wage, so that the field of application *ratione personae* of the Community rules on this subject might vary from one Member State to another."[25] Article 45 TFEU covers all activities that are effective and genuine, to the exclusion only of "activities on such a small scale as to be regarded as purely marginal and ancillary."[26]

Neither the fact that an individual only works a few hours a week nor the fact that a worker receives very low wages is determinative of the status as a worker.[27] In *Kempf* (1986), the Court held that an individual working part-time as a music teacher and receiving supplementary benefits is a worker.[28] The fact that Mr. Kempf was supplementing his income with social assistance financed out of public funds did not impair

---

23 Case 66/85, *Lawrie-Blum* [1986] ECR 2121, paras. 16–17; Case C-138/02, *Collins* [2004] ECR I-2703, para. 26.
24 Case 13/76, *Donà* [1976] ECR 1333, paras. 12–13.   25 Case 53/81, *Levin* [1982] ECR 1035, para. 11.
26 See also Case C-317/93, *Nolte* [1995] ECR I-4625, para. 19.
27 Case C-456/02, *Trojani* [2004] ECR I-7573, para. 16; *Levin*, para. 16; *Nolte*, para. 19.
28 Case 139/85, *Kempf* [1986] ECR 1741.

his status as a worker. In *Bernini* (1992), the Court held that an individual who worked for ten weeks as a paid trainee must be regarded as a worker, although it argued that the national court could examine whether the person has "completed a sufficient number of hours in order to familiarize himself with the work."[29] If that was not the case, the educational element would predominate, and the individual could not be classified as a worker. In *Ninni-Orasche* (2003), the Court ruled that "[t]he fact that a national of a Member State has worked for a temporary period of two and a half months in the territory of another Member State, of which he is not a national, can confer on him the status of a worker."[30] Generally, the fact that an activity does have an educational or training component does not exclude the applicability of Article 45 TFEU. The Court held in *Kranemann* (2005) that a trainee lawyer who is undergoing part of his preparatory legal training in a Member State other than that of which he is a national is covered by Article 45 TFEU, as the individual performs services for and under the direction of another person and receives remuneration in return.[31] The same is true for trainee teachers (*Lawrie-Blum*, 1986). It is irrelevant whether the remuneration is coming directly from the employer or from another source, as long as it is paid in consideration for services provided under the direction of another person.[32] In *Raccanelli* (2008), the Court ruled that a doctoral student working on his thesis on the basis of a grant contract with the German Max-Planck-Gesellschaft, a research institute, is a worker only when he works under the direction of and subordinate to the institute and receives remuneration for this.[33]

While the concept of "worker" is broad, certain activities remain excluded. In *Bettray* (1989), the Court held that work in an institution that provides employment and training to individuals suffering from drug addiction cannot be regarded as an effective and genuine economic activity if it constitutes merely a means of reha-bilitation or reintegration. In *Trojani* (2004), the Court added that employment that is part of a rehabilitation or reintegration effort constitutes effective and genuine economic activity only if the occupation could be regarded as "forming part of the normal labour market."[34]

As the essential characteristic of an employment relationship within the meaning of Article 45 TFEU is the fact that a person performs services for and under the direction of another person in return for remuneration, any activity which a person performs outside a relationship of subordination must be classified as an activity pursued in a self-employed capacity (*Nadin*, 2005).[35] The definition of an activity under national law is irrelevant for the applicability of Article 45 TFEU. The term "worker" for the purposes of Union law has an autonomous meaning specific to Union law, as the Court first held in the decision *Hoekstra*.

29 Case C-3/90, *Bernini* [1992] ECR I-1071, para. 16.
30 Case C-413/01, *Ninni-Orasche* [2003] ECR I-13187, para. 32.
31 Case C-109/04, *Kranemann* [2005] ECR I-2421, para. 18.
32 Case 344/87, *Bettray* [1989] ECR 1621, para. 15.   33 Case C-94/07, *Raccanelli* [2008] ECR I-5939.
34 *Trojani*, para. 24.   35 Case C-151/04, *Nadin* [2005] ECR I-11203, para. 31.

Case C-75/63, Hoekstra (née Unger) (1964)

Ms. Hoekstra, a German citizen living in the Netherlands, was not currently employed because she was pregnant, but she had previously been employed. She visited her parents in Germany, where she fell ill. Subsequently, the Dutch social security authorities refused to pay for her expenses. Under an EEC Regulation, insurance coverage was provided in such cases, but only if the affected person is a worker. Under the national definition, Ms. Hoekstra would not be considered a "worker."

Does the concept of a "worker" have a supranational meaning independent of the legislation of the Member States?

Yes.

The concept of "worker" has a Union law meaning and must not be interpreted by the legislation of each Member State. The Court stated:

If the definition of this term were a matter within the competence of national law, it would therefore be possible for each Member State to modify the meaning of the concept of 'migrant worker' and to eliminate at will the protection afforded by the Treaty to certain categories of person ... Articles (45–48 TFEU) would therefore be deprived of all effect and the above-mentioned objectives of the Treaty would be frustrated if the meaning of such a term could be unilaterally fixed and modified by national law. The concept of 'workers' in the said Articles does not therefore relate to national law, but to Community law.[36]

Additional beneficiaries covered by Article 45 TFEU

According to EU law and to the Court's case law, groups other than workers can invoke Article 45 TFEU under certain circumstances. First, individuals may retain their status as a worker after the termination of their employment. Job-seekers can invoke certain rights under Article 45 TFEU, as can employers. Posted workers, on the other hand, cannot invoke Article 45 TFEU.

Job-seekers

Job-seekers enjoy the right to equal treatment laid down in Article 45(2) TFEU.[37] This includes, *inter alia*, the right of entry and to move freely within a Member State for the purposes of seeking employment.[38] Job-seekers also have equal access to social benefits of a financial nature intended to facilitate access to employment in the labor market of a Member State, such as a "tideover allowance" granted to

---

36 Case 75/63, *Hoekstra* [1964] ECR 177, 184.
37 Case C-258/04, *Ioannidis* [2005] ECR I-8275, para. 21; Joined Cases C-22/08 and C-23/08, *Vatsouras* [2009] ECR I-4585, para. 36.
38 Case C-292/89, *Antonissen* [1991] ECR I-745, para. 13.

bridge the time between completion of secondary education and the first employment (*Ioannidis*, 2005; *D'Hoop*, 2002).[39] It is, however, legitimate for a Member State to grant such an allowance only after it has been possible to establish a real link between the job-seeker and the labor market of that state (e.g. *Vatsouras*, 2009).[40]

A Member State may limit the period of time for which a job-seeker is authorized to stay within its territory. The Citizenship Directive's right of short-term residence for up to three months provides a lower limit: individuals – and members of their family accompanying or joining them – have the right to stay in the territory of another Member State for up to three months without having to fulfill the requirement of an occupational activity or of sufficient financial means (Article 6 Citizenship Directive). The right of job-seekers extends beyond the three-month period. In *Commission* v. *Belgium* (1995), the Court found that a Belgian law that ordered job-seekers to leave the country after a period of three months violated Article 45 TFEU.[41] In *Antonissen* (1991), the Court found that, under certain conditions, a limit of six months is compatible with Article 45 TFEU.

Case C-292/89, Antonissen (1991)

Mr. Antonissen, a Belgian national, had lived in the United Kingdom since 1984 and remained unemployed until he was arrested in 1987 for the possession of cocaine. Subsequently, Mr. Antonissen's expulsion was ordered. He appealed against the expulsion order. UK law allowed the expulsion after six months of unemployment.

Can national legislation limit the length of stay for job-seekers?

Yes.

The Court found that:

[I]t is not contrary to the provisions of Community law governing the free movement of workers for the legislation of a Member State to provide that a national of another Member State who entered the first State in order to seek employment may be required to leave the territory of that State (subject to appeal) if he has not found employment there after six months, unless the person concerned provides evidence that he is continuing to seek employment and that he has genuine chances of being engaged.[42]

The individual must have the opportunity to provide evidence to this effect, and an expulsion order on this ground must be subject to appeal.

---

39 *Collins*, para. 63; *Ioannidis*, para. 22.
40 Case C-224/98, *D'Hoop* [2002] ECR I-6191, para. 38; *Ioannidis*, para. 30; *Vatsouras*, para. 38.
41 Case C-344/95, *Commission* v. *Belgium* [1995] ECR I-1035.   42 *Antonissen*, para. 22.

While job-seekers have the right to move and reside freely in another Member State and to equal access to employment, they do not share the employees' right to equal access to social or tax advantages (*Lebon*, 1987), with the exception of benefits that are granted to job-seekers such as the tideover allowance in *D'Hoop*.[43]

Employers

Employers may also invoke Article 45 TFEU when they hire nationals from other Member States, as the Court held in *Clean Car* (1998).[44] The Clean Car GmbH was denied registration in Austria because its manager did not reside in Austria, as the law stipulated. According to the Court, this was a violation of Article 45 TFEU. The right of workers to be engaged and employed without discrimination necessarily entails as a corollary the employer's entitlement to engage non-nationals. Private-sector recruitment agencies can also invoke Article 45 TFEU, as the Court held in *ITC* (2007).[45] Germany allowed private agencies to provide job recruitment services. According to German law, a private agency received a fee if it helped a job-seeker to gain employment that met certain minimum standards, including a minimum period of employment of three months and compulsory social security contributions. ITC found a job that met these standards for a client at a company located in the Netherlands. However, the German authorities refused to award the premium to ITC, arguing that the job had to be subject to compulsory social security contributions in Germany. The Court found that such restriction conflicted with Article 45 TFEU.

Retention of worker status after employment

The right to residence is subject to the condition that the status as a worker or job-seeker is retained.[46] However, the Court held in such cases as *Collins* (2004) and *Ninni-Orasche* (2003) that "migrant workers are guaranteed certain rights linked to the status as a worker even when they are no longer in an employment relationship."[47] According to Article 7(3)(a) Citizenship Directive, a worker who has become involuntarily unemployed after having been employed for more than one year retains the status of a worker if registered as a job-seeker with the relevant employment office. According to Article 7(3)(c), a worker who has become involuntarily unemployed during the first twelve months after completing a fixed-term employment contract of less than a year likewise retains that status for a minimum period of six months if registered as a job-seeker with the relevant employment office. In *Vatsouras* (2009), the Court found that an individual retains the status of a worker even when the initial employment lasted for less than two months. But, in

43 Case 316/85, *Lebon* [1987] ECR 2811, para. 26; Case C-278/94, *Commission* v. *Belgium* [1996] ECR I-4307, paras. 39–40.
44 Case C-350/96, *Clean Car* [1998] ECR I-3075.   45 Case C-208/05, *ITC* [2007] ECR I-181, para. 25.
46 Joined Cases C-482/01 and C-493/01, *Orfanopoulos* [2004] ECR I-5257, para. 49.   47 *Collins*, para. 27.

Collins (2004), the Court held that, after seventeen years of absence from the UK labor market, the status could no longer be retained.

Groups not covered by Article 45 TFEU

The following groups do not fall under the worker provisions of the Treaty:

- *Posted workers.* Posted workers are employed by a company that provides services in another Member State. The company posts the employees temporarily in another Member State. The Court has ruled that posted workers do not enter the host state's labor market because their stay is only temporary and they return to their country of origin after the completion of their work (*Rush Portuguesa*, 1990).[48] The situation of posted workers is regulated by a specific Directive, the Posted Workers Directive (see below).
- *Self-employed.* The situation of the self-employed falls under the provisions on the freedom of establishment or the free movement of services.

MATERIAL SCOPE

Cross-border element

Article 45 TFEU can be invoked only in situations that feature a cross-border element. As the Court ruled for the first time in *Saunders* (1979), the provisions do not apply to situations that are purely internal to a Member State.[49] These are defined as "activities which have no factor linking them with any of the situations governed by Community law and which are confined in all relevant respects within a single Member State" (*Flemish Insurance*, 2008).[50] An individual who has not exercised the right of free movement cannot rely on Article 45 TFEU. In *Moser* (1984), the Court held that a German student who was refused access to post-university training in Germany because of his membership of the communist party could not invoke Article 45 TFEU.

Case 180/83, Moser (1984)

The German Land Baden-Württemberg refused the application of Mr. Moser, a German national, for admission to post-graduate training necessary to become a teacher. The refusal was based on the fact that Mr. Moser was a member of the German Communist Party (DKP). Mr. Moser invoked Article 45 TFEU on the ground

---

48 Case C-113/89, *Rush Portuguesa* [1990] ECR I-1417, para. 15.
49 Case 175/78, *Saunders* [1979] ECR 1129, para. 11.
50 Case C-212/06, *Flemish Insurance* [2008] ECR I-1683, para. 33.

that – in the future – he may be unable to apply for a teaching job in another Member State if he could not complete his education in Germany.

Can a plaintiff in a law suit against his home country rely on Article 45 TFEU arguing that the Member State's denial may in the future deprive him of the possibility to work as a teacher in another Member State?

No.

According to the Court, Article 45 TFEU "does not apply to situations which are wholly internal to a Member State, such as that of a national of a Member State who has never resided or worked in another Member State. Such a person may not rely on Article [45 TFEU] to prevent the application to him of the legislation of his own country."

In *Uecker and Jacquet* (1997), two foreign language assistants employed at German universities – one from Norway, the other from Russia, and both married to German citizens – tried to challenge their disadvantageous, time-limited contracts.[51] The Court held, however, that they could not invoke privileges as family members of workers as their spouses had not exercised their right to free movement. In *Morson and Jhanjan* (1982), the Court refused Dutch workers residing in the Netherlands the right to be joined by their family, as they had not exercised their right of mobility.[52] We have seen in the recent case *McCarthy* (2011) that the Court has not moved on this point. Union citizens have no right to be joined by family members who are third-country nationals under the Treaty's provisions if they have not exercised their mobility right.

The Court applies Article 45 TFEU not only to situations where workers move to another Member State, but also to situations where workers were employed in another Member State and subsequently return to their home state and face disadvantages by reason of their having exercised their mobility right (*Terhoeve*, 1999).[53] A common case is that of frontier workers, who work in a different Member State to that in which they reside (e.g. *Hartmann*, 2007). An individual who initially resided and worked in his home country, and subsequently takes up residence in another Member State while continuing to work in the home country, acquires the status of a migrant worker (*Hendrix*, 2007).[54]

The continuing relevance of the cross-border element is manifestly restated in *Flemish Insurance* (2008). Belgium has three regions (the Flemish, the Walloon, and the Brussels region) and three "communities" (the Flemish, the French, and the German) as governing entities, the latter being responsible for "aid to persons," among other fields. The Flemish community introduced a care insurance

51 Joined Cases C-64/96 and C-65/96, *Uecker and Jacquet* [1997] ECR I-3171.
52 Joined Cases 35/82 and 36/82, *Morson and Jhanjan* [1982] ECR 3723.
53 Case C-18/95, *Terhoeve* [1999] ECR I-345, para. 27; Case C-419/92, *Scholz* [1994] ECR I-505, para. 9.
54 Case C-287/05, *Hendrix* [2007] ECR I-6909, para. 46.

that provided for persons facing prolonged disability. The personal scope was restricted to individuals residing in the Flemish or Brussels regions. After the Commission had opened infringement proceedings in 2002, the personal scope was extended to include also individuals working in the Flemish or Brussels regions, but residing outside of Belgium. The only group effectively excluded were individuals working in the Flemish or Brussels regions but residing in the Walloon region. While the Commission abandoned further infringement procedures, the measure was challenged in the national courts by the Walloon government and the French-speaking community. The Court distinguished between two situations: (1) The situation of Belgian citizens living in the Walloon region and working in the Flemish or Brussels regions who have never exercised their mobility rights is "purely internal," so that Article 45 TFEU cannot apply.[55] (2) For Belgian citizens who have at some point exercised their mobility rights (and afterwards returned to Belgium), or for Union citizens residing in the Walloon region and working in the Flemish or Brussels regions, on the other hand, Article 45 TFEU is applicable. The Court ultimately ruled that the Flemish care insurance provision constituted a restriction of Article 45 TFEU, but only with regard to the second group.

Even if a situation features a cross-border element, the Court has ruled from time to time that Article 45 TFEU is not applicable if the effects of a measure on the internal market are too uncertain and indirect to be capable of being regarded as liable to hinder freedom of movement for workers (*Graf*, 2000).[56] Generally, however, the Court applies a rather generous understanding of what it considers a cross-border situation.

ADDRESSEES

Member States

Article 45 TFEU obliges Member States to abolish any discrimination on the ground of nationality and any restrictions on the freedom of movement of workers. Individuals can invoke Article 45 TFEU against both the host state and the home state.

Non-state actors

Under certain conditions, Article 45 TFEU is binding not only upon Member States, but also upon non-state actors. The Court held in *Angonese* (2000) that "the principle of non-discrimination set out in [Article 45 TFEU] is drafted in general

---

55 *Flemish Insurance*, para. 38.   56 Case C-190/98, *Graf* [2000] ECR I-493, paras. 24–25.

terms and is not specifically addressed to the Member States."[57] Obligations for non-state actors may arise in two situations: non-state actors may be bound either by secondary law, or on the ground of direct horizontal effect of Article 45 TFEU.

Secondary law addressed to non-state actors

The obligation to accord equal treatment with regard to employment and work conditions laid down in Article 7 Regulation 492/2011 applies not only to the Member States, but also to employers and employers' associations. According to Article 7, clauses in individual or collective agreements which are discriminatory or which authorize discriminatory conditions are void (see e.g. *Erny*, 2012).[58]

Horizontal direct effect of Article 45 TFEU

Due to its horizontal direct effect, Article 45 TFEU can be invoked by individuals against non-state actors, such as employers, employers' organizations, professional organizations such as bar associations and labor unions. The Court first held in *Walrave* (1974) that the provision is applicable not only to the Member States, but also "to rules of any other nature aimed at regulating in a collective manner gainful employment and the provision of services."[59]

Case 36/74, Walrave and Koch v. Union Cycliste Internationale (1974)

The Union Cycliste Internationale (UCI), the world governing body for sports cycling, organizes international competitions such as the world championships. Until the mid 1990s, the UCI held so-called motor-paced racing competitions, where the athlete ("stayer") cycles in the slipstream behind a motorcycle ("pacer"). According to a UCI rule, the stayer and the pacer had to be of the same nationality. The rule was challenged by two Dutch pacers.

Can a nationality requirement of an international sporting association be challenged under Article 45 TFEU?

Yes.

Sport is subject to Union law in so far as it constitutes an economic activity.[60] The prohibition of discrimination on grounds of nationality "does not apply only to the action of public authorities, but extends likewise to rules of any other nature aimed at regulating in a collective manner gainful employment and the provision of services."[61] The Court further held that:

The abolition as between Member States of obstacles to freedom of movement for persons and to freedom to provide services ... would be compromised if the abolition

---

57 Case C-281/98, *Angonese* [2000] ECR I-4139, para. 30.   58 Case C-172/11, *Erny* [2012] ECR I-00000.
59 Case 36/74, *Walrave and Koch* [1974] ECR 1405, para. 31.   60 *Ibid.*, para. 4.   61 *Ibid.*, para. 17.

of barriers of national origin could be neutralized by obstacles resulting from the exercise of their legal autonomy by associations or organizations which do not come under public law. Since, moreover, working conditions in the various Member States are governed sometimes by means of provisions laid down by law or regulation and sometimes by agreements and other acts concluded or adopted by private persons, to limit the prohibitions in question to acts of a public authority would risk creating inequality in their application.[62]

Therefore, the Treaty provisions "may be taken into account by the national court in judging the validity or the effects of a provision inserted in the rules of a sporting organization."[63]

This broad applicability of Article 45 TFEU to any rules aimed at regulating in a collective manner gainful employment has subsequently been confirmed in numerous cases (*Donà*, 1976; *Bosman*, 1995; *Olympique Lyonnais*, 2010).[64] The decisions often concern the rules of international sporting organizations, which are – while organized privately – the dominant governance bodies for the sporting discipline concerned. They have significant power, as a professional sporting career outside their realm is virtually impossible in practice. While organizations like the UCI (*Walrave*) or UEFA (*Bosman*) are privately organized bodies, they constitute a hierarchical governance structure where the rules are made at the level above that of teams and athletes. In a sense, such organizations perform quasi-governmental functions. However, the applicability of Article 45 TFEU is not restricted to such entities.

In *Angonese* (2000), an Italian citizen who had studied in Vienna challenged an employment practice, common in the region of Bolzano, of requiring a specific certificate of Italian and German bilingualism. Employers routinely required prospective employees to produce such certificate, administered by the public authorities in Bolzano. Mr. Angonese's application for a job at a bank was rejected because he failed to produce such a certificate, despite the fact that he was perfectly bilingual. The Court held that Article 45 TFEU must apply to "all agreements intended to regulate paid labour collectively, as well as to contracts between individuals."[65] As the certificate in question can only be acquired in Bolzano, demanding it as the only means of proving bilingualism constitutes an indirect discrimination. The Court argued that "[p]ersons not resident in that province therefore have little chance of acquiring the Certificate and it will be difficult, or even impossible, for them to gain access to the employment in question."[66] And: "even though requiring an applicant for a post to have a certain level of linguistic

---

62 *Ibid.*, paras. 18–19.   63 *Ibid.*, para. 25.
64 Case 13/76, *Dona* [1976] ECR 1333; Case C-415/93, *Bosman* [1995] ECR I-4921; Case C-325/08, *Olympique Lyonnais* [2010] ECR I-2177.
65 *Angonese*, para. 34.   66 *Ibid.*, para. 39.

knowledge may be legitimate and possession of a diploma such as the Certificate may constitute a criterion for assessing that knowledge, the fact that it is impossible to submit proof of the required linguistic knowledge by any other means, in particular by equivalent qualifications obtained in other Member States, must be considered disproportionate in relation to the aim in view."[67] Even though the Court explained at that time that the requirement constituted discrimination on the ground of nationality,[68] this is not in fact the case, as Mr. Angonese is both an Italian citizen *and* resident in Bolzano; he had merely studied in Austria. From the perspective of where the Court's case law stands today, the employment practice in question would be an infringement of Article 45 TFEU because it puts Mr. Angonese, as a mobile Union citizen, at a disadvantage. This is the approach the Court has continued to pursue in later decisions, for example in *Casteels* (2011). The claimant Maurits Casteels, a Belgian national, had worked for British Airways (BA) continuously since 1974 in Belgium, Germany and France. While he was stationed in Germany, he was affiliated with a supplementary pension scheme. According to the relevant collective agreement, supplementary pension rights could be acquired only after serving a minimum period of time under this specific scheme. Before he met this requirement, however, he transferred to France. The Court ruled that the collective agreement breaches Article 45 TFEU because it does not take into account the time Mr. Casteels had served with the same employer in another Member State. Therefore, he was put at a disadvantage in comparison to workers employed with BA for the same period of time who had always stayed in Germany.[69] Advocate General Kokott held:

In quite general terms, the provisions of the TFEU relating to the freedom of movement are intended to facilitate the pursuit by nationals of the Member States of occupational activities of all kinds throughout the European Union, and preclude measures which might place Union citizens at a disadvantage when they wish to pursue an economic activity in the territory of another Member State. Collectively agreed rules such as those [in question] make it less attractive for employees to leave their establishment and move to another which is affiliated to a different old-age pension scheme or no such scheme at all.[70]

APPLYING ARTICLE 45 TFEU: THE PROHIBITION OF DISCRIMINATION AND OF RESTRICTIONS

Article 45(2) TFEU provides that the "freedom of movement shall entail the abolition of any discrimination based on nationality between workers of the Member States as regards employment, remuneration and other conditions of work and employment."

---

67 *Ibid.*, para. 44.   68 *Ibid.*, para. 45.   69 Case C-379/09, *Casteels* [2011] ECR I-1379, paras. 25–26.
70 *Casteels*, Opinion of Advocate General Kokott, paras. 42–43.

The Court applies this provision as a prohibition of both direct and indirect discrimination. However, the wording of Article 45(3) TFEU suggests an even broader interpretation of the rights of workers. It holds that the freedom of movement for workers entails the right to accept employment offers, move freely and stay in another Member State, and to remain after employment. This could be read as a prohibition of national measures that create restrictions on the (substantive) ability of workers to exercise their mobility, even though the restrictions are nondiscriminatory. The Court has in fact moved in this direction since the mid 1990s, in particular in the decision in *Bosman* (1995).

Direct discrimination

Direct discrimination occurs when a measure explicitly treats workers who are EU citizens of another Member State less favorably than its own nationals. Article 45 TFEU provides a general prohibition of discrimination on the ground of nationality as regards employment, remuneration and other conditions of work and employment.[71] Regulation 492/2011 specifies this prohibition for various employment-related situations. The prohibition of discrimination includes a prohibition of quotas for EU citizens. In *French Sailors* (1974), the Court found that a law reserving employment at the bridge and in the engine and wireless rooms aboard French merchant marine ships exclusively to French citizens violated Article 45 TFEU.

Indirect discrimination

A measure that is neutral on its face but creates adverse effects for non-nationals constitutes an indirect discrimination. The Court holds that "rules regarding equal treatment forbid not only overt discrimination by reason of nationality but also all covert forms of discrimination which, by the application of other criteria of differentiation, lead in fact to the same result" (*Commission* v. *Greece – Real Estate Tax Exemption*, 2011).[72] A national measure is "indirectly discriminatory if it is intrinsically liable to affect migrant workers more than national workers and if there is a consequent risk that it will place the former at a particular disadvantage."[73] A typical example for national measures that the Court routinely finds to be indirectly discriminatory are residence requirements (*Petersen*).

71 Case 167/73, *Commission* v. *France – French Sailors* [1974] ECR 359, para. 44.
72 Case C-155/09, *Commission* v. *Greece – Real Estate Tax Exemption* [2011] ECR I-65, para. 45; Case C-152/73, *Sotgiu* [1974] ECR 153, para. 11.
73 Case C-228/07, *Petersen* [2008] ECR I-6989, para. 54.

Case C-228/07, Petersen (2008)

Mr. Petersen, a German national who was employed in Austria, applied in 2000 to the Austrian pension benefits authority for an incapacity pension under the statutory retirement pension scheme. After applying, he moved from Austria back to Germany. The application for the pension was refused by the Austrian authorities.

Can the incapacity pension be denied to Mr. Petersen because he is no longer resident in Austria?

No.

A residence requirement is indirectly discriminatory because it can be met more easily by national workers than by those from other Member States.

According to settled case law, the aims of [Article 45 TFEU] would not be attained if, as a consequence of the exercise of their right to freedom of movement, workers were to lose the social security advantages guaranteed them by the legislation of one Member State, especially where those advantages represent the counterpart of contributions which they have paid. Such a consequence might discourage [Union] workers from exercising their right to freedom of movement and would therefore constitute an obstacle to that freedom.[74]

A residence requirement is often indirectly discriminatory because it "can be more easily met by national workers than by those from other Member States, since the latter workers above all, particularly in the case of unemployment or invalidity, tend to leave the country in which they were formerly employed to return to their countries of origin."[75]

Prohibition of restrictions

Discriminatory rules are the most obvious obstacles to mobility. If migrant workers do not have the same rights in a Member State as are enjoyed by nationals of that state, they face major impediments. But, after the Member States had started to gradually abolish discriminatory national measures, the Court started to encounter situations where worker mobility was impeded, despite the fact that national rules did neither overtly nor covertly differentiate on grounds of nationality. Such impediments often arise when the specific situation of mobile workers is not sufficiently taken into account by the national legislation. This has led the Court to essentially adapt the *Dassonville* formula for the field of workers, arguing that Article 45 TFEU prohibits rules that impede the freedom of movement for workers, even if they apply irrespective of their nationality.[76] This approach – which could be termed the "prohibition of restrictions" – was first adopted by the Court in the decision in *Bosman*.

---

74 *Ibid.*, para. 43.   75 *Ibid.*, para. 55.

76 Case C-190/98, *Graf* [2000] ECR I-493, para. 18; Case C-387/01, *Weigel* [2004] ECR I-4981, paras. 50–51; Case C-464/02, *Commission* v. *Denmark* [2005] ECR I-7929, para. 45; Case C-269/07, *Commission* v. *Germany* [2009] ECR I-7811, para. 107.

Case C-415/93, Bosman (1995)

Mr. Bosman was a Belgian football player, playing for the Belgian first division club, RC Liège. As the club wanted to reduce his salary to the minimum allowed, Mr. Bosman refused to sign for another season, and was subsequently put on the transfer list. US Dunkerque, a French second division club, wanted to engage him, but would have had to pay a very high compensation fee for training according to the rules of UEFA, the European governing body for professional football.

Does Article 45 TFEU preclude the application of rules laid down by sporting associations, under which a professional footballer who is a national of one Member State may not, on the expiry of his contract with a club, be employed by a club of another Member State unless the latter club has paid to the former a transfer, training or development fee?

Yes.

Provisions which preclude or deter a national of a Member State from leaving his or her country of origin in order to exercise the right to freedom of movement constitute an obstacle to that freedom even if they apply without regard to the nationality of the workers concerned. The Court held:

It is sufficient to note that, although the rules in issue in the main proceedings apply also to transfers between clubs belonging to different national associations within the same Member State and are similar to those governing transfers between clubs belonging to the same national association, they still directly affect players' access to the employment market in other Member States and are thus capable of impeding freedom of movement for workers.

The Court held that the Treaty freedoms

preclude measures which might place Community citizens at a disadvantage when they wish to pursue an economic activity in the territory of another Member State … In that context, nationals of Member States have in particular the right, which they derive directly from the Treaty, to leave their country of origin to enter the territory of another Member State and reside there in order there to pursue an economic activity … Provisions which preclude or deter a national of a Member State from leaving his country of origin in order to exercise his right to freedom of movement therefore constitute an obstacle to that freedom even if they apply without regard to the nationality of the workers concerned.[77]

The prohibition of restrictions is relevant in situations where the disadvantage to the mobile worker does not stem from the differential treatment of nationals and non-nationals, but from other factors:

---

77 *Bosman*, paras. 94 *et seq.*

- In the *taxation cases*, problems often arise because the specific situation of mobile workers (in particular, frontier workers) is not sufficiently taken into account (*Schumacker*, 1995).
- In *return cases*, workers return to their home country from employment abroad and find that they are put at a disadvantage in comparison to workers who have remained in the home country. This is the case, for example, if the time a worker is affiliated with a foreign social insurance is not taken into account in the calculation of benefits. While they are not discriminated against on the grounds of their nationality, they nonetheless face disadvantages because they have exercised their right to freedom of movement (*Öberg*, 2006).
- In the professional qualifications cases, mobile workers (irrespective of their nationality) are put at a disadvantage because the equivalence of their qualifications to the required national standards is not evaluated on the basis of a sufficiently flexible approach (*Bobadilla*, 1999).[78]

JUSTIFICATIONS

A measure that discriminates on the ground of nationality or otherwise restricts the free movement of workers can be justified if it is designed to achieve legitimate ends and fulfills the proportionality requirement. There are three types of justification: (1) the justifications of Article 45(3) TFEU dealing with public policy, security and health; (2) the public service exception of Article 45(4) TFEU; and (3) other justifications in the general interest developed in the Court's case law. The Court has routinely held limitations on the market freedoms have to be interpreted strictly (e.g. *Lawrie-Blum*, 1986). In *Rutili* (1975), the Court ruled that the scope of these exceptions cannot be determined unilaterally by each Member State without being subject to control by the institutions of the Union.[79]

Public policy, public security and public health

According to Article 45(3) TFEU, restrictions to the free movement of workers can be justified on grounds of public policy, public security or public health. The restrictions on mobility and residence are subject to the limitations laid out in the Citizenship Directive, as discussed above.

Public service exception

Article 45(4) TFEU states that the provisions on the free movement of workers shall not apply to employment in the public service. This concept does not simply refer to

---

78 Case C-234/97, *Bobadilla* [1999] ECR I-4773.   79 Case 36/75, *Rutili* [1975] ECR 1219, para. 27.

what the Member States consider to constitute their "public service"; rather, it has an autonomous meaning in EU law. According to the Court, the exception applies only to those fields of public service which are entrusted with the exercise of powers conferred by public law and with responsibility for safeguarding the general interests of the state.[80] The fact that certain services are performed by governmental bodies or public entities does not bring them under the public services exemption of Article 45(4) TFEU, as the Court held for example in *Commission* v. *Belgium – Public Services* (1982). In this case, the Commission brought an infringement procedure for failure to comply with Treaty obligations against Belgium, challenging various job advertisements made by the national railway company, the city of Brussels and other bodies, because they required Belgian nationality. The Commission considered this practice to be in conflict with the free movement of workers. The Court held that the exception of Article 45(4) TFEU applies only to those fields of public service which are entrusted with the exercise of powers conferred by public law and with responsibility for safeguarding the general interests of the state. In *Lawrie-Blum* (1986), a British national finished her studies at a German university and applied for the "*Vorbereitungsdienst*," a post-graduate training qualification necessary to become a teacher in Baden-Württemberg. She was refused admission to the training course on the ground of her nationality and appealed. Baden-Württemberg argued that a trainee teacher's work contributes toward the safeguarding of the general interest of the state, which encompasses education. The Court found that the job of a trainee teacher is not covered by the exception of Article 45(4) TFEU. The exception only covers posts "which involve direct or indirect participation in the exercise of powers conferred by public law and in the discharge of functions whose purpose is to safeguard the general interests of the state or of other public authorities and which therefore require a special relationship of allegiance to the state on the part of persons occupying them and reciprocity of rights and duties which form the foundation of the bond of nationality."[81]

Jobs that cannot be considered a public service within the meaning of Article 45(4) TFEU include:

- trainee locomotive drivers, loaders, plate-layers, shunters and unskilled workers on railways (*Commission* v. *Belgium – Public Services*, 1982);
- city employees such as plumbers, carpenters, electricians and gardeners (*Commission* v. *Belgium – Public Services*, 1982);
- nurses (*Commission* v. *France*, 1986);[82]
- teachers and teaching assistants (*ÖGB*, 2000; *Lawrie-Blum*, 1986);
- legal trainees in Germany ("*Rechtsreferererendariat*"), even when employed in the public sector (*Pesla*, 2009; *Kranemann*, 2005);[83]

---

80 Case 149/79, *Commission* v. *Belgium – Public Service* [1982] ECR 1845.   81 *Lawrie-Blum*, para. 27.
82 Case 307/84, *Commission* v. *France* [1986] ECR 1725.   83 Case C-345/08, *Pesla* [2009] ECR I-11677, para. 29.

- masters and chief mates on ships flying the flag of a Member State, unless the public powers conferred on these rights are in fact exercised on a regular basis by those holders and do not represent a very minor part of their activities (*Colegio de Oficiales de la Marina Mercante Espanola*, 2003);[84]
- jobs in public utility companies, such as water, electricity and gas companies (*Commission* v. *Belgium – Utility Providers*, 1996).[85]

Employment by a private natural or legal person, on the other hand, generally excludes the application of Article 45(4) TFEU, regardless of the duties of the employee.[86] Private security guards, for example, do not form part of the public service.[87] Article 45(4) TFEU allows for differential treatment on the ground of nationality in public service only as regards access to employment. Once non-citizens are employed in the public service, however, discrimination can no longer be justified under that provision (*Sotgiu*, 1974).[88]

Since the late 1980s, the Commission has increasingly been pushing against an expansive interpretation of the public services exception by the Member States.[89] According to the Commission, jobs in certain areas will usually come under the exception of Article 45(4) TFEU because they are generally seen as being in close connection with the exercise of public authority.[90] This includes the police, the armed service, tax authorities, the judiciary and the diplomatic corps. The Commission emphasized, however, that not all posts in these fields imply the exercise of public authority. This includes administrative and technical tasks or maintenance. The Commission held that posts in the following areas are usually not covered by the public service exception because they rarely consist of tasks involving the exercise of public authority: public utilities such as public transport, electricity and gas, airlines and shipping lines, post and telecommunication services, radio and television companies, public healthcare services, public educational establishments and civil research.

Commission v. *Greece* (2008) dealt with a Greek law that provided that the captain and the chief officer of ships sailing under Greek flag must be of Greek nationality.[91] Greece argued that captains and first officers were granted specific tasks related to the exercise of public power under Greek law, including the maintenance of order on the vessel, the right to coerce and punish offenders, notarial tasks and tasks covered by civil law. Additionally, even civilian vessels had an important role to play in case of a war, considering the great number of

---

84 Case C-405/01, *Colegio de Oficiales de la Marina Mercante Espanola* [2003] ECR I-10391, para. 44; see also Case C-47/02, *Anker* [2003] ECR I-10447.
85 Case C-173/94, *Commission* v. *Belgium* [1996] ECR I-3265.   86 *Pesla*, para. 29.
87 Case C-283/99, *Commission* v. *Italy – Private Security Guards* [2001] ECR I-4363.   88 *Sotgiu*, para. 6.
89 Freedom of movement of workers and access to employment in the public service of Member States – Commission action in respect of the application of Article 48(4) of the EEC Treaty, [1988] OJ C72/2.
90 Communication from the Commission, Free Movement of Workers – Achieving the full benefits and potential, COM(2002) 694 final, December 11, 2002.
91 Case C-460/08, *Commission* v. *Greece* [2009] ECR I-216; see also Case C-94/08, *Commission* v. *Spain* [2008] I-160; Case C-447/07, *Commission* v. *Italy* [2008] ECR I-160.

islands in Greece. The Court ruled, however, that captains exercise these functions only in very exceptional cases. Derogation under Article 45(4) TFEU can only be justified if public power is regularly exercised by the institution in question. Prior to this case, the Court had struck down similar rules in every other Member State in the Mediterranean.

Justification by overriding requirements of the general interest

While the Treaty explicitly mentions only the public policy, security, health and public service exceptions, modern states pass regulations in a much broader range of policy areas. As the scope of Article 45 TFEU is very extensive (catching all national regulations liable to hinder or make less attractive the exercise of free movement rights), the number of national measures that could at least potentially infringe upon the rights of workers is very considerable. The Court therefore has to strike a balance between the freedom of movement of workers on the one hand, and legitimate regulatory interests of the Member States – for example, in labor market regulation or social affairs – on the other. According to the Court's case law, indirectly discriminatory or restrictive national measures can be justified on overriding requirements of the general interest. These measures must conform to the proportionality requirement. What regulatory goals are considered to be important lies in the discretion of the Member States, subject to an appraisal by the Court attempting to strike a balance between the competing interests involved. A typical way of phrasing the task of the balancing exercise is the following quote from the decision in *ITC* (2007), which deals with the regulation of unemployment services in Germany:

[I]t must be pointed out that the Member States are required to choose measures likely to attain the objectives pursued in the field of employment. The Court has recognized that the Member States have a broad margin of discretion in exercising that power. In addition, encouragement of recruitment constitutes a legitimate aim of social policy . . . However, the broad margin of discretion which the Member States enjoy in matters of social policy may not have the effect of undermining the rights granted to individuals by the Treaty provisions in which their fundamental freedoms are enshrined.[92]

In *Anton Las* (2013), the Court had to deal with a requirement imposed by the Flemish community in Belgium that all employers established in that entity's territory had to draft cross-border employment contracts exclusively in the official language of that community.[93] Contracts that failed to follow this requirement were declared null and void. The Court held that "the objective of promoting and encouraging the use of Dutch, which is one of the official languages of the Kingdom of Belgium, constitutes a legitimate interest which, in principle, justifies a restriction on the obligations imposed by Article 45 TFEU."[94] However, as the

92 *ITC*, paras. 39–40.   93 Case C-202/11, *Anton Las* [2013] ECR I-00000.   94 *Ibid.*, para. 27.

parties to an employment contract do not necessarily have knowledge of the Dutch language, the requirement impairs free and informed consent among the parties. The Court suggested that allowing the parties to draft an authentic version of the contract in their language of choice alongside a contract in Dutch would constitute a less restrictive means that would nonetheless be appropriate for securing the objectives pursued by that legislation.

Legitimate objectives that may justify restrictive national measures recognized by the Court include the encouragement of recruitment (*ITC*, 2007),[95] the protection of workers (*Rush Portuguesa*, 1990),[96] avoiding disruption to the labor market (*Commission* v. *Luxembourg*, 2004),[97] combating illegal employment (*Commission* v. *France*, 2006)[98] and monitoring the employment and family situation of unemployed persons (*De Cuyper*, 2006).[99]

RIGHTS OF WORKERS: SECONDARY LAW AND CASE LAW

The general requirements of Article 45 TFEU – the prohibition of discrimination and of restrictions to the freedom of movement – are substantiated in secondary law and in the Court's case law. The most important secondary law sources for the rights of workers are Regulation 492/2011 (ex-Regulation 1612/68)[100] and the Citizenship Directive. In essence, Regulation 492/2011 spells out the general obligation of Member States to treat nationals and non-nationals equally in all aspects related to work. This obligation is to be understood broadly: the basic idea is that mobility necessitates equal treatment not only with regard to access to jobs in other Member States but in a broad number of social and other related fields as well. The Court essentially argues that migrant workers will likely be hindered in their right to mobility if they are not treated equally in all aspects affecting workers, including social issues, housing issues and access to representative organizations. In this section, we will discuss substantive rights of workers which are based either on secondary law, or on the Court's interpretation of Article 45 TFEU. Table 5.3 sets out an overview of the provisions of Regulation 492/2011.

The right to enter another Member State, to reside there and to leave

The free movement of natural persons – including those covered by Article 45 TFEU – is consolidated in one single act of secondary law, the Citizenship Directive (2004/38/EC) (see Chapter 4 above). Under certain circumstances, mobility

---

95 *ITC*, para. 39.   96 *Rush Portuguesa*, para. 18.

97 Case C-445/03, *Commission* v. *Luxembourg* [2004] ECR I-10191, para. 38.

98 Case C-255/04, *Commission* v. *France* [2006] ECR I-5251, para. 52.

99 Case C-406/04, *De Cuyper* [2006] ECR I-6947, para. 41.

100 Regulation 492/2011 of the European Parliament and of the Council of 5 April 2011 on freedom of movement for workers within the Union, [2011] OJ L141/1.

Provision	Subject-matter
Art. 1	Equal treatment in taking up employment
Art. 2	Right to exchange applications and offers of employment
Art. 3	Inapplicability of discriminatory or restrictive national provisions
Art. 4	Prohibition of quotas of Union citizens in undertakings
Art. 5	Equal treatment in regard to the assistance afforded to job seekers by employment offices
Art. 6	No discriminatory medical or vocational requirements
Art. 7(1)	Right to equal treatment, in particular as regards remuneration, dismissal and, should the worker become unemployed, reinstatement or re-employment
Art. 7(2)	Equal treatment in regard to social and tax advantages
Art. 7(3)	Equal access to training in vocational schools and training centers (this includes, according to the case law, universities)
Art. 7(4)	The prohibition of discriminatory clauses also applies to collective and individual agreements (thus, to private work contracts)
Art. 8	Equal treatment as regards membership in trade unions
Art. 9	Equal treatment as regards housing
Art. 10	Equal access of the children of workers to education
Arts. 11–34	Cooperation and coordination between Member States as regards the clearing of vacancies and employment within the EU

Table 5.3 Overview of the provisions of Regulation 492/2011

and residence rights may be based on other provisions as well – either directly on Article 45 TFEU (if the Citizenship Directive is not applicable) or on Regulation 492/2011, as was the case in the decision in *Nimco Hassan Ibrahim* (2010) and the similar case of *Teixeira* (2010).[101]

Case C-310/08, Nimco Hassan Ibrahim (2010)

Ms. Ibrahim was a Somali citizen married to a Danish citizen, Mr. Yusuf. Mr. Yusuf worked in the United Kingdom, and was joined by his wife and by their children, who are of Danish nationality. Mr. Yusuf ceased working and left the United Kingdom, while Ms. Ibrahim and her children stayed. The children went to school in the United Kingdom. Ms. Ibrahim did not work, and relied on social assistance; she also did not have comprehensive health coverage, and relied on the National

101 Case C-310/08, *Nimco Hassan Ibrahim* [2010] ECR I-1065.

Health Service (NHS). When she applied for housing assistance for her family, the UK authorities rejected her application, because Ms. Ibrahim could not be considered to be legally resident in the United Kingdom under EU law: Ms. Ibrahim was not employed and had neither sufficient resources nor comprehensive health coverage, making the Citizenship Directive inapplicable. She argued, however, that she had a right of residence deriving from Regulation 492/2011. Because she was the caregiver of children schooled in the United Kingdom, and the children's father is a Union citizen who had worked in the United Kingdom, she had a right of residence under Article 10 Regulation 492/2011 (ex-Article 12 Regulation 1612/68).

Does the mother of children of a worker schooled in the United Kingdom have a right of residence based on Article 10 Regulation 492/2011?

Yes.

Article 10 Regulation 492/2011 provides for the right of children of workers to equal treatment with regard to the host state's educational system. Once they have entered the educational system, they retain that right even if their parents subsequently lose the status of worker or divorce. The Court argued: "[W]here the children enjoy, under [Article 10 Regulation 492/2011], the right to continue their education in the host Member State although the parents who are their carers are at risk of losing their rights of residence, a refusal to allow those parents to remain in the host Member State during the period of their children's education might deprive those children of a right which has been granted to them by the legislature of the European Union."[102] The restrictions imposed by the Citizenship Directive (sufficient resources, health coverage) cannot limit the residence rights derived from Article 10 Regulation 492/2011. As the primary caregiver of children schooled in the United Kingdom on the basis of Article 10, Ms. Ibrahim has a right of residence that is not subject to the restrictions set up by the Citizenship Directive.

The Court held in *Alarape* (2013) that a parent's right of residence derived from that of a student covered by Article 10 Regulation 492/2011 (ex-Article 12 Regulation 1612/68) may continue even beyond the moment when the student has reached the age of majority "if that child remains in need of the presence and care of that parent in order to be able to continue and to complete his or her education."[103]

The right to leave the home state, and to return to the home state

The Court has ruled in *ITC* (2007) that "[n]ational provisions which preclude or deter a national of a Member State from leaving his country of origin in order to

---

102 *Ibid.*, para. 30; see also Case C-413/99, *Baumbast* [2002] ECR I-7091, para. 71.
103 Case C-529/11, *Alarape* [2013] ECR I-00000, para. 31; the Court held in *Czop* that Art. 10 Regulation 492/2011 applies only if the parents of the child relying on the provision have been employed at some point, whereas it does not apply if they have been self-employed. See Joined Cases C-147/11 and C-148/11, *Czop* [2012] ECR I-00000, paras. 31–33.

exercise his right to freedom of movement constitute an obstacle to that freedom even if they apply without regard to the nationality of the workers concerned."[104] Restrictive measures may emanate either from Member States or, as in *Olympique Lyonnais* (2010), from non-state entities that regulate employment in a collective manner.

Case C-325/08, Olympique Lyonnais (2010)

Olivier Bernard was a "*joueur espoir*" with the French football team, Olympique Lyonnais. These "*joueurs*" are young trainees with a professional football club. According to the "Chartre du football professional" – the collective agreement for football players in France – the club can require the "*joueur*" to sign a contract as a professional player upon expiry of the trainee contract, as the club has invested money into the training of the young player. However, Bernard refused, and signed with the English team, Newcastle United FC instead. Olympique Lyonnais sued Bernard for €53 000 in damages.

Does the obligation to sign the first professional contract with the club which provided the training conflict with Article 45 TFEU?

Yes.

The Court held:

Rules such as those at issue in the main proceedings, according to which a '*joueur espoir*', at the end of his training period, is required, under pain of being sued for damages, to sign a professional contract with the club which trained him are likely to discourage that player from exercising his right of free movement. Even though ... such rules do not formally prevent the player from signing a professional contract with a club in another Member State, it none the less makes the exercise of that right less attractive.[105]

However, "the objective of encouraging the recruitment and training of young players must be accepted as legitimate."[106] Accordingly, a system where the club that has trained young players receives compensation for its effort may, in principle, be justifiable. A compensation scheme like the one in question must ascertain, however, that the damages are calculated on the basis of the actual costs of the training.

The Court regularly holds that measures that make returning to the home state after employment abroad more difficult may also breach the obligations under the Treaty. Most of these cases concern social and tax advantages, as we will see below: national measures that put individuals at a disadvantage for the sole reason that they have exercised their right of mobility constitute an infringement of the right to free movement of workers. In *Eind* (2007), a Dutch national was employed

---

104 *ITC*, para. 33; *Bosman*, para. 96; *Terhoeve*, para. 39; *Graf*, para. 23.   105 *Olympique Lyonnais*, paras. 35–36.
106 *Ibid.*, para. 39.

in the United Kingdom, and was subsequently joined by his daughter, a Surinamese citizen, who arrived directly from Surinam. Both were granted residence rights under Regulation 1612/68 (now Regulation 492/2011). When Mr. Eind returned to the Netherlands, however, he suffered from ill health, was not working and had to rely on social assistance. Therefore, the Dutch authorities argued that he was not a worker under Union law, so that his daughter did not have a right to join him in the Netherlands. The Court dismissed the contention, considering that such a measure was liable to deter individuals from returning to their Member States of origin, thereby undermining the right to free movement.[107] The Court concluded that, "in circumstances such as those in the case before the referring court, Miss Eind has the right to install herself with her father, Mr. Eind, in the Netherlands, even if the latter is not economically active."[108]

Equal access to employment

Article 45(2) TFEU provides:

[The free movement of workers] shall entail the abolition of any discrimination based on nationality between workers of the Member States as regards employment, remuneration and other conditions of work and employment.

Article 1 Regulation 492/2011 explicitly reiterates the principle of nondiscrimination with regard to access to employment: "Any national of a Member State shall, irrespective of his place of residence, have the right to take up an activity as an employed person, and to pursue such activity, within the territory of another Member State in accordance with the provisions laid down by law, regulation or administrative action governing the employment of nationals of that State." This includes a prohibition of preferential treatment for nationals (Article 1(2) Regulation 492/2011), and of any restriction on employers and potential employees to exchange job offers and applications (Article 2 Regulation 492/2011). Article 3 Regulation 492/2011 declares national laws inapplicable that limit application for and offers of employment, the rights of non-nationals to take up work, special recruitment procedures for non-nationals, a limitation of advertising vacancies to the territory of the Member State, etc. Article 3 Regulation 492/2011 prohibits direct and indirect discrimination, holding that national laws are inapplicable if, "though applicable irrespective of nationality, their exclusive or principal aim or effect is to keep nationals of other Member States away from the employment offered." Article 4 Regulation 492/2011 prohibits any kind of quota on EU citizens. A national of a Member State who seeks employment in the territory of another Member State shall receive the same assistance there as that afforded by the employment offices in that state to their own nationals seeking employment (Article 5 Regulation 492/2011).

107 Case C-291/05, *Eind* [2007] ECR I-10719, paras. 35–37.   108 *Ibid.*, para. 38.

Article 3 Regulation 492/2011 contains an exception with regard to language skills, as the provisions "shall not apply to conditions relating to linguistic knowledge required by reason of the nature of the post to be filled." Such exemption was the issue in *Groener*.

Case 379/87, Groener v. Ministry of Education (1989)

Ms. Groener, a Dutch national, sought employment as an arts teacher in Ireland. For this reason, she had to pass an Irish language test, which she failed. She instituted proceedings against the Ministry of Education, claiming that the requirement was contrary to Article 45 TFEU and to Regulation 492/2011.

Can the requirement for a teacher to know the Irish language be justified, although such knowledge is not required to fulfill the duties attached to the job?

Yes.

An Irish language requirement constitutes an indirect discrimination, as it is more likely to be met by Irish than by non-Irish citizens. However, such measure can be justified if it is designed to achieve legitimate ends and is both necessary and appropriate for that purpose. Union law does not preclude a Member State from adopting measures to promote the national language. Because teachers also play a role in the daily life of the school and its students, knowledge of the Irish language is required by reason of the nature of the post.

Equal treatment in employment

A worker may not be treated differently by reason of his nationality with respect to any conditions of employment and work, in particular as regards remuneration, dismissal, reinstatement or re-employment (Article 7(1) Regulation 492/2011).[109] An early case in this regard was *Südmilch AG* v. *Ugliola* (1969). A German law stipulated that a worker who interrupted his employment for the purpose of military service was entitled to have the time spent in the military service taken into account in calculating his seniority. This rule applied only to German nationals. The Court found that a law intended to protect a worker from the disadvantages caused by his absence due to military service falls within the context of conditions of work and employment, and therefore falls within the provisions of the equal treatment of migrant workers of Regulation 492/2011. The national law on time spent in the military needs to be applied equally to nationals and to EU migrant workers.

As we have already seen, the equal treatment requirement of Article 45 TFEU extends also to collective and even individual agreements. Article 7(4) Regulation 492/2011 provides:

---

109 Case C-276/07, *Delay* [2008] ECR I-3635.

Any clause of a collective or individual agreement or of any other collective regulation concerning eligibility for employment, remuneration and other conditions of work or dismissal shall be null and void in so far as it lays down or authorises discriminatory conditions in respect of workers who are nationals of the other Member States.

Accordingly, the Court applies an expansive interpretation of the scope of Article 45 TFEU, arguing that it applies to all rules aimed at regulating gainful employment in a collective manner (*Bosman*, 1995; *Olympique Lyonnais*, 2010).[110]

Case C-15/96, Schönig-Kougebetopoulou v. Freie und Hansestadt Hamburg (1998)

Ms. Schönig-Kougebetopoulou, a Greek national, was employed as a specialist doctor by the city of Hamburg. Pursuant to the applicable collective agreement ("BAT") specialist doctors would be promoted after eight years of practice under the BAT. The BAT covered many, but not all, hospitals in Germany. Ms. Schönig-Kougebetopoulou had served for a number of years as a doctor in Greek public service. However, this period was not taken into account in calculating her seniority, as she had not been employed in a hospital covered by the BAT. Germany argued that even employment performed in Germany, but not under the BAT, was not taken into account for the purpose of promotion; thus, this clause would not be discriminatory on the ground of nationality.

Does Union law preclude a clause in a collective agreement that does not take into account the time spent in a similar employment in another Member State?

Yes.

The BAT applies to a large number of specialist doctors in Germany, not only to those employed by the city of Hamburg. By contrast, it does not cover any hospitals outside of Germany. According to the Court, "the conditions for promotion on grounds of seniority laid down in the BAT ... manifestly work to the detriment of migrant workers who have spent part of their careers in the public service of another Member State."[111] While the rule is worded neutrally, it nevertheless privileges Germans over non-Germans because the conditions for promotion are harder to fulfill for the latter, as they are more likely to have gained prior work experience in hospitals outside of Germany not covered by the BAT.

A number of cases deal with language assistants employed by universities. They often received contracts for only limited periods of time (*Delay*, 2008, *Allué*, 1993;

---

110 *Olympique Lyonnais*, para. 30.   111 Case C-15/96, *Schöning-Kougebetopoulou* [1998] ECR I-47, para. 23.

Spotti, 1993).[112] The Court held that Union law does not *per se* prevent universities from employing assistants for fixed periods, if the need for such arrangement can be objectively justified. This, however, is not the case when contracts with teachers other than language assistants are regularly concluded for indeterminate periods of time.

Article 45 TFEU and Article 7(1) Regulation. 492/2011 preclude periods of employment, in a comparable field of activity, completed by one of those workers in one Member State from not being taken into account by the administration of another Member State in the determination of conditions of employment, such as remuneration, grade or promotion prospects, whereas experience gained in the civil service of the second state would be taken into account.[113] In *Greek Orchestras* (1998), Greek authorities refused to take into account a musician's employment with the Nice municipal orchestra in France for the purpose of his grading on the salary scale and the award of additional seniority, whereas that period would have been taken into account if it had been served in a municipal orchestra in Greece.[114] According to the Court, this contravened the principle of nondiscrimination enshrined in Article 45 TFEU and Article 7(1) Regulation 492/2011.[115] Similarly, the Court found in the *Italian Civil Service* case (2006) that the failure to take into account the professional experience or seniority gained in a comparable activity within the public administration of another Member State contravened the freedom of movement of workers.[116]

Equal treatment with regard to social advantages

Article 7(2) Regulation 492/2011 provides that workers from other Member States "shall enjoy the same social and tax advantages as national workers." Social advantages are to be understood as all advantages which, whether or not linked to a contract of employment, are generally granted to national workers because of their objective status as workers or by virtue of the mere fact of their residence on the national territory, and whose extension to workers who are nationals of other Member States therefore seems likely to facilitate their mobility within the EU (e.g. *Even*, 1979).[117] This includes, for example, a child-raising allowance (*Öberg*, 2006)[118] or reinstatement and re-employment measures in case the worker becomes unemployed (Article 7(1) Regulation 492/2011). The Court held that Article 7(2) "is the particular expression, in the specific area of the grant of social advantages, of the principle of equal treatment enshrined in Article 45(2) TFEU, and must be accorded

112 Joined Cases C-259/91, C-331/91 and C-332/91, *Allué* [1993] ECR I-4309; Case C-272/92, *Spotti* [1993] ECR I-05185.
113 Case C-371/04, *Commission v. Italy – Italian Civil Service* [2006] ECR I-10257, para. 12.
114 Case C-187/96, *Commission v. Greece – Greek Orchestra* [1998] ECR I-1095.   115 *Ibid.*, para. 21.
116 Case C-371/04, *Commission v. Italy – Italian Civil Service* [2006] ECR I-10257, para. 12.
117 Case 207/78, *Even* [1979] ECR 2019, para. 22; Case C-213/05, *Wendy Geven* [2007] ECR I-6347, para. 12.
118 Case C-185/04, *Öberg* [2006] ECR I-1453; Case C-85/96, *Martínez Sala* [1998] ECR I-2691, para. 26.

the same interpretation as that provision" (*Giersch*, 2013).[119] Family members have been entitled to invoke this provision, provided the advantage is of some benefit to the worker as well (*Lebon*, 1987). There must be at least some connection of the social advantage to the goal of promoting labor mobility. The Court employs a broad interpretation of the concept of social advantage. The concept of social advantage in Article 7(2) covers virtually all types of social benefits, not just those that are closely connected to employment. The concept of social advantage includes, as the Court held in *Reina* (1982), "not only the benefits accorded by virtue of a right but also those granted on a discretionary basis."[120] It includes social benefits for dependent family members, as the Court held in *Inzirillo*.[121]

Case 63/76, Inzirillo (1976)

An Italian national employed in France, residing there with his disabled adult son, was denied an allowance for disabled adults.

Does national legislation granting an allowance for disabled adults also apply to a citizen from another Member State who has never worked in this state but is dependent on his working father?

Yes.

If the host state does not provide protection for an adult disabled child, a migrant worker would be induced not to remain in this state. This would run counter to the objectives of the free movement of workers. According to the Court, the equality of treatment cannot end when the son ceases to be a minor, if the child by reason of his disability is himself prevented from acquiring the status of employed person. The Court held that "[i]n the light of the equality of treatment which Regulation [492/2011] seeks to bring about and taking account of the provisions of that Regulation as a whole, the matters covered by Art. 7(2) must be defined in such a way as to include every social and tax advantage, whether or not linked to a contract of employment, such as an allowance for disabled adults provided by a Member State to its own nationals."[122]

Whereas workers have the right of equal access to virtually all social benefits, some remain excluded. For example benefits that are based on primarily military considerations or considerations based on national loyalty do not constitute social advantages within the meaning of Article 7(2), as the Court held for example in *Even*.

---

119 Case C-20/12, *Giersch* [2013] ECR I-00000, para. 35.   120 Case 65/81, *Reina* [1982] ECR 33, para. 17.
121 Case 63/76, *Inzirillo* [1976] ECR 2057.   122 *Ibid.*, para. 21.

Case 207/78, Ministère Public v. Even (1979)

Mr. Even, a French worker, received an early retirement pension in Belgium. For every year of retirement before the normal retirement age of sixty-five, 5 percent of the pension was deducted. Only Belgian nationals receiving a Second World War invalidity pension paid by an Allied nation were granted early retirement without reduction. Mr. Even had served in the French army and was the recipient of a French invalidity pension.

Is this benefit a social advantage within the meaning of Article 7(2) Regulation 492/ 2011?

No.

Social advantages within the meaning of Article 7(2) are those which are generally granted to national workers primarily because of their objective status as workers or residents. The aim of the national legislation in question is to give nationals a social benefit by reason of the hardships suffered for that country. It is not primarily granted because of the status of worker or resident. Therefore, the social advantage in question is not covered by Article 7(2).

In *De Vos* (1996), the Court dealt with a German measure according to which German nationals serving in the military are entitled to have payments of the contributions to the supplementary old-age and survivors' pension scheme for workers in the public service continued, while non-nationals do not.[123] To the Court, however, the differential treatment is not prohibited under Union law because it serves as partial compensation for any detriment suffered as a result of their obligation to perform military service, and constitutes no social advantage. In *Hartmann* (2007),[124] a German citizen worked in Germany while residing in Austria. His spouse, an Austrian citizen, and the children had never lived in Germany. The Court ruled that, as a frontier worker, he is covered by Article 7(2) Regulation 492/2011, and therefore his spouse may apply for a German child-raising allowance. In *Wendy Geven* (2007), decided the same day as *Hartmann*, however, the Court declared that a Member State may exclude those frontier workers from receiving a child-raising allowance who merely are in minor employ-ment (in this case, between three and fourteen hours a week) and have never had permanent or ordinary residence in that state.

The case of *Giersch* (2013) dealt with residence-based restrictions on financial aid for students.[125] According to Luxembourg law, students resident in Luxembourg received financial aid regardless of nationality. The measure was challenged on the basis of Article 7(2) Regulation 1612/68 (now Regulation 492/2011), which requires equal

---

123　Case C-315/94, *De Vos* [1996] ECR I-1417.　　124　Case C-212/05, *Hartmann* [2007] ECR I-6303.
125　Case C-20/12, *Giersch* [2013] ECR I-00000.

treatment with regard to social advantages. The plaintiffs were children of frontier workers employed in Luxembourg, who, however, were not entitled to receive student aid because they had not resided in Luxembourg. The Court found the residence requirement to be indirectly discriminatory. Luxembourg sought to justify the measure as a means of "increasing the proportion of residents with a higher education degree in order to promote the development of the economy." The Court not only accepted this as a legitimate objective apt to justify differential treatment, but also recognized that a residence requirement could be an appropriate instrument to achieve that goal. We have seen that, in *Bidar* (2005), the Court had held that a Member State may reserve student aid to individuals with a sufficiently close connection to that Member State. However, the Luxembourg measure failed the necessity test because it employed residency as the sole indicator of such connection. As the measure does not take into account the situation of the children of frontier workers who do not reside in Luxembourg, the measure fails the least-restrictive-means requirement. According to the Court, the measure "precludes the taking into account of other elements potentially representative of the actual degree of attachment of the applicant for the financial aid with the society or with the labour market of the Member State concerned, such as the fact that one of the parents, who continues to support the student, is a frontier worker who has stable employment in that Member State and has already worked there for a significant period of time."[126]

In *L. N.* (2013), the Court had to deal with the situation of a European citizen employed in Denmark who was denied education assistance because, as the Danish authorities suspected, L. N. had entered Denmark for the sole purpose of taking up studies there.[127] The individual had applied to the Copenhagen Business School prior to March 2009, entered Denmark in June 2009 and took up employment on a full-time basis with an international wholesale firm later that month. L. N. was issued a certificate of registration as a worker by the Danish authorities at the end of the month. In August 2009, L. N. applied for education assistance, and began studies in September. The individual then resigned from the full-time job, and took up other part-time employment. As L. N. had entered the country solely for the purpose of studying, the Danish government argued that the person could not be considered to be a "worker" within the meaning of the Treaty, so that L. N. could not claim equal treatment with regard to the education assistance by reference to Article 7(2) Regulation 492/2011. The Court responded, however, that the concept of "worker" has an autonomous meaning specific to EU law. Whether L. N. must be considered to be a "worker" depends on whether the person has pursued effective and genuine employment activities. Whether the individual has entered an employment relationship with the intention of getting access to education

---

126 *Ibid.*, para. 83; see also Joined Cases C-523/11 and C-585/11, *Prinz* [2013] ECR I-00000; Case C-542/09, *Commission* v. *Netherlands – Three-Out-of-Six-Years Rule* [2012] ECR I-00000; Case C-75/11, *Commission* v. *Austria – Reduced Public Transport Fares* [2012] ECR I-00000.

127 Case C-46/12, *L. N.* [2013] ECR I-00000.

assistance, on the other hand, must not be taken into consideration.[128] Assuming that L. N. was in fact engaged in effective and genuine employment activities, the individual can in fact rely on the equal treatment requirement of Article 7(2) with regard to social advantages.

Examples of benefits considered to be "social advantages" include: student grants (*L. N.*, 2013), rehabilitation measures for disabled workers (*Michel*, 1973),[129] allowances for disabled adults who are dependents of the worker (*Inzirillo*, 1976), separation allowance granted to workers allocated to posts away from their place of residence (*Sotgiu*, 1974), reduced fare train tickets for large families (*Cristini*, 1975),[130] an old-age allowance for the mother of a worker who is a dependent (*Frascogna*, 1987),[131] interest-free loans granted on childbirth to low-income families with a view to stimulating the birth rate (*Reina*, 1982), social assistance (*Hoeckx*, 1985)[132] and parental benefits (*Öberg*, 2006).

The Court has interpreted the concept of "social advantage" in such a way that it does not merely include social benefits in a narrow sense, but all types of rights that facilitate integration in the host state's society. In *Reed* (1986), the Court ruled that a refusal to grant residence rights to the unmarried partner of a worker constitutes unequal treatment with regard to social advantages. As unmarried partners were not treated as "family members" under the old Regulation 1612/68 and therefore had no residence rights, the Court chose this other route, defining the right to be accompanied by the partner as a social advantage within the meaning of Article 7(2). This decision retains some importance today: according to Article 2(2) Citizenship Directive, only spouses and registered partners equivalent to marriage are considered "family members," whereas unmarried partners still are not.[133]

Other examples of a broad interpretation of the term of "social advantages" include:

- the right to have criminal proceedings conducted in a language other than the language normally used in proceedings if workers who are nationals of the host Member State have that right in the same circumstances (*Mutsch*, 1985);[134]
- protection against dismissal (*Marsman*, 1972);[135]
- a funeral payment to cover the cost incurred on the occasion of a death in the family (*O'Flynn*, 1996).[136]

These decisions, reflecting a very broad interpretation, may appear to be stretching the concept of "social advantages" beyond the limit of the term's literal meaning. This may be explained by reason of the Court's tendency to read the provisions on the free movement of persons functionally, aimed at establishing a general principle of equal treatment between nationals and non-nationals. Article 7 Regulation

---

128 *Ibid.*, para. 47.   129 Case 76/72, *Michel* [1973] ECR 457.
130 Case 32/75, *Cristini* [1975] ECR 1085, para. 19.
131 Joined Cases 157/84 and 256/86, *Frascogna* [1987] ECR 1739.   132 Case 249/83, *Hoeckx* [1985] ECR 973.
133 See, however, C-356/98, *Arben Kaba* v. *Secretary of State for the Home Department* [2000] ECR I-2623.
134 Case 137/84, *Mutsch* [1985] ECR 2681, para. 18.   135 Case 44/72, *Marsman* [1972] ECR 1243.
136 Case C-237/94, *O'Flynn* [1996] ECR I-2617.

492/2011 is also intended to protect children of workers, as the Court has held for example in *Meeusen* (1999): "Those descendants can thus rely on Article 7(2) in order to obtain study finance under the same conditions as are applicable to children of national workers"[137] (see below).

In cases where Regulation 492/2011 does not apply, the equal treatment requirement with regard to social advantages may derive directly from Article 45 TFEU. In *Radziejewski* (2012), for example, the Court found that Swedish legislation granting debt relief solely to persons who are resident in Sweden constituted an infringement of Article 45 TFEU.[138]

Social benefits related to unemployment

According to Article 4 Regulation 883/2004 on the coordination of social security systems, workers enjoy the same benefits, including unemployment benefits, and are subject to the same obligations under the legislation of any Member State as the nationals thereof. This means that workers from other Member States can claim unemployment benefits under the same conditions as workers who are nationals of that Member State. Moreover, Member States must take into account periods of insurance completed in other Member States as though they were completed under its own legislation (Article 61(1) Regulation 883/2004). Measures that subject workers from other Member States to different conditions for claiming unemployment benefits than domestic workers are prohibited, as the Court held for example in *Chateignier* (2006). In that case, under Belgian legislation, workers from other Member States had to complete at least a day's work in Belgium before they could claim unemployment benefits, whereas Belgian nationals were not subject to the same condition. The Court found that the principle of equal treatment of Article 4 Regulation 883/2004 and Article 45 TFEU precludes national legislation that subjects citizens from other Member States who claim unemployment benefits to the condition of completing a specified period of employment in Belgium if there is no such requirement for Belgian nationals. The right of equal treatment applies not only to benefits from contributory unemployment systems (i.e. when claims are based on the completion of prior periods of employment), but also to other benefits for job-seekers, which are often means-based and which require beneficiaries to be actively seeking work (e.g. the *Arbeitslosengeld II* (known as "Hartz IV") in Germany and the contribution-based job-seeker's allowance in the United Kingdom). The Court has held that benefits of a financial nature intended to facilitate access to employment in the labor market of a Member State are subject to the equal treatment requirement (*Vatsouras*, 2009).[139] However, Member States can limit access to such benefits under certain conditions (see below).

137 Case C-337/97, *Meeusen* [1999] ECR I-3289, para. 22.
138 Case C-461/11, *Radziejewski* [2012] ECR I-00000.
139 *Vatsouras*, para. 37. See also *Collins*, para. 63, and *Ioannidis*, para. 22.

Employing Article 7(2) against the home state

The previous cases mostly dealt with situations where a worker demands equal treatment by the host state. However, the provision applies equally to situations where mobile citizens return to their home state and face disadvantages because they have exercised their mobility rights. In *Öberg* (2006), the Court held that "provisions which preclude or deter a national of a Member State from leaving his country of origin to exercise his right to freedom of movement constitute an obstacle to that freedom even if they apply without regard to the nationality of the workers concerned."[140] A similar situation arose in the decision in *Bergström* (2011).

Case C-257/10, Bergström (2011)

According to the 1999 Agreement between the EU and Switzerland,[141] the free movement of persons essentially extends to Switzerland. The Preamble to the Agreement provides that the EU and Switzerland are "[r]esolved to bring about the free movement of persons between them on the basis of the rules applying in the European Community." This objective implies, *inter alia*, the application of the Regulation on the coordination of social security systems.[142] Ms. Bergström, a Swedish national, worked and resided in Switzerland between 1994 and 2002, when she moved back to Sweden with her husband and gave birth to her daughter. In Sweden, she remained unemployed in order to take care of her daughter and applied for parental benefit. The Swedish authority awarded her only the basic parental benefit, determining her to be ineligible for the more extensive, income-based benefits, as she had not been employed in Sweden for the 240 days prior to the birth.[143]

Must the time spent in employment in Switzerland be recognized for the calculation of the Swedish parental benefit?

Yes.

The free movement of persons between the EU and Switzerland would be impeded "if a national of a Contracting Party were to be placed at a disadvantage in his country of origin solely for having exercised his right of movement."[144] The EU Regulation on the coordination of social security systems (referred to by the agreement between Switzerland and the EU) contains the principle of aggregation: the time period spent under the social security system of one state is relevant for the calculation of benefits in other Member States as well. Consequently, the Swedish insurance must take the periods completed in Switzerland into account for the calculation of the parental benefit.

---

140 *Öberg*, para. 15.
141 Agreement between the European Community and its Member States, of the one part, and the Swiss Confederation, of the other, on the free movement of persons, signed at Luxembourg on June 21, 1999, [2002] OJ L114/6.
142 Regulation 883/2004 (ex-Regulation 1408/71) on the coordination of social security systems.
143 Case C-257/10, *Bergström* [2011] ECR I-00000.   144 *Bergström*, para. 28.

Limitations to the principle of equal treatment with regard to social advantages

Article 24(2) Citizenship Directive holds that Member States are not obliged to grant social assistance for the first three months of residence or for the time a Union citizen first seeks employment in the host state. If the benefit in question is intended to facilitate access to the labor market, then it does not constitute "social assistance" within the meaning of the Citizenship Directive. This means that job-seekers cannot generally be excluded from social benefits.[145] As shown above, however, the Court has acknowledged, that Member States can limit entitlements to such benefits to those job-seekers who have a "real link" to the labor market of that state (*D'Hoop*, 2002). In *Collins* (2004), an Irish-American individual had resided in the United Kingdom in 1980–1981, doing part time work and "casual work" in pubs and in sales.[146] He returned to the United Kingdom in 1998, claiming a job-seeker's allowance (a noncontributory benefit). The Court held that Mr. Collins had lost his status as a worker during his seventeen years of absence, having no right to receive the job-seeker's allowance: "In the absence of a sufficiently close connection with the United Kingdom employment market, Mr. Collins' position in 1998 must therefore be compared with that of any national of a Member State looking for his first job in another Member State."[147] This approach resembles the Court's reasoning in the student mobility cases of *Grzelczyk* (2001) and *Bidar* (2005), where the Court found that a "genuine link" of a student to the society of the host state constituted the basis for a right to equal treatment as regards certain social benefits. A requirement for a minimum period of residence may be a suitable tool to establish whether a sufficiently close link between the job-seeker and the host state's labor market exists; however, it is up to the host state to show that such condition is proportionate.[148]

In *Ioannidis* (2005), the Court again dealt with the Belgian tideover allowance (as in the earlier case *D'Hoop*, 2002), which was granted to graduates seeking their first employment. The measure was restricted to individuals who had completed their secondary education in a Belgian institution. Mr. Ioannidis had completed his secondary education in Greece, and had only subsequently studied in Belgium. This condition – which is more easily met by Belgians than by non-Belgian nationals – constituted a restriction of Article 45 TFEU. The Court held that it is a legitimate concern to grant social benefits only to individuals who have a certain link to the Member State: "[I]t is legitimate for the national legislature to wish to ensure that there is a real link between the applicant for that allowance and the geographic employment market concerned."[149] However, the place of completion of the secondary education is a too constricted condition; the difference in treatment was therefore not justified. In *Prete* (2012), the Court held that a precondition for receiving the tideover allowance of having completed six years of

---

145 *Vatsouras*, para. 45.   146 *Collins*, para. 18.   147 *Ibid.*, para. 29.
148 *Vatsouras*, Opinion of Advocate General Colomer, para. 49; *Trojani*, paras. 42–45.
149 *Ioannidis*, para. 30; see also *D'Hoop*, para. 38.

secondary education in a Belgian educational establishment also fails to meet the requirements of the proportionality test.[150] The case concerned a French national who had completed her education in France, and subsequently married a Belgian national and moved to Belgium. By focusing exclusively on the period spent in the Belgian education system, the measure failed to acknowledge other possible links of the claimant to Belgian society.[151]

The Court has routinely held that – while social benefits may be limited to individuals with a sufficient link to the society of the Member State in question – migrant workers and frontier workers must generally be considered to have such sufficient link because they have participated in the employment market of that state.[152] In *Caves Krier Frères* (2012), the Court found that a Luxembourg measure infringed Article 45 TFEU which made the grant to employers of a subsidy for the recruitment of unemployed persons aged over forty-five years subject to the condition that the unemployed person recruited had been registered as a job-seeker in that same Member State, in the case where such registration is subject to a condition of residence in the national territory.[153] A residence requirement must be considered "inappropriate as regards migrant workers and frontier workers" because workers have a "sufficient link of integration with the society" of the host state: "The link of integration arises, in particular, from the fact that, through the taxes which they pay in the host Member State by virtue of their employment there, migrant and frontier workers also contribute to the financing of the social policies of that State."[154]

According to Regulation 883/2004, certain social benefits (which are explicitly listed in the Regulation) can be limited to residents, "in particular as regards special benefits linked to the economic and social context of the person involved."[155] In *Hendrix* (2007), the Netherlands paid a benefit for young people who suffered from long-term full or partial incapacity for work before joining the labor force. It was restricted to individuals who resided in the Netherlands. Mr. Hendrix, who moved to Belgium while remaining employed in the Netherlands, lost his benefit. The Court found that such a limitation is justified because it concerns a benefit where Regulation 883/2004 explicitly allows for a residence requirement.[156]

Equal treatment with regard to tax advantages

Article 7(2) Regulation 492/2011 holds that migrant workers from other Member States shall enjoy the same tax advantages as national workers.[157] The case law mostly concerns direct taxation, particularly income tax. In practice, migrant workers

150 Case C-367/11, *Prete* [2012] ECR I-00000, para. 52.   151 *Ibid.*, paras. 50–51.
152 Case C-379/11, *Caves Krier Frères* [2012] ECR I-00000, para. 53.   153 *Ibid.*, para. 55.
154 *Ibid.*, para. 53.   155 Regulation 883/2004, Preamble, recital 16.   156 *Hendrix*, para. 52.
157 See e.g. Case C-544/11, *Petersen* [2013] ECR I-00000.

tend to face two types of disadvantages with regard to taxation. First, migrant workers – and in particular frontier workers who work and reside in different Member States – may face disadvantages because a tax benefit is conditional on a residence requirement. Second, migrant workers may face difficulties because the peculiarity of their transnational situation is taken into account in neither the state of employment nor the state of residence. The decision in *Schumacker* (1995) exemplifies both problems.

Case C-279/93, Schumacker (1995)

Germany established a beneficial tax regime for married couples, the so-called "splitting" procedure. According to this procedure, the income of both spouses is aggregated, and each spouse is attributed half of the aggregated income for the purpose of calculating income tax. Income tax is progressive, which means that high incomes are subject to a higher tax rate than lower incomes. If one spouse earns considerably more than the other, the "splitting" procedure has the effect that the overall income tax burden for the couple is lower. Whereas permanent residents are subject to income tax in Germany with their full income ("unlimited taxation"), nonresidents are subject to the same tax only on that part of their income arising in Germany ("limited taxation"). The "splitting" procedure is available only if both spouses are permanent residents in Germany and thereby subject to unlimited taxation. Mr. Schumacker, a Belgian national, worked in Germany, but resided with his family in Belgium. Accordingly, Mr. Schumacker could not request to be taxed according to the "splitting" procedure. As a resident, Mr. Schumacker's total income was subject to unlimited taxation in Belgium, with the exception of the income already taxed in Germany. However, as Mr. Schumacker received no significant additional income in Belgium and therefore was not subject to any significant taxation there, Belgium was not in a position to grant him the benefits resulting from the taking into account of his personal and family circumstances.

Is a provision under which a non-resident worker is subject to higher taxation than a resident worker contrary to Article 45 TFEU if he receives most of his income in that state?

Yes.

According to the Court, "[t]he situation of a resident is different in so far as the major part of his income is normally concentrated in the State of residence. Moreover, that State generally has available all the information needed to assess the taxpayer's overall ability to pay, taking account of his personal and family circumstances."[158] Consequently, the Court held, "the fact that a Member State does not grant to a

---

158 Case C-279/93, *Schumacker* [1995] ECR I-225, para. 33.

non-resident certain tax benefits which it grants to a resident is not, as a rule, discriminatory since those two categories of taxpayer are not in a comparable situation."[159] However, the situation is different "in a case such as this one where the non-resident receives no significant income in the State of his residence and obtains the major part of his taxable income from an activity performed in the State of employment, with the result that the State of his residence is not in a position to grant him the benefits resulting from the taking into account of his personal and family circumstances."[160] In such a situation, "[t]here is no objective difference between the situations of such a non-resident and a resident engaged in comparable employment, such as to justify different treatment as regards the taking into account for taxation purposes of the taxpayer's personal and family circumstances."[161] Accordingly, differential treatment constitutes a restriction of Article 45 TFEU.

Member States insisted, however, that differential treatment of residents and non-residents should not generally be considered to exhibit illicit motives. Residents and non-residents may in fact be in objectively different situations, which would justify differential treatment. In reviewing its own case law in *Turpeinen* (2006), the Court agreed, holding that, "in relation to direct taxes, the Court has accepted that the situations of residents and of non-residents are not, as a rule, comparable."[162] A case where the Court in fact adopted such a position was *Gschwind* (1999). The case dealt again with the German "splitting" procedure. However, following the *Schumacker* (1995) decision, Germany had reformed its tax law, which now allowed resident as well as non-resident couples to apply for the "splitting" procedure if 90 percent of the family income was subject to taxation in Germany. Mr. Gschwind, a Dutch national, lived in the Netherlands, but worked in Germany. His wife was employed in the Netherlands. Mr. Gschwind could not apply for application of the "splitting" procedure as the wage he earned in Germany amounted to only 58 percent of the family income. Residence is usually the main factor for allocating powers of taxation in international tax conventions. The Court found that the reformed German tax provision was justifiable. The Gschwind family benefited from tax deductions similar to the "splitting" procedure in the Netherlands, as they had a sufficient tax base there. By contrast, in the *Schumacker* case, the family's income had derived entirely from Germany. Therefore, tax deductions would be lost for Mr. Schumacker if they were not taken into account for his German income. The fact that a Member State does not grant to a nonresident certain tax benefits which it grants to a resident is not, as a rule, discriminatory since, as regards direct taxation, those two categories of taxpayer are not in a comparable situation. Specifically, a nonresident married couple – one of whom works in the state of taxation in question and who may, owing to the existence of a sufficient tax base in the state of residence, have personal and family

---

159 *Ibid.*, para. 34.   160 *Ibid.*, para. 36.   161 *Ibid.*, para. 37.   162 *Turpeinen*, para. 26; *Schumacker*, para. 31.

circumstances taken into account by its tax authorities – is not in a situation comparable to that of a resident married couple, even if one of the spouses works in another Member State.

While the Court has held that, as a general rule, residents and nonresidents are considered to be in objectively different situations, it has held that states must treat nonresidents equally to residents if they receive almost all of their taxable income in that state. In *Renneberg* (2008), the Court emphasized this principle with regard to the case of an individual who resided in Belgium but earned almost all of his income in the Netherlands. The Court found that a tax rule is contrary to Article 45 TFEU if it prevents the worker from deducting negative income relating to a house owned and used by him in Belgium while it would authorize such deduction if the house were located within the Netherlands.

Disadvantages with regard to taxation may not only occur in the host Member State where migrant workers receive less beneficial treatment than nationals, but also in the home Member State that treats transnational situations worse than purely national ones (e.g. *Ritter-Coulais*, 2006). A German law that provided for a tax deduction for school fees only when the school was situated in Germany was found to conflict with the Treaty freedoms (*Schwarz and Gootjes-Schwarz*, 2007). In *Filipiak* (2009),[163] a Polish law granted the right to deduct expenses for health insurance from the taxable income, but only if these expenses were incurred in Poland. Krzysztof Filipiak was a Polish citizen paying taxes in Poland but working in the Netherlands. According to Dutch law, he had to pay health insurance there, but he did not have the right to deduct such payments from tax in Poland. The Court held that this constituted a breach of Article 45 TFEU. Many other taxation cases feature a similar structure: the Member State grants tax reductions only for domestic expenses, but not for similar expenses in other Member States. In *Lakebrink* (2007),[164] for example, Luxembourg granted tax reductions for negative rental income for property if it was situated in Luxembourg, but not if it was situated in another Member State. This was found to be contrary to Article 45 TFEU.

In the area of taxation, the Court is navigating in very difficult terrain. As direct taxation (unlike indirect taxation) is not harmonized in the EU, mobile individuals are confronted with very different tax systems in the various Member States. Some of the disadvantages that individuals face simply arise from these differences. In light of these differences, the Court opted for a strategy of relative restraint. In *Schulz-Delzers and Schulz* (2011), it argued that "the Treaty offers no guarantee to a citizen of the Union that transferring his activities to a Member State other than that in which he previously resided will be neutral as regards taxation. Given the relevant disparities in the tax legislation of the Member States, such a transfer may be to the citizen's advantage or not, according to circumstances."[165] Even double

---

163 Case C-314/08, *Filipiak* [2009] ECR I-11049.   164 Case C-182/06, *Lakebrink* [2007] ECR I-6705.
165 Case C-240/10, *Schulz-Delzers and Schulz* [2011] ECR I-8531, para. 42.

taxation of the same situation by two Member States does not always constitute a restriction of the Treaty freedoms, as the Court held in *Commission* v. *Hungary* (2011): "[I]n the current stage of the development of EU law, the Member States enjoy a certain autonomy in the area of taxation provided they comply with EU law, and are not obliged therefore to adapt their own tax systems to the different systems of tax of the other Member States in order, *inter alia*, to eliminate the double taxation."[166]

Another difficult situation that the Court faces is tax rules where certain tax benefits correspond with tax obligations. This was the situation in *Bachmann* (1992).[167] The Belgian case dealt with tax deductions for contributions to sickness and invalidity insurance. The individuals had the choice between two models:

- they could have the contributions deducted from the income tax *now* and then pay tax on the future benefits paid by the insurer *later*; or
- they could choose not to have the contributions deducted from tax *now* and then not pay tax on the future benefits paid by the insurer *later*.

The effect of this system was that payments to the insurance would be taxed only once, and the individual could opt whether the benefits *or* the contributions would be taxed. Mr. Bachmann, a German working in Belgium, had paid contributions for sickness and invalidity insurance in Germany, which he was not allowed to deduct from his occupational income in Belgium. As Belgium could not tax benefits paid at some point in the future to a German resident, it prohibited Mr. Bachmann from opting into the first model. The Court found that this restriction was justifiable: the benefit (not having the contributions deducted from the income) was only a corollary to a later tax obligation, and denying this option to Mr. Bachmann would be justified by the need to safeguard the "cohesion of the tax system." Mr. Bachmann was not deprived of a tax benefit; the Belgian measure merely ensured that the transaction would not evade taxation in Belgium completely. The justificatory ground of ensuring the "cohesion of the tax system" can only be invoked if a direct link between the tax advantage and the offsetting of that advantage by a particular tax levy can be established, as the Court held for example in *Commission* v. *Hungary* (2011).[168] Other public interest considerations that can potentially justify unequal treatment with regard to tax benefits include the preservation of the effectiveness of fiscal supervision (*Futura Participations*, 1997),[169] ensuring the effective collection of income tax (*Scorpio Konzertproduktionen*, 2006)[170] and preventing "wholly artificial arrangements aimed at circumventing the application of the legislation of the Member State concerned" (*Cadbury Schweppes*, 2006).[171]

---

166 Case C-253/09, *Commission* v. *Hungary* [2011] ECR I-00000, para. 83.
167 Case C-204/90, *Bachmann* [1992] ECR I-249.
168 Case C-253/09, *Commission* v. *Hungary* [2011] ECR I-00000, para. 72.
169 Case C-250/95, *Futura Participations* [1997] ECR I-2471, para. 31.
170 Case C-290/04, *Scorpio Konzertproduktionen* [2006] ECR I-9461, para. 35.
171 Case C-196/04, *Cadbury Schweppes* [2006] ECR I-4027, para. 51.

Educational rights

Article 7(3) Regulation 492/2011 provides that migrant workers have the same access to training in vocational schools and retraining centers – including universities – as workers who are citizens. On the basis of Article 7(2), workers also have a right to equal access to scholarships and financial assistance with regard to education. The Court found in *Matteucci* (1988) that an Italian national born and raised in Belgium who worked in Belgium as a music teacher cannot be refused a scholarship to study in Germany under a scheme that is based on a bilateral agreement between the countries and is open only to Belgian nationals.[172] In *Bernini* (1992),[173] the Court dealt with the case of an Italian national who grew up in the Netherlands, was employed there for ten weeks as a paid trainee, and subsequently enrolled in Naples, Italy, to study architecture. The Court ruled that Bernini enjoyed the same entitlement to financial assistance as Dutch nationals, provided the education had some relation to Bernini's previous occupation.

Rights after employment

Migrant workers retain their status as workers even when they are no longer in an employment relationship (Article 7(3) Citizenship Directive). Article 7(1) Regulation 492/2011 holds that the equal treatment requirement also applies to reinstatement or re-employment measures if the worker becomes unemployed. According to settled case law, individuals retain their status as workers with regard to access to vocational training and education maintenance grants if there is a relationship between the purpose of the studies and the previous occupational activity (*Lair*, 1988).[174] The same applies to beneficial provisions in retirement plans. The equal treatment provisions pertaining to the free movement of workers apply even to retired individuals. A retiree's pension is connected to the individual's previous status as a worker, and thus the pension provisions must not be directly or indirectly discriminatory (*Commission* v. *France*, 1998).[175] The worker status does not, however, remain indefinitely. In *Collins* (2004), the individual concerned – having dual US and Irish citizenship – had worked casually in bars and in sales in the United Kingdom for a ten-month period in 1981. He returned to the United Kingdom seventeen years later and demanded job-seeker's allowance according to Article 7(2) Regulation 492/2011. The Court decided that this interim period was too long for Mr. Collins to have retained his worker status.

---

172 Case 235/87, *Matteucci* [1988] ECR 5589.   173 Case C-3/90, *Bernini* [1992] ECR I-1071.
174 Case 39/86, *Lair* [1988] ECR 3161, para. 36.
175 Case C-35/97, *Commission* v. *France* [1998] ECR I-5325, para. 41.

Workers' families

Since the early days of the EEC, workers' families were granted considerable rights of equal treatment. Articles 10 and 11 Regulation 1612/68 (now repealed) granted the right of residence and employment to the spouse and dependent relatives in the descending and ascending line. Today, the Citizenship Directive (discussed in Chapter 4 above) grants extensive rights of equal treatment to family members of workers. Article 7(2) Citizenship Directive grants a right of residence to family members of Union citizens, and Article 23 grants them a right to take up employment or self-employment. This means, for example, equal access to the medical profession without additional administrative burdens, as the Court has held in *Gül* (1986), a case of a Turkish national married to a Union citizen.[176] Article 24 Citizenship Directive extends the general right of equal treatment to family members of Union citizens.

Article 10 of Regulation 492/2011 grants equal treatment to the children of workers to be admitted to the host state's educational system, including apprenticeship and vocational training courses, under the same conditions as the nationals of that state. This includes training, vocational rehabilitation and retraining of disabled individuals, as the Court held in *Michel* (1973). It also covers the right to equal treatment with regard to educational grants, as the Court held in *Di Leo* (1990).[177] Ms. Di Leo, an Italian citizen, was the daughter of an Italian worker employed in Germany. After finishing her primary and secondary education in Germany, she enrolled to study medicine in Siena, Italy. The German authorities refused to award her the educational grant BAFöG, which was granted for the attendance of courses outside Germany, but only to German nationals. The Court held that, according to Article 10 of Regulation 492/2011, children of migrant workers must be treated as nationals not only with regard to education in the host state, but also with regard to educational grants for education pursued in another Member State. Consequently, Ms. Di Leo had a right to equal treatment with regard to the BAFöG even when she studied in Italy, being an Italian national.

Article 7 Regulation 492/2011 is applicable to the family members of workers. The Court held in *Ioannidis* (2005): "According to settled case law, the principle of equal treatment laid down in Article 7 of Regulation No. [492/2011], which extends to all the advantages which, whether or not linked to a contract of employment, are generally granted to national workers primarily because of their objective status as workers or by virtue of the mere fact of their residence on the national territory, is also intended to prevent discrimination to the detriment of descendants dependent on the worker."[178] In *Deak* (1985), the Court ruled that the child of an Italian worker in Belgium who has not yet worked has a right to unemployment benefits under Article 7(2) Regulation 492/2011.

---

176 Case 131/85, *Gül* [1986] ECR 1573.   177 Case C-309/89, *Di Leo* [1990] ECR I-4185.   178 *Ioannidis*, para. 35.

IMPORTANT SECONDARY LAW

The right to free movement of workers within the Union laid down in Article 45 TFEU is implemented and further specified in secondary law. The most important piece of legislation in this regard is Regulation 492/2011 (ex-Regulation 1612/68), which we have already discussed extensively above, and the Citizenship Directive, discussed in Chapter 4 above. Other important pieces of legislation include the Regulation on the coordination of social security systems, the works council Directive and the health and safety Directives. In this chapter, we will provide a brief overview of a few of the most important acts. Article 46 TFEU is the legal basis for measures "required to bring about freedom of movement for workers" (Regulation 492/2011 and the Citizenship Directive are based on Article 46 TFEU), and Article 48 TFEU authorizes the European legislators to enact measures to coordinate the national social security systems. Other legislative acts relevant for worker mobility include Articles 165 and 166 TFEU for cooperation with regard to education. In principle, harmonizing measures can also be based on Articles 114 and 115 TFEU. However, harmonization on the basis of Article 114 TFEU – which requires only qualified majority in the Council – is precluded for provisions relating to the free movement of persons and to the rights and interests of employed persons (Article 114(2) TFEU).

Coordination of social security systems

If employed or self-employed persons move from one Member State to another, they move into a different social security system as well. Regulation 883/2004[179] provides a coordination mechanism between the different social security systems. According to its Preamble, the Regulation aims at guaranteeing "that persons moving within the Community and their dependants and survivors retain the rights and the advantages acquired and in the course of being acquired."[180] This means in particular that the time spent under one Member State's social security system are to be recognized for the calculation of benefits in other Member States as well. The legislation applicable to individuals is that of the Member State where they pursue employment or self-employment (Article 11).

The coordination of social security systems is governed by the following principles:

- The principle of the exportability of social security benefits.[181] This means that individuals are entitled to receive benefits from the Member State where they were

---

179 See also Regulation 987/2009 of the European Parliament and of the Council of 16 September 2009 laying down the procedure for implementing Regulation 883/2004 on the coordination of social security systems, [2009] L 284/1.
180 Regulation 883/2004, Preamble, recital 13.   181 *Ibid.*, recital 37.

acquired also in other Member States. Residence requirements are generally prohibited. This principle can be derogated from only with regard to specific, noncontributory benefits.

- Aggregation of periods (Article 6). Periods of insurance, employment, self-employment or residence completed under the legislation of any other Member State should be taken into account as though they were periods completed under the applicable legislation.
- The principle of equal treatment of benefits, income, facts or events (Article 5). If the receipt of social benefits has certain legal effects, or if legal effects are attributed to certain facts or events, it should be irrelevant whether the benefits have been acquired or the facts have occurred in another Member State.
- Prevention of overlapping of benefits (Article 10). Individuals should not be able to claim several benefits of the same kind for the same period of compulsory insurance.

The Regulation covers all major contributory and noncontributory benefits, including sickness benefits, maternity and equivalent paternity benefits, invalidity benefits, old-age benefits, survivors' benefits, benefits in respect of accidents at work and occupational diseases, death grants, unemployment benefits, pre-retirement benefits and family benefits. It does not, however, cover social assistance. By way of example, Table 5.4 sets out the rules related to sickness benefits.

Table 5.4 Example: the rules related to sickness benefits

Situation	Entitlement
Insured person resides in Member State other than the Member State where he or she is insured (Art. 17)	Insured person receives benefits in kind (e.g. hospital treatment) by the institution of the place of residence as though he or she was insured there, on behalf of the competent institution.
Insured person travels from the competent Member State to another Member State and suddenly requires medical attention (Art. 19)	Insured person is entitled to the benefits in kind which become necessary on medical grounds during his or her stay. They are provided by the institution of the place of stay, on behalf of the competent institution.
Insured person travels to other Member State with the purpose of receiving medical treatment (Art. 20)	Insured person has to seek authorization from the competent authority prior to the treatment. This, however, applies solely to services typically provided in hospitals, as the Court has consistently ruled since the decisions in *Kohll* and *Decker* (1998). For non-hospital services received abroad, he or she can demand reimbursement from the competent institution without prior authorization (on these patient mobility cases, see below).

Works Council Directive

Works councils represent employees at the level of a firm. While works councils often cooperate with labor unions, they are distinct types of organization. Works councils are instituted by law, whereas labor unions are usually private organizations. Depending on the Member State, the organization and the competences of works councils vary widely. The most far-reaching system exists in Germany, where workers elect 50 percent of the members of the supervisory board ("*Aufsichtsrat*") in all capital companies of over 2,000 employees.

Establishing functional relations between employers and employees has been an important political concern in the EU. In particular, in the 1980s, the European Commission under Jacques Delors tried to push forward the institutionalization of industrial relations in Europe. The Commission believed that a system of coordination between employers and employees had an important economic function.[182] One attempt to strengthen industrial relations was the adoption of the Works Council Directive.[183] It created a framework for informing and consulting employees in "Union-scale" undertakings. The Directive provides that either a European Works Council (EWC) or a procedure for informing and consulting employees shall be established in every "Union-scale" undertaking. A "Union-scale" undertaking is an undertaking with at least 1,000 employees within the Member States and at least 150 employees in each of at least two Member States. The EWCs do not replace the national works councils in the undertaking. Their competences are restricted to transnational issues. The Directive does not provide for a specific form of EWC. Rather, it merely institutes a system where the undertaking's central management or its employees can launch negotiations on the establishment of an EWC or an informing and consulting procedure.

Work, health and safety regulation

Since the 1980s, the EU has passed a considerable number of measures regulating standards for health and safety at work and other employment terms and conditions such as working time and parental leave. This was the consequence of increased calls since the 1980s for a "social dimension" to European integration. Table 5.5 provides an overview of some areas of regulation that are of importance for the freedom of movement for workers.

---

182 Committee for the Study of Economic and Monetary Union, "Report on Economic and Monetary Union in the European Community" ("Delors Report"), presented April 17, 1989, http://aei.pitt.edu/1007/1/monetary_delors.pdf (accessed February 18, 2014), p. 20.

183 Directive 2009/38/EC of the European Parliament and of the Council of 6 May 2009 on the establishment of a European Works Council or a procedure in Community-scale undertakings and Community-scale groups of undertakings for the purposes of informing and consulting employees (Recast) [2009] OJ L122/28.

Table 5.5 Some relevant secondary law measures

Measure	Subject-matter
Working Time Directive	The general Working Time Directive establishes minimum standards (e.g. a minimum daily rest period of eleven hours per twenty-four hours and paid annual leave of four weeks), but allows for derogations for certain situations and in certain industries.[a] Additionally, there are directives for specific industries, e.g. for the road transport sector[b] and for civil aviation.[c]
Parental Leave Directive	The directive establishes, *inter alia*, a right to parental leave of at least four months.[d]
Part-Time Work Directive	The directive aims at removing discrimination against part-time workers.[e]
Temporary Agency Work Directive	Temporary workers (employees of temporary work agencies who are posted temporarily at undertakings) are a particularly vulnerable group, as they work alongside permanent employees in undertakings without having the same rights and career opportunities.[f] The directive on temporary agency work establishes a general right of equal treatment, in particular in regard to working time (holidays, working time, overtime, rest periods, etc.) and pay. Moreover, it aims at giving temporary workers the opportunity to get into permanent employment. For this reason, they must be kept informed about job openings and encouraged to take part in training programs.
Health and Safety at Work Directives	The directives establish minimum safety and health requirements in a multiplicity of areas, from training and information requirements to issues like room temperature, ventilation and lighting, or standards for emergencies. In addition to the general framework Directive from 1989,[g] the EU has passed directives in a number of specific areas, including health and safety at temporary work sites[h] and fishing vessels,[i] protection of young people at work[j] and numerous directives on chemical safety (e.g. exposure to asbestos or carcinogens[k]).

a   Directive 2003/88/EC of the European Parliament and of the Council of 4 November 2003 concerning certain aspects of the organization of working time, [2003] OJ L299/9.
b   Directive 2002/15/EC of the European Parliament and of the Council of 11 March 2002 on the organization of the working time of persons performing mobile road transport activities, [2002] OJ L80/35.
c   Council Directive 2000/79/EC of 27 November 2000 concerning the European Agreement on the Organization of Working Time of Mobile Workers in Civil Aviation concluded by the Association of European Airlines (AEA), the European Transport Workers' Federation (ETF), the European Cockpit Association (ECA), the European Regions Airline Association (ERA) and the International Air Carrier Association (IACA), [2000] OJ L302/57.
d   Council Directive 2010/18/EU of 8 March 2010 implementing the revised Framework Agreement on parental leave concluded by BUSINESSEUROPE, UEAPME, CEEP and ETUC and repealing Directive 96/34/EC, [2010] OJ L68/13.
e   Council Directive 97/81/EC of 15 December 1997 concerning the Framework Agreement on part-time work concluded by UNICE, CEEP and the ETUC, Annex: Framework agreement on part-time work, [1998] OJ L14/9.
f   Directive 2008/104/EC of the European Parliament and of the Council of 19 November 2008 on temporary agency work, [2008] OJ L327/9.
g   Council Directive 89/391/EEC of 12 June 1989 on the introduction of measures to encourage improvements in the safety and health of workers at work, [1989] OJ L183/1.
h   Council Directive 92/57/EEC of 24 June 1992 on the implementation of minimum safety and health requirements at temporary or mobile work sites (eighth individual Directive within the meaning of Article 16 of Directive 89/391/EEC), [1992] OJ L245/6.
i   Council Directive 93/103/EC of 23 November 1993 concerning the minimum safety and health requirements for work on board fishing vessels (thirteenth individual Directive within the meaning of Article 16(1) of Directive 89/391/EEC), [1993] OJ L307/1.
j   Council Directive 94/33/EC of 22 June 1994 on the protection of young people at work, [1994] OJ L216/12
k   Directive 2009/148/EC of 30 November 2009 on the protection of workers from the risks related to exposure to asbestos at work, [2009] OJ L330/28; Directive 2004/37/EC of 29 April 2004 on the protection of workers from the risks related to exposure to carcinogens or mutagens at work (sixth individual Directive within the meaning of Article 16 of Directive 89/391/EEC), [2004] OJ L229/23.

Further reading

ASHIAGBOR, DIAMOND, "Unravelling the Embedded Liberal Bargain: Labour and Social Welfare Law in the Context of EU Market Integration" (2013) 19 *European Law Journal* 303

DØLVIK, JON ERIK, and VISSER, JELLE, "Free Movement, Equal Treatment and Workers' Rights: Can the European Union Solve Its Trilemma of Fundamental Principles?" (2009) 40 *Industrial Relations Journal* 491

KRINGS, TORBEN, "A Race to the Bottom? Trade Unions, EU Enlargement and the Free Movement of Labour" (2009) 15 *European Journal of Industrial Relations* 49

PASKALIA, VICKI, "Co-ordination of Social Security in the European Union: An Overview of recent case law" (2009) 46 *Common Market Law Review* 1177

SOMEK, ALEXANDER, "From Workers to Migrants, from Distributive Justice to Inclusion: Exploring the Changing Social Democratic Imagination" (2012) 18 *European Law Journal* 711

TEZCAN-IDRIZ, NARIN, "Free Movement of Persons Between Turkey and the EU: To Move or Not to Move? The Response of the Judiciary" (2009) 46 *Common Market Law Review* 1621

TRYFONIDOU, ALINA, "In Search of the Aim of the EC Free Movement of Persons Provisions: Has the Court of Justice Missed the Point?" (2009) 46 *Common Market Law Review* 1591

WHITE, ROBIN, "Revisiting Free Movement of Workers" (2011) 33 *Fordham International Law Journal* 1564

WIESBROCK, ANJA, "Political Reluctance and Judicial Activism in the Area of Free Movement of Persons: The Court as the Motor of EU–Turkey Relations?" (2013) 19 *European Law Journal* 422

Freedom of establishment
6 (Articles 49–55 TFEU)

INTRODUCTION

Article 49(1) TFEU provides:

Within the framework of the provisions set out below, restrictions on the freedom of establishment of nationals of a Member State in the territory of another Member State shall be prohibited. Such prohibition shall also apply to restrictions on the setting-up of agencies, branches or subsidiaries by nationals of any Member State established in the territory of any Member State.

It grants individuals the right to establish themselves in another Member State to pursue an economic activity on a self-employed basis. The Court held in *Gebhard* (1995) that the rationale of the freedom of establishment is "allowing a [Union] national to participate, on a stable and continuous basis, in the economic life of a Member State other than his State of origin and to profit therefrom, so contributing to economic and social interpenetration within the [Union] in the sphere of activities as self-employed persons."[1]

According to the EEC Treaty, freedom of establishment had to be implemented over the course of the transitional period, which ended in December 1969. This process was laid down in the "General Programme for the abolition of restrictions on freedom of establishment" (1962).[2] In particular, the General Programme mapped out the liberalization of the various economic sectors through numerous legislative measures. By the early 1970s, broad economic sectors, including commerce, industry and crafts, had been opened up to European competition.[3] After the transitional period had ended, the freedom of establishment became directly effective. As a consequence, the Court became increasingly relevant in the continuing integration of the European markets. This was particularly the case in areas where no consensus among the Member States for harmonizing measures could be found.

Article 54 TFEU extends the right to establishment to companies. The rationale behind this provision has been described by US scholar Eric Stein as follows:

---

1 Case C-55/94, *Gebhard* [1995] ECR I-4165, para. 25.
2 General Programme for the abolition of restrictions on freedom of establishment, [1962] OJ 2/36.
3 Cesare Maestripieri, "Freedom of Establishment and Freedom to Supply Services" (1973) 10 *Common Market Law Review* 150, 168.

The authors of the EEC Treaty recognized that if companies are to help integrate national markets into a common market – much as US corporations have helped to create a single continental market in the United States – the legal order must enable such companies to progress from the classic import-export pattern to a stage at which they create relatively permanent "establishments" beyond their own states' borders. In American constitutional parlance, the company which has been engaged only in "interstate" business must be free to "enter" another state with a view to doing "intrastate" business there. In order to be able to effect this entry, however, the company must be "recognized" as a legal person in the receiving state; otherwise it will not be able legally to carry on business there, to make contracts, or to sue and be sued in local courts. An analogous situation prevails in the EEC. If a company organized in one member state wishes to do business in another member state, it must be "recognized" in the receiving state as a legal person.[4]

In the decades following the signature of the Treaty of Rome, multiple legislative initiatives to coordinate or harmonize the various laws of the Member States that affect the operation of companies were set in motion. This includes measures like the convention on the mutual recognition of companies and legal persons (1968) and the various Directives harmonizing aspects of company law, which will be discussed briefly later in this chapter. However, the realization of the free movement of companies was constrained by the significant differences that existed between the various national systems, and which made a legislative compromise between the Member States difficult. The logjam was shaken up by a series of judgments by the Court, starting with *Centros* in 1999. These decisions greatly facilitated cross-border company mobility. The criticism has, however, been made that the Court's approach has come at the expense of the protection of the interests of creditors, employees and taxpayers, a discussion that has continued to this day.

Main Treaty provisions at a glance

Article 49 TFEU prohibits restrictions on the freedom of establishment. This applies, as the provision explicitly states, both to primary establishment and to secondary establishment, i.e. the "setting-up of agencies, branches or subsidiaries." Article 49 in conjunction with Article 54 TFEU extends the freedom of establishment to companies and firms. Article 50 as well as Article 53 TFEU authorize various secondary law measures. Articles 51 and 52 TFEU recognize certain exemptions to the freedom of establishment. Table 6.1 sets out the main Treaty provisions.

Direct effect

Article 49 TFEU has had direct effect since the end of the transitional period, as the Court held in *Reyners* (1974).[5] The case concerned a Dutch national who was born

---

4 Eric Stein, "Conflict-of-Laws Rules by Treaty: Recognition of Companies in a Regional Market" (1969–1970) 68 *Michigan Law Review* 1327, 1329.
5 Case 2/74, *Reyners* [1974] ECR 631, para. 30.

Provision	Content
Table 6.1 Overview of the main Treaty provisions with regard to the freedom of establishment	
Art. 49 TFEU	Prohibition of restrictions of the freedom of (primary and secondary) establishment, both for natural persons and legal persons (the latter in conjunction with Art. 54)
Art. 50 TFEU	Authorization for various secondary law measures
Art. 51 TFEU	Exception for activities related to the exercise of public authority
Art. 52 TFEU	Justification for restrictions on grounds of public policy, public security or public health
Art. 53 TFEU	Authorization to pass EU law measures in regard to the mutual recognition of professional qualifications
Art. 54 TFEU	Freedom of establishment extended to legal persons
Art. 55 TFEU	Equal treatment requirement in regard to participation in the capital of companies

and raised in Belgium, and who had also received his legal diploma in Belgium. Because of his nationality, he was not admitted to the practice of the profession of an advocate. As Articles 50 and 53 TFEU (ex-Articles 54 and 57 EEC) provided for the implementation of the freedom of establishment through Directives, Belgium argued that Article 49 TFEU could not be assumed to be sufficiently clear and precise in its meaning, and therefore could not be assumed to have direct effect.[6] However, the Court held that Article 49 TFEU "has ... the character of a provision which is complete in itself and legally perfect."[7] The provision therefore has direct effect. According to the Court, the freedom of establishment would be facilitated by implementing measures such as those provided for by Articles 50 and 53 TFEU, but could not be made dependent on them.[8]

PERSONAL SCOPE (BENEFICIARIES)

Natural persons

Natural persons who are Union citizens have the right to establish themselves in another Member State.[9] Citizens of the EEA (Article 31 EEA Agreement) and Swiss citizens (EU–Swiss Agreement on the free movement of persons)[10] have a comparable right to establishment in the EU.

---

6 *Ibid.*, paras. 4–7 (see also *ibid.*, 642).   7 *Ibid.*, para. 12.   8 *Ibid.*, paras. 25–32.

9 Case C-70/09, *Hengartner and Gasser* [2010] ECR I-7233, para. 25.

10 Agreement between the European Community and its Member States, of the one part, and the Swiss Confederation, of the other, on the free movement of persons, [2002] OJ L114/6, Art. 4.

The rights of Turkish citizens with regard to the freedom of establishment and to provide services

The Association Agreement between Turkey and the EU (1963, Articles 13–14) as well as the Additional Protocol (1970, Article 41(2)) aimed at the abolition of any restrictions on the freedom of establishment and the freedom to provide services for its citizens, guided by the Treaty freedom provisions of the TFEU. These goals have not yet been fully implemented, and the provisions do not have direct effect. However, Article 41(1) Additional Protocol established a standstill clause that has been found to have direct effect: "The Contracting Parties shall refrain from introducing between themselves any new restrictions on the freedom of establishment and the freedom to provide services." This means that EU Member States cannot apply stricter rules to Turkish citizens than those that were in place when the Protocol first entered into force for the respective Member State (for the United Kingdom, for example, this is January 1, 1973, the date it acceded to the EU and its international agreements).[11] The standstill clause does not grant substantive rights to self-employed persons (*Oguz*, 2011).[12] According to the Court, "the Additional Protocol is not, in itself, capable of conferring on Turkish nationals – on the basis of European Union legislation alone – a right of establishment or, as a corollary, a right of residence, or indeed a right of freedom to provide services or to enter the territory of a Member State."[13] However, it prohibits new restrictions with regard both to the entry of a Member State's territory as well as to the access to professional activity.[14] The Court has found that Article 41(1) has direct effect, so that Turkish nationals can rely on it before national courts to prevent the application of national law that is more restrictive than the law that was in place when the Protocol entered into force (*Savas*, 2000).[15] The Court held in *Abatay* (2003) that the principles enshrined in the Treaty freedom provisions "must be extended, so far as possible, to Turkish nationals to eliminate restrictions on the freedom to provide services between the contracting parties."[16] By contrast, the Court has rejected attempts to apply Article 41(1) to the situation of Turkish service recipients. Consequently, Turkish individuals cannot invoke Article 41(1) against a visa requirement even though they are recipients of services in the host Member State, for example as tourists (*Demirkan*, 2013).

Companies

Article 54(1) TFEU extends the right of establishment to "companies or firms formed in accordance with the law of a Member State and having their registered office, central administration or principal place of business." They shall be "treated in the

---

11 Case C-186/10, *Oguz* [2011] ECR I-6957, para. 8.   12 *Ibid.*, para. 26.
13 Case C-221/11, *Leyla Ecem Demirkan* [2013] ECR I-00000, para. 54.
14 Case C-228/06, *Soysal* [2009] ECR I-1031, para. 50.
15 Case C-37/98, *Savas* [2000] ECR I-2927, paras. 46–54; see also *Soysal*, para. 45.
16 Joined Cases C-317/01 and C-369/01, *Abatay* [2003] ECR I-12301, para. 112.

same way as natural persons who are nationals of Member States." Article 54(2) TFEU defines "companies or firms" as legal entities constituted under civil or commercial law of a Member State, including cooperative societies, and other legal persons governed by public or private law, save for those which are non-profitmaking. Additionally, the company must have its registered office, central administration or principal place of business within the Union. The EEA Agreement extends the right to establishment to companies from the EEA Member States.[17] Under the EU–Swiss Agreement, on the other hand, legal persons are not granted a right of establishment.[18]

MATERIAL SCOPE

Self-employment

The provisions on the freedom of establishment apply to self-employed individuals, whereas employed individuals are covered by Article 45 TFEU. Individuals who own shares in a public limited company usually fall under the free movement of capital provisions (Article 63 TFEU). Only a situation in which a "[Union] national lives in one Member State and has a shareholding in the capital of a company established in another Member State which gives him substantial influence over the company's decisions and allows him to determine its activities . . . may . . . fall within the freedom of establishment." (*N*, 2006).[19]

Cross-border element

According to the Court, national legislation falls under Article 49 TFEU "only to the extent that it applies to situations connected with trade between Member States" (*Duomo Gpa*, 2012).[20] This means that the Treaty provisions on the freedom of establishment are only applicable to situations that feature a cross-border element. By contrast, Article 49 TFEU "cannot be applied to activities which are confined in all respects within a single Member State" (*Höfner and Elsner*, 1991).[21] For example, in *Geurts* (2007), the Court held that Article 49 TFEU applies in cases where a person had a business established in the home state and subsequently moved his personal residence to another Member State. As this created a cross-border situation, Article 49 TFEU became applicable. In this regard the Court held that "the situation of a [Union] national who, since the transfer of his residence, has been living in one Member State and holding the majority of the shares in companies

---

17 Art. 34 EEA Agreement.   18 Case C-541/08, *Fokus Invest* [2010] ECR I-1025, para. 34.
19 Case C-470/04, *N* [2006] ECR I-7409, para. 27.
20 Joined Cases C-357/10 to C-359/10, *Duomo Gpa* [2012] ECR I-00000, para. 26, with further references.
21 Case C-41/90, *Höfner* [1991] ECR I-1979, para. 37.

established in another Member State, has fallen within the scope of [Article 49 TFEU] since that transfer" (*Geurts*, 2007).[22]

In certain cases, the Court finds Article 49 TFEU to be applicable even though all the facts in the main proceedings are confined within a single Member State.[23] This is the case when the Court concludes that the national provision in question could at least potentially affect cross-border situations. For example, the Court usually finds tender procedures to be of potential cross-border relevance. In *Duomo Gpa* (2012), the question concerned a public procurement tender procedure established by an Italian municipality in which only Italian companies participated. The Court argued that, even though all the facts of the case were confined to Italy, it nonetheless had jurisdiction to rule on Article 49 TFEU because "in the present case it is far from inconceivable that companies established in Member States other than the Italian Republic have been or are interested in pursuing, in Italy, activities such as those covered by the contracts at issue in the main proceedings."[24] Moreover, "the interpretation of [Articles 49 and 54 TFEU] sought by the referring court may be useful to it if its national law were to require it to grant an Italian operator the same rights as those which an operator of another Member State would derive from EU law in the same situation."[25]

The temporal criterion: permanent establishment

The establishment provisions apply to individuals and companies who wish to establish themselves in another Member State on a permanent basis. According to the Court, "the concept of establishment means that the operator offers its services on a stable and continuous basis from an establishment in the Member State of destination."[26] The temporal criterion is the main standard for distinguishing between situations that fall under the establishment provisions and those covered by the service provisions. The Court clarified the distinction in *Gebhard*.

Case C-55/94, Gebhard (1995)

Mr. Gebhard, a German national, had been authorized to practice as a *Rechtsanwalt* (attorney) in Germany since 1977, and was a member of a bar association in Germany. He pursued a professional activity in Italy since 1978, initially as a collaborator in a set of chambers of lawyers in Milan, and subsequently, from 1980 until 1989, as an associate member of those chambers. No criticism had been made of him in relation to his activities in those chambers. In 1989, Mr. Gebhard opened his own chambers in Milan, and employed the title *"avvocato."* The Milan Bar Council prohibited him from using the title and opened disciplinary proceedings against

22 Case C-464/05, *Geurts* [2007] ECR I-9325, para. 14.
23 See e.g. Case C-347/06, *Brescia* [2008] ECR I-5641, paras. 57–59.   24 *Duomo Gpa*, para. 26.
25 *Ibid.*, para. 28.   26 *Ibid.*, para. 31.

him. According to the Bar Council, Mr. Gebhard had contravened his obligations under an Italian law, which held:

[Nationals of Member States authorized to practise as lawyers in their home Member State] shall be permitted to pursue lawyers' professional activities on a temporary basis . . . in contentious and non-contentious matters in accordance with the detailed rules laid down in this title.

For the purpose of the pursuit of the professional activities referred to in the preceding paragraph, the establishment on the territory of the Republic either of chambers or of a principal or branch office is not permitted.[27]

Is Article 49 TFEU applicable even though Italian law expressly prohibits establishment?

Yes.

Whether Article 49 TFEU is applicable does not depend on the national rules, but on European law alone. According to the Court, the "concept of establishment within the meaning of the Treaty is . . . a very broad one, allowing a Community national to participate, on a stable and continuous basis, in the economic life of a Member State other than his State of origin and to profit therefrom, so contributing to economic and social interpenetration within the Community in the sphere of activities as self-employed persons."[28] In contrast, the services provisions are applicable if the service is pursued "on a temporary basis."[29] The Court held:

[T]he temporary nature of the activities in question has to be determined in the light, not only of the duration of the provision of the service, but also of its regularity, periodicity or continuity. The fact that the provision of services is temporary does not mean that the provider of services within the meaning of the Treaty may not equip himself with some form of infrastructure in the host Member State (including an office, chambers or consulting rooms) in so far as such infrastructure is necessary for the purposes of performing the services in question.[30]

As Mr. Gebhard pursued his activity on a stable and continuous basis, the establishment provisions are applicable to him. The Court emphasized that Member States continue to be competent to regulate self-employment: "[T]he taking-up and pursuit of certain self-employed activities may be conditional on complying with certain provisions laid down by law, regulation or administrative action justified by the general good, such as rules relating to organization, qualifications, professional ethics, supervision and liability."[31] However, these conditions must satisfy the proportionality requirement: "[N]ational measures liable to hinder or make less attractive the exercise of fundamental freedoms guaranteed by the Treaty must fulfil four conditions: they must be applied in a non-discriminatory manner; they must be justified by imperative requirements in the general interest; they must be suitable for securing the attainment of the objective which they pursue; and they must not go beyond what is necessary in order to attain it."[32]

---

27 *Gebhard*, para. 17.   28 *Ibid.*, para. 25.   29 *Ibid.*, para. 26.   30 *Ibid.*, para. 27.   31 *Ibid.*, para. 35.
32 *Ibid.*, para. 37.

Whether Article 49 TFEU or Article 56 TFEU is applicable depends on the specific circumstances of a case. According to the Court, "no provision of the [EU] Treaty affords a means of determining, in an abstract manner, the duration or frequency beyond which the supply of a service or of a certain type of service can no longer be regarded as the provision of services, and accordingly 'services' within the meaning of the Treaty may cover services varying widely in nature, including services which are provided over an extended period, even over several years" (*Duomo Gpa*, 2012).[33] Table 6.2 sets out an overview of establishment and services as established by the Court in *Gebhard* (1995).

Table 6.2 Overview: establishment and services (*Gebhard*, 1995)		
	Establishment	**Services**
Duration?	Pursuit of a professional activity "on a stable and continuous basis"	Provision of services "on a temporary basis", to be established "not only of the duration of the provision of the service, but also of its regularity, periodicity or continuity"
Infrastructure?	Infrastructure may be acquired	Service provider "may equip himself in the host Member State with the infrastructure necessary for the purposes of performing the services"[a]

a   *Gebhard* (1995), para. 39.

ADDRESSEES

Host state

Article 49 TFEU is explicitly addressed to the host Member State, as it prohibits "restrictions on the freedom of establishment of nationals of a Member State in the territory of another Member State." The Member States are obliged to prevent discrimination of nationals and companies from other Member States on the ground of nationality as well as restrictions of their right to permanently establish themselves on their territory.

Home state

Article 49 TFEU applies not only to the host state, but also to the home state. The Court held in *National Grid Indus* (2011): "Even though, according to their wording, the Treaty provisions on freedom of establishment are aimed at ensuring that

---

33 *Duomo Gpa*, para. 32.

foreign nationals are treated in the host Member State in the same way as nationals of that State, they also prohibit the Member State of origin from hindering the establishment in another Member State of one of its nationals or of a company incorporated under its legislation."[34]

Non-state actors

Article 49 TFEU also applies to non-state actors. In *Wouters* (2002), the Court held that "compliance with [Articles 49 and 56 TFEU] is also required in the case of rules which are not public in nature but which are designed to regulate, collectively, self-employment and the provision of services. The abolition, as between Member States, of obstacles to freedom of movement for persons would be compromised if the abolition of State barriers could be neutralized by obstacles resulting from the exercise of their legal autonomy by associations or organizations not governed by public law."[35] According to the Court in *Viking* (2007), the Treaty freedoms were compromised "if the abolition of State barriers could be neutralized by obstacles resulting from the exercise, by associations or organizations not governed by public law, of their legal autonomy."[36] In *Wouters*, the Court held that Article 49 TFEU is applicable to regulations passed by the Dutch bar association. And, in *Viking*, the Court found industrial action initiated by a labor union to be subject to Article 49 TFEU.

Case C-438/05, Viking (2007)

Viking Lines was a company that operated a ferry line between Finland and Estonia. The company, established in Finland, attempted to re-register one of its ships, the *Rosella*, in Estonia in order to hire a crew that was paid a lower wage. The Finnish labor union FSU, however, sought to renew its collective agreement with Viking Lines and initiated collective action in order to avert relocation. The Finnish labor union was supported by the International Transport Workers' Federation (ITF) as well as by the Estonian labor union. Transport unions have long fought against so-called "flags of convenience," where, in order to avoid regulation, the ship is registered in a different country to that in which the owner is registered.

Is the collective action by the Finnish labor union and the ITF subject to Article 49 TFEU?

Yes.

---

34 Case C-371/10, *National Grid Indus* [2011] ECR I-12273, para. 35.
35 Case C-309/99, *Wouters* [2002] ECR I-1577, para. 120.
36 Case C-438/05, *International Transport Workers' Federation and The Finnish Seamen's Union* [2007] ECR I-10779, paras. 57–66.

According to the Court, "the collective action taken by FSU and ITF is aimed at the conclusion of an agreement which is meant to regulate the work of Viking's employees collectively, and, that those two trade unions are organizations which are not public law entities but exercise the legal autonomy conferred on them, *inter alia*, by national law."[37] Accordingly, Article 49 TFEU "must be interpreted as meaning that, in circumstances such as those in the main proceedings, it may be relied on by a private undertaking against a trade union or an association of trade unions."[38] The Court found the actions of the Finnish labor union to constitute a restriction of the freedom of establishment, which includes the freedom to relocate a ship to another Member State. Such a restriction may be justified on grounds of the protection of workers. In particular, the Court acknowledged that collective action by employees is a long-recognized fundamental right.[39] However, the Court emphasized that the labor union is subject to the proportionality requirement. Before initiating strike action, the labor union was required to exhaust all other, less restrictive options in order to bring to a successful conclusion the collective negotiations.[40] (*Viking* was a hugely controversial judgment by the Court. We will discuss the political context of the decision and some of the arguments of its critics in Chapter 7.)

APPLYING ARTICLE 49 TFEU: PROHIBITION OF DISCRIMINATION AND OF RESTRICTIONS

Article 49 TFEU prohibits both direct and indirect discrimination as well as indistinctly applicable measures that constitute restrictions of the freedom of establishment.

Prohibition of discrimination

The establishment provisions prohibit discrimination on the ground of nationality. According to Article 49 TFEU, the "[f]reedom of establishment shall include the right to take up and pursue activities as self-employed persons and to set up and manage undertakings ... under the conditions laid down for its own nationals by the law of the country where such establishment is effected." The Court held in *Commission* v. *Austria* (2008) that Article 49 TFEU "prohibits the Member States from laying down in their laws conditions for the pursuit of activities by persons exercising their right of establishment which differ from those laid down for its own nationals."[41] The case concerned an Austrian measure that required nationals from the new Member States who wished to register a partnership or company in the commercial register to obtain a certificate from the Austrian employment agency

---

37 *Ibid.*, para. 60.   38 *Ibid.*, para. 61.   39 *Ibid.*, para. 86.   40 *Ibid.*, para. 87.
41 Case C-161/07, *Commission* v. *Austria* [2008] ECR I-10671, para. 28.

that verified that they were indeed self-employed. As Austria restricted labor market access of workers from the new Member States during the transitional period after the accession of these countries to the EU, the measure aimed at preventing "false" self-employment that circumvented this restriction. According to the Court, the measure constituted differential treatment, as Austrian nationals were not subject to the same requirement. It was therefore prohibited by Article 49 TFEU. In *Commission* v. *Italy – Private Security Guards* (2001), the Court ruled that an Italian provision holding that only Italian citizens could acquire the license necessary to provide private security services was directly discriminatory and therefore prohibited under the freedom of establishment (and services) provisions.[42] With regard to companies, the relevant criterion is not nationality, but their seat. The Court held in *Truck Center* (2008) that "[f]reedom of establishment . . . aims to guarantee the benefit of national treatment in the host Member State, by prohibiting any discrimination based on the place in which companies have their seat."[43]

The prohibition of Article 49 TFEU encompasses both direct and indirect discrimination. Already the "General Programme for the abolition of restrictions on freedom of establishment" of 1962 called for the elimination of national measures if, "although applicable irrespective of nationality, their effect is exclusively or principally, to hinder the taking up or pursuit of such activity by foreign nationals."[44] Residence requirements are usually considered to be indirectly discriminatory. The Court held in *Ciola* (1999) that "[i]t is settled case law that national rules under which a distinction is drawn on the basis of residence are liable to operate mainly to the detriment of nationals of other Member States, as non-residents are in the majority of cases foreigners."[45]

Prohibition of restrictions

The establishment provisions preclude any national measure which, even though it is applicable without distinction on the ground of nationality, is liable to hinder or render less attractive the exercise by Union nationals of the fundamental freedoms guaranteed by the Treaty.[46] An early case where the Court interpreted Article 49 TFEU as a prohibition of such nondiscriminatory restrictions was *Kraus* (1993). The case dealt with a German law that required holders of foreign academic titles to obtain an administrative authorization prior to using the title on German territory. Mr. Kraus, a German national, had received an LLM degree from the University of Edinburgh. The Court found the German measure to be liable to hamper or to render less attractive the exercise of Article 49 TFEU. According to the Court, an

42 Case C-283/99, *Commission* v. *Italy – Private Security Guards* [2001] ECR I-4363, para. 22.
43 Case C-282/07, *Belgian State–SPF Finances* v. *Truck Center SA* [2008] ECR I-10767, para. 32.
44 General Programme for the abolition of restrictions on freedom of establishment, [1962] OJ 2/36, Title III, para. B; see also Case C-71/76, *Thieffry* [1977] ECR 765, para. 13.
45 Case C-224/97, *Ciola* [1999] ECR I-2517, para. 14.
46 Case C-456/05, *Commission* v. *Germany – Psychotherapists* [2007] ECR I-10517, para. 49.

authorization requirement, even though it applied to nationals and non-nationals alike, could only be justified if it "is intended solely to verify whether the post-graduate academic title was properly awarded, that the procedure is easily accessible and does not call for the payment of excessive administrative fees, that any refusal of authorization is capable of being subject to proceedings, that the person concerned is able to ascertain the reasons for the decision and that the penalties prescribed for non-compliance with the authorization procedure are not disproportionate to the gravity of the offence."[47]

Over the past decades, the Court has applied different tests to identify restrictions of the freedom of establishment. In the 1990s, the Court sometimes applied the *Keck* formula (initially developed with regard to Article 34 TFEU) to cases concerning Article 49 TFEU. In *Semeraro Casa Uno* (1996), for example, the Court argued that Sunday trading rules breached neither the free movement of goods nor the establishment provisions. It argued that "[a]s far as Article 52 [now Article 49 TFEU] is concerned, suffice it to state that ... the legislation in question is applicable to all traders exercising their activity on national territory; that its purpose is not to regulate the conditions concerning the establishment of the undertakings concerned; and that any restrictive effects which it might have on freedom of establishment are too uncertain and indirect for the obligation laid down to be regarded as being capable of hindering that freedom."[48] The practice of employing the *Keck* formula in establishment cases has later been discontinued. Currently, the Court frequently applies a market access test, which, however, retains important elements of the *Keck* formula. The market access test holds that indistinctly applicable measures constitute restrictions only if they make it more difficult for new competitors to enter a national market. An example is the case of *CaixaBank France*.

Case C-442/02, CaixaBank France (2004)

A French law prohibited banks from paying interest on sight accounts (that is, on accounts against which the depositor can immediately draw). The prohibition applies to all banks concluding contracts with French residents. CaixaBank France, a subsidiary of the Spanish CaixaBank, paid interest at the rate of 2 percent per year. The French banking regulation authority prohibited this practice, and CaixaBank appealed.

Does the prohibition to pay interest on sight accounts conflict with the freedom of establishment?

Yes.

According to the Court, the prohibition hinders CaixaBank from effectively gaining access to the French market. It "hinders credit institutions which are subsidiaries of

---

47 C-19/92, *Dieter Kraus* v. *Land Baden-Württemberg* [1993] ECR I-1663, para. 42.
48 Case C-418/93, *Semeraro Casa Uno* [1996] ECR I-2975, para. 32.

foreign companies in raising capital from the public, by depriving them of the possibility of competing more effectively, by paying [interest] on sight accounts, with the credit institutions traditionally established in the Member State of establishment, which have an extensive network of branches and therefore greater opportunities than those subsidiaries for raising capital from the public."[49] According to Advocate General Tizzano, prohibiting the company from offering a better return on savings than the long-established companies deprives foreign banks "of the only effective means of acquiring customers in the French market."[50] Accordingly, the national measure constitutes a restriction of Article 49 TFEU.

Attanasio (2010)[51] is another example where the Court employed the market access test to identify restrictions of Article 49 TFEU. An Italian law provided that new gas stations could only be constructed if they were located at a minimum distance from existing gas stations. The Court found that the rule makes it difficult for new operators to enter the Italian market, and therefore protected the providers already present on the market.[52] The rule – although nondiscriminatory – therefore constituted an obstacle to the freedom of establishment.

JUSTIFICATIONS

Measures that restrict the freedom of establishment can be justified on the following grounds:

- exercise of official authority (Article 51 TFEU);
- grounds of public policy, public security or public health (Article 52 TFEU);
- overriding reasons in the public interest.

The first two exceptions are explicitly recognized by the Treaty, and can justify indistinctly applicable measures as well as directly or indirectly discriminatory measures. The Court has recognized other justifications in the public interest as well. They can justify indirectly discriminatory and indistinctly applicable measures. The Court held that it is for the Member States to decide the level at which they intend to ensure the protection of the general interest as well as the means to achieve them. However, "they can do so only within the limits set by the Treaty and, in particular, they must observe the principle of proportionality, which requires that the measures adopted be appropriate for ensuring attainment of the objective which they pursue and do not go beyond what is necessary for that purpose" (*Commission* v. *Netherlands*, 2004).[53]

---

49 Case C-442/02, *CaixaBank France* [2004] ECR I-8961, para. 13.
50 *Ibid.*, Opinion of Advocate General Tizzano, para. 89.   51 Case C-384/08, *Attanasio* [2010] ECR I-2055.
52 *Ibid.*, para. 45.   53 Case C-299/02, *Commission* v. *Netherlands* [2004] ECR I-9761, para. 18.

Public policy, public security and public health

Article 52(1) TFEU provides:

The provisions of this Chapter and measures taken in pursuance thereof shall not prejudice the applicability of provisions laid down by law, regulation or administrative action providing for special treatment for foreign nationals on grounds of public policy, public security or public health.

These derogations justify direct and indirect discrimination as well as nondiscriminatory restrictions.[54] The Court interprets the exceptions narrowly. However, the Court generally accepts that Member States have considerable discretion to define the requirements of public policy, public security and public health. The Court held for example with regard to the public health exception that "it is for the Member States to determine the level of protection which they wish to afford to public health and the way in which that level is to be achieved. Since the level may vary from one Member State to another, Member States should be allowed a measure of discretion" (*Blanco Pérez*, 2010).[55]

National measures must comply with the proportionality requirement. This means, *inter alia*, that the criteria applied by the Member States must be transparent and known in advance, as the Court held for example in *Commission* v. *Italy – Veto on Acquisition of Shares* (2009).[56] According to an Italian measure, the finance minister had the power to oppose the acquisition by investors of significant shareholdings representing at least 5 percent of voting rights of companies directly or indirectly controlled by the state, including Telecom Italia, ENI (petrochemical industry) and ENEL (energy, of notoriety from the *Costa* v. *ENEL* case). The Court held that such a measure restricts the freedom of establishment, as it affects the power of shareholders to influence the management of the companies concerned and to determine their activities.[57] The Court accepted that, "with regard to bodies operating in the oil, telecommunications and electricity sectors, that the object of ensuring a secure supply of such services in the case of a crisis in the territory of the Member State concerned may constitute a reason of public security and, therefore, justify a restriction of a fundamental freedom."[58] However, the Court stipulated that a veto right such as the one in question must conform to certain procedural standards that ensure the proportionality of such measure. In particular, the state must lay down criteria based on objectively verifiable conditions in advance on which basis such a decision is made. As the Italian measure does not provide details on the actual circumstances in which the power of veto may be exercised, the Court found it to be disproportionate, and therefore not justifiable.

---

54 See e.g. Joined Cases C-65/95 and C-111/95, *Mann Singh Shingara* [1997] ECR I-3343, para. 28.
55 Joined Cases C-570/07 and C-571/07, *Blanco Pérez* [2010] ECR I-4629, para. 44.
56 Case C-326/07, *Commission* v. *Italy – Veto on Acquisition of Shares* [2009] ECR I-2291.   57 *Ibid.*, para. 56.
58 *Ibid.*, para. 69.

Exercise of official authority

Article 51 TFEU provides:

The provisions of this Chapter shall not apply, so far as any given Member State is concerned, to activities which in that State are connected, even occasionally, with the exercise of official authority.

As was already discussed with regard to the "public service" exception in Article 45(4) TFEU, the Court employs a narrow interpretation of the official authority derogation. The mere fact that in a Member State some tasks are traditionally fulfilled by public authorities cannot by itself lead to the conclusion that they also exercise official authority within the meaning of Article 51 TFEU.

The Court has ruled a number of times that private security companies generally cannot be considered to exercise official authority within the meaning of Article 51 TFEU (e.g. *Commission* v. *Italy – Private Security Guards*, 2001).[59] In *Commission* v. *Spain – Private Security Guards* (1998),[60] the Court held:

Merely making a contribution to the maintenance of public security, which any individual may be called upon to do, does not constitute exercise of official authority.[61]

For the public authority derogation to apply, the activity in question must be "directly and specifically connected with the exercise of official authority" (*Commission* v. *Spain – Private Security Guards*, 1998).[62] Equally, the activities of advocates cannot be considered to constitute an exercise of official authority, as the Court first held in *Reyners* (1974): "The most typical activities of the profession of avocat, in particular, such as consultation and legal assistance and also representation and the defence of parties in court, even when the intervention or assistance of the avocat is compulsory or is a legal monopoly, cannot be considered as connected with the exercise of official authority."[63] More recently, in 2011, the Court has decided in a series of decisions against Germany, France, Belgium, Greece, Austria, Portugal, Luxembourg and the Netherlands that civil law notaries are not protected by the public authority derogation.[64] Accordingly, the national rules that reserved the function of a civil law notary to nationals of these Member States infringed Article 51 TFEU. The activities of private vocational training schools or private home tutors also do not constitute an exercise of official authority (*Commission* v. *Greece – Private Schools*, 1988).[65]

---

59 Case C-283/99, *Commission* v. *Italy – Private Security Guards* [2001] ECR I-4363, paras. 19–22.
60 Case C-114/97, *Commission* v. *Spain – Private Security Guards* [1998] ECR I-6717.   61 *Ibid.*, para. 37.
62 *Ibid.*, para. 35.   63 *Reyners*, para. 52.
64 Case C-157/09, *Commission* v. *Netherlands – Notaries* [2011] ECR I-00000, para. 90; see also Case C-47/08, *Commission* v. *Belgium* [2011] ECR I-4105; Case C-50/08, *Commission* v. *France* [2011] ECR I-4195; Case C-51/08, *Commission* v. *Luxembourg* [2011] ECR I-4231; Case C-52/08, *Commission* v. *Portugal* [2011] ECR I-4275; Case C-53/08, *Commission* v. *Austria* [2011] ECR I-4309; Case C-54/08, *Commission* v. *Germany* [2011] ECR I-4355; Case C-61/08, *Commission* v. *Greece* [2011] ECR I-4399.
65 Case 147/86, *Commission* v. *Greece – Private Schools* [1988] ECR 1637, para. 9.

Justifications on overriding grounds in the public interest

National measures that are indirectly discriminatory or indistinctly applicable restrictions can be justified on overriding grounds in the public interest. These measures must be proportionate. Justifications accepted by the Court in the field of establishment include the protection of consumers (*CaixaBank France*, 2004);[66] the protection of the interests of creditors, minority shareholders, employees and the taxation authorities (*Überseering*, 2002);[67] road safety and environmental protection (*Attanasio*, 2010);[68] the prevention of both fraud and incitement to squander money on gaming (*Placanica*, 2007)[69] and the aim of ensuring high standards of university education (*Neri*, 2003).[70]

Mutual recognition

We have seen that the Member States are allowed to impose requirements on self-employed persons from other Member States if these requirements are justified on overriding grounds in the public interest. Where the field of regulation has not been fully harmonized, the Court regularly holds that Member States have the right to choose the level of protection of public interest they wish to accord. However, the principle of mutual recognition requires the Member States to take into account the requirements that a person is already subject to in his home state. Only if it can be shown by the Member State that the requirements a person is subject to in the home state are not equivalent to its own requirements can it require adherence to its own standards.

The concept of mutual recognition originated in Article 57 Treaty of Rome (now Article 53 TFEU). It held:

> In order to make it easier for persons to take up and pursue activities as self-employed persons, the Council shall, on a proposal from the Commission and after consulting the Assembly [European Parliament], acting unanimously during the first stage and by a qualified majority thereafter, issue directives for the mutual recognition of diplomas, certificates and other evidence of formal qualifications.

We have already seen that the Court had found in *Reyners* (1974) that the principle of mutual recognition of qualifications followed directly from the freedom of establishment, and applies even without such implementing measures.

The principle of mutual recognition requires active engagement by the Member States. The Court held in *Gebhard* (1995): "[I]n applying their national provisions, Member States may not ignore the knowledge and qualifications already acquired

---

66 *CaixaBank France*, para. 21.   67 Case C-208/00, *Überseering* [2002] ECR I-9919, para. 92.
68 *Attanasio*, para. 50.
69 Joined Cases C-338/04, C-359/04 and C-360/04, *Placanica* [2007] ECR I-1891, para. 46.
70 Case C-153/02, *Neri* [2003] ECR I-13555, para. 46.

by the person concerned in another Member State. Consequently, they must take account of the equivalence of diplomas and, if necessary, proceed to a comparison of the knowledge and qualifications required by their national rules and those of the person concerned."[71] The principle of mutual recognition, therefore, requires Member States to actively account for requirements that persons are already subject to in their home country, and to provide suitable procedures that allow for an evaluation of their equivalence to domestic requirements.

RIGHTS UNDER ARTICLE 49 TFEU: SECONDARY LAW AND CASE LAW

The right to enter another Member State, to reside there and to leave

The Court has held that, under Article 49 TFEU, "every national of a Member State is assured of freedom both to enter another Member State in order to pursue an employed or self-employed activity and to reside there after having pursued such an activity" (*Commission* v. *France – Registration of Vessels*, 1996).[72] These rights of self-employed persons to enter, reside in and to leave other Member States are consolidated in the Citizenship Directive 2004/38/EC, which was discussed in Chapter 4 above.

The requirement to have not more than one chamber, office or shop

In a number of cases, the Court had to deal with national provisions that prohibited self-employed individuals from operating more than one chamber, office or shop. Such provisions cannot be considered to be directly discriminatory if they apply to nationals and non-nationals alike. However, they are nonetheless liable to restrict intra-Union mobility because they put individuals at a disadvantage who have already established themselves in another Member State, and who are therefore barred from opening another office in the Member State in question. In *Klopp* (1984), for example, the Paris Bar Council refused registration to Mr. Klopp, a German advocate, because he was simultaneously retaining his chamber in Germany.[73] The Court found this decision to restrict the freedom of (secondary) establishment. According to the Court, the freedom of establishment "includes freedom to set up and maintain, subject to observance of the professional rules of conduct, more than one place of work within the [Union]."[74] A Greek law that prohibited opticians from operating more than one shop was similarly found to be

---

71 *Gebhard*, para. 38.
72 Case C-334/94, *Commission* v. *France – Registration of Vessels* [1996] ECR I-1307, para. 21.
73 Case 107/83, *Klopp* [1984] ECR 2971.   74 *Ibid.*, para. 19.

in breach of Article 49 TFEU (*Commission* v. *Greece*, 2005).[75] A French measure that prohibited biologists from holding shares in more than two companies formed in order to operate jointly one or more biomedical analysis laboratories was found to infringe Article 49 TFEU (*Commission* v. *France – Biomedical Laboratories*, 2010).[76] The Court's case law has subsequently been codified in the Services Directive. According to its Article 14(2), operators who wish to establish themselves in another Member State must not be made subject to a "prohibition on having an establishment in more than one Member State or on being entered in the registers or enrolled with professional bodies or associations of more than one Member State."

A ban on having more than one establishment in the same Member State (as opposed to in the EU as a whole, which is, as shown, prohibited) is considered to be what could be called a "suspect" provision under Article 15(2)(e) Services Directive (parts of which apply, contrary to what the name of the Directive suggests, also to the freedom of establishment; the Directive is discussed in detail in Chapter 7 below). The article lists eight types of measure and calls on the Member States to evaluate whether their national system makes access to a service activity dependent on any of them. Member States are required to ensure that these measures are justified on public interest grounds and are proportionate. In *Susisalo* (2012), the Court had to deal with a Finnish measure that allowed pharmacists to run up to three branch pharmacies, but made an exception for the University of Helsinki, which was authorized to operate up to sixteen branch pharmacies.[77] According to the Finnish measure, the university pharmacy was required to train pharmacy students and to carry out research on pharmaceutical products, as well as to sell medicine. The Court found the preferential treatment of the university pharmacy to be justified in light of its specific obligation, which aims at the protection of public health.[78]

Geographical protection

Exclusive rights to provide a service in a certain geographical area may constitute a restriction of the right to establishment. In *Commission* v. *France – Bovine Insemination* (2008), a French rule granted exclusive regional rights to insemination centers providing the service of artificial insemination of bovine animals. As these exclusive rights had been awarded for an unlimited duration, it was difficult for new operators to enter the French market. The Court concluded that "the national measures at issue, on account of their nature, render it difficult, if not impossible or, in any event, less attractive, to exercise freedom of establishment

75 Case C-140/03, *Commission* v. *Greece* [2005] ECR I-3177, para. 38.
76 Case C-89/09, *Commission* v. *France – Biomedical Laboratories* [2010] ECR I-12941, para. 103.
77 Case C-84/11, *Susisalo* [2012] ECR I-00000.   78 *Ibid.*, paras. 42–44.

with a view to carrying on, in French territory, the distribution and insemination of bovine semen."[79]

The geographical protection of pharmacies, on the other hand, has been found to be justifiable by the Court. In *Blanco Pérez* (2010), a Spanish measure specified that one pharmacy may be opened for every 2,800 inhabitants, and that new pharmacies must be located at least 250 meters away from existing pharmacies.[80] The measure constituted a restriction of Article 49 TFEU, as it had the effect "to hinder and render less attractive the exercise by pharmacists from other Member States of their activities on Spanish territory through a fixed place of business."[81] However, the Court found the measure to be justifiable on grounds of public health. It held that "it is not inconceivable that, if this field were wholly unregulated, pharmacists would become concentrated in the areas considered to be attractive, so that certain other less attractive areas would suffer from a shortfall in the number of pharmacists needed to ensure a pharmaceutical service which is reliable and of good quality."[82] Similarly, the Court found an Italian rule that defined a minimum distance between opticians' shops of 300 meters as well as a limitation to one shop per 8,000 inhabitants potentially justifiable on the ground of public health (*Ottica New Line*, 2013). However, comparing opticians' shops to pharmacies that were at issue in *Blanco Pérez*, the Court pointed out that "the need for rapid access to [optical] products is less great than is inherently the case for the provision of many medicinal products, with the result that the interest in having an optician's shop close by is not as acute as is the case with the distribution of medicinal products."[83]

Authorization requirements

In order to operate a business, authorizations either by public bodies or by professional organizations are often required. Such authorization requirements may constitute a considerable obstacle to the freedom of establishment. The Court held in *Hartlauer* (2009) that "[a] national rule under which the establishment of an undertaking from another Member State is subject to the issue of a prior authorization constitutes a restriction within the meaning of [Article 49 TFEU], since it is capable of hindering the exercise by that undertaking of freedom of establishment by preventing it from freely carrying on its activities through a fixed place of business."[84]

Authorization requirements can be justified if they are proportionate. According to Article 9(1) Services Directive, authorization schemes must fulfill three requirements: (1) they must be nondiscriminatory; (2) they must be justified by an

79 Case C-389/05, *Commission* v. *France – Bovine Insemination* [2008] ECR I-5337, para. 55.
80 Joined Cases C-570/07 and C-571/07, *Blanco Pérez* [2010] ECR I-4629.   81 *Ibid.*, para. 59.
82 *Ibid.*, para. 73.   83 Case C-539/11, *Ottica New Line* [2013] ECR I-00000, para. 43.
84 Case C-169/07, *Hartlauer* [2009] ECR I-1721, para. 34.

overriding reason relating to the public interest; and (3) they cannot be attained by means of a less restrictive measure. According to the provision, an *a posteriori* inspection must be considered to constitute a less restrictive means unless it "would take place too late to be genuinely effective." According to the Preamble to the Services Directive, the concept of an "authorization scheme" is supposed to cover, *inter alia*, "the administrative procedures for granting authorizations, licences, approvals or concessions, and also the obligation, in order to be eligible to exercise the activity, to be registered as a member of a profession or entered in a register, roll or database, to be officially appointed to a body or to obtain a card attesting to membership of a particular profession."[85] Articles 10 and 13 Services Directive further elaborate the requirements that authorization schemes are subject to, essentially defining procedural minimum standards. The criteria used in authorization schemes must be (1) clear and unambiguous; (2) objective; (3) made public in advance; and (4) transparent and accessible. Moreover, they must (5) not "duplicate requirements and controls which are equivalent or essentially comparable as regards their purpose to which the provider is already subject in another Member State or in the same Member State" (Article 10(4)). The Member States are therefore subject to a mutual recognition requirement with regard to authorization schemes. Negative decisions under an authorization scheme must be open to appeal (Article 10(6)).

Registration requirements for ships and aircraft

The Court applies the right to establishment also to the registration of ships and aircraft. The case of *Factortame* (1991) arose in the context of the EU's Common Fisheries Policy, which sets fishing quotas for each Member State. In 1988, the United Kingdom introduced the Merchant Shipping Act "to put a stop to the practice known as 'quota hopping' whereby, according to the United Kingdom, its fishing quotas are 'plundered' by vessels flying the British flag but lacking any genuine link with the United Kingdom."[86] According to this legislation, a fishing vessel can be registered in the new register if 75 percent of the ship is owned by British citizens resident and domiciled in the United Kingdom or by companies that are in turn owned and managed by British citizens. Moreover, the ship must be managed from within the United Kingdom and operated by British citizens or companies. The Court held that Article 49 TFEU also applies to the registration of ships: "[W]here the vessel constitutes an instrument for pursuing an economic activity which involves a fixed establishment in the Member State concerned, the registration of that vessel cannot be dissociated from the exercise of the freedom of establishment."[87] Nationality or residence requirements as a precondition to the

---

85 Services Directive, Preamble, recital 39.   86 Case C-221/89, *Factortame* [1991] ECR I-3905, para. 4.
87 *Ibid.*, para. 22.

registration of a fishing vessel therefore constitute an infringement of Article 49 TFEU.[88] In *Commission* v. *Belgium – Registration of Aircraft* (1999), the Court found that a requirement for operators to be resident or established for at least one year in Belgium before they can register aircraft there infringed Article 49 TFEU.[89]

Residence requirements

Article 14(1)(b) Services Directive prohibits "a requirement that the provider, his staff, persons holding the share capital or members of the provider's management or supervisory bodies be resident within the territory." In *Commission* v. *Italy – Dentists* (2001), the Court had to deal with a national measure that made registration of dentists with the dental association subject to the requirement that the individual reside within the district of the professional association with which they seek registration. The registration is a precondition to practicing dentistry in Italy. According to the Court, this constitutes a restriction of the freedom of establishment, "in that such a requirement prevents dentists established or resident in another Member State from setting up a second dental surgery in the first State or practising as employees there."[90] Sometimes national laws required the managers of a company to reside in that Member State. In *Commission* v. *Spain – Private Security Guards* (1998), a Spanish measure required directors and managers of security companies providing security services in Spain to reside there.[91] The provision was found to be indirectly discriminatory by the Court.

Access to professional organizations

Many self-employed activities require admission to a professional organization as a prerequisite for practicing the profession: lawyers need to be members of the bar association, architects and civil engineers of the technical chamber, etc. Over the years, the Court has dealt with numerous cases on the access to professional organizations. These cases regularly concern measures that prescribe conditions of admission that are difficult for non-nationals to meet, and are therefore indirectly discriminatory.[92] This was the case, for example, in *Thieffry* (1977).[93] Jean Thieffry, a Belgian advocate, held a Belgian diploma of doctor of laws, which has been recognized by a French university as equivalent to the French degree in law. He was therefore allowed to take the lawyers' exam, passed it in accordance with French legislation and obtained the qualifying certificate for the profession of

---

88 See also Cases C-151/96, *Commission* v. *Ireland – Registration of Vessels* [1997] ECR I-3327; Case C-62/96, *Commission* v. *Greece – Registration of Vessels* [1997] ECR I-6725.
89 Case C-203/98, *Commission* v. *Belgium – Registration of Aircraft* [1999] ECR I-4899, para. 15.
90 Case C-162/99, *Commission* v. *Italy – Dentists* [2001] ECR I-541, para. 20.
91 Case C-114/97, *Commission* v. *Spain – Private Security Guards* [1998] ECR I-6717.
92 For an example of a directly discriminatory measure, see Case 38/87, *Commission* v. *Greece – Liberal Professions* [1988] ECR 4415.
93 Case 71/76, *Thieffry* [1977] ECR 765.

advocate. His subsequent application for admission to the Paris bar, however, was rejected on the ground that he did not hold the prescribed *French* law degree. The Court found that the conditions of admission to the Paris bar conflicted with Article 49 TFEU. The provision was indirectly discriminatory, as it is much more likely that French citizens would hold a French law degree than citizens of other Member States.

Member States may require individuals to join a professional organization in order to practice a regulated profession. Such requirement does not infringe EU law as long as citizens from other Member States can join under the same conditions as nationals of that state (*Gebhard*, 1995).[94] This applies, *inter alia*, to lawyers. The Court held in *Ebert* (2011) that Hungary may require a German lawyer established in Budapest to become a member of the Hungarian bar association in order to practice the profession of lawyer under the professional title of that state.[95]

Restrictions on the acquisition and use of real estate

National rules that prohibit the acquisition of immovable property by self-employed citizens of other Member States infringe Article 49 TFEU.[96] In *Commission* v. *Greece – Immovable Property* (1989), the Court had to deal with a Greek law that prohibited the acquisition by foreign natural or legal persons of immovable property situated in Greek border regions.[97] The Court found that this measure infringed Article 49 TFEU. According to the Court, the scope of Article 49 TFEU is not limited to rules regulating the pursuit of an occupation, but extends also to measures which "are of assistance in the pursuit of that occupation."[98] In *Commission* v. *Italy – Social Housing* (1988), the Court found a measure that reserved access to social housing and reduced-rate mortgage loans to Italian nationals to breach Article 49 TFEU.[99] Article 49 TFEU also applies with regard to the renting of premises for business purposes (*Steinhauser*, 1985).[100]

The Court also had to deal with restrictions on the freedom of establishment that stemmed from measures related to regional planning. In *Commission* v. *Spain – Shopping Centers* (2011), the authorities in the province of Catalonia had passed a number of measures that limited the establishment of very large retail stores, also known as "hypermarkets."[101] Measures challenged by the Commission included limits on the location (not outside consolidated urban areas) and on the size of these shopping centers, but also measures detailing different aspects of the licensing procedure. The Commission claimed that these measures would restrict the right to

94 *Gebhard*, paras. 35–37.   95 Case C-359/09, *Ebert* [2011] ECR I-269, para. 42.
96 Service providers have the same right of equal treatment under Art. 56 TFEU, and workers under Art. 45 TFEU as well as Art. 9 Regulation 492/2011.
97 Case 305/87, *Commission* v. *Greece – Immovable Property* [1989] ECR 1461.   98 *Ibid.*, para. 21.
99 Case 63/86, *Commission* v. *Italy – Social Housing* [1988] ECR 29, para. 20; see also Case C-155/09, *Commission* v. *Greece – Transfer Tax Exemption* [2011] ECR I-65.
100 Case 197/84, *Steinhauser* [1985] ECR 1819.
101 Case C-400/08, *Commission* v. *Spain – Shopping Centers* [2011] ECR I-1915.

establishment, arguing that "[m]ost economic operators wishing to set up medium-sized retail establishments are of Spanish nationality, whereas those wishing to set up large retail establishments are more usually from other Member States."[102] The Court accepted that such measures might in principle be justified on grounds of the public interest, for example relating to urban planning or environmental protection.[103] However, it found that Spain had produced insufficient evidence to demonstrate that the concrete measures would in fact be necessary to achieve these goals.

Lawyers

Directive 98/5/EC regulates the practice of the profession of lawyer on a permanent basis in a Member State other than that in which the professional qualification was obtained.[104] It applies to both employed and self-employed lawyers (Article 1). According to the Directive, lawyers are entitled to practice under their home country professional title in other Member States on a permanent basis, though confusion with the professional title of the host Member State must be avoided. This means that a German "*Rechtsanwalt*" can practice under this title for example in France, where the professional title of lawyers is "*avocat.*" According to Article 5(1), "a lawyer practising under his home-country professional title carries on the same professional activities as a lawyer practising under the relevant professional title used in the host Member State and may, *inter alia*, give advice on the law of his home Member State, on [Union] law, on international law and on the law of the host Member State." Member States may, however, reserve the pursuit of activities relating to the representation or defense of a client in legal proceedings to lawyers practicing under the professional title of the host state, so that a lawyer practicing under their home country title has to cooperate with a lawyer practicing under the title of the host state (Article 5(3)). Member States may also lay down specific rules for access to supreme courts.

Lawyers who practice under their home state titles are subject to the rules of professional conduct applicable to lawyers in the host state (Article 6). According to the Court, the Directive does not preclude "the application, to any person practising the profession of lawyer in a Member State, particularly as regards the taking up or pursuit thereof, of national provisions laid down by law, regulation or administrative action justified by the general good, such as rules relating to organization, qualifications, professional ethics, supervision and liability" (*Ebert*, 2011).[105] In particular, Member States are not prohibited from requiring lawyers who wish to practice the profession of lawyer under the title of lawyer of the host Member State to become members of the local bar association.[106] Lawyers may have their home

---

102 *Ibid.*, para. 55.   103 *Ibid.*, paras. 73–76 and 80.
104 Directive 98/5/EC of the European Parliament and of the Council to facilitate practice of the profession of lawyer on a permanent basis in a Member State other than that in which the qualification was obtained, [1998] OJ L77/36.
105 Case C-359/09, *Ebert* [2011] ECR I-269, para. 40.   106 *Ibid.*, para. 42.

state diploma recognized in accordance with the Professional Qualifications Directive (see below). If they have practiced as lawyers under their home state professional title "effectively and regularly" for at least three years they may also obtain from the competent authority of that state admission to the profession of lawyer in the host Member State and the right to practice it under the professional title corresponding to the profession in that Member State, without having to meet the conditions of the Professional Qualifications Directive (Article 10).

RIGHTS OF COMPANIES: SECONDARY LAW AND CASE LAW

Article 49 TFEU in conjunction with Article 54 TFEU grants the right to all European citizens to incorporate a company in a Member State under the same conditions that apply to the nationals of that Member State (primary establishment). Furthermore, companies incorporated in one Member State have the right to establish "agencies, branches or subsidiaries" in other Member States (secondary establishment). In this section, we will look at some of the main questions that affect the right of establishment of companies. Most of the case law we discuss here arose because of the fact that company law remains relatively unharmonized in Europe (see below for an overview of company law harmonization measures in the EU), that is, company law remains mostly within the national jurisdiction. This means that, when companies are active across borders, Member States are confronted with legal persons that were created on the basis of a different legal system, and which might not conform to the requirements of their own company law. Internal market law had to find ways to facilitate the mobility of legal persons, while trying to ensure that the regulatory objectives of the various national company laws were not undermined. Generally speaking, national company laws are characterized by two, partly contradictory, regulatory objectives: on the one hand, company law seeks to facilitate business activities, for example by limiting the liability of capital owners; on the other hand, it seeks to prevent the externalization of costs from some parties onto others.[107] It aims to protect the interests of groups such as creditors, shareholders, employees, tort victims and tax authorities who have little or no influence on the business decisions of the companies. These diverse regulatory objectives have to be acknowledged within the context of the internal market. We will see that the Court has developed a two-pronged strategy to handle these divergent requirements. With regard to the status of companies (i.e. under which conditions a company is recognized as a legal person), the Court applies a rigorous home state perspective: companies lawfully incorporated in their home state must be fully recognized, and cannot be subject to any additional or disadvantageous requirements in the host state. We will discuss this

---

107 John Armour and Wolf-Georg Ringe, "European Company Law 1999–2010: Renaissance and Crisis" (2011) 48 *Common Market Law Review* 125, 127.

approach with regard to the Court's case law on secondary establishment. With regard to all other aspects of company law and adjacent legal fields, the Court applies a host state perspective: in the unharmonized areas, Member States remain free to organize company law according to the regulatory objectives they prefer. They cannot, however, apply a different regime for domestic situations on the one hand and cross-border situations on the other, unless such differential treatment is justified on grounds in the public interest.

The right to primary establishment

Article 49(2) TFEU provides:

Freedom of establishment shall include the right to take up and pursue activities as self-employed persons and to set up and manage undertakings, in particular companies or firms within the meaning of the second paragraph of Article 54, under the conditions laid down for its own nationals by the law of the country where such establishment is effected, subject to the provisions of the Chapter relating to capital.

Article 54 TFEU adds:

Companies or firms formed in accordance with the law of a Member State and having their registered office, central administration or principal place of business within the Union shall, for the purposes of this Chapter, be treated in the same way as natural persons who are nationals of Member States. "Companies or firms" means companies or firms constituted under civil or commercial law, including cooperative societies, and other legal persons governed by public or private law, save for those which are non-profit-making.

Whether a company can be incorporated in a Member State depends exclusively on the law of that state, provided that the same conditions apply to nationals and non-nationals alike. In *Daily Mail* (1988), the Court explained that "companies are creatures of the law and, in the present state of [Union] law, creatures of national law. They exist only by virtue of the varying national legislation which determines their incorporation and functioning."[108] The law of the Member States on the incorporation of legal persons varies widely. Usually two paradigmatic types of company law are distinguished: those following the "real seat doctrine," and those following the "incorporation doctrine."[109] The minority of Member States, in particular the United Kingdom and the Netherlands, follows the latter doctrine. These countries allow companies to incorporate under their law independently of the factual location of its business activities. "Real seat" countries, on the other hand, require the company to have a "connecting factor," such as the central administration or the head office (i.e. a "real seat"), within its territory in order to incorporate under their law.[110] The "real seat doctrine" implies that a company has to be wound up under national law if the "connecting factor" no longer exists. The Court dealt with this issue in *Daily Mail*.

108 Case 81/87, *Daily Mail* [1988] ECR 5483, para. 19.
109 Stephan Rammeloo, *Corporations in Private International Law*, Oxford University Press, 2001, p. 95.
110 Andrew Johnston and Phil Syrpis, "Regulatory Competition in European Company Law After Cartesio" (2009) 34 *European Law Review* 378, 381.

Case 81/87, Daily Mail (1988)

According to UK tax legislation, companies were liable to pay corporation tax in the United Kingdom if they were resident for tax purposes. A company was resident for tax purposes in the place in which its central management and control was located. UK law prohibited companies resident for tax purposes in the United Kingdom from moving the central management and control to another country without the consent of the Treasury while retaining its legal personality and remaining a company incorporated under UK law. In order to avoid corporation tax, Daily Mail, a private limited company established in the United Kingdom, wanted to move its central management and control to the Netherlands while retaining its legal form. It opened an investment management office in the Netherlands without waiting for the consent of the Treasury.

Do Articles 49 and 54 TFEU give a company that is incorporated under the legislation of one Member State and has its registered office there the right to transfer its central management and control to another Member State without a prior consent?

No.

The right of establishment is exercised by the setting up of agencies, branches or subsidiaries but may also be exercised by establishing a company in another Member State. However, "unlike natural persons, companies are creatures of the law and, in the present state of [Union] law, creatures of national law. They exist only by virtue of the varying national legislation which determines their incorporation and functioning."[111] The Court held that:

[T]he legislation of the Member States varies widely with regard to both the factor providing a connection to the national territory required for the incorporation of a company and the question whether a company incorporated under the legislation of a Member State may subsequently modify that connecting factor. Certain States require that not merely the registered office but also the real head office, that is to say the central administration of the company, should be situated on their territory, and the removal of the central administration from that territory thus presupposes the winding-up of the company with all the consequences that winding-up entails in company law and tax law. The legislation of other States permits companies to transfer their central administration to a foreign country but certain of them, such as the United Kingdom, make that right subject to certain restrictions, and the legal consequences of a transfer, particularly with regard to taxation, vary from one Member State to another.[112]

Accordingly, Articles 49 and 54 TFEU "cannot be interpreted as conferring on companies incorporated under the law of a Member State a right to transfer their central management and control and their central administration to another Member State while retaining their status as companies incorporated under the legislation of the first Member State."[113]

---

111 *Daily Mail*, para. 19.   112 *Ibid.*, para. 20.   113 *Ibid.*, para. 24.

The Court held in *Daily Mail* that rules on the incorporation of companies are for the Member States to decide, as long as there is no European harmonization in place. A company cannot move its central management to another Member State while retaining its legal form if the company law of the home state does not allow for such a possibility. If the company insists on moving its central management abroad, it has no other option than to wind up in the first state and reincorporate in another Member State.

Because the Court has, since *Daily Mail* (1988), developed far-reaching rights of secondary establishment in cases like *Centros* (see below), there was some expectation among company law scholars that the Court would eventually over-turn *Daily Mail*. However, exactly 30 years after *Daily Mail*, the Court confirmed in its decision in *Cartesio* (2008)[114] that a Member State may prohibit a company from moving its primary establishment to another Member State while main-taining its legal form. The case concerned a Hungarian company wishing to move its primary establishment to Italy while maintaining its Hungarian legal form. The Court decided that the Hungarian law did not breach the freedom of estab-lishment. The Court held:

> [I]n the absence of a uniform [Union] law definition of the companies which may enjoy the right of establishment on the basis of a single connecting factor determining the national law applicable to a company, the question whether [Article 49 TFEU] applies to a company which seeks to rely on the fundamental freedom enshrined in that article – like the question whether a natural person is a national of a Member State, hence entitled to enjoy that freedom – is a preliminary matter which, as [Union] law now stands, can only be resolved by the applicable national law. In consequence, the question whether the company is faced with a restriction on the freedom of establishment, within the meaning of [Article 49 TFEU], can arise only if it has been established, in the light of the conditions laid down in [Article 54 TFEU], that the company actually has a right to that freedom. Thus a Member State has the power to define both the connecting factor required of a company if it is to be regarded as incorporated under the law of that Member State and, as such, capable of enjoying the right of establishment, and that required if the company is to be able subsequently to maintain that status. That power includes the possibility for that Member State not to permit a company governed by its law to retain that status if the company intends to reorganize itself in another Member State by moving its seat to the territory of the latter, thereby breaking the connecting factor required under the national law of the Member State of incorporation.[115]

While the Court confirmed its hands-off approach with regard to primary establish-ment in *Cartesio* (2008), companies are nonetheless in a rather different situation today than they were in the 1980s. Since then, the European legislators and the Court have developed a number of possibilities for companies to "move" to other Member States, as we will see in the following sections. This is possible through cross-border mergers and transformations, as well as on the basis of the SE Regulation. What remains impossible, however, is to move the central administration or head office to another Member State while retaining the legal form if the company law of the home

---

114 Case C-210/06, *Cartesio* [2008] ECR I-9641.   115 *Ibid.*, paras. 109–110.

state prohibits this. In this sense, Member States can continue to apply the real seat doctrine.

The right to secondary establishment

According to Articles 49 and 54 TFEU, companies have the right to secondary establishment in another Member State, i.e. to set up "agencies, branches or subsidiaries." The Court has interpreted the right to secondary establishment of companies as an obligation on the Member States to fully accept the legal status of companies created according to the laws of another Member State and to grant them full rights under the Treaty. It prohibits Member States from applying their own rules on the legal status of companies if this would hinder them from enjoying the rights granted under the Treaty. Member States are, as we have seen, exclusively competent to define under which conditions companies can be created and when they cease to exist (primary establishment). However, Member States cannot restrict the mobility of companies that have been legally created under the laws of another Member State (secondary establishment). The Court first put forward this understanding of the right of secondary establishment of companies in the decision in *Centros*.

Case C-212/97, Centros (1999)

Centros was a private limited company registered in the United Kingdom. Its shares were held by Mr. and Mrs. Bryde, Danish nationals. The minimum share capital necessary for a private limited company in the United Kingdom was significantly lower than in Denmark. Centros did not do business in the United Kingdom, but planned to do so in Denmark. The Danish Trade and Companies Board accused Mr. and Mrs. Bryde of circumvention of the Danish company law. The board argued that the Brydes had established the company in the United Kingdom for the sole reason of avoiding the higher minimum share capital. It refused to register a branch, arguing that Centros was in fact seeking primary establishment in Denmark.

Is it contrary to Articles 49 and 54 TFEU for a Member State to refuse to register a branch of a company formed in accordance with the laws of another Member State for the reason that the company did not do any business in the Member State of primary establishment and intended to conduct its entire business in the Member State of secondary establishment?

Yes.

The fact that a company does not conduct any business in the Member State where it has its registered office does not in itself constitute abuse or fraudulent conduct that would entitle the host Member State to restrict the company's freedom of establishment. The Court emphasized that "it is immaterial that the company was formed in the first

Member State only for the purpose of establishing itself in the second [Member State], where its main, or indeed entire, business is to be conducted."[116] Accordingly, the refusal to register the branch is an obstacle to the exercise of the freedom of establishment.

Member States must fully acknowledge the status of companies lawfully incorporated in another Member State and must grant full rights of secondary establishment. As regards the recognition of their status, Member States cannot subject companies from other Member States to any additional requirements. The Court acknowledges that Member States retain full rights to prohibit fraudulent or abusive behavior by any company that is active on its territory (see below). However, the Member States cannot subject companies lawfully established in other Member States to any requirements that affect their status as bearers of full establishment rights.

The different approach of the Court with regard to primary and secondary establishment could be compared to its case law on national and European citizenship.[117] As we have seen, the Court holds that it is up to the Member States to decide who receives and who loses national citizenship. The respective rules of the Member States can vary widely in this regard. Similarly, it is for the Member States to decide under which conditions companies can be incorporated and when they cease to exist. The situation is completely different, however, with regard to secondary establishment. Just as Member States must recognize that individuals have acquired the nationality of another Member State (and thereby have become European citizens) and cannot apply their own laws on nationality to establish their legal status, they must recognize that legal persons have been correctly incorporated in another Member State, and cannot apply their own company law to them as regards their status. Table 6.3 sets out

Table 6.3 Schematic comparison of the Court's case law on the status of natural and legal persons		
	Primary establishment	**Secondary establishment**
The Court's adjudication as regards companies	Member States decide under which conditions companies can be created and when they cease to exist, as long as both nationals and non-nationals incorporating a company are treated equally.	The legal status of a company depends exclusively on the laws of the Member State where the company has been incorporated. Other Member States cannot apply their own standards in this regard.
Parallels to the Court's adjudication on nationality (i.e. the legal status of a natural person)	Member States retain the right to define under which conditions individuals acquire nationality.	Member States must grant full mobility rights under the Treaty to nationals of other Member States, and cannot apply their own nationality law on them.

116 Case C-212/97, *Centros* [1999] ECR I-1459, para. 17.
117 See also Armour and Ringe, "European Company Law 1999–2010," 137–139.

a schematic comparison of the Court's case law on the status of natural and legal persons.

The obligation to recognize and accept the legal status that companies have acquired through incorporation in another Member State puts certain limits on the company law of the host Member State. The host Member State may be obliged to grant rights to companies lawfully incorporated in another Member State even though its own company law would not permit this. This can be seen in the decision in *Überseering*.

Case C-208/00, Überseering v. Nordic Construction Company (2002)

Überseering was a company incorporated under Dutch law when it was bought by two Germans living in Germany. When it brought an action against a business partner in a German court (claiming compensation for defective work), the court ruled that Überseering did not have the capacity to be a party to legal proceedings. According to German law, a company's legal capacity is determined by reference to the law applicable in the place where its actual center of administration is established (real seat principle). The national court dismissed the action as inadmissible, as Überseering did not have the legal capacity to bring legal proceedings. It held that when Überseering was acquired by Germans living in Germany, its actual center of administration was transferred to Germany, where it was not, however, incorporated. Accordingly, the company no longer existed under German law (though it remained validly incorporated under Dutch law). It therefore lacked legal capacity, and would have to reincorporate in Germany in order to be able to sue in a German court.

Do Articles 49 and 54 TFEU preclude a Member State from denying legal capacity to a company which has its registered office in another Member State and which has moved its actual center of administration to its territory?

Yes.

According to the Court, "[a] necessary precondition for the exercise of the freedom of establishment is the recognition of those companies by any Member State in which they wish to establish themselves."[118] Überseering is validly incorporated under Dutch law and has its registered office there. It is entitled to exercise its freedom of establishment in Germany as a company incorporated under Dutch law. The Court found that "[t]he requirement of reincorporation of the same company in Germany is . . . tantamount to outright negation of freedom of establishment."[119] Accordingly, the refusal by Germany to recognize the legal existence of Überseering, which was formed in accordance with Dutch law and has its registered office there, constitutes a restriction on the freedom of establishment.[120]

---

118 *Überseering*, para. 59.   119 *Ibid.*, para. 81.   120 *Ibid.*, para. 82.

The Court also clarified the relation between its case law on primary establishment (such as *Daily Mail*) and on secondary establishment (such as *Überseering*). It held that, in *Daily Mail*,

the Court confined itself to holding that the question whether a company formed in accordance with the legislation of one Member State could transfer its registered office or its actual centre of administration to another Member State without losing its legal personality under the law of the Member State of incorporation and, in certain circumstances, the rules relating to that transfer were determined by the national law in accordance with which the company had been incorporated. It concluded that a Member State was able, in the case of a company incorporated under its law, to make the company's right to retain its legal personality under the law of that State subject to restrictions on the transfer of the company's actual centre of administration to a foreign country.[121]

By contrast,

the Court did not intend to recognize a Member State as having the power, *vis-à-vis* companies validly incorporated in other Member States and found by it to have transferred their seat to its territory, to subject those companies' effective exercise in its territory of the freedom of establishment to compliance with its domestic company law.[122]

In *Überseering*, the Court did not reject the real seat principle on which German company law was based. Germany could still apply it to companies incorporating under its law. However, Germany could not reject the right of a company to be party in legal proceedings if it was formed in accordance with the law of another Member State.

Centros and *Überseering* dealt with situations where the law of the host state does not acknowledge the legal status of companies granted under the laws of the Member State of incorporation, thereby undermining the very ability of these companies to exercise their rights under the Treaty. In *Inspire Art* (2003), the Court also found national rules to infringe Article 49 TFEU which did not prevent secondary establishment as such, but nonetheless made secondary establishment less attractive.

Case C-167/01, Inspire Art (2003)

According to Dutch law, a "formally foreign company" is defined as "a capital company formed under laws other than those of the Netherlands and having legal personality, which carries on its activities entirely or almost entirely in the Netherlands and also does not have any real connection with the State within which the law under which the company was formed applies."[123] A "formally foreign company" was subject to a number of disclosure requirements: it had to be registered in the commercial register as such and had to give an indication of that status in all the documents produced by it. Moreover, the subscribed capital as well as the paid-up share capital of a "formally foreign company" had to be at least equal to the minimum amount required of Netherlands limited companies, which at that time was €18,000.[124] The directors of the company were personally liable until the registration and the minimum capital requirements were satisfied.[125]

---

121 *Ibid.*, para. 70.   122 *Ibid.*, para. 72.   123 Case C-167/01, *Inspire Art* [2003] ECR I-10155, para. 22.
124 *Ibid.*, para. 27.   125 *Ibid.*, paras. 25 and 28.

The minimum share capital for a UK limited company is lower than that required to establish a similar company in the Netherlands. Inspire Art was founded as a limited company in the United Kingdom; its director was resident in The Hague in the Netherlands. It then established a branch in Amsterdam, without doing any business in the United Kingdom. Inspire Art was registered in the commercial register of the Dutch Chamber of Commerce without any indication of the fact that it is a "formally foreign company." Because Inspire Art traded exclusively in the Netherlands, the Dutch Chamber of Commerce applied to a court to add in the commercial register that Inspire Art is a "formally foreign company."

Is it contrary to Articles 49 and 54 TFEU for national legislation to impose on companies formed in accordance with the law of another Member State the requirement to be registered as a "formally foreign company" as well as requirements relating to minimum capital and directors' liability?
Yes.

According to the Court, "the fact that Inspire Art was formed in the United Kingdom for the purpose of circumventing Netherlands company law which lays down stricter rules with regard in particular to minimum capital and the paying-up of shares does not mean that that company's establishment of a branch in the Netherlands is not covered by freedom of establishment as provided for by [Articles 49 and 54 TFEU]."[126] While the Dutch legislation does not prevent companies such as Inspire Art from establishing themselves in the Netherlands, it "has the effect of impeding the exercise by those companies of the freedom of establishment conferred by the Treaty."[127] The legislation therefore constitutes a restriction of the freedom of establishment.

As already briefly mentioned with regard to *Centros*, Member States retain the right to prosecute criminal activities and to prevent fraudulent or abusive behavior. The Court regularly emphasizes that "a Member State is entitled to take measures designed to prevent certain of its nationals from attempting, under cover of the rights created by the Treaty, improperly to circumvent their national legislation or to prevent individuals from improperly or fraudulently taking advantage of provisions of [Union] law" (*Centros*).[128] For example, the Court has found measures taken by Member States to prevent "wholly artificial arrangements aimed at circumventing the application of the legislation of the Member State concerned" to be justifiable (*Cadbury Schweppes*, 2006).[129] However, the Court emphasized that "the fact that [a] company was established in a Member State for the purpose of benefiting from more favourable legislation does not in itself suffice to constitute abuse of that freedom."[130] This includes establishment that seeks to profit from tax advantages in force in the host Member State (*Cadbury Schweppes*).[131]

---

126 *Ibid.*, para. 98.   127 *Ibid.*, para. 101.   128 *Centros*, para. 24.
129 Case C-196/04, *Cadbury Schweppes* [2006] ECR I-4027, para. 51.   130 *Ibid.*, para. 37.   131 *Ibid.*, para. 36.

The effect of the case law since *Centros* is that entrepreneurs can freely choose for newly established companies the company law they wish to be subject to. By incorporating under the law of country A and then opening a secondary establishment in country B, the legal form of country A can essentially be "exported" to country B. This, of course, applies only to company statutes of Member States that apply the incorporation doctrine, i.e. they do not require the "real seat" of the company to remain within

The concept of regulatory competition: enabling a race to the bottom?

Economic theory assumes that competition between producers is beneficial for consumers as well as for society in general because it forces companies to lower prices, to increase efficiency and to innovate.[132] Some scholars advanced the idea that public institutions should equally be subject to competition, assuming that this would have beneficial effects for the public as well. In particular, it has been argued that regulatory competition between different national company statutes would lead to beneficial results.[133] If companies could pick and choose the national company law that they are subject to, countries would be forced to adapt their laws according to the needs of businesses. In the past years, the UK "private limited company" (Ltd) was particularly attractive for companies in the EU, as it did not require any minimum capital, unlike the company forms of most other countries in the EU. One of the problems of conceptualizing corporate mobility in terms of a "market" for regulation is that relocation is usually decided upon by the management and the shareholders, whereas company law is usually intended to protect other groups as well, including creditors, employees, taxpayers and consumers. Critics of the concept of "regulatory competition" point out that countries that have to attract the interest of companies will likely reduce the protective standards for these groups.[134] The minimum capital requirement, for example, is designed to protect creditors, who cannot bring direct claims against the owners of a limited liability company in case of insolvency. Abolishing minimum capital requirements will thus leave creditors increasingly vulnerable. It is for this reason that critics of "regulatory competition" fear that this may lead to a "race to the bottom," where all Member States are factually forced to lower their protective standards. Moreover, the question remains whether legal rules should be forced into competition at all: after all, they serve a variety of regulatory goals and values set by the legislator that go beyond the maximization of company profits.[135]

---

132 On regulatory competition, see e.g. Simon Deakin, "Legal Diversity and Regulatory Competition: Which Model for Europe" (2006) 12 *European Law Journal* 440; Eva-Maria Kieninger, "The Legal Framework of Regulatory Competition Based on Company Mobility: EU and US Compared" (2005) 6 *German Law Journal* 741; in support of regulatory competition, see e.g. Bratton, McCahery and Vermeulen, "How Does Corporate Mobility Affect Lawmaking? A Comparative Analysis" (2009) 57 *American Journal of Comparative Law* 347.
133 See e.g. *Centros*, Opinion of Advocate General La Pergola, para. 20.
134 Lucian Bebchuk, "The Desirable Limits in State Competition in Corporate Law" (1992) 105 *Harvard Law Review* 1435.
135 See e.g. Deakin, "Legal Diversity and Regulatory Competition," p. 441.

their jurisdiction. In particular, the UK private limited company (Ltd) has become a popular company form.

Cross-border transformations and mergers

We have seen that Member States must allow Union citizens to incorporate companies in their territory under the same conditions as to its own citizens. In the decisions in *SEVIC* (2005) and *VALE* (2012), the Court has expanded this approach to cross-border mergers and transformations. Member States must allow cross-border mergers and transformations to the same extent as in internal situations.

Case C-411/03, SEVIC (2005)

SEVIC Systems AG, a company established in Germany, and Security Vision, a company established in Luxembourg concluded a merger contract in 2002. The aim was the dissolution without liquidation of Security Vision, and the transfer of the whole of its assets to SEVIC. The German court rejected the application for registration of the merger in the commercial register, as the German law on transforming companies (*Umwandlungsgesetz*) provided exclusively for mergers between companies established in Germany. There was no equivalent provision on cross-border mergers such as that planned by SEVIC and Security Vision.

Does a measure of a Member State that precludes registration in the national commercial register of the merger of two companies where one company is established in another Member State infringe Articles 49 and 54 TFEU, if such registration is possible if both companies are established in the first Member State?
Yes.

The Court held that cross-border mergers "constitute particular methods of exercise of the freedom of establishment, important for the proper functioning of the internal market, and are therefore amongst those economic activities in respect of which Member States are required to comply with the freedom of establishment laid down by [Article 49 TFEU]."[136] According to the Court, "German law establishes a difference in treatment between companies according to the internal or cross-border nature of the merger, which is likely to deter the exercise of the freedom of establishment laid down by the Treaty."[137] The German government contended that the procedure of the *Umwandlungsgesetz* was designed specifically for the situation of internal mergers "to protect the interests of creditors, minority shareholders and employees, and to preserve the effectiveness of fiscal supervision and the fairness of commercial transactions."[138] Cross-border mergers, however, create different types of problems, which should be solved by a harmonized procedure on

---

136 Case C-411/03, *SEVIC Systems AG* [2005] ECR I-10805, para. 19.   137 *Ibid.*, para. 22.   138 *Ibid.*, para. 24.

the Union level. The Court responded that the lack of harmonization in this field could not restrict the implementation of the freedom of establishment. While Germany's concerns could justify restrictive measures, a general refusal to register cross-border mergers would go beyond what is necessary to protect those interests.

The Court follows an approach that is similar to the one adopted by the European legislators in the Directive 2005/56/EC on cross-border mergers of limited liability companies.[139] The Directive requires Member States to allow the merger of a national limited liability company with a limited liability company from another Member State if the same merger would be allowed between two domestic companies. According to its Article 4(1)(b), "a company taking part in a cross-border merger shall comply with the provisions and formalities of the national law to which it is subject." In a merger between companies located in different Member States, the merger must conform to the rules and procedures of both Member States (Article 11).

The Court chose a similar approach in *VALE* (2012) with regard to the cross-border transformation (i.e. the change of the legal form) of a company. Member States must allow the transformation of a company originally established in another Member State into a domestic company under the same conditions that it requires such transformations for domestic companies.

Case C-378/10, VALE Epítési (2012)

VALE Construzioni Srl, a limited liability company governed by Italian law, decided in 2006 to transfer its seat to Hungary and thereby to change the applicable national law, while maintaining the legal personality of the company (cross-border conversion). It asked to be removed from the Italian commercial register, and the entry was subsequently deleted by the authorities in February 2006. In November 2006, the director of VALE Construzioni and another person adopted the articles of association of VALE Epítési kft, a limited liability company governed by Hungarian law, with a view to registration in the Hungarian commercial register. The share capital was paid up to the extent required under Hungarian law for registration. In January 2007, a representative of VALE Epítési applied to the Hungarian commercial court to register the company in accordance with Hungarian law. In the application, the representative stated that VALE Construzioni was the predecessor in law to VALE Epítési. The application was rejected. The court held that a company which was incorporated and registered in Italy cannot, by virtue of Hungarian company law, transfer its seat to Hungary and cannot obtain registration there in the form requested, as a company which is not Hungarian cannot be listed as a predecessor in law.

---

139 Directive 2005/56/EC of the European Parliament and of the Council on cross-border mergers of limited liability companies, [2005] OJ L310/1.

Does the refusal to register VALE Epítési infringe Articles 49 and 54 TFEU?

Yes.

Hungarian law provides only for conversion of companies which already have their seat in Hungary. By contrast, it does not allow a company incorporated in accordance with the law of another Member State to convert to a company governed by Hungarian law. This constitutes a restriction of Articles 49 and 54 TFEU, as it likely deters companies which have their seat in another Member State from exercising the freedom of establishment laid down by the Treaty. While such difference in treatment can be justified in principle, the Court did not identify overriding reasons of justification in the public interest in this case.

Member States are not obliged to grant rights with regard to cross-border conversions if such rights are not granted with regard to domestic conversions. The Court held in *VALE* that if the legislation of a Member State requires strict legal and economic continuity between the predecessor company which applied to be converted and the converted successor company in the context of a domestic conversion, such a requirement may also be imposed in the context of a cross-border conversion. Table 6.4 sets out an overview of how companies can "move" from one Member State to another.

Table 6.4 Overview: how companies can "move" to another Member State		
Right	**Legal foundation and leading cases**	**Effect**
Primary establishment	Arts. 49 and 54 TFEU	European citizens can create companies in other Member States
Secondary establishment	Arts. 49 and 54 TFEU; *Centros*, *Überseering*, *Inspire Art*	Companies established in a Member State can take up business in other Member States. It is irrelevant whether the company has been incorporated in the first Member State for the sole reason of gaining access to a more beneficial legal regime. Legal forms (such as the UK private limited company) can be "exported" by creating a secondary establishment in another Member State.
Cross-border merger	*SEVIC*, Cross-Border Merger Directive	Company A from one Member State can merge into another (either existing or newly formed) company of Member State B, and thereby change its legal form.
Societas Europaea	SE Regulation[a]	Registered office of an SE can be transferred to another Member State (Art. 8 SE Regulation).
Seamless "reincorporation"	VALE	Company from Member State A can transform into a company in Member State B if the latter would allow such transformation in a domestic situation.

a   Council Regulation 2157/2001 on the Statute for a European Company (SE) [2001] OJ L294/1.

"Exit taxes"

According to the principle of territoriality that governs international tax law, states may tax income generated on its territory. A special problem arises when capital gains are unrealized, i.e. when the gains only exist on the books. If, for example, the value of a claim rises because of a change in the currency exchange rates (*National Grid Indus*, 2011), then the gain remains unrealized until the claim is settled. If persons move their residence to another state in the meantime, the originating state will wish to tax the unrealized gains on the basis of the principle of fiscal territoriality. This, however, may put the mobile person at a disadvantage in comparison to a non-mobile person, as the latter may often be able to control when and in what form a gain is realized. For this reason, the taxation of unrealized gains upon relocation of a person is sometimes termed an "exit tax."

The Court has recognized the right of states to tax unrealized gains upon exit of the taxable person (*N*, 2006).[140] However, the Court emphasized that national measures must be proportionate to attain the purported goal. In *N*, for example, the Netherlands granted deferred payment of the exit tax to an individual, but required the person to provide security until the payment of the tax debts. The Court found the measure to be excessive, as the Netherlands had other, less restrictive means at its disposal, most notably certain harmonized instruments on assistance by the tax authorities of other Member States and on the recovery of tax debts.[141] Moreover, the Court held that "a system for recovering tax ... would have to take full account of reductions in value capable of arising after the transfer of residence by the taxpayer concerned, unless such reductions have already been taken into account in the host Member State."[142]

Requirement for minimum capital or for a specific legal form

In *Commission* v. *Spain – Private Security Guards* (2006), private security providers were subject to a requirement for a minimum share capital, among other require-ments such as the obligation to be constituted as legal persons, the obligation to lodge security and the obligation to employ a minimum number of staff.[143] The Court found these requirements to infringe Articles 49 and 56 TFEU. The case of *Duomo Gpa* (2012) dealt with a public procurement tender procedure launched by the Comune di Baranzate, a municipality near Milan, for a service concession for the administration, assessment and collection of certain taxes and other local revenue for a five-year period.[144] The estimated value of these services was €57,000. One of the requirements of the tender was that the bidding company had a fully paid-up share capital of at least €10 million. The Court found the measure to render the exercise of the freedom of establishment and of the freedom

---

140 Case C-470/04, *N* [2006] ECR I-7409, paras. 41–50.   141 *Ibid.*, paras. 51–53.   142 *Ibid.*, para. 54.
143 Case C-514/03, *Commission* v. *Spain – Private Security Guards* [2006] ECR I-963.   144 *Duomo Gpa*, para. 11.

to provide services less attractive, and therefore to constitute a restriction of the Treaty freedoms. Italy attempted to justify the measure as a protection of public authorities against possible nonperformance by the concession holder.[145] According to the Comune di Baranzate, the real financial risk was not the value of the service itself, but the handling of millions of euros of collected taxes. The concession holders make their profit by investing the collected taxes on the financial market before passing it on to the Comune di Baranzate. The Court found the national measure to be disproportionate, arguing that it goes far beyond what is necessary to protect public authorities from nonperformance by concession holders. The Court argued that a less restrictive means could be that the minimum threshold for fully paid capital could be made variable, depending on the value of the concessions, or general proof of creditworthiness and solvency.[146] In *Engelmann* (2010), an Austrian measure held that operators of gaming establishments would have to adopt the legal form of a public limited company.[147] The Court found this requirement to constitute a restriction of Article 49 TFEU, as "[s]uch a condition prevents, *inter alia*, operators who are natural persons and undertakings which, in the country in which they are established, have chosen another corporate form from setting up a secondary establishment in Austria."[148]

SECONDARY LAW

The legal basis for secondary law measures in the field of establishment is Article 53 TFEU as well as the general harmonization provisions of Articles 114 and 115 TFEU. Important secondary law includes the Professional Qualifications Directive, which we will discuss in detail below, and various harmonization measures in the field of company law. Numerous other Directives exist for different economic sectors, including banking, insurance, postal services, television and e-commerce. Table 6.5 gives examples of secondary law in the field of establishment and their legal bases.

The recognition of qualifications: the Professional Qualifications Directive

The Professional Qualifications Directive 2005/36/EC regulates the conditions under which Member States must recognize diploma and professional experience acquired by an individual in another Member State.[149] The recognition of professional qualifications is a significant precondition of the mobility of natural

---

145 *Ibid.*, para. 40.   146 *Ibid.*, para. 44.   147 Case C-64/08, *Engelmann* [2010] ECR I-8219, para. 28.
148 *Ibid.*, para. 28.
149 Directive 2005/36/EC of the European Parliament and of the Council on the recognition of professional qualifications, [2005] OJ L255/22.

Table 6.5 Examples of secondary law in the field of establishment and their legal bases	
Legal act	**Legal basis**
Directive[a] on a common regulatory framework for electronic communications networks and services	Art. 114 TFEU (harmonization)
Directive on markets in financial instruments[b]	Art. 53 TFEU
Directive to facilitate practice of the profession of lawyer[c] on a permanent basis in a Member State other than that in which the qualification was obtained	Art. 46 TFEU (workers), Art. 53 TFEU
Directive on the full accomplishment of the internal market of Community postal services[d]	Art. 53 TFEU, Art. 62 TFEU (services), Art. 114 TFEU (harmonization)

a   Directive 2002/21/EC of the European Parliament and of the Council on a common regulatory framework for electronic communications networks and services, [2002] OJ L108/33.
b   Directive 2004/39/EC of the European Parliament and of the Council on markets in financial instruments amending Council Directives 85/611/EEC and 93/6/EEC and Directive 2000/12/EC of the European Parliament and of the Council and repealing Council Directive 93/22/EEC, [2004] OJ L145/1.
c   Directive 98/5/EC of the European Parliament and of the Council of 16 February 1998 to facilitate practice of the profession of lawyer on a permanent basis in a Member State other than that in which the qualification was obtained, [1998] OJ L77/36.
d   Directive 2008/6/EC of the European Parliament and of the Council amending Directive 97/67/EC with regard to the full accomplishment of the internal market of Community postal services, [2008] OJ L52/3.

persons. The central importance of the recognition of qualifications for mobility was already acknowledged in the Treaty of Rome: Article 57 EEC required the Council to "issue Directives for the mutual recognition of diplomas, certificates and other evidence of formal qualifications" during the transitional phase. Since then, the Court has repeatedly ruled that Member States are obliged under the Treaty freedoms to recognize professional qualifications gained in other Member States that are essentially equivalent to their own. Over the past decades, the European legislators have passed numerous measures on various aspects of the recognition of qualifications.[150] These measures, as well as the Court's case law, were later integrated in a comprehensive act, the Professional Qualifications Directive. Before we analyze the Directive in detail, we will look at some of the Court's case law on the recognition of qualifications.

CASE LAW

In *Patrick* (1977), a British architect requested authorization to practice his profession in France.[151] No bilateral agreement existed between the United Kingdom

---

150 For an overview, see Julia Laslett, "The Mutual Recognition of Diplomas, Certificates and Other Evidence of Formal Qualifications in the European Community" (1990) 17 *Legal Issues of Eur. Integration* 1.
151 Case 11/77, *Patrick* [1977] ECR 1199.

and France, and no Directive on the recognition of qualifications of architects had yet been issued. France denied authorization, referring to the fact that no Directive on mutual recognition existed. The Court held that the failure of the Council to enact such measures would not entitle a Member State to deny the practical benefits of Article 49 TFEU to Union citizens. The Directives "have become super-fluous with regard to implementing the rule on nationality, since this is henceforth sanctioned by the Treaty itself with direct effect."[152] In *Thieffry* (1977), the Court emphasized the principle of mutual recognition of qualifications (see Article 57 EEC): a non-national holding a diploma found to be equivalent to the national diploma must be granted the same rights. Even though the Paris Bar Association required a French law diploma, the Court held that Mr. Thieffry, holding a Belgian law diploma found to be equivalent, had to be admitted to the bar. In *Vlassopoulou* (1991), a Greek lawyer was registered with the Athens bar, worked in Germany as a legal adviser and had acquired her doctorate there.[153] Her application to admission as a lawyer in Germany was rejected on the ground that she would not have the necessary qualifications: she had not studied in Germany, had not passed the two "state examinations" and had not completed the preparatory training. The Court, however, ruled that the national authorities could not simply stick to the letter of their national law, but would have to examine the qualifications of the individual: "If those diplomas correspond only partially, the national authorities in question are entitled to require the person concerned to prove that he has acquired the knowledge and qualifications which are lacking. In this regard the said authorities must assess whether the knowledge acquired in the host Member State, either during a course of study or by way of practical experience, is sufficient in order to prove possession of the knowledge which is lacking." Additionally, such a decision in an individual case must be open to judicial review. The principle of mutual recognition prevents a Member State from adhering in a formalistic manner to its national requirements, without taking qualifications acquired in other Member States into account that are formally different, but substantially compa-rable. Member States have an obligation to individually assess the comparability of the foreign with the national qualifications.[154]

The Court has also clarified the limits of mutual recognition of qualifications. In *Consiglio Nazionale degli Ingegneri* (2009), an Italian citizen, Marco Cavallera, had completed his education as a mechanical engineer in Italy.[155] He subse-quently applied for homologation of his qualification in Spain, which authorized him to become a member of the chamber of engineers in Catalonia. He never studied or worked in Spain. Subsequently, he applied in Italy for recognition of his Spanish certificate in order to be enrolled in the Italian register of engineers.

152 *Ibid.*, para. 13.   153 Case C-340/89, *Vlassopoulou* [1991] ECR I-2357.
154 Case C-586/08, *Rubino* [2009] ECR I-12013.
155 Case C-311/06, *Consiglio Nazionale degli Ingegneri* [2009] ECR I-415.

This would have allowed him to skip the state examination required in Italy to enter the register of engineers. He was enrolled by the ministry, but the decision was challenged by the National council of engineers. The Court held that Marco Cavallera could not rely on Union law to use his Spanish certificate for access to a regulated profession, as the certificate did not attest any education, examination or work experience acquired in Spain. In *Pesla* (2009), a Polish law graduate applied for a legal traineeship in Germany.[156] The German authorities argued that – additionally to his Polish law degree – he had to prove sufficient working knowledge of German law, and required him to pass an aptitude test. The Court confirmed the decision. The Court ruled that the examination of equivalence must be carried out in light of the academic and professional training as a whole which the person concerned is able to demonstrate, in order to assess whether that overall assessment may be regarded as satisfying, even in part, the conditions required for access to the activity concerned. Even though Mr. Pesla has earned a law degree, he also needs to provide proof for the qualification necessary for the specific task.

Provisions on establishment

The Professional Qualifications Directive deals with the mutual recognition of qualifications. The Directive applies to all nationals of a Member State wishing to pursue a "regulated profession" in a Member State other than that in which they obtained their professional qualifications on either a self-employed or an employed basis (Article 2(1)). The Directive contains three different systems of recognition, reminiscent of the previously disparate approaches to recognition measures which were replaced by the current Directive.

(1) *System of automatic recognition of qualifications for specific professions (Chapter III).*
   With regard to certain professions, minimum qualifications are harmonized among the Member States. Accordingly, each Member State must automatically recognize diplomas from other Member States. This applies to doctors, nurses, dental practitioners, midwives, veterinarians, pharmacists and architects.

(2) *System of automatic recognition of qualifications attested by professional experience (Chapter II).* Chapter II provides for a system of automatic recognition of qualifications attested by professional experience. It applies to a broad list of activities enumerated in the Directive's Annex IV. Article 16 of the Directive holds that "[i]f, in a Member State, access to or pursuit of one of the activities listed in Annex IV is contingent upon possession of general, commercial or professional knowledge and aptitudes, that Member State shall recognize previous pursuit of the activity in another Member State as sufficient proof of such knowledge and

---

156 Case C-345/08, *Pesla* [2009] ECR I-11677.

aptitudes." Articles 17–19 lay down conditions concerning the duration and form of professional experience required as sufficient proof within the meaning of Article 16.

(3) *General system for the recognition of professional qualifications (Chapter I).* The general system for the recognition of professional qualifications is based on the principle of mutual recognition. The competent authority in this state must allow access to and pursuit of the profession under the same conditions as for nationals. Chapter I contains fallback clauses for professions to which Chapters II and III do not apply. If a profession in the host state requires a specific professional qualification . . .

- . . . *and* the profession is also regulated in the individual's home state, then the individual has the right to work in the host state if he holds a professional qualification roughly equivalent to the qualification required by the host state (Article 13(1))

- . . . *but*, if the profession is *not* regulated in the individual's home state: then the individual has the right to work in this profession in the host state if he has 2 years of working experience in this job *plus* some sort of attestation of competence or a document providing formal qualifications (Article 13(2)).

The following box shows the requirements that Article 17 lays down for self-employment in areas enumerated in List I of Annex IV. The list covers a wide range of manufacturing and industrial activities, including the manufacture of textiles, footwear and wooden furniture. These activities can be exercised in the host state on a self-employed basis if one of the conditions enumerated in the box is fulfilled.

Recognition of professional experience according to Article 17

- six consecutive years on a self-employed basis or as a manager of an undertaking
- three consecutive years as a self-employed/manager *plus* three certified years of professional training
- four consecutive years as a self-employed/manager *plus* two certified years professional training
- three consecutive years self-employed *plus* five years employed in industry
- five consecutive years in an executive position (three of which require technical duties *plus* being responsible for a department in the company) *plus* three certified years of professional training

Provisions on service providers

The Directive provides that Member States shall not restrict, for any reason relating to professional qualifications, the free provision of services in another Member State (Article 5(1) Professional Qualifications Directive). In particular, the following rules apply:

- No minimum qualification requirements apply if the service provider does not physically cross the border (Article 5(1)(a) Professional Qualifications Directive).
- No minimum qualification requirements apply if the profession or the education and training leading to the profession is regulated in the home state (Article 5(1)(b) Professional Qualifications Directive).
- If the profession is not regulated in the home state, the service provider must have two years of professional experience (Article 5(1)(b) Professional Qualifications Directive).

The host Member State shall exempt service providers established in another Member State from the requirements which it places on professionals established in its territory with regard to authorization or registration requirements and registration with a public social security body (Article 6 Professional Qualifications Directive).

Harmonization of company law and corporate governance

The EU has issued numerous measures to harmonize national company law and corporate governance (the term "corporate governance" denotes the legal rules that define how a company is managed, and how different players – such as the management, the board, shareholders and employee representatives – interact). The rationale behind company law harmonization is manifold, as Advocate General Trstenjak explained in *Idryma Typou AE* (2010):

> There are various reasons for the efforts to approximate the company law rules which exist in the individual Member States. A central link is the principle of freedom of establishment ... according to which restrictions on the right of establishment of nationals of one Member State in other Member States must be removed. Specifically in the case of companies, however, they can and will in fact exercise their right of establishment only if there is a harmonised legal environment. A further impetus for legal harmonisation is the realisation that decisions on location should be taken in the interest of the European Union economy as a whole, on the basis of rational economic factors, and not according to where the environment is most favourable for undertakings from the point of view of company law. Furthermore, the approximation of national legal orders is intended to ensure that competitive conditions are as equal as possible for undertakings in the European Union. Lastly, the existence of comparable legal environments helps to ensure that cross-border investments by undertakings ... are made for the benefit of economic and social development in the European Union.[157]

The legislative basis of harmonization measures in the field of company law is Article 50(2)(g) TFEU, according to which Directives can be enacted that aim at "coordinating to the necessary extent the safeguards which, for the protection of the interests of members and others, are required by Member States of companies or firms ... with a view to making such safeguards equivalent throughout the Union."

---

157 Case C-81/09, *Idryma Typou AE* [2010] ECR I-10161, Opinion of Advocate General Trstenjak, para. 30.

The earliest harmonization measure, the First Company Law Directive, was enacted in 1968, and more than a dozen followed over the next decades (see the overview in Table 6.6). Company law harmonization aims at creating certain minimum standards for the different legal forms of companies existing in the various Member States, without fully erasing the regulatory diversity.

Table 6.6 Overview: important company law harmonization measures	
Measure	**Subject-matter**
Directive 2009/101/EC on the coordination of safeguards (replacing First Company Law Directive 68/151/EEC)	Disclosure requirements in regard to, *inter alia*, the company's constitution and statutes and its representatives (Art. 1); obligation to establish company register (Arts. 3–7); rules on power of representation (Arts. 8–10); nullity of the company (Arts. 11–13)
Directive 2012/30/EU (replacing Second Company Law Directive 77/91/EEC)	Minimum safeguards in regard to public limited companies, such as a minimum capital requirement of €25,000 (Art. 6)
Directive 2011/35/EU (replacing Third Company Law Directive 78/855/EEC)	Rules on the merger of public limited liability companies
Directive 2013/34/EU (replacing Fourth Company Law Directive 78/660/EEC and Seventh Company Law Directive 83/349/EEC)	Rules on the annual financial statements and related reports of private and public limited companies
Sixth Company Law Directive 82/891/EEC	Rules concerning the division of public limited liability companies
Eleventh Company Law Directive 89/666/EEC	Disclosure requirements in respect of branches opened in a Member State governed by the law of another State
Directive 2009/102/EC (replacing Twelfth Company Law Directive 89/667/EEC)	Rules on single-member private limited liability companies
Regulation 2157/2001	On the statute for a European company (SE)
Directive 2004/25/EC	On takeover bids
Directive 2005/56/EC	Cross-border mergers of limited liability companies
Directive 2007/36/EC	Exercise of certain rights of shareholders in listed companies ("Shareholders Rights Directive")

Societas Europaea: the European Company Statute

The Societas Europaea (SE) is a form of organization for European companies, established by Regulation 2157/2001 ("SE Regulation").[158] The process of creating a European company statute took more than three decades: the first Commission

---

158 Regulation 2157/2001; Directive 86/2001; Rose, "The New Corporate Vehicle Societas Europaea (SE): Consequences for European Corporate Governance" (2007) 15 *Corporate Governance* 112; Eidenmüller, Engert and Hornuf, "Incorporating Under European Law: The Societas Europaea as a Vehicle for Legal Arbitrage" (2009) 10 *European Business Organization Law Review* 1.

proposal for a European public limited-liability company was issued in 1970.[159] As of September 2013, over 1,900 SEs have been established.[160] The SE is modeled as a public limited-liability company: it has legal personality, and its capital is divided into shares (Article 1 SE Regulation). An SE can be formed by two or more existing companies either by merger or by creating an SE holding company or an SE subsidiary, or by reorganizing an existing company as an SE (Article 2 SE Regulation). Important features of the SE Regulation are:

- The registered office (which must be the real place of the central administration) of an SE may be transferred to another Member State (Article 8 SE Regulation).
- An SE is governed by the SE Regulation. If the SE Regulation provides no rules on a specific issue, the rules on public limited companies of the Member State apply where the company has its registered office (Article 9(1)(c) SE Regulation).
- The SE may have either a two-tier system (featuring a supervisory organ and a management organ like the *Aktiengesellschaften* in Germany and Austria) or a one-tier system (featuring a single administrative organ like the board of directors in a UK public limited company) (Article 38(b) SE Regulation).

Further reading

ARMOUR, JOHN, and RINGE, WOLF-GEORG, "European Company Law 1999–2010: Renaissance and Crisis" (2011) 48 *Common Market Law Review* 125

BRATTON, WILLIAM, MCCAHERY, JOSEPH, and VERMEULEN, ERIK, "How Does Corporate Mobility Affect Lawmaking? A Comparative Analysis" (2009) 57 *American Journal of Comparative Law* 347

DEAKIN, SIMON, "Legal Diversity and Regulatory Competition: Which Model for Europe" (2006) 12 *European Law Journal* 440

EIDENMÜLLER, HORST, ENGERT, ANDREAS, and HORNUF, LARS, "Incorporating under European Law: The Societas Europaea as a Vehicle for Legal Arbitrage" (2009) 10 *European Business Organization Law Review* 1

HORN, LAURA, "Corporate Governance in Crisis? The Politics of EU Corporate Governance Regulation" (2012) 18 *European Law Journal* 83

JOHNSTON, ANDREW, and SYRPIS, PHIL, "Regulatory Competition in European Company Law After Cartesio" (2009) 34 *European Law Review* 378

KIENINGER, EVA-MARIA, "The Legal Framework of Regulatory Competition Based on Company Mobility: EU and US Compared" (2005) 6 *German Law Journal* 741

MÖRSDORF, OLIVER, "The Legal Mobility of Companies Within the European Union Through Cross-Border Conversion" (2012) 49 *Common Market Law Review* 629

PANAYI, CHRISTIANA, "Exit Taxation as an Obstacle to Corporate Emigration from the Spectre of EU Tax Law" (2010–2011) 13 *Cambridge Yearbook of European Legal Studies* 245

ROSE, CASPAR, "The New Corporate Vehicle Societas Europaea (SE): Consequences for European Corporate Governance" (2007) 15 *Corporate Governance* 112

SNELL, JUKKA, "Varieties of Capitalism and the Limits of European Economic Integration" (2010–2011) 13 *Cambridge Yearbook of European Legal Studies* 415

---

159 SE Regulation, Preamble, recital 9.
160 European Trade Union Institute, "European Company (SE) Database" (2014), http://ecdb.worker-participation.eu.

7 Freedom to provide and receive services (Articles 56–62 TFEU)

INTRODUCTION

Article 56(1) TFEU provides:

Within the framework of the provisions set out below, restrictions on freedom to provide services within the Union shall be prohibited in respect of nationals of Member States who are established in a Member State other than that of the person for whom the services are intended.

The concept of "services" is a relatively recent one, both in economic and in legal terms. While from today's perspective the provision of services has always been an important field of the economy, it was only in the 1940s and 1950s that scholars started to conceptualize services as a distinct economic sector.[1] In comparison to trade in goods, the legal framework for transnational trade in services began to evolve with a significant time lag. Negotiations for a global agreement on trade in services were initiated only in the 1980s, during the Uruguay Round of multilateral trade negotiations, and the General Agreement on Trade in Services (GATS) which emerged from them, came into force in 1995. The number of the Court's cases in the field of services grew significantly during the same period.

Over the past decade, legislation and adjudication on the free movement of services has been one of the most dynamic, but also one of the most controversial, of the Treaty freedoms. The dynamic character of the field is owed to the fact that the integration of a European market in services essentially dates back only to the 1980s and 1990s. This means that a considerable number of regulatory questions are not yet fully settled, and that the legal framework has not yet been fully stabilized. Consequently, controversies persist, as unsolved regulatory questions are liable to attract different, sometimes conflicting, answers. A central field of controversy has been the area of public services. The main question in this regard has been the following: what does EU law require in a situation where a private provider wishes to offer the same service as is offered by a public provider? The question has important implications, because the issue of public services has been the center of a political conflict since the 1980s: some policymakers believed that

---

1 V. Hatzopoulos, *Regulating Services in the European Union*, Oxford University Press, 2012, p. 4, with further references.

241

private enterprises could provide public services more efficiently than public operators, whereas others believed that public operators were more efficient and could serve the public interest better.

Another controversial issue was the relationship between national labor and social standards and the free movement of services. If, for example, an operator brought its employees temporarily to another Member State to perform a service, such as the construction of a building, would the wage standards of the home state (where the workers are employed) or the host state (where the workers actually do their job) apply? Whereas, especially in the wake of the accession of ten new Member States in 2004, some feared social dumping and exploitation of labor forces from low-wage countries, others claimed that the full application of the wage levels of the host state would constitute a form of protectionism practiced by the high-wage countries. While many of the regulatory conflicts will eventually be settled over time, it should not be ignored that the question of how the European and the national societies should best regulate the provision of services has no definitive answer, and therefore will always be open to political contestation.

Main Treaty provisions at a glance

Article 56 TFEU prohibits restrictions on the freedom to provide services (according to the case law, this also implies the freedom to receive services). Article 57 TFEU defines the concept of "services," and Article 59 TFEU authorizes secondary law measures that liberalize the provision of services. Article 62 TFEU makes certain Treaty provisions from the section on establishment applicable, including the exceptions with regard to the exercise of public authority and the exceptions on grounds of public policy, public security and public health. Table 7.1 sets out an overview of the main Treaty provisions with regard to the freedom to provide and receive services.

Table 7.1 Overview of the main Treaty provisions with regard to the freedom to provide and receive services	
Provision	**Subject-matter**
Art. 56 TFEU	Prohibits restrictions on the freedom to provide services
Art. 57 TFEU	Defines the concept of "services"
Art. 58 TFEU	Art. 58(1): in regard to transport services, the Treaty provisions on transport are *lex specialis* to the services provisions
Art. 59 TFEU	Authorizes secondary law measures to liberalize specific services
Art. 60 TFEU	Encourages Member States to liberalize services beyond the scope stipulated by secondary law measures
Art. 61 TFEU	Prohibits discrimination on grounds of nationality or residence

Table 7.1 *(cont.)*	
Provision	**Subject-matter**
Art. 62 TFEU	Arts. 51–54 TFEU also apply to services
Arts. 62 and 51 TFEU	Public authority exception
Arts. 62 and 52 TFEU	Exceptions on grounds of public policy, public security or public health
Arts. 62 and 53 TFEU	Authorizes harmonization measures in regard to professional qualifications
Arts. 62 and 54 TFEU	Extends freedom to provide services to legal persons

Direct effect

The Court first found Article 56 TFEU to have direct effect in *Van Binsbergen* (1974).[2] The case dealt with the situation of Mr. Kortmann, a Dutch national, who practiced in the Netherlands as a representative in social security matters. He was engaged by Mr. van Binsbergen, another Dutch national, as his legal representative before a Dutch social security court. During the proceedings, Mr. Kortmann moved from the Netherlands to Belgium whereupon the court registrar informed him that he could no longer act for his client because only persons residing in the Netherlands could represent other individuals in social security matters. The Court held that Article 56 TFEU, which it found to have direct effect, prohibited Member States from denying persons established in another Member State the right to provide a service by imposing a requirement of habitual residence within its territory.

PERSONAL SCOPE (BENEFICIARIES)

Nationality and residence

Article 56 TFEU can be invoked by individuals who are Union citizens as well as by companies having their registered office, central administration or principal place of business within the Union. According to the Court, Article 56 TFEU applies only if the service is provided within the Union (*Scorpio Konzertproduktionen*, 2006).[3] The Court held in the same case that Article 56 TFEU cannot be invoked by service providers who are nationals of nonmember countries, even if they are established within the Union.[4] Under Article 56(2) TFEU, the freedom to provide services may be extended to include nationals of a third country who provide services and who are established within the Union. However, the European Parliament and the

2 Case 33/74, *Van Binsbergen* [1974] ECR 1299.
3 Case C-290/04, *Scorpio Konzertproduktionen* [2006] ECR I-9461, paras. 67–68.   4 *Ibid.*, para. 68.

Council have not yet passed such a measure.[5] EEA and Swiss citizens have an equivalent right.[6]

Self-employed service providers

Article 56 TFEU can be invoked by natural persons who are self-employed and by companies providing a service. "Self-employed" means that the activities are "performed outside the ties of a contract of employment" (*Walrave and Koch*, 1974).[7]

Recipients of services

According to its wording, Article 56 TFEU appears to apply solely to service *providers*. However, the Court has consistently ruled that the right to provide services is by necessity linked to a reciprocal right to receive services. The right of service recipients has also long been enshrined in secondary legislation.[8] Service recipients therefore can invoke Article 56 TFEU. Typical situations include tourists (*Donatella Calfa*, 1999)[9] and recipients of medical services (*Kohll*, 1998).[10]

Case C-348/96, Donatella Calfa (1999)

Donatella Calfa, an Italian national on vacation in Greece, was charged with possession and use of prohibited drugs. A Greek criminal court found her guilty and sentenced her to three months' imprisonment and ordered her to be expelled for life from Greece. Ms. Calfa appealed against the decision, claiming that the expulsion order contravened Article 56 TFEU because a comparable measure could not be taken against a Greek citizen.

Can Donatella Calfa invoke Article 56 TFEU as a tourist?

Yes.

The freedom to provide services includes the freedom for the recipients of services to go to another Member State in order to receive a service there. Tourists such as

---

5 However, there have been proposals to enact such a measure: see Proposal COM(1999) 3 by the Commission for a Directive of the European Parliament and of the Council on the posting of workers who are third-country nationals for the provision of cross-border services, [1999] OJ C67/12.

6 Legal persons have certain rights with regard to the provision of services as well. See Art. 5(1) of the EU–Swiss Agreement and Art. 18 of its Annex I. The rights of self-employed Turkish citizens have been discussed in Chapter 6 above.

7 Case 36/74, *Walrave and Koch* [1974] ECR 1405, para. 23.

8 See e.g. Art. 1(1) Council Directive 64/221/EEC on the co-ordination of special measures concerning the movement and residence of foreign nationals which are justified on grounds of public policy, public security or public health, [1964] OJ 56/850.

9 Case C-348/96, *Calfa* [1999] ECR I-11; see also Joined Cases 286/82 and 26/83 *Luisi and Carbone* [1984] ECR 377; Case 186/87, *Cowan* [1989] ECR 195.

10 Case C-158/96, *Kohll* [1998] ECR I-1931.

Donatella Calfa must be regarded as recipients of services. According to the Court, "the penalty of expulsion for life from the territory, which is applicable to the nationals of other Member States in the event of conviction for obtaining and being in possession of drugs for their own use, clearly constitutes an obstacle to the freedom to provide services recognized in [Article 56 TFEU], since it is the very negation of that freedom."[11] An expulsion order could be made against a Union citizen such as Ms. Calfa only if her personal conduct created a genuine and sufficiently serious threat affecting one of the fundamental interests of society, which was not the case. Thus, the penalty was not justified by the public policy derogation.

MATERIAL SCOPE

What are "services"?

Article 57 TFEU provides:

Services shall be considered to be "services" within the meaning of the Treaties where they are normally provided for remuneration, in so far as they are not governed by the provisions relating to freedom of movement for goods, capital and persons.

The definition of "services" is therefore residual: only services not covered by the other freedoms fall under Article 56 TFEU. This concerns only the classification of an activity, however, and "does not establish any order of priority between the freedom to provide services and the other fundamental freedoms" (*Fidium Finanz*, 2006).[12] Article 57 TFEU sets out a non-exhaustive list of activities that are considered to be "services" within the meaning of the Treaty: activities of an industrial character; activities of a commercial character; activities of craftsmen; and activities of the professions.

The Services Directive[13] classifies "services" as follows:

- *Business services*, such as management consultancy, certification and testing; facilities management, including office maintenance; advertising; recruitment services; and the services of commercial agents.
- *Services provided both to businesses and to consumers*, such as legal or fiscal advice; real estate services such as estate agencies; construction, including the services of architects; distributive trades; the organization of trade fairs; car rental; and travel agencies.
- *Consumer services*, such as those in the field of tourism, including tour guides; leisure services, sports centers and amusement parks.
- *Household support services*, such as help for the elderly.

11 *Donatella Calfa*, para. 18.   12 Case C-452/04, *Fidium Finanz* [2006] ECR I-9521, para. 32.
13 Services Directive, Preamble, recital 33.

Activities covered by Article 56 TFEU include making fishing waters available to third parties for consideration (*Jägerskiöld*, 1999),[14] the transmission of radio or television programs (*Stichting Collectieve Antennevoorziening Gouda*, 1991),[15] healthcare services (*Kohll*, 1998),[16] the provision of insurance (*Safir*, 1998)[17] and the activities of a temporary workers' agency (*Webb*, 1981).[18] Sport may constitute an economic activity if it is exercised for remuneration.[19] According to the Court, this is usually the case with regard to the activities of semi-professional or professional athletes (*Meca-Medina*, 2006).[20]

The GATS and the EU

The liberalization of trade in services became an increasingly important political demand not only on the European level, but on the global level as well. The Uruguay round of multilateral trade negotiations that started in 1986 aimed at expanding the logic developed within the framework of the General Agreement on Tariffs and Trade (GATT) to the field of services. Nine years later, the General Agreement on Trade in Services (GATS) came into effect under the umbrella of the newly created World Trade Organization (WTO).[21]

Like the GATT, the GATS features a most-favored-nation provision (Article II GATS), which holds that states must immediately and unconditionally grant the most beneficial treatment it accords to service providers from any state to operators from all other states. This includes market access (Article XVI GATS) and national treatment (Article XVII GATS). Article XVI GATS (market access) essentially prohibits measures that create quantitative restrictions, such as limitations on the total number of service providers or of the total value of service transactions or quantitative limits on the participation of foreign capital.[22] Article XVII GATS (national treatment) requires states to treat domestic and non-domestic service providers alike. It essentially prohibits direct and indirect discrimination.

Similar to the GATT, in the GATS framework, states commit in trade negotiations to the liberalization of trade in certain sectors: in other words, the states themselves decide which service sectors they are willing to liberalize, and offer

---

14 Case C-97/98, *Jägerskiöld* [1999] ECR I-7319, para. 36.
15 Case C-288/89, *Stichting Collectieve Antennevoorziening Gouda* [1991] ECR I-4007.   16 *Kohll*, para. 29.
17 Case C-118/96, *Safir* [1998] ECR I-1897, para. 22.   18 Case 279/80, *Webb* [1981] ECR 3305, para. 9.
19 Case C-519/04P, *Meca-Medina* [2006] ECR I-6991, para. 22.   20 *Ibid.*, para. 23.
21 For a general analysis, see Friedl Weiss, "The General Agreement on Trade in Services" (1995) 32 *Common Market Law Review* 1177–1225.
22 Aaditya Mattoo, "National Treatment in the GATS: Corner-Stone or Pandora's Box," Staff Working Paper TISD-96-02 (2009), p. 3.

these concessions in trade negotiations. States may also choose to offer limited liberalization in a sector: they can offer a full commitment (with no restrictions allowed) or define limitations, or remain "unbound," which means that they are free to introduce limitations. States may also choose to liberalize only some "modes" of provision. The GATS distinguishes four modes of supply (Article I (2) GATS): (a) cross-border provision (the service is provided cross-border, but the service provider and the consumer remain in their respective states); (b) consumption abroad (the service is provided in the home state of the provider to a consumer who has crossed the border); (c) commercial presence (the service provider has a commercial presence in another state, where the service is provided); and (d) presence of natural person (the service provider crosses the border to provide a service, and is physically present in the host state). By contrast, trade in goods under the GATT covers only the first mode of supply; in this sense, the GATS reaches much further. Many states have granted concessions in fields such as tourism (95 percent of states), financial (81 percent), business services (78 percent) and telecommunications (71 percent).[23] In other fields, such as education and health services, relatively few states have offered concessions (around 39 percent). On average, states have granted concessions in one-third of the 160 services sectors covered by the GATS.[24]

The GATS was the subject of immense political controversy in the 1990s and the 2000s. A global political movement, most notably associated with the World Social Forums, criticized the trend of growing commodification of public services such as education or water supply, and held the WTO responsible (among other global institutions such as the International Monetary Fund). One of the earliest events that brought the criticism of the GATS to public attention were the protests against the WTO Ministerial Conference in Seattle in 1999, which has become known as the "Battle of Seattle."[25]

The current round of trade negotiation, the Doha Round that commenced in 2001, has since stalled. Since then, many states have resorted to bilateral agreements to further the goal of liberalizing trade in services (so-called "preferential trade agreements," or PTAs). Since the early 1990s, the number of PTAs has steadily increased. As of 2012, over 500 PTAs were notified to the WTO.[26] The EU has so far signed over thirty PTAs.[27] While most (particularly the older) PTAs concern goods only, the number of agreements that include services is on the rise.

---

23 Rudolf Adlung and Martin Roy, "Turning Hills into Mountains? Current Commitments under the GATS and Prospects for Change," WTO Staff Working Paper No. ERSD-2005-01, p. 8.
24 Adlung and Roy, "Turning Hills into Mountains," p. 9.
25 See e.g. Jackie Smith, "Globalizing Resistance: The Battle of Seattle and the Future of Social Movements" (2001) 6 *Mobilization: An International Quarterly* 1.
26 For an overview, see www.wto.org/english/tratop_e/region_e/region_e.htm (accessed July 11, 2013).
27 See http://rtais.wto.org (accessed July 11, 2013).

Cross-border element

According to the Court, Article 56 TFEU applies "whenever a provider of services offers services in a Member State other than the one in which he is established" (*ITC*, 2007).[28] Contrariwise, "the Treaty provisions relating to the freedom to provide services do not apply to situations where all the relevant facts are confined within a single Member State" (*Omalet*, 2010).[29]

Examples of the cross-border provision of services include:

- a Latvian company provides a construction service in Sweden (*Laval*, 2007);
- a Luxembourg national receives a medical service in Germany (*Kohll*, 1998);
- a company established in the United Kingdom provides services to companies in Italy through the Internet (*Gambelli*, 2003);[30]
- a Dutch national residing in the Netherlands provides a service to another Dutch national in the Netherlands, and subsequently moves to Belgium while continuing to provide the service (*Van Binsbergen*, 1974).

Similar to the case law on establishment, the Court sometimes holds Article 56 TFEU to be applicable even though all the facts in the main proceedings are confined within a single Member State. That is the case when the national provision in question could at least potentially affect cross-border situations as well. In *Parking Brixen* (2005), for example, the Court found a tender procedure for a public concession was not purely internal to the Member State because "[i]t is possible that, in the main proceedings, undertakings established in Member States other than the Italian Republic might have been interested in providing the services concerned."[31]

Remuneration

Article 57 TFEU provides that "[s]ervices shall be considered to be 'services' within the meaning of this Treaty where they are *normally provided for remuneration*." The Court holds that "the concept of 'services' within the meaning of [Article 57 TFEU] implies that they are ordinarily provided for remuneration and that the remuneration constitutes consideration for the service in question and is agreed upon between the provider and the recipient of the service" (*Stopover Tax*, 2009).[32] In other words, "the decisive factor which brings an activity within the ambit of the Treaty provisions on the freedom to provide services is its economic character, that

---

28 Case C-208/05, *ITC* [2007] ECR I-181, para. 56.   29 Case C-245/09, *Omalet* [2010] ECR I-13771, para. 12.
30 Case C-243/01, *Gambelli* [2003] ECR I-13031, para. 54.
31 Case C-458/03, *Parking Brixen* [2005] ECR I-8585, para. 55.
32 Case C-169/08, *Presidente del Consiglio dei Ministri* v. *Regione Sardegna – Stopover Tax* [2009] ECR I-10821, para. 23.

is to say, the activity must not be provided for nothing" (*Jundt*, 2007).[33] In *Danner* (2002)[34] and *Skandia* (2003),[35] the Court ruled that payments for a complementary old-age insurance constitute remuneration although the service (the payment of the pension) is performed only decades later.

Whether an operator is profit-seeking or not is irrelevant.[36] The case *Smits and Peerbooms* (2001) dealt with the question of reimbursement by the sickness insurance fund of hospital costs incurred by a patient for treatment received abroad. The Court held that payments made by the social insurance to hospitals, even if set at a flat rate, constitute consideration for services. Accordingly, hospitals are engaged in economic activity, and Article 56 TFEU applies. The Court has held in *Jany* (2001) that prostitution constitutes a service, as it "satisfies a request by the beneficiary in return for consideration without producing or transferring material goods."[37] In *Grogan* (1991), the Court found that the "termination of pregnancy, as lawfully practised in several Member States, is a medical activity which is normally provided for remuneration and may be carried out as part of a professional activity."[38] It therefore constitutes a service within the meaning of Article 56 TFEU.

The service recipient usually pays the remuneration directly to the provider of a service. In some instances, however, this situation may become triangular, where somebody other than the service recipient pays for the provision of the service. In *Deliège* (2000),[39] an athlete's participation in a competition was regarded as the provision of services for remuneration, even though the athlete is not paid by the organizers of the tournament, but by the sponsors.

The payment of a fee (e.g. a tuition or enrollment fee) does not in itself constitute remuneration when the service is still essentially financed by the public (*Humbel*, 1988).[40] The Court held, for example, that, "by establishing and maintaining such a system of public education, financed as a general rule by the public budget and not by pupils or their parents, the State did not intend to involve itself in remunerated activities, but was carrying out its task in the social, cultural and educational fields towards its population" (*Schwarz*, 2007).[41] By contrast, "educational establishments essentially financed by private funds, notably by students and their parents, constitute services within the meaning of [Article 57 TFEU], since the aim of those establishments is to offer a service for remuneration."[42]

33 Case C-281/06, *Jundt* [2007] ECR I-12231, para. 32.
34 Case C-136/00, *Rolf Dieter Danner* [2002] ECR I-8147, para. 27.
35 Case C-422/01, *Skandia* [2003] ECR I-6817, para. 24.   36 *Jundt*, para. 33.
37 Case C-268/99, *Malgorzata Jany* [2001] ECR I-8615, para. 48.
38 Case C-159/90, *Grogan* [1991] ECR I-4685, para. 18.
39 Joined Cases C-51/96 and C-191/97, *Deliège* [2000] ECR I-2549.
40 Case 263/86, *Humbel* [1988] ECR 5365, paras. 16–20; see also Case C-109/92, *Wirth* [1993] ECR I-6447, para. 19.
41 Case C-76/05, *Schwarz and Gootjes-Schwarz* [2007] ECR I-6849, para. 39.   42 *Ibid.*, para. 40.

Cases C-51/96 and C-191/97, Deliège (2000)

Ms. Deliège was a Belgian judoka. Although she was a successful athlete – winning the national and the European championships – the national Judo federation did not nominate her for a tournament in Paris. Ms. Deliège brought an action against the national Judo federation, arguing that the selection process for international tournaments would encroach upon the right of judokas to provide services.

Do the activities of professional athletes constitute a service provided for remuneration within the meaning of Article 57 TFEU even though the service provider (the athlete) is not directly paid by the recipient of the service, but by a third party (the sponsors)?

Yes.

Sport is subject to Union law only in so far as it constitutes an economic activity within the meaning of the Treaty. The Court held that:

[S]porting activities and, in particular, a high-ranking athlete's participation in an international competition are capable of involving the provision of a number of separate, but closely related, services which may fall within the scope of [Article 56 TFEU] even if some of those services are not paid for by those for whom they are performed. For example, an organizer of such a competition may offer athletes an opportunity of engaging in their sporting activity in competition with others and, at the same time, the athletes, by participating in the competition, enable the organizer to put on a sports event which the public may attend, which television broadcasters may retransmit and which may be of interest to advertisers and sponsors. Moreover, the athletes provide their sponsors with publicity the basis for which is the sporting activity itself.[43]

Temporary nature

According to the wording of Article 57 TFEU, the provision of services is "temporary."[44] In the 1980s, the Court had ruled that any type of infrastructure that an operator establishes in another Member State (e.g. an office) makes the provisions on establishment applicable.[45] The Court ruled in *Gebhard* (1995), however, that the establishment of permanent infrastructure is not the key element in deciding whether the service or the establishment provisions are to apply, but held instead that the temporary character is decisive. However, the mere fact that the provision of a service (e.g. the construction of a building) requires an extended period of time, sometimes even years, does not automatically make the services provisions

---

43 *Ibid.*, paras. 56–57.
44 On the following, see Vassilis Hatzopoulos and Thien Uyen Do, "The Case Law of the ECJ Concerning the Free Provision of Services: 2000–2005" (2006) **43** *Common Market Law Review* 923, 927.
45 Case 205/84, *Commission* v. *Germany – Insurances* [1986] ECR 3755, para. 21.

inapplicable (*Schnitzer*, 2003):[46] rather, the question has to be decided with regard to "not only the duration of the provision of the service, but also its regularity, periodicity or continuity." Thus, persons providing a service in another Member State on a regular and continuous basis will fall under the establishment provisions, whereas operators providing services in another Member State only occasionally and on an irregular basis will fall under the services provisions. The Court has, however, not always employed the temporal criterion to establish whether an activity is to be considered a "service" within the meaning of Article 56 TFEU. Certain services (such as television broadcasting, transport or telecommunications) have always been held to fall under Article 56 TFEU, even though the provision of these services is typically not temporally limited.[47]

ADDRESSEES

Host state

Article 56 TFEU applies to the host Member State, i.e. the state where the service is provided.

Home state

Article 56 TFEU also creates obligations for the home state of the service provider. In *Alpine Investments* (1995) (discussed more extensively below), a Dutch law prohibited Dutch companies from cold-calling customers (i.e. calling them without prior notification) to sell risky financial products, regardless of where the customer is located. The Court ruled that this law of the service provider's home state restricted the provision of services (although it subsequently found the prohibition justifiable on the ground of consumer protection).

Non-state actors

Article 56 TFEU not only applies to the Member States, but may also apply to non-state actors. This is the case when these actors have the power to collectively regulate the provision of services. In *Laval* (2007), the Court held:

[C]ompliance with [Article 56 TFEU] is also required in the case of rules which are not public in nature but which are designed to regulate, collectively, the provision of services. The abolition, as between Member States, of obstacles to the freedom to provide services would be

---

46 Case C-215/01, *Bruno Schnitzer* [2003] ECR I-14847, para. 30.
47 Hatzopoulos and Do, "The Case Law of the ECJ," 927; see e.g. Case C-17/00, *De Coster* [2001] ECR I-9445; Joined Cases C-544/03 and C-545/03, *Mobistar* [2005] ECR I-7723; Case C-92/01, *Stylianakis* [2003] ECR I-1291.

compromised if the abolition of State barriers could be neutralized by obstacles resulting from the exercise of their legal autonomy by associations or organizations not governed by public law.[48]

This includes, for example, the rules of international sports associations, if they are "aimed at regulating gainful employment and the provision of services in a collective manner" (*Deliège*, 2000).[49] It may also include the activities of labor unions, as the Court found in *Laval* (2007).

APPLYING ARTICLE 56 TFEU: PROHIBITION OF DISCRIMINATION AND OF RESTRICTIONS

Prohibition of discrimination

Article 56 TFEU prohibits directly and indirectly discriminatory national measures. A national measure is directly discriminatory if it establishes a formal distinction on the basis of nationality (or, in the case of a legal person, the location of the seat) that puts a non-domestic service provider at a disadvantage. A national measure is indirectly discriminatory if, while not discriminating on the face of it, it nonetheless puts non-domestic service providers at a disadvantage. An example of a directly discriminatory measure can be found in *Commission* v. *Germany – Temp Work Agencies* (2007).[50] A German law required non-domestic temporary employment agencies that posted workers in Germany to report both (1) the initial placement and (2) every subsequent change. German agencies, on the other hand, had to conform solely to the first requirement. This provision was found to be directly discriminatory, as it formally differentiated between temporary work agencies located in Germany and those that are not.

Article 56 TFEU also prohibits indirectly discriminatory measures, i.e. measures that formally apply to nationals and non-nationals alike, but nonetheless put the latter at a disadvantage. In *Ciola* (1999), the Court had to deal with an Austrian provision that established a maximum quota of moorings on Lake Constance which may be rented to boat-owners resident in another Member State. The Court held that "[i]t is settled case law that national rules under which a distinction is drawn on the basis of residence are liable to operate mainly to the detriment of nationals of other Member States, as non-residents are in the majority of cases foreigners."[51]

---

48 Case C-341/05, *Laval* [2007] ECR I-11767, para. 98.   49 *Deliège*, para. 47.
50 C-490/04, *Commission* v. *Germany – Temp Work Agencies* [2007] ECR I-6095.
51 Case C-224/97, *Ciola* [1999] ECR I-2517, para. 14.

Prohibition of restrictions

Article 56 TFEU requires not only the elimination of all discrimination against a person on the ground of nationality, but has, from the Court's earliest decisions, been found to have a broader meaning.[52] In *Van Binsbergen* (1974), the Court held that "[t]he restrictions to be abolished pursuant to [Articles 56 and 57 TFEU] include all requirements ... which may prevent or otherwise obstruct the activities of the person providing the service."[53] In *Säger* (1991), the Court clarified that this broad interpretation of Article 56 TFEU would cover a measure that applies without distinction to national providers of services and to those of other Member States "when it is liable to prohibit or otherwise impede the activities of a provider of services established in another Member State where he lawfully provides similar services."[54] In more recent decisions, the Court often uses the formula that national measures constitute a restriction on the freedom to provide services within the meaning of Article 56 TFEU if the measure "is liable to make it less attractive, or more difficult" (e.g. *Laval*, 2007).[55]

Case C-76/90, Säger (1991)

Dennemeyer & Co. Ltd was a UK company specializing in patent renewal services. Its business was to notify its (especially German) clients by means of a computerized system when the fees for renewing the patents they were holding were due. If the clients requested so, Dennemeyer then paid the renewal fees on their behalf. Mr. Säger, a patent lawyer in Munich, claimed that this practice infringed the *Rechtsberatungsgesetz*, a German law that reserved the right to attend to legal affairs for third parties or pay fees on their behalf to licensed patent lawyers.

Does the *Rechtsberatungsgesetz* infringe Article 56 TFEU, even though the law is indistinctly applicable to both nationals and non-nationals alike?
Yes.

According to the Court, Article 56 TFEU requires not only the elimination of all discrimination against a person providing services on the ground of his nationality, but also of measures that are indistinctly applicable to nationals and non-nationals alike if they are "liable to prohibit or otherwise impede the activities of a provider of services established in another Member State where he lawfully provides similar services."[56] In order to legally provide its patent renewal services in Germany, the company would have to comply with all the rules that national patent lawyers need

---

52 Hatzopoulos, *Regulating Services in the European Union*, p. 103.   53 *Van Binsbergen*, para. 10.
54 Case C-76/90, *Säger* [1991] ECR I-4221, para. 12.   55 *Laval*, para. 99.   56 *Ibid.*, para. 12.

to comply with as well. The Court held, however, that a "Member State may not make the provision of services in its territory subject to compliance with all the conditions required for establishment."[57] This would "deprive of all practical effectiveness the provisions of the Treaty whose object is, precisely, to guarantee the freedom to provide services."[58] This is all the more true as "the service is supplied without its being necessary for the person providing it to visit the territory of the Member State where it is provided."[59] Accordingly, the *Rechtsberatungsgesetz* constitutes a restriction of the freedom to provide services.

The broad reading of Article 56 TFEU is similar to the one the Court has employed since its decision in *Dassonville* with regard to the free movement of goods. Similar to the field of goods, almost any national rule can in principle be challenged under Article 56 TFEU. Unlike with regard to Article 34 TFEU, however, the Court has so far not developed a general *prima facie* rule comparable to the *Keck* formula that would allow distinguishing between national measures that are generally assumed not to improperly impair the provision of services, and those that do. One possible reason is that the distinction employed under Article 34 TFEU between rules affecting the product itself (product requirements) and those merely concerning the conditions of sale (selling arrangements) is often not applicable when it comes to services. Rules affecting services often regulate the service provider, not the service itself (e.g. professional qualifications). Therefore, the concepts of product requirements and selling arrangements often do not provide a useful distinction in the context of Article 56 TFEU. Instead, the Court has applied various alternative tests to identify restrictions on the freedom to provide and receive services. These include a test whether the situation for non-domestic providers is "more difficult," the market access test and the double burden test. These tests are not mutually exclusive; they are used – sometimes cumulatively – to establish whether a national measure has restrictive effects.

More difficulties for non-domestic providers (or additional benefits for domestic providers)

The Court sometimes holds that Article 56 TFEU "precludes the application of any national rules which have the effect of making the provision of services between Member States more difficult than the provision of services purely within one Member State" (*Cipolla*, 2006).[60] The national measure may equally constitute a restriction of Article 56 TFEU if it grants an advantage to domestic operators alone. In *Stopover Tax* (2009),[61] the Court held that a tax imposed by the Italian

---

57 *Ibid.*, para. 13.   58 *Ibid.*   59 *Ibid.*

60 Joined Cases C-94/04 and C-202/04, *Cipolla* [2006] ECR I-11421, para. 57; see also Case C-17/00, *De Coster* [2001] ECR I-9445, para. 30; Joined Cases C-544/03 and C-545/03, *Mobistar* [2005] ECR I-7723, para. 30.

61 Case C-169/08, *Presidente del Consiglio dei Ministri* v. *Regione Sardegna – Stopover Tax* [2009] ECR I-10821.

region of Sardinia solely on stopovers by vessels or aircraft whose operators do not have their tax domicile in that region constituted a restriction of Article 56 TFEU. According to the Court, "[s]uch legislation introduces an additional cost for stopovers made by aircraft or boats operated by persons having their tax domicile outside the territory of the region and established in other Member States, and thus creates an advantage for some categories of undertaking established in that territory."[62] In *De Coster* (2001), the Court had to deal with a municipal tax that was levied on satellite dishes, but not on cable television. As the number of channels available by cable is limited, this tax mainly affected non-Belgian channels and therefore gave "an advantage to the internal Belgian market and to radio and television distribution within that Member State."[63]

The Court has held, however, that measures that merely raise the cost of the provision of services while they affect intra-state and the cross-border provision of a service alike do not constitute a restriction. In *Mobistar* (2005), the Court had to rule on a tax by a Belgian municipality on transmission pylons, masts and antennae for cell phone service. The Court argued:

[S]uch taxes apply without distinction to all owners of mobile telephone installations within the commune in question, and ... foreign operators are not, either in fact or in law, more adversely affected by those measures than national operators. Nor do the tax measures in question make cross-border service provision more difficult than national service provision. Admittedly, introducing a tax on pylons, masts and antennae can make tariffs for mobile telephone communications to Belgium from abroad and *vice versa* more expensive. However, national telephone service provision is, to the same extent, subject to the risk that the tax will have an impact on tariffs.[64]

Double burden

Without harmonization, it is possible that an operator providing a cross-border service would be subject to two sets of regulations, those of the home state and those of the host state. Such double regulation may constitute a considerable obstacle for the service provider, or may even make a cross-border provision of services impossible in practice. The Court does not consider the existence of different forms of regulation in the various Member States as a problem as such: in fact, such regulatory diversity is a necessary by-product of a federal system that is not fully centralized. Member States retain the right to decide autonomously on the regulatory standards they wish to apply in non-harmonized fields. However, Member States cannot require full compliance with their regulations without taking into account the regulatory standards that a service provider already complies with in its home state. Member States therefore have to provide sufficient administrative procedures to ensure that these regulatory standards are taken into account. The lack of such procedures to ensure mutual recognition, and not the divergence in

---

62 *Ibid.*, para. 32.   63 *De Coster*, para. 35.   64 *Mobistar*, paras. 32–33.

regulatory standards as such, constitutes a restriction of Article 56 TFEU.[65] A national measure can be justified if the Member State shows that the regulatory standards a service provider is subject to in its home state are not equivalent to its own standards (see the section below on mutual recognition).

An example of a case where a double burden was found to constitute a restriction of Article 56 TFEU is *Seco* (1982). Luxembourg required employers to pay social security contributions imposed on persons providing services within their national territory even if they were established in another Member State and were already liable under the legislation of that state for similar contributions in respect of the same workers and the same periods of employment. While working at a project in Luxembourg, the employers had to pay their contributions twice, once to their state of establishment, and once to Luxembourg. The Court held that "in such a case the legislation of the State in which the service is provided proves in economic terms to be more onerous for employers established in another Member State, who in fact have to bear a heavier burden than those established within the national territory."[66]

Market access

National measures may be nondiscriminatory, and yet constitute an obstacle on service providers from other Member States by making market access more difficult.[67] We have already encountered a number of examples in the previous chapter on the right to establishment: in *CaixaBank France* (2004), it will be remembered, the Court found a rule that prohibited offering sight accounts that paid interest to conflict with Article 56 TFEU. The measure prevented new competitors from offering a new service to attract customers, and thereby made it difficult for non-domestic service providers to enter the French market. The market access approach is often compared to the *Keck* formula: the idea behind both approaches is that national rules that regulate market behavior in a general way and do not put non-domestic products at a disadvantage should not be considered restrictions; however, rules that specifically hinder a service provider from entering the market in the first place should be scrutinized under the Treaty freedoms (with the possibility of a justification). However, in many situations it is simply not clear whether a national rule should be understood as regulating the access to, or as regulating behavior in, the market. The market access approach is best understood as an obligation of the Member State to actively ensure that its laws allow service providers from other Member States to enter its market.

---

65 See e.g. *Laval*, para. 116; see also Hatzopoulos, *Regulating Services in the European Union*, p. 112.
66 Case 62/81, *Seco* [1982] ECR I-223, para. 9.
67 Case C-288/89, *Stichting Collectieve Antennevoorziening Gouda* [1991] ECR I-4007, para. 10.

JUSTIFICATIONS

Discriminatory or restrictive measures may be justified under certain conditions. Measures that directly discriminate on the ground of nationality or seat can be justified only by the grounds explicitly recognized in Article 62 TFEU in conjunction with Articles 51 and 52 TFEU. These are public policy, public security and public health as well as the exercise of official authority. Indirectly discriminatory and indistinctly applicable measures can be justified both by the justificatory grounds provided in the treaty and by overriding reasons in the common interest. All national measures are subject to a proportionality requirement.

Public policy, public security and public health

According to Article 62 TFEU in conjunction with Article 52 TFEU, directly discriminatory or restrictive measures can be justified on grounds of public policy, public security and public health.[68] In *Corsica Ferries France* (1998), the Court had to deal with an exclusive concession that had been granted to a provider for mooring services in the port of Genoa.[69] The Court found the measure to be justified on the ground of public security:

> With regard to the possible existence of a restriction on [the] freedom to provide maritime transport services, it must be observed that the mooring service constitutes a technical nautical service which is essential to the maintenance of safety in port waters and has the characteristics of a public service (universality, continuity, satisfaction of public-interest requirements, regulation and supervision by the public authorities). Accordingly, provided that the price supplement in relation to the actual cost of the service does indeed correspond to the additional cost occasioned by the need to maintain a universal mooring service, the requirement to have recourse to a local mooring service, even if it were capable of constituting a hindrance or impediment to freedom to provide maritime transport services, could be justified ... by the considerations of public security relied on by the mooring groups, on the basis of which the national legislation on mooring was adopted.[70]

Exercise of official authority

According to Article 62 TFEU in conjunction with Article 51 TFEU, national measures are exempted from the scope of the provisions on the free movement of services if they "are connected, even occasionally, with the exercise of official authority" (see "Justifications" in Chapter 6 above).

---

68 Case C-546/07, *Commission* v. *Germany* [2010] ECR I-439, para. 48.
69 Case C-266/96, *Corsica Ferries France* [1998] ECR I-3949.   70 *Ibid.*, para. 60.

Justifications on overriding grounds in the public interest

Restrictive national measures that are indistinctly applicable can be justified on overriding grounds in the public interest. Justifications accepted by the Court include the protection of workers (*Arblade*, 1999),[71] the maintenance of media pluralism (*United Pan-Europe*, 2007)[72] and the protection of fundamental rights (*Omega Spielhallen*, 2004).[73] In *Sky Italia* (2013), the Court had to deal with an Italian law that laid down shorter hourly advertising limits for pay-TV broadcasters than for free-to-air broadcasters.[74] The Court held that the protection of consumers from excessive advertising could justify restrictions of the freedom to provide services. As pay-TV broadcasters already receive remuneration from their consumers whereas free-to-air broadcasters do not, the broadcasters are in an objectively different situation.[75] This means that different rules on advertising limits for pay-TV on the one hand and free-to-air on the other may conform to the proportionality requirement.

Principle of mutual recognition

The principle of mutual recognition requires Member States to take the requirements into account that service providers already conform to in their home state. The Court held that "a restriction of [Article 56 TFEU] can be justified only to the extent that the public interest sought to be protected by national legislation is not safeguarded by the rules to which the service provider is subject in the Member State of establishment." (*Commission* v. *Portugal – Construction Sector*, 2010).[76] In particular, "a national authorization scheme goes beyond what is necessary where the requirements to which the issue of authorization is subject duplicate the equivalent evidence and safeguards required in the Member State of establishment, inferring in particular an obligation on the part of the host Member State to take account of controls and verifications already carried out in the Member State of establishment."[77]

In practice, the principle of mutual recognition shifts the burden of proof from the service provider to the host Member State, as can be seen for example in *Commission* v. *Portugal – Construction Sector* (2010). Portugal required all providers of construction services to acquire an authorization by the public authority. This authorization was granted to providers that conformed to certain requirements, which related to commercial aptitude, technical capacity and economic and financial capacity. The measures applied regardless of whether the provider was permanently established in Portugal or merely provided a temporary service in Portugal. The Court held that

71 Joined Cases C-369/96 and C-376/96, *Arblade* [1999] ECR I-8453, para. 60.
72 Case C-250/06, *United Pan-Europe Communications* [2007] ECR I-11135, para. 42.
73 Case C-36/02, *Omega Spielhallen* [2004] ECR I-9609, para. 35.
74 Case C-234/12, *Sky Italia* [2013] ECR I-00000.   75 *Ibid.*, paras. 20–21 and 24–26.
76 Case C-458/08, *Commission* v. *Portugal – Construction Sector* [2010] ECR I-11599, para. 100.
77 *Commission* v. *Portugal – Construction Sector*, para. 100.

Member States are, in principle, allowed to require non-domestic service providers to conform to their national requirements if this is justified on grounds of the public interest. Portugal argued that the measure was justified on the grounds of, among others, ensuring the soundness and safety of buildings as well as protecting the users of those buildings.[78] According to Portuguese law, it is the obligation of the service provider to prove that its service conforms to the national requirements that ensure these public interest objectives. However, the principle of mutual recognition shifts the burden of proof: it is for the host Member State to show that it is indeed necessary to subject non-domestic service providers to its national rules, as these providers already conform to the requirements of their state of establishment, which may essentially provide for an equivalent level of protection. Only if the host Member State can show that the service provider is not subject to an equivalent regulatory standard can it require a service provider to conform to its national requirements. The principle of mutual recognition requires the Member States to actively account for the regulation a service provider is already subject to in other Member States. The Portuguese measure failed the proportionality test because it did not allow for such considerations. The Court held:

> By requiring construction undertakings established in another Member State to satisfy all the requirements imposed by the national scheme and ... in order to obtain authorization to exercise, in Portugal, an activity in the construction sector, the scheme precludes the possibility of account being duly taken of equivalent obligations to which such an undertaking is subject in the Member State of establishment or of the verifications already carried out in that regard by the authorities of that Member State.[79]

The principle of mutual recognition also applies with regard to documents and certifications, as the Court held, for example, in *Arblade* (1999). The case concerned a French company that posted French workers to a site in Belgium to perform construction services. The authorities required the French company to produce a number of social documents required under Belgian legislation. In this regard, the Court held:

> The items of information respectively required by the rules of the Member State of establishment and by those of the host Member State concerning, in particular, the employer, the worker, working conditions and remuneration may differ to such an extent that the monitoring required under the rules of the host Member State cannot be carried out on the basis of documents kept in accordance with the rules of the Member State of establishment. On the other hand, the mere fact that there are certain differences of form or content cannot justify the keeping of two sets of documents, one of which conforms to the rules of the Member State of establishment and the other to those of the host Member State, if the information provided, as a whole, by the documents required under the rules of the Member State of establishment is adequate to enable the controls needed in the host Member State to be carried out. Consequently, the authorities and, if need be, the courts of the host Member State must verify in turn, before demanding that social or labour documents complying with their own rules be drawn up and kept in the territory of that State, that the social protection for workers which may justify those requirements is not sufficiently safeguarded by the production, within a

---

78 *Ibid.*, para. 89.   79 *Ibid.*, para. 101.

reasonable time, of originals or copies of the documents kept in the Member State of establishment or, failing that, by keeping the originals or copies of those documents available on site or in an accessible and clearly identified place in the territory of the host Member State.[80]

Finally, the principle of mutual recognition also applies with regard to diplomas and other professional qualifications. The Court held in *Commission* v. *Spain – Tourist Guides* (1994):

In that respect, it should be recalled that the Court has consistently held that a Member State which receives a request to admit a person to a profession to which access, under national law, depends upon the possession of a diploma or a professional qualification must take into consideration the diplomas, certificates and other evidence of qualifications which the person concerned has acquired in order to exercise the same profession in another Member State, by making a comparison between the specialized knowledge and abilities certified by those diplomas and the knowledge and qualifications required by the national rules. That examination procedure must enable the authorities of the host Member State to assure themselves, on an objective basis, that the foreign diploma certifies that its holder has knowledge and qualifications which are, if not identical, at least equivalent to those certified by the national diploma. That assessment of the equivalence of the foreign diploma must be carried out exclusively in the light of the level of knowledge and qualifications which its holder can be assumed to possess in the light of that diploma, having regard to the nature and duration of the studies and practical training to which the diploma relates.[81]

The essence of the principle of mutual recognition is that requirements on service providers should not be duplicated. According to the Court, national requirements imposed on service providers "may not duplicate equivalent statutory conditions which have already been satisfied in the State in which the undertaking is established." Moreover, "the supervisory authority of the State in which the service is provided must take into account supervision and verifications which have already been carried out in the Member State of establishment" (*Commission* v. *Germany – Insurances*, 1986).[82] From a procedural perspective it means that national requirements can be applied to non-domestic service providers only if the host Member State can show that it has taken the conditions the provider is subject to in its home state sufficiently into account.

RIGHTS UNDER ARTICLE 56 TFEU: SECONDARY LAW AND CASE LAW

The right to enter another Member State, to reside there and to leave

The free movement of natural persons – including those covered by Article 56 TFEU – is consolidated in one single Directive, the Citizenship Directive (2004/38/EC), which

80 Joined Cases C-369/96 and C-376/96, *Arblade* [1999] ECR I-8453, paras. 63–65.
81 Case C-375/92, *Commission* v. *Spain – Tourist Guides* [1994] ECR I-923, paras. 12–13.
82 Case 205/84, *Commission* v. *Germany – Insurances* [1986] ECR 3755, para. 47.

we discussed in Chapter 4. As we will see in the section on "posted workers" below, the right to enter and reside in another Member State also extends to the workforce of a company that exercises its rights under Article 56 TFEU, even though the workforce may not be Union citizens themselves.

Prohibition of disproportionate requirements

The Court has generally held that service providers must not be made subject to the same requirements as persons wishing to establish themselves permanently in another Member State. The Court held in *Säger* (1991) that "a Member State may not make the provision of services in its territory subject to compliance with all the conditions required for establishment and thereby deprive of all practical effectiveness the provisions of the Treaty whose object is, precisely, to guarantee the freedom to provide services."[83] The Court argues that the freedom to provide services would be rendered factually meaningless if service providers (especially those which only occasionally provide services in other Member States) would have to fulfil every single criterion that established providers have to fulfill. Thus, generally, the provision of services must not be made subject to disproportionate requirements. Requirements caught under this prohibition include, for example, registration and authorization requirements (see below).

Establishment, residence or seat requirements

Requirements that oblige operators to be established in a Member State in order to provide certain services are generally incompatible with Article 56 TFEU. The Court has held that "the requirement of a permanent establishment is the very negation of that freedom [to provide services]."[84] The Court has dismissed residence requirements, for example, for companies providing temporary labor,[85] private security[86] and extrajudicial debt recovery,[87] for boiler and pressure tank inspectors[88] and for lawyers. The prohibition of an establishment requirement for service providers has been codified in Article 16(2)(a) Services Directive. In *Commission* v. *Austria – Inspection of Organic Production* (2007), the Court had to deal with an Austrian law that established a system of inspection of organically farmed products operated by private bodies.[89] The law required these private bodies to maintain an establishment in Austria which had to satisfy minimum standards relating to

---

83 *Säger*, para. 13.   84 *Fidium Finanz*, para. 46.
85 Case C-279/00, *Commission* v. *Italy – Temp Work* [2002] ECR I-1425.
86 Case C-465/05, *Commission* v. *Italy – Security Guards* [2007] ECR I-11091, para. 84.
87 Case C-134/05, *Commission* v. *Italy – Extrajudicial Debt Recovery* [2007] ECR I-6251, para. 43.
88 Case C-257/05, *Commission* v. *Austria – Boiler Inspectors* [2006] ECR I-134.
89 Case C-393/05, *Commission* v. *Austria – Inspection of Organic Production* [2007] ECR I-10195; see also
   Case C-404/05, *Commission* v. *Germany – Inspection of Organic Production* [2007] ECR I-10239.

staff as well as to administrative and technical facilities. The Court found that such a requirement to maintain an establishment in Austria infringed Article 56 TFEU which also prohibits national measures which require an establishment in a specific region. An Italian law required companies pursuing the activity of extrajudicial debt recovery to have premises in each region in which they want to carry on their business (*Commission* v. *Italy – Extrajudicial Debt Recovery*, 2007).[90] The Court found this measure to constitute an infringement of Article 56 TFEU.

Authorization and registration requirements

Authorization and registration requirements are usually not directly discriminatory if they apply to all providers of a specific service alike. However, they may nonetheless constitute restrictions that are liable to hinder or make less attractive the cross-border provision of services. The Court has ruled, for example, that an obligation for a service provider to be entered in the trades register is precluded under Article 56 TFEU if it "delays, complicates or renders more onerous the provision of its services in the host Member State" (*Schnitzer*, 2003).[91] Legislation making the marketing of satellite decoders and connected services subject to prior authorization constitutes a restriction of Article 56 TFEU as well as of the freedom to provide goods (*Canal Satéllite Digital*, 2002).[92] The prohibition of authorization requirements for service providers is now explicitly codified in Article 16 Services Directive. Article 16(2)(b) Services Directive prohibits Member States from imposing "an obligation on the provider to obtain an authorization from their competent authorities including entry in a register or registration with a professional body or association in their territory, except where provided for in this Directive or other instruments of [Union] law." This condition is much stricter than the one Member States are allowed to apply to operators who wish to establish themselves on their territory: we have already seen that Article 9 Services Directive allows Member States to apply authorization schemes to operators who establish themselves permanently in their territory if the measure is justified on public interest grounds and is proportionate.

Compulsory minimum fees and authorization requirements for insurance rate increases

In *Commission* v. *Italy – Security Guards* (2007),[93] the Court ruled that compulsory minimum fees or a price scheme for the services of security guards is a restriction on the freedom to provide services. In *Cipolla* (2006),[94] the Court ruled that

---

90 Case C-134/05, *Commission* v. *Italy – Extrajudicial Debt Recovery* [2007] ECR I-6251.
91 Case C-215/01, *Bruno Schnitzer* [2003] ECR I-14847, para. 40.
92 Case C-390/99, *Canal Satéllite Digital* [2002] ECR I-607.
93 Case C-465/05, *Commission* v. *Italy – Security Guards* [2007] ECR I-11091.
94 Joined Cases C-94/04 and C-202/04, *Cipolla* [2006] ECR I-11421.

minimum fees for lawyers set by the bar association without the possibility of derogation by individual contract are in breach of Article 56 TFEU, but may be justified on the ground of consumer protection. In response, Italy repealed the fixed or minimum tariffs applicable to lawyers' fees, but kept a system of maximum tariffs in place. The maximum tariffs are flexible, however, allowing for an increase of the maximum fees by a factor of four, and for lawyers to conclude special agreements with their clients to fix the amount of the fees. The Commission challenged the system in 2011 (*Commission* v. *Italy – Lawyer Tariffs*, 2011), arguing that the rule discourages lawyers established in other Member States from establishing themselves in Italy or from temporarily providing services there.[95] According to the Commission, the restrictions result from the additional costs generated by the application of the "extremely complex" scale of tariffs; and from the fact that it prevents lawyers from offering their services who, for example because of the superior quality of their services, claim higher fees.[96] More generally, the Commission argued that the Italian system runs counter to "the contractual freedom of lawyers by preventing *ad hoc* offers in certain situations and/or to individual clients."[97] They are therefore denied effective means to gain access to the Italian market. However, the Court rejected the Commission's line of argument. While indistinctly applicable measures that affect market access constitute a restriction covered by Article 56 TFEU, it argued that "rules of a Member State do not constitute a restriction within the meaning of the [TFEU] solely by virtue of the fact that other Member States apply less strict, or more commercially favourable, rules to providers of similar services established in their territory."[98] The fact that lawyers need to become accustomed to different rules for the calculation of their fees does not, by itself, indicate a restriction. As the Italian system grants considerable flexibility in departing from the maximum tariffs, it does not deprive lawyers from other Member States of the opportunity to gain market access.

In *DKV Belgium* (2013), the Court had to deal with a Belgian authorization requirement for certain insurance premiums.[99] According to Belgian law, insurers could alter annually the premium on the basis of the consumer price index (or, if increases in the service costs exceeded the increase in the consumer price index, certain other indices). If the insurance is unable to cover expected losses with those rate increases, it can apply to the Banking, Finance and Insurance Commission to "authorize the undertaking to take measures in order to balance its premium rates."[100] In 2009, DKV Belgium had requested authorization for a rate increase of 7.84 percent, which was rejected. The Court found the measure to constitute a restriction on the freedom of establishment and the freedom to provide services, which, however, was justified on grounds of consumer protection. The authorization requirement did not prevent insurers from freely setting their premiums and

95 Case C-565/08, *Commission* v. *Italy – Lawyer Tariffs* [2011] ECR I-2101.   96 *Ibid.*, paras. 29–30.
97 *Ibid.*, para. 31.   98 *Ibid.*, para. 49.   99 Case C-577/11, *DKV Belgium* [2013] ECR I-00000.
100 *Ibid.*, para. 8.

to increase rates; it merely provided for an authorization requirement for rate increases that went beyond general cost increases in the market, as indicated by the consumer price index. It thereby established a system to protect "consumers against sharp, unexpected increases in insurance premiums."[101]

Gambling and betting

Gambling and betting has been and continues to be subject to relatively extensive public regulation, which may range from outright prohibition or monopolies to concession systems. These national regulations have come under increased scrutiny over the past two decades. The Court first found in *Schindler* (1994) that lotteries are services within the meaning of the Treaty.[102] The Court had to deal with the case of two independent agents of a public German lottery, Gerhart and Joerg Schindler. They dispatched envelopes from the Netherlands to the United Kingdom containing advertisements and application forms for the lottery. According to UK law, the importation of such advertisements was illegal: the United Kingdom generally prohibited lotteries, with the exception of small-scale lotteries for charitable purposes and (since 1993) the national lottery.[103] The Court found that Article 56 TFEU is applicable, arguing that the "services at issue are those provided by the operator of the lottery to enable purchasers of tickets to participate in a game of chance with the hope of winning, by arranging for that purpose for the stakes to be collected, the draws to be organized and the prizes or winnings to be ascertained and paid out."[104] They are normally provided for remuneration, and are cross-border services because they have been offered in a Member State other than that in which the lottery operator is established.

The Court explicitly addressed the issue of national market regulation, as the United Kingdom formally prohibited lotteries, though with considerable exceptions. The Court held:

> Admittedly, as some Member States point out, lotteries are subject to particularly strict regulation and close control by the public authorities in the various Member States of the Community. However, they are not totally prohibited in those States. On the contrary, they are commonplace. In particular, although in principle lotteries are prohibited in the United Kingdom, small-scale lotteries for charitable and similar purposes are permitted, and, since the enactment of the appropriate law in 1993, so is the national lottery.[105]

Because lotteries are neither completely prohibited in the United Kingdom nor in any other Member State, they cannot be exempted from the application of Article 56 TFEU. Legislation that prohibits the promotion of lotteries located in another Member State therefore constitutes an obstacle to the freedom to provide services. However, the Court recognized the concerns of the Member States with regard to

---

101 *Ibid.*, para. 49.   102 Case C-275/92, *Schindler* [1994] ECR I-1039, para. 25.   103 *Ibid.*, para. 31.
104 *Ibid.*, para. 27.   105 *Ibid.*, para. 31.

gambling, and found that restrictions or even outright prohibitions of gambling were justifiable. The Court held:

> First of all, it is not possible to disregard the moral, religious or cultural aspects of lotteries, like other types of gambling, in all the Member States. The general tendency of the Member States is to restrict, or even prohibit, the practice of gambling and to prevent it from being a source of private profit. Secondly, lotteries involve a high risk of crime or fraud, given the size of the amounts which can be staked and of the winnings which they can hold out to the players, particularly when they are operated on a large scale. Thirdly, they are an incitement to spend which may have damaging individual and social consequences. A final ground which is not without relevance, although it cannot in itself be regarded as an objective justification, is that lotteries may make a significant contribution to the financing of benevolent or public interest activities such as social works, charitable works, sport or culture.[106]

The prohibition of the import of promotional material for a lottery was therefore justifiable.[107] The Court established a relatively broad degree of latitude for the national authorities with regard to gambling, and has upheld it ever since. However, the Court has increasingly emphasized the requirement that restrictions on gambling and betting operations are justifiable only if they are in fact consistent with the policy goal they purport to serve. Public interest grounds accepted by the Court include consumer protection and "the prevention of both fraud and incitement to squander money on gambling" (*Carmen Media Group*, 2010).[108] The consistency of a national regulation is scrutinized within the framework of the proportionality test. Member States that wish to combat compulsive gambling or criminality associated with gambling do not necessarily have to enact an outright ban, as the Court held for example in *Zeturf* (2011): "A Member State that is seeking to ensure a particularly high level of consumer protection in the gambling sector may be justified in taking the view that it is only by granting exclusive rights to a single body, subject to strict control by the public authorities, that it can tackle the risks connected with that sector and pursue the objective of preventing incitement to squander money on gambling and of combating addiction to gambling with sufficient effectiveness."[109] A public monopoly may be better suited to confine "the desire to gamble and the exploitation of gambling within controlled channels,"[110] as the Court stated in *Läärä* (1999), which dealt with a public monopoly for the operation of slot machines. Even the promotion and expansion of gambling operations may be justified under certain conditions, as the Court held in *Placanica* (2007): "[I]t is possible that a policy of controlled expansion in the betting and gaming sector may be entirely consistent with the objective of drawing players away from clandestine betting and gaming – and, as such, activities which are prohibited – to activities which are authorized and regulated."[111] National measures like authorization or concession schemes have to be "consistent with

---

106 *Ibid.*, para. 60.   107 *Ibid.*, para. 63.
108 Case C-46/08, *Carmen Media Group* [2010] ECR I-8149, para. 55.
109 Case C-212/08, *Zeturf* [2011] ECR I-5633, para. 72.   110 Case C-124/97, *Läärä* [1999] ECR I-6067, para. 37.
111 Joined Cases C-338/04, C-359/04 and C-360/04, *Placanica* [2007] ECR I-1891, para. 55.

the principle of equal treatment and to meet the obligation of transparency which flows from that principle" (*SIA Garkalns*, 2012).[112] Such schemes "must be based on objective, non-discriminatory criteria known in advance, in such a way as to circumscribe the exercise by the authorities of their discretion so that it is not used arbitrarily."[113] The Court reiterated in *Stanleybet* (2013) that restrictions on gambling and betting on overriding grounds in the public interest must be implemented in a way that is "consistent and systematic" with the objectives sought. In that case, Greece had granted the exclusive right to offer gambling and betting to OPAP, a listed public limited company. The Court found that Greece exercised only superficial actual oversight, and suggested that this might undermine the consistency of the Greek measure with the purported goals of restricting the supply of games of chance and to combat criminality.[114]

Advertising prohibitions

Restrictions or bans on advertisements are a recurrent theme in the Court's adjudication on Article 56 TFEU. While advertisement restrictions are often indistinctly applicable to domestic and non-domestic operators alike, they may nonetheless have a disproportionate impact on new competitors, and therefore may put non-domestic service providers at a disadvantage. With restrictions on advertisements, the incumbents on the market may have an advantage because the restrictions create difficulties for new competitors to become better known. At the same time, advertisement restrictions may serve important public policy goals. Advertisements are not neutral sources of information, but may shape the demands and desires of consumers in a way that could be found incompatible with the public interest. The EU itself, for example, enacted a ban on the advertisement of cigarettes.[115] Advertisement restrictions or bans can be justifiable if they serve legitimate public interest goals, but have to be proportionate and consistent. In *Corporación Dermoestética* (2008), the Court dealt with an Italian prohibition on advertising medical and surgical treatments on national television networks. The Court held that such a measure, while indistinctly applicable, makes it more difficult for non-domestic operators to enter the Italian market.[116] The measure could in principle be justified on the ground of public health protection. However, the ban was found to be inconsistent, as it applied to national networks only, and did not prohibit such advertisements on local channels. The measure was therefore found to be an unjustifiable restriction of Article 56 TFEU.

112 Case C-470/11, *SIA Garkalns* [2012] ECR I-00000, para. 42.   113 *Ibid.*, para. 42.
114 Joined Cases C-186/11 and C-209/11, *Stanleybet* [2013] ECR I-00000, paras. 33–36.
115 Directive 2003/33/EC of the European Parliament and of the Council on the approximation of the laws, regulations and administrative provisions of the Member States relating to the advertising and sponsorship of tobacco products, [2003] OJ L152/16.
116 Case C-500/06, *Corporación Dermoestética* [2008] ECR I-5785, paras. 33 and 39.

The Services Directive prohibits "all total prohibitions on commercial communications by the regulated professions" (Article 24(1) Services Directive). This affects, for example, bans on advertisements for professions such as lawyers and doctors that had been in place in many Member States, and which had the effect of protecting incumbent providers. In *Société fiduciaire nationale d'expertise comptable* (2011), the Court had to deal with legislation prohibiting qualified accountants, a regulated profession, from engaging in canvassing.[117] As canvassing – the unsolicited personal offer of goods or services to a certain natural or legal person – is a commercial communication, its prohibition is precluded by Article 24 Services Directive.

Posted workers

Posted workers are workers employed by an undertaking established in one Member State who are temporarily sent by the employer to another Member State to perform services and who return to their country of origin after the completion of their work. As a general rule, migrant workers who take up employment in a host state are subject to the social and labor standards of that state. The situation is different, however, for posted workers, as the Court first held in *Rush Portuguesa* (1990). According to the Court, the right to free provision of services entails that the service provider may temporarily pursue his activity in the host state "under the same conditions as are imposed by that State on its own nationals." Member States expressed disquiet about the risks of social dumping, as they feared that service providers take advantage of cheaper labor standards in their home state to win a contract in the host state to the detriment of employees there. For this reason, the Posted Workers Directive was enacted, allowing Member States to impose certain minimum standards for workers posted on their territory.

The Posted Workers Directive
The Posted Workers Directive 96/71/EC applies to undertakings established in a Member State which, in the framework of the transnational provision of services, post workers to the territory of another Member State. The Directive covers three forms of posting (Article 1(3) Posted Workers Directive): (1) posting under a contract concluded between the undertaking making the posting and the party for whom the services are intended (this was the situation in *Rush Portuguesa*, 1990); (2) posting to an establishment or an undertaking owned by the same group (intra-group mobility); and (3) posting by a

---

117 Case C-119/09, *Société fiduciaire nationale d'expertise comptable* [2011] ECR I-2551.

temporary employment or placement agency to an undertaking established or operating in the territory of another Member State, provided there is an employment relationship between the agency and the worker during the period of the posting.

The Directive provides that host Member States can impose minimum standards in certain work-related areas. These areas include: minimum rates of pay; maximum work and minimum rest periods; minimum paid annual holidays; conditions of temporary work; health, safety and hygiene standards at work; conditions of employment concerning pregnant women or women who have recently given birth, and of young people; and measures concerning nondiscrimination. These minimum standards can be established by law or regulation or by collective agreements which are generally applicable, i.e. they must be observed by all undertakings in the geographical area and in the industry concerned (Article 3(1) and (8) Posted Workers Directive). In a series of judgments in 2007 and 2008, the Court determined that the formal limitations established by the Posted Workers Directive are to be interpreted strictly. In *Laval* (2007), the Court emphasized that working conditions for posted workers can be prescribed by law or by universally applicable collective agreements alone. In *Rüffert* (2008), the Court held that a public procurement measure requiring contractors to pay their employees the remuneration prescribed by a designated collective agreement, which, however, was not declared universally applicable, infringed the Posted Workers Directive.[118]

Member States are not allowed to demand prior authorization of posted workers entering their territory. This includes, for example, a requirement for administrative visas for the posted workers (*Commission* v. *Germany – Work Visa Regime*, 2006).[119] Member States may require, however, a prior declaration from the service provider certifying that the situation of the workers concerned is lawful, particularly in light of the requirements of residence, work visas and social security cover in the Member State where that provider employs them.[120] Member States may also oblige employers to keep available for the national authorities copies of relevant social and labor documents during the time of the posting, and also to send those copies to the authorities at the end of that period (*Dos Santos Palhota*, 2010).[121] Member States have the power to verify compliance with national and Union law. These controls must not be of such an extent, however, as to render the freedom to provide services illusory (*Commission* v. *Germany – Work Visa Regime*, 2006).[122]

---

118 Case C-346/06, *Rüffert* [2008] ECR I-1989, para. 33.
119 Case C-244/04, *Commission* v. *Germany – Work Visa Regime* [2006] ECR I-885, para. 34.
120 *Ibid.*, para. 41.   121 Case C-515/08, *Dos Santos Palhota* [2010] ECR I-9133, para. 61.
122 *Commission* v. *Germany – Work Visa Regime*, para. 36.

Laval, Viking and the tension between internal market law and national labor market organization

The 2007/2008 decisions in *Laval* and *Viking* have been subject to severe criticism, in particular from labor unions, as well as from many labor law scholars.[123] *Laval* concerned the freedom to provide services as well as the Posted Workers Directive, whereas *Viking* concerned the freedom of establishment. In both cases, the Court found collective action by labor unions to be disproportionate in light of the Treaty freedoms. In practice, this made the trade unions potentially liable for damages. From a political perspective, the Court was blamed for unduly supporting the interests of employers, to the detriment of employees. According to one commentator, "this case law and the mere threat of trade union liability for damages will have a 'chilling effect' on industrial action and trade union activity."[124]

From a labor law perspective, the central criticism was that the Court had not sufficiently respected the autonomous traditions of the various national labor law systems. The Swedish model of labor market organization, which was under scrutiny in *Laval*, relied mainly on flexible agreements between labor unions and employers on the firm level, and less on legally established standards or on collective agreements on the regional or national level. In applying a narrow interpretation of the Posted Workers Directive, the Court found the Swedish system to contravene European law. This made a major overhaul of Swedish labor law necessary.[125] Because of this, the Court was criticized for enforcing a specific idea of how labor markets are or should be typically organized, thereby ignoring the broad diversity of regulatory systems in Europe.[126] Scholars have long argued that there is not one "correct" way of organizing markets;[127] instead, there are different varieties, characterized by different institutional and legal settings.[128] Often, three main types are distinguished, which differ considerably in their institutional setup: the Anglo-Saxon, the Continental and the Nordic models. The plurality of regulatory models is held to be beneficial by some scholars, as these models are believed to respond to the specific requirements of each region. Moreover, they may be understood as "laboratories" that develop innovations that can subsequently be adopted in other regions as well.

123 See e.g. Christian Joerges and Florian Rödl, "Informal Politics, Formalised Law and the 'Social Deficit' of European Integration: Reflections After the Judgments of the ECJ in Viking and Laval" (2009) 15 *European Law Journal* 1; for an overview of the political conflict surrounding the *Laval* and *Viking* decisions, see Nicole Lindstrom, "Service Liberalization in the Enlarged EU: A Race to the Bottom or the Emergence of Transnational Political Conflict?" (2010) 48 *Journal of Common Market Studies* 1307.
124 Mia Rönnmar, "Laval Returns to Sweden: The Final Judgment of the Swedish Labour Court and Swedish Legislative Reforms" (2010) 39 *Industrial Law Journal* 280, 286.
125 *Ibid.*
126 See e.g. Martin Höpner and Armin Schäfer, "A New Phase of European Integration: Organised Capitalisms in Post-Ricardian Europe" (2010) 33 *West European Politics* 344.
127 See e.g. Neil Fligstein, *The Architecture of Markets: An Economic Sociology of Twenty-First-Century Capitalist Societies*, Princeton University Press, 2002.
128 This is the basic assumption of a research approach known as "Varieties of Capitalism" (VoC). On VoC from a perspective of European law, see Jukka Snell, "Varieties of Capitalism and the Limits of European Economic Integration" (2010–2011) 13 *Cambridge Yearbook of European Legal Studies* 415.

Taxation

While direct taxation falls within the legislative competence of the Member States, the Court routinely holds that they have to exercise this competence consistently with EU law (e.g. *Waypoint Aviation*, 2011).[129] National tax rules may prohibit, impede or render less attractive the exercise of the freedom to provide services,[130] and therefore may constitute restrictions to Article 56 TFEU. At the same time, the Court has consistently held that disadvantages that are the result of differences in the tax system of the Member States do not as such constitute an obstacle to the Treaty freedoms.[131] According to the Court, the Treaty freedoms do not grant a right to tax-neutral mobility.

A number of cases have dealt with tax advantages that were granted only for investments within the territory of a certain Member State. Measures that the Court has found to be precluded by Article 56 TFEU include tax rules that facilitated the acquisition of assets by domestic companies only. In *Waypoint Aviation* (2011), Belgium applied a favorable tax regime to income from loans financing the acquisition of assets used by a company established in the national territory, but not to companies that transferred the right to use that asset to companies established in another Member State. In the case, a Belgian company had acquired two Airbus aircraft, and subsequently leased them to Air France, a company established in another Member State. The Belgian tax authorities refused to grant the favorable tax regime on income from this loan. The Court found the national measure to be precluded by Article 56 TFEU.

Under certain conditions, tax measures may include distinctions based on residence or on the place where capital is invested (Article 65(1) TFEU). They do not violate the Treaty freedoms if the distinction is based on objective grounds (*Bachmann*, 1992). A common reason for a distinction based on location is the attempt to restrain tax evasion and to ensure the effectiveness of fiscal supervision. As the national taxation systems remain unharmonized, and supranational collaboration of tax authorities is still underdeveloped, restrictive tax measures may be justifiable on these grounds. In *SIAT* (2012), the Court had to deal with a Belgium tax measure on the deductibility of payments for supplies or services. As a general rule, these expenses could be deducted from the taxable income, and the tax authorities presumed that the expenditure is necessary for acquiring or retaining taxable income, with the additional condition that the amount of that expenditure must not exceed business needs to an unreasonable extent.[132] As a special rule, however, payments are not regarded as deductible business expenses if they are made to a non-domestic supplier "which, by virtue of the legislation of the country of establishment, is not subject there to a tax on income or is subject there to a tax regime which is appreciably more advantageous than the applicable tax regime in Belgium, unless the taxpayer proves, by any legal means, that such payments relate to genuine and proper transactions and do not exceed the normal limits."[133] In essence, this rule reverses the burden of proof: in the latter case,

---

129 Case C-9/11, *Waypoint Aviation* [2011] ECR I-9697, para. 19.   130 *Ibid.*, para. 22.
131 See e.g. Case C-403/03, *Schempp* [2005] ECR I-6421, para. 45.   132 Case C-318/10, *SIAT* [2012], para. 21.
133 *Ibid.*, para. 6.

the taxpayer has to convince the tax authority that the payments are genuine and do not merely constitute a "simulation of business transactions," i.e. tax evasion.[134] The rule therefore constitutes a restriction of Article 56 TFEU, as it dissuades service recipients from making use of the services of providers established in another Member State.[135] The Court then held that such measure may be justified on the grounds of preventing tax evasion and of ensuring the effectiveness of fiscal supervision. However, the measure does not pass the proportionality test: the criteria applied by the tax authorities to establish whether the special rule is applicable are not laid down in advance, and the assessment is carried out on a case-by-case basis instead.[136] According to the Court, "[s]uch a rule does not, therefore, meet the requirements of the principle of legal certainty, in accordance with which rules of law must be clear, precise and predictable as regards their effects, in particular where they may have unfavourable consequences for individuals and undertakings."[137]

RIGHTS OF SERVICE RECIPIENTS

According to the Court, "[Article 56 TFEU] confers rights not only on the provider of services but also on the recipient" (*Dijkman*, 2010).[138] The Court had already held in *Luisi and Carbone* (1984): "[T]he freedom to provide services includes the freedom, for the recipients of services, to go to another Member State in order to receive a service there, without being obstructed by restrictions, even in relation to payments and that tourists, persons receiving medical treatment and persons travelling for the purpose of education or business are to be regarded as recipients of services."[139]

Right to enter another Member State to receive services

Service recipients have the right to enter another Member State to receive a service. For example, tourists are considered to be service recipients who can rely on Article 56 TFEU, as the Court held for example in *Cowan* (1989).[140] The rights of natural persons to move to and reside in another Member State are consolidated in the Citizenship Directive (see above).

Right to receive services under the same conditions as nationals

Service recipients have the right to discrimination-free access to services. In *Commission* v. *Spain – Access to Museums* (1993),[141] a Spanish law provided that only Spanish nationals, residents in Spain and teenagers under the age of twenty-one

---

134 *Ibid.*, para. 22.   135 *Ibid.*, para. 28.   136 *Ibid.*, para. 26.   137 *Ibid.*, para. 58.
138 Case C-233/09, *Dijkman* [2010] ECR I-6649, para. 24.
139 Joined Cases 286/82 and 26/83, *Luisi and Carbone* [1984] ECR 377, para. 16.
140 Case 186/87, *Cowan* [1989] ECR 195, para. 15.
141 Case C-45/93, *Commission* v. *Spain – Access to Museums* [1994] ECR I-911; see also Case C-388/01, *Commission*
    v. *Italy – Access to Museums* [2003] ECR I-721.

could visit state museums without charge. The Court found the measure to be discriminatory, ruling that Article 56 TFEU incorporates the right of Union citizens to receive services in another Member State under the same conditions as the nationals of that state.

In *Stopover Tax* (2009),[142] the Court had to deal with a tax that the Italian region of Sardinia had established on stopovers for tourism purposes of aircraft used for the private transportation of persons or for recreational use, which was imposed solely on operators whose tax domicile was outside the territory of that region. As regards companies that offer such aviation services for remuneration or rent out recreational aircraft, Article 56 TFEU is clearly applicable.[143] However, the Court also held that Article 56 TFEU is even applicable to individuals who fly their aircraft to Sardinia for purely private reasons, namely, as the recipients of services: "[P]ersons operating a means of transport . . . receive a number of services on the territory of the Region of Sardinia, such as the services provided at the airports and ports. Consequently, the stopover is a necessary condition for receiving such services and the regional tax on stopovers has a certain link with their provision."[144] The tax was then found unjustifiable by the Court with regard both to operators who provide transportation services and to operators who use the aircraft for purely private reasons as recipients of services.

The right to access healthcare in another Member State

According to the Court, medical treatment constitutes a service within the meaning of Article 56 TFEU which also applies to social security systems where patients receive the treatment free of charge. Even though in these situations the healthcare providers receive the remuneration not from the patient, but from the public insurance, the service is nonetheless provided for remuneration, which means that Article 56 TFEU is applicable.[145]

Because healthcare services are often costly and individuals pay considerable contributions to social security systems, the question whether the costs of treatment in another Member State are covered by the home state insurance is highly relevant in the decision of patients to get treatment abroad. Since the 1970s, Regulation 1408/71 (now Regulation 883/2004) on the coordination of national social security provides for the possibility of Union citizens to receive healthcare services in another Member State. However, treatment in another Member State requires, except in cases of emergency, prior authorization by the competent institution of the home state (Article 20 Regulation 883/2004). While in the original provision of Regulation 1408/71 the authorization decision was entirely up to the competent institution, the current Regulation provides certain minimum

---

142 Case C-169/08, *Presidente del Consiglio dei Ministri* v. *Regione Sardegna – Stopover Tax* [2009] ECR I-10821.
143 *Ibid.*, para. 27.   144 *Ibid.*, para. 26.   145 Case C-157/99, *Smits* v. *Peerbooms* [2001] ECR I-5473, para. 58.

requirements, based on the Court's case law. The authorization must be accorded when two conditions are fulfilled: (1) where the treatment in question is among the benefits provided for by the legislation in the Member State where the person concerned resides; and (2) where the treatment cannot be provided within a time-limit which is medically justifiable, taking into account the patient's current state of health and the probable course of the illness.

Since the 1990s, the Court has held that patients have a right to reimbursement of the costs of a treatment in another Member State even without prior authorization. According to the Court, this right is based on Article 56 TFEU. The first decision where the Court ruled in this regard was *Kohll*.

Case C-158/96, Kohll (1998)

Raymond Kohll, a Luxembourg national, requested authorization by his insurer, UCM, for his daughter to receive treatment from an orthodontist established in Germany. UCM rejected the request, arguing that the treatment was not urgent and that it could be provided in Luxembourg as well.

Does the authorization requirement for treatment in another Member State breach Article 56 TFEU?

Yes.

According to the Court, the authorization requirements "deter insured persons from approaching providers of medical services established in another Member State and constitute, for them and their patients, a barrier to freedom to provide services."[146] To justify the restriction, UCM argued that the "requirement of prior authorization constitutes the only effective and least restrictive means of controlling expenditure on health and balancing the budget of the social security system."[147] Mr. Kohll denied that these concerns were relevant in the present case. As he had asked only for reimbursement at the rate applied in Luxembourg, the financial burden for UCM would be the same regardless of whether the treatment was performed by a domestic orthodontist or one established in another Member State.[148] The Court agreed, arguing that "it is clear that reimbursement of the costs of dental treatment provided in other Member States in accordance with the tariff of the State of insurance has no significant effect on the financing of the social security system."[149]

On the same day the Court handed down its decision in *Kohll*, it also gave its decision in *Decker* (1998), which was an analogous case concerning the free movement of goods.[150] Mr. Decker was a Luxembourg citizen who bought a pair

---

146 *Kohll*, para. 35.   147 *Ibid.*, para. 37.   148 *Ibid.*, para. 40.   149 *Ibid.*, para. 42.
150 Case C-120/95, *Decker* [1998] ECR I-1831.

of glasses in Belgium, and was refused reimbursement by his insurer because he had not sought prior authorization. The Court held that such an authorization requirement constitutes a restriction of Article 34 TFEU.

Patients therefore have two independent rights to reimbursement for their medical expenses for treatments received in other Member States: if they seek prior authorization by their insurer based on Article 20 Regulation 883/2004, they receive the benefit in kind by the institution in the host state on behalf of the patient's insurer. If they do not seek prior authorization or if it is refused, they can still claim reimbursement at the rate applied by their insurer on the basis of Article 56 TFEU.

The decisions in *Kohll* and *Decker* required Member States and social insurance institutions to rethink the regulatory instruments they used to provide efficient healthcare while controlling expenditure. A control mechanism based strictly on national boundaries was no longer viable in light of the Court's decisions. At the same time, the ability to effectively plan for the long-term and to prevent excessive cost increases continued to be necessary requirements for national health policies. The Court acknowledged these needs in *Kohll* and in its later case law. The Court held that "it cannot be excluded that the possible risk of seriously undermining a social security system's financial balance may constitute an overriding reason in the general interest capable of justifying a barrier to the principle of freedom to provide services" (*Smits* v. *Peerbooms*, 2001).[151] Moreover, the "objective of maintaining a balanced medical and hospital service open to all ... even if intrinsically linked to the method of financing the social security system, may also fall within the derogations on grounds of public health ... in so far as it contributes to the attainment of a high level of health protection" (*Smits* v. *Peerbooms*, 2001)[152] And, finally, "the Treaty permits Member States to restrict the freedom to provide medical and hospital services in so far as the maintenance of treatment capacity or medical competence on national territory is essential for the public health, and even the survival of, the population" (*Smits* v. *Peerbooms*, 2001).[153] The issue became particularly relevant with regard to hospital care.

In *Smits* v. *Peerbooms* (2001),[154] the Court addressed the question whether an authorization requirement for hospital care in another Member State can be justified on grounds relating to the public interest. The Court acknowledged the challenges Member States faced with regard to upkeeping an efficient system of hospitals:

[B]y comparison with medical services provided by practitioners in their surgeries or at the patient's home, medical services provided in a hospital take place within an infrastructure with, undoubtedly, certain very distinct characteristics. It is thus well known that the number of hospitals, their geographical distribution, the mode of their organization and the equipment with which they are provided, and even the nature of the medical services which they are able to offer, are all matters for which planning must be possible.[155]

---

151 *Smits* v. *Peerbooms*, para. 72.   152 *Ibid.*, para. 73.   153 *Ibid.*, para. 74.
154 See also Case C-368/98, *Vanbraekel* [2001] ECR I-5363.   155 *Smits* v. *Peerbooms*, para. 76.

The Court went on to argue that "it is clear that, if insured persons were at liberty, regardless of the circumstances, to use the services of hospitals with which their sickness insurance fund had no contractual arrangements, whether they were situated in the Netherlands or in another Member State, all the planning which goes into the contractual system in an effort to guarantee a rationalized, stable, balanced and accessible supply of hospital services would be jeopardized at a stroke."[156] On these grounds, the Court found that an authorization requirement for hospital care is justifiable, though the conditions attached to the grant of such authorization must be necessary and proportionate with regard to the invoked grounds of public interest.[157] The Court's case law on the reimbursement of costs was codified in 2011 in the Patient Rights Directive (Articles 7 and 8).[158] The Directive also clarifies the applicable law in the cross-border provision of healthcare services. According to Article 4, cross-border healthcare is subject to the legislation and standards of the Member State where the treatment occurs.

SECONDARY LAW

Legal basis for services liberalization and harmonization

The legal basis for secondary law measures in the field of services liberalization and harmonization is Article 62 TFEU in conjunction with Articles 53 and 59 TFEU as well as the general harmonization provisions of Articles 114 and 115 TFEU. One of the central secondary law measures is the Services Directive.

Services Directive

The Services Directive 2006/123/EC aims at removing obstacles to the freedom to provide services and to the freedom of establishment of service providers.[159] It combines a number of rather different regulatory approaches. First, the Services Directive initiated a review process that required Member States to evaluate various aspects of their national law relating to the provision of services and report the results to the Commission.[160] Second, the Directive proposed a number of procedural innovations aimed at facilitating the cross-border provision of services and establishment. This included, most notably, the establishment of "points of single contact" in each Member State where non-domestic service providers can complete the most relevant formalities and procedures required to start operations. And,

---

156 *Ibid.*, para. 81.   157 See also *ibid.*, para. 108.
158 Directive 2011/24/EU of the European Parliament and of the Council on the application of patients' rights in cross-border healthcare, [2012] OJ L88/45.
159 Directive 2006/123/EC of the European Parliament and of the Council on services in the internal market, [2006] OJ L376/36.
160 Arts. 5, 9(2), 15(5), 25(3) and 39 Services Directive.

third, the Directive also has a considerable importance in substantive terms, defining and clarifying the meaning of Articles 49 and 56 TFEU. Some of the substantive provisions of the Directive have already been mentioned in the preceding sections. It is this third dimension of the Services Directive that has been the subject of considerable political dispute prior to its inception.

History of the Services Directive

While the market in services now accounts for over two-thirds of the EU's GDP, it remained relatively fragmented until recently. In 2000, the European heads of state and governments proclaimed the so-called Lisbon Strategy. The European Council stated:

The Union has today set itself a new strategic goal for the next decade: to become the most competitive and dynamic knowledge-based economy in the world capable of sustainable economic growth with more and better jobs and greater social cohesion.[161]

Following the Lisbon Strategy, the Commission issued a proposal for a services Directive in 2004, which was dubbed the "Bolkestein Directive" after then-Commissioner for the Internal Market, Frits Bolkestein. The proposal contained a very broad country-of-origin principle, according to which a service provider is subject only to the law of his country of establishment, but not to the laws of the country of destination.[162] Critics of the principle feared that this would lead to a regulatory race to the bottom, as service providers could simply establish themselves in a Member State with low labor, social, environmental and other regulatory standards and "export" these standards to other Member States. After considerable protests by, among others, labor unions and NGOs like ATTAC, the European Parliament watered down the proposal, causing the Commission to issue a new, more conciliatory Directive. Criticism of the Services Directive was partly rooted in a more general conflict on the socio-economic orientation of the EU. Should the internal market rules promote regulatory competition among the Member States, or should Member States be allowed to ensure a high level of protection of consumers and workers even at the expense of a certain degree of mobility of service providers? While the original proposal seemed to favor the former model, the revised version attempted to reconcile the two. However, being the result of a delicate political compromise, critics point out that the final version suffers from some poor drafting and lacks the focus of the original.[163]

---

161 Lisbon European Council, March 23 and 24, 2000, Presidency Conclusions, para. 5.
162 Berend Drijber, "'The Country-of-Origin Principle' Hearing Before the Committee Internal Market and Consumer Protection on the Proposed Directive on Services in the Internal Market," www.europarl.europa.eu/hear-ings/20041111/imco/contributions_en.htm (2004) (accessed February 9, 2013), pp. 3–4; see also Kalypso Nicolaïdis and Susanne Schmidt, "Mutual Recognition on 'Trial': The Long Road to Services Liberalization" (2007) 14 *Journal of European Public Policy* 717, 729.
163 Catherine Barnard, "Unravelling the Services Directive" (2008) 45 *Common Market Law Review* 323, 323–324.

Evaluation of national law relating to the provision of services

The Treaty freedoms create legal remedies that Union citizens can rely on when they challenge restrictive national measures. However, legal proceedings tend to be expensive and cumbersome, and cannot but yield very limited results. The integration of the services market therefore requires active steps by the Member States to adapt their national systems in such a way as to facilitate the cross-border provision of services and establishment. The Services Directive stipulates various requirements for the Member States to evaluate their national laws and to adapt them in ways to support the functioning of the integrated market in services.[164] Article 5 requires the Member States to "simplify" the procedures and formalities applicable to access to and exercise of a service activity. With regard to the right of establishment, Member States are required to review their authorization schemes (Article 9(2)) as well as other requirements listed in Article 15 Services Directive.

Procedural innovations

Article 5(3) Services Directive provides:

> Where Member States require a provider or recipient to supply a certificate, attestation or any other document proving that a requirement has been satisfied, they shall accept any document from another Member State which serves an equivalent purpose or from which it is clear that the requirement in question has been satisfied.

Formal specifications like a requirement to produce the original, certified copies or certified translations are prohibited unless justified on grounds of the public interest. The provision lays down a principle of mutual recognition: if a certain attestation is required from a service provider, Member States must accept functionally equivalent documents from other Member States. It is aimed at reducing unnecessary bureaucratic obstacles for service providers, while upholding the right of Member States to subject them to their specific requirements. The principle of mutual recognition requires an active engagement of the Member States: they must provide an environment in which public institutions are both willing and able to deal with documentation from different Member States.

Another procedural innovation is the requirement that Member States need to create a "point of single contact" (Article 6 Services Directive), where operators can complete all formalities to access and exercise their service activities, and where they can access the essential information in this regard. All Member States have created websites for this purpose.[165]

Material scope of the Services Directive

The material scope of the Services Directive is a rather complex matter. On the one hand, Article 2(1) Services Directive states that the Directive applies to all services

---

164 Arts. 5, 9(2), 15(5), 25(3) and 39 Services Directive.
165 See http://ec.europa.eu/internal_market/eu-go/index_en.htm (accessed July 11, 2013).

supplied by providers established in a Member State. On the other hand, the Directive provides for numerous exceptions. The fractured nature of the Directive's scope is an expression of the difficult political and complex regulatory character of this field, and of the competing legal-political concepts that govern it. The concept of services is so broad that it covers activities ranging from roofing to healthcare, from hairdressing to open heart surgery, and from massage to security services. While it is true that the Directive lacks doctrinal simplicity, as some commentators have criticized, it could be argued that its complex nature reflects the divergent nature of the fields it touches.

The scope of the Services Directive is limited by its Articles 2 and 3. The former excludes certain activities and economic sectors (such as noneconomic services of general interest or social services); the latter holds that more specific secondary law provisions on the access or exercise of a service (such as the Posted Workers Directive) prevail over the provisions of the Services Directive. Article 17 provides further derogations, which apply solely to the freedom to provide services (i.e. not establishment). The doctrinal effect is that the Services Directive does not apply to services covered by these exceptions. Instead, other secondary law applies, or, in the absence of harmonization, the Treaty freedom provisions apply directly.

We can distinguish roughly between the following types of exceptions: (1) fields excluded because they are already harmonized on the European level (e.g. financial services, electronic communication services); and (2) fields where, for a variety of legal and political reasons, a regulatory logic distinct from that of the Directive applies (for example, social services). A case that dealt with the scope of the Services Directive is *Femarbel* (2013).[166] The referring court inquired whether day- and night-care centers providing assistance and care to elderly persons are exempted from the scope of the Services Directive. The Court suggested that these services could be exempted from the scope of the Services Directive because they provide healthcare services or social services (Article 2(2)(f) and (j) Services Directive). It emphasized that "[t]he centres would be exempt from the rules established in that Directive only if such activities constitute their principal activity."[167] Activities constitute "social services" within the meaning of the Directive if they are "essential in order to guarantee the fundamental right to human dignity and integrity and are a manifestation of the principles of social cohesion and solidarity."[168] The service provider must be "the State itself, a charity recognized as such by the State, or a private service provider mandated by the State."[169]

Provisions concerning the right of establishment

The Services Directive has three major substantive parts related to the freedom of establishment. Articles 9–13 Services Directive deal with national schemes regulating the authorization of the access to and exercise of a service activity. As

---

166 Case C-57/12, *Femarbel* [2013] ECR I-00000.   167 *Ibid.*, para. 33.   168 *Ibid.*, para. 43.
169 *Ibid.*, para. 44.

we have already seen, these schemes are subject to a general proportionality requirement: authorization schemes are prohibited unless they are nondiscriminatory, justified by an overriding reason relating to the public interest, and proportionate.

Article 14 Services Directive prohibits a number of requirements on service providers. This includes directly and indirectly discriminatory requirements based on nationality or, in case of companies, the location of the registered office; nationality or residence requirements for the staff, shareholders or management, the prohibition of being enrolled with a professional body in more than one Member State; the case-by-case application of an economic test making the granting of authorization subject to proof of the existence of an economic need or market demand, or other criteria; and the obligation to provide or participate in a financial guarantee or to take out insurance from a provider or body established in their territory, etc. These prohibitions are largely codifications of the Court's case law.

Article 15 Services Directive provides a list of "suspect" requirements imposed on service providers that are not prohibited, but shall be subjected by the Member States to a review in order to ensure that these requirements comply with the general proportionality requirement. Article 15(7) establishes a notification requirement for any newly enacted national provision covered by Article 15 Services Directive. The Member States must notify the Commission of such measures and justify them. Within three months, and after examining the compatibility with EU law of the notified measures, the Commission may request the Member State to refrain from adopting these measures or to abolish them. The procedure in Article 15(7) resembles the very successful notification requirement that was discussed with regard to the free movement of goods. Suspect requirements include: quantitative or territorial restrictions, in particular in the form of limits fixed according to population or of a minimum geographical distance between providers; an obligation on a provider to take a specific legal form; a ban on having more than one establishment in the territory of the same state; requirements fixing a minimum number of employees; and an obligation on the provider to supply other specific services jointly with his service.

Provisions with regard to the provision of services

Article 16(2) Services Directive provides a list of prohibited requirements. Service providers shall not be required to comply with these as a precondition for market access or for the exercise of a service activity. They include an obligation on the provider to have an establishment in their territory; an obligation on the provider to obtain an authorization from their competent authorities including entry in a register or registration with a professional body or association in their territory, except where provided for in the Directive or other instruments of Community law; a ban on the provider setting up a certain form or type of infrastructure in their territory, including an office or chambers, which the provider needs in order to supply the services in question; and requirements, except for those necessary for health and safety at work, which affect the use of equipment and material which are an integral part of the service provided. Any such or other restriction on service providers can be justified only on grounds of public policy, public security, public health or the protection of the environment, and must be nondiscriminatory, necessary and proportionate. Other public interests can justify restrictions only under Article 18, which provides for "case-by-case derogations" in "exceptional circumstances" with regard to measures relating to the safety of services.

Public services

In both public and scholarly debate, society is often casually conceptualized in a dichotomic form: the market on the one side, the state on the other. However, the reality is often much more complicated than this clear-cut distinction would suggest. In fact, the two spheres are intrinsically connected in many ways: for example, public institutions routinely buy their equipment from private suppliers, or contract out services to private operators. Public services may also be delegated to privately organized entities that are either owned by a public authority, or receive public funding. In fact, most areas commonly understood to be "public services" are in fact intricate regulatory networks of market-based and nonmarket organization (and, conversely, markets require a complex and sophisticated regulatory framework to function). Health care systems, for example, are often organized on the basis of public regulation and semi-public insurances while at the same time employing various forms of market-based mechanisms, for example, in the acquisition of pharmaceutical products from private suppliers or contracts with for-profit or non-profit service providers, self-employed doctors and other medical professionals. These mixed systems are the consequence of regulatory choices: based on economic assumptions, practical experience and political compromises, the EU and the Member States have opted to organize certain tasks as markets, and others in a nonmarket form. In parts, these choices are subject to a political cycle: for example, many European countries nationalized significant segments of their economy in the first half of the twentieth century and after the Second World War. Since the 1980s, however, many Member States have moved toward greater involvement of private actors in fields previously organized as exclusively public systems; with the break-down of the trust in market-based solutions in the wake of the economic crisis, the pendulum may well, yet again, move in a different direction in the future. The European Union has to navigate this complex regulatory landscape, ensuring the application of its rules in areas that are organized as markets, while at the same time protecting regulatory choices for nonmarket solutions.

A vast number of activities may potentially be organized as public services: they may range from police, the judiciary, social security, social assistance and education to the maintenance and universal accessibility of traffic systems, public transport, water supply, waste management, electricity, telephone and Internet services. Accordingly, the European regulatory system that applies to public services is relatively complex, and encompasses internal market and competition rules, secondary legislation as well as soft law. In particular, public services usually touch the following EU law questions:

- Is internal market law applicable to the activities of a specific service provider?
- Is competition law applicable to the activities of a specific service provider?
- Under which conditions can a public service provider be compensated (state aid)?
- Under which conditions can public services be contracted out (public procurement, concessions)?

Types of public services

In EU law, usually three types of public services are distinguished: (1) regular services (which, however, are performed by public institutions); (2) services of general economic interest (SGEIs); and (3) noneconomic services of general interest (NESGIs). In EU law jargon, an additional abbreviation is sometimes used, SGI, which stands for "services of general interest." It encompasses both SGEIs and NESGIs, in contrast to "regular" services.[170] Table 7.2 sets out the types of public service and their applicable law.

Table 7.2 Types of public service and their applicable law	
Type of service	**Which law applies**
"Regular" services	No exceptions; internal market law, competition law, public procurement law apply
SGEIs	Internal market law, competition law, procurement law apply, but with exceptions (e.g. Art. 106(2) TFEU, *Altmark Trans* case law, secondary law)
NESGIs	Procurement law applies

(1) *"Regular" services.* For the applicability of internal market law and competition law it is irrelevant whether a service is provided by a public or a private institution. In other words, the legal status of the operator is not decisive.[171] Internal market law applies if the activity is economic in nature. Competition law (including state aid) applies to "undertakings," which in turn are defined to be engaged in "economic activities," which include "any activity consisting in offering goods and services on a given market."[172] If a public entity decides to contract out a service to a private operator, public procurement rules apply.

---

170 Hatzopoulos, *Regulating Services in the European Union*, p. 42.
171 Case C-41/90, *Höfner* [1991] ECR I-1979, para. 21.
172 Case C-35/96, *Commission* v. *Italy – Customs Agents* [1998] ECR I-3851, para. 36.

(2) *Services of general economic interest (SGEIs).* According to the Court, SGEIs are services that have "special characteristics" as compared to other economic activities.[173] In *Corsica Ferries France* (1998), the Court held for example that mooring operations in ports "are obliged to provide at any time and to any user a universal mooring service, for reasons of safety in port waters."[174] This requirement sets them apart from "regular" services. While internal market law and competition law apply to these services in principle, their application is limited by a number of exceptions. These exceptions can be based either on Article 106(2) TFEU or on secondary law.

(3) *Non-economic services of general interest (NESGIs).* Certain public services are understood to be excluded from the scope of European economic law, either generally or in parts. If the entity is not considered to be an "undertaking" because it is not engaged in economic activities, competition law does not apply. The Court has found that the exercise of public authority as well as solidarity-based social

The special role of public services

European legislators have emphasized the special role they assign to public services on many occasions:

- Article 106(2) TFEU provides: "Undertakings entrusted with the operation of services of general economic interest or having the character of a revenue-producing monopoly shall be subject to the rules contained in the Treaties, in particular to the rules on competition, in so far as the application of such rules does not obstruct the performance, in law or in fact, of the particular tasks assigned to them. The development of trade must not be affected to such an extent as would be contrary to the interests of the Union."
- Article 14 TFEU emphasizes with regard to SGIs that the Member States and the Union "shall take care that such services operate on the basis of principles and conditions, particularly economic and financial conditions, which enable them to fulfil their missions."
- Articles 34–36 Charter of Fundamental Rights emphasize the importance of access to social security benefits, social services, healthcare and services of general economic interest.
- Article 1 Protocol No. 26 "On Services of General Interest" emphasizes, *inter alia*, "the wide discretion of national, regional and local authorities in providing, commissioning and organizing services of general economic interest." Article 2 adds that "[t]he provisions of the Treaties do not affect in any way the competence of Member States to provide, commission and organize non-economic services of general interest."

---

173 Case C-266/96, *Corsica Ferries France* [1998] ECR I-3949, para. 45.   174 *Ibid.*, para. 45.

security systems fall outside the scope of competition law.[175] Internal market law remains inapplicable if the activity is not a "service" within the meaning of the services provisions, i.e. if it is not "normally provided for remuneration." We have already seen, for example, that the Court has found that internal market law does not apply to public education (*Humbel*, 1988).[176] Procurement law applies only to a limited extent to services such as education, health and social services.[177]

Compensation for public service: the Altmark criteria

As mentioned, SGEIs differ from regular services because they exhibit "special characteristics." These special features are the reason why service providers may require compensation by the public that goes beyond the price that is charged for the service. Compensation for services paid by a public authority to a service provider falls under the state aid rules of the Treaty. Article 107 TFEU prohibits any aid granted by a Member State to certain undertakings which distorts or threatens to distort competition. The scope of measures that can constitute state aid is broad. According to the Court: "[M]easures which, whatever their form, are likely directly or indirectly to favour certain undertakings or are to be regarded as an economic advantage which the recipient undertaking would not have obtained under normal market conditions, are regarded as aid" (*Altmark Trans*, 2003).[178] This includes, for example, tax deductions or subsidies for social housing operators (*Eric Libert*, 2013).[179] This is not the case, however, "where a State measure must be regarded as compensation for the services provided by the recipient undertakings in order to discharge public service obligations, so that those undertakings do not enjoy a real financial advantage and the measure thus does not have the effect of putting them in a more favourable competitive position than the undertakings competing with them" (*Eric Libert*, 2013).[180] The Court defined in *Altmark Trans* (2003) under which conditions compensation for public service does not constitute state aid, and therefore is not caught by Article 107 TFEU. In particular, the Court defined four criteria:

- "[T]he recipient undertaking must actually have public service obligations to discharge, and the obligations must be clearly defined."[181]
- "[T]he parameters on the basis of which the compensation is calculated must be established in advance in an objective and transparent manner, to avoid it conferring an economic advantage which may favour the recipient undertaking over competing undertakings."[182]

---

175 On solidarity-based social security, see Case C-159/91, *Poucet* [1993] ECR I-637; on the exercise of public authority, see Case C-364/92, *SAT Fluggesellschaft* [1994] ECR I-43, para. 28.
176 Case 263/86, *Humbel* [1988] ECR 5365, paras. 16–20.   177 Directive 2004/18/EC, Annex II B.
178 Case C-280/00, *Altmark* [2003] ECR I-7747, para. 84.
179 Joined Cases C-197/11 and C-203/11, *Libert* [2013] ECR I-00000, para. 102.   180 *Ibid.*, para. 84.
181 *Altmark*, para. 89.   182 *Ibid.*, para. 90.

- "[T]he compensation cannot exceed what is necessary to cover all or part of the costs incurred in the discharge of public service obligations, taking into account the relevant receipts and a reasonable profit for discharging those obligations."[183]
- The undertaking which is to discharge public service obligations is to be chosen by a public procurement procedure; if this is not the case, then the "level of compensation needed must be determined on the basis of an analysis of the costs which a typical undertaking, well run and adequately provided with means of transport so as to be able to meet the necessary public service requirements, would have incurred in discharging those obligations, taking into account the relevant receipts and a reasonable profit for discharging the obligations."[184]

The Court has stressed that the "Member States have a wide margin of discretion with regard to the definition of services that could be classified as being services of general economic interest" (*Eric Libert*, 2013).[185] The doctrinal consequence of the *Altmark* criteria applying to compensation for a public service is that the payment is not considered to be state aid within the meaning of Article 107 TFEU at all. Measures that do not meet the *Altmark* criteria constitute state aid, but can nonetheless be compatible with the Treaty based on Article 106(2) TFEU.

Public procurement

Public procurement describes the acquisition by a public authority of goods and services on the market. Examples are a municipality that commissions a construction company to build a school (a public works contract), a public hospital that acquires medical supplies (a public supply contract) or a ministry that awards a contract to maintain its facilities to a service provider (a public service contract). Public procurement constitutes a significant part of overall market activity. Accordingly, it is necessary to ensure that contracts are awarded according to nondiscriminatory criteria, and to ensure that non-domestic providers have a fair chance to bid for public contracts.

The European legislator has issued Directives on the procurement of public works contracts, public supply contracts and public service contracts (2004/18/EC)[186] as well as on procurement in the water, energy, transport and postal services sectors (2004/17/EC).[187] The Directives apply to all public authorities. This includes all

183 *Ibid.*, para. 92.   184 *Ibid.*, para. 93.   185 *Eric Libert*, para. 98.
186 Directive 2004/18/EC of the European Parliament and of the Council on the coordination of procedures for the award of public works contracts, public supply contracts and public service contracts, [2004] OJ L134/114.
187 Directive 2004/17/EC of the European Parliament and of the Council coordinating the procurement procedures of entities operating in the water, energy, transport and postal services sectors, [2004] OJ L134/1; see also Directive 2009/81/EC of the European Parliament and of the Council of 13 July 2009 on the coordination of procedures for the award of certain works contracts, supply contracts and service contracts by contracting authorities or entities in the fields of defence and security, and amending Directives 2004/17/EC and 2004/18/EC, [2009] OJ L216/76.

state and local authorities and organizations financed or supervised mainly by them. These contracting authorities must treat all economic operators equally and must act in a transparent way. The Directive requires the contracting authorities to advertise their calls for tenders if the value of the service lies above a certain threshold. These notices are published on a Commission website, ted.europa.eu. This means that potential suppliers from all over Europe (including EEA countries) are able to obtain information and to participate in tender procedures to bid for the award of contracts.

Public authorities are exempted from the requirement to initiate a tender procedure if (1) it awards the contract to an entity over which it exercises control similar to that which it exercises over its own departments and (2) the entity carries out the essential part of its activities with the contracting authorities to which it belongs (*Teckal*, 1999).[188] These are called "in-house" providers, as the providers, even though they are organized as distinct entities, function essentially as sub-divisions of the public authority. Municipalities often perform public services such as the distribution of water, gas and district heating as well as waste disposal through publicly owned companies (see e.g. *Econord*, 2012).[189] The Court has pointed out, however, that the providers must be exclusively in public ownership. It ruled in *Stadt Halle and RPL Recyclingpark Lochau* (2005): "[T]he participation, even as a minority, of a private undertaking in the capital of a company in which the contracting authority in question is also a participant excludes in any event the possibility of that contracting authority exercising over that company a control similar to that which it exercises over its own departments."[190]

The procuring authority has various possibilities to ensure compliance with economic and social standards. In particular, Member States do not necessarily have to base the award of public contracts solely on the lowest price. According to Article 53(1)(a) Directive 2004/18/EC, Member States may also employ various other criteria, including environmental considerations. Member States may also require proof by contractors that they have paid their taxes and the required social security contributions in both the home and the host state (Article 45(2)). This was confirmed by the Court in *Bâtiments et Ponts Construction* (2010),[191] which dealt with construction work related to the renovation of the Berlaymont building in Brussels, which houses the European Commission.

Service concessions

A concession is a contract in which a public authority authorizes an economic operator to provide services and to receive remuneration from the recipients of the

---

188 Case C-107/98, *Teckal* [1999] ECR I-8121, para. 50.
189 Joined Cases C-182/11 and C-183/11, *Econord* [2012] ECR I-00000.
190 Case C-26/03, *Stadt Halle and RPL Recyclingpark Lochau* [2005] ECR I-1, para. 49.
191 Case C-74/09, *Bâtiments et Ponts Construction* [2010] ECR I-7271, para. 53.

service. Unlike public procurement, where the public authority itself remunerates the service provider, in a concession the service provider levies charges on the users. According to the Court, "[a] service concession is present where the agreed method of remuneration consists in the right to exploit the service and the provider takes the risk of operating the services in question" (*Acoset*, 2009).[192] Examples of services concessions are arrangements where the service provider's remuneration came from payments made by users of a public parking lot (*Parking Brixen*, 2005),[193] the public transport system (*ANAV*, 2006)[194] or a cable television network (*Coditel Brabant*, 2008).[195]

The public procurement Directives did not apply to services concessions, which consequently were regulated by the Treaty freedoms alone, with Articles 49 and 56 TFEU being the central provisions.[196] On the basis of these Treaty freedoms, the Court developed a system essentially analogous to that in force for public procurement, with much of the case law being relevant for both public service contracts and service concessions. This includes the obligation to put the service concession out to tender.[197] The Court also applied the same exceptions with regard to this obligation that it had applied with regard to public service contracts. It held in *Acoset* (2009) that:

[T]he application of the rules set out in [Articles 18, 49 and 56 TFEU], as well as the general principles of which they are the specific expression, is excluded if the control exercised over the concessionaire by the concession-granting public authority is comparable to that which the authority exercises over its own departments and if, at the same time, that entity carries out the essential part of its activities with the controlling authority. In such a case, an invitation to tender is not mandatory, even if the other party to the contract is an entity that is legally distinct from the contracting authority.[198]

The in-house rules apply, however, only if the provider is exclusively held by the public authority. The Court held in *ANAV* (2006): "[I]n so far as the concessionaire is a company which is open, even in part, to private capital, that fact precludes it from being regarded as a structure for the 'in-house' management of a public service on behalf of the controlling local authority."[199]

The regulation of public works and service concessions is the subject of a proposed Directive on the award of concession contracts.[200] The Directive will require public authorities to put concessions out to tender if their value is above a certain threshold. The calls for tenders are to be advertised on a European-wide basis.

---

192 Case C-196/08, *Acoset* [2009] ECR I-9913, para. 39.
193 Case C-458/03, *Parking Brixen* [2005] ECR I-8585, para. 40.
194 Case C-410/04, *ANAV* [2006] ECR I-3303, para. 16.
195 Case C-324/07, *Coditel Brabant* [2008] ECR I-8457, para. 24.   196 *Acoset*, para. 47.   197 *Ibid.*, para. 50.
198 *Ibid.*, para. 51.   199 *ANAV*, para. 32.
200 Proposal for a Directive of the European Parliament and of the Council on the award of concession contracts,
[2011] COM(2011) 897 final.

Further reading

BARNARD, CATHERINE, "Unravelling the Services Directive" (2008) 45 *Common Market Law Review* 323

ENCHELMAIER, STEFAN, "Always at Your Service (Within Limits): The ECJ's Case Law on Article 56 TFEU" (2006–2011) 36 *European Law Review* 615

GIUBBONI, STEFANO, "Social Rights and Market Freedom in the European Constitution: A Re-Appraisal" (2010) 1 *European Labour Law Journal* 161

HATZOPOULOS, VASSILIS, *Regulating Services in the European Union*, Oxford University Press, 2012

The Court's Approach to Services (2006–2012): From Case Law to Case Load?" (2013) 50 *Common Market Law Review* 459

"The Case Law of the ECJ Concerning the Free Provision of Services: 2000–2005" (2006) 43 *Common Market Law Review* 923

LIANOS, IOANNIS, and ODUDU, OKEOGHENE (eds.), *Regulating Trade in Services in the EU and the WTO: Trust, Distrust and Economic Integration*, Cambridge University Press, 2012

NEERGAARD, ULLA, SZYSZCZAK, ERIKA, VAN DE GRONDEN, JOHAN, and KRAJEWSKI, MARKUS (eds.), *Legal Issues of Services of General Interest, Social Services of General Interest in the EU*, The Hague: TMC Asser Press, 2013

NICOLAÏDIS, KALYPSO, and SCHMIDT, SUSANNE, "Mutual Recognition on 'Trial': The Long Road to Services Liberalization" (2007) 14 *Journal of European Public Policy* 717

SNELL, JUKKA, "The Notion of Market Access: A Concept or a Slogan?" (2010) 47 *Common Market Law Review* 437

Free movement of capital and payments

8 (Articles 63–66 TFEU)

INTRODUCTION

Article 63 TFEU deals with the free movement of capital and of payments. The former concept describes any kind of investments in bonds, shares or real estate as well as loans, gifts, inheritances and other transfers. The latter describes transactions that constitute remuneration for goods, employed or self-employed services or capital provided, and therefore are a necessary correlate to the other Treaty freedoms.

While the free movement of capital was not fully implemented until the late 1980s, the movement of payments was already liberalized in the decade that followed the signature of the Treaty of Rome. Article 106 EEC required Member States "to authorise, in the currency of the Member State in which the creditor or the beneficiary resides, any payments connected with the movement of goods, services or capital, and any transfers of capital and earnings, to the extent that the movement of goods, services, capital and persons between Member States has been liberalised pursuant to this Treaty." As the Treaty freedoms had to be realized by the end of the transitional period in 1969, Member States could no longer restrict the movement of payments from this point onward.

The Treaty of Rome (1957) already aimed at a considerable degree of capital mobility as well. It envisaged that, during the transitional period, the "Member States shall progressively abolish between themselves all restrictions on the movement of capital," however only "to the extent necessary to ensure the proper functioning of the common market" (Article 67(1) Treaty of Rome). After the end of the transitional period, Member States were supposed to "be as liberal as possible in granting such exchange authorisations" (Article 68(1) Treaty of Rome). And, indeed, the First Directive for the implementation of Article 67 EEC of 1960 required Member States to grant authorizations for a far-reaching list of capital movements.[1] This included important areas such as direct investment, investment in real estate and securities dealt in on a stock exchange.[2] However, the Treaty of

---

1 First Directive for the implementation of Article 67 of the Treaty, [1960] OJ 43/921.
2 Arts. 1 and 2 of the Directive in conjunction with Lists A and B of Annex I. Transactions itemized in List C allowed Member States to maintain or reimpose exchange restrictions, and transactions scheduled in List D were not subject to a liberalization requirement at all. See also Case C-203/80, *Casati* [1981] ECR 2595, para. 11.

Rome did not aim at a full liberalization of capital movements. Accordingly, and in contrast to other Treaty freedoms, the Court did not find the free movement of capital provisions to have direct effect until the early 1990s. Instead, secondary law measures remained necessary to implement the provision.

From an economic perspective, the free movement of capital was, as one commentator noted, "necessary to ensure that the maximum efficiency in production was achieved."[3] Moreover, it was a factual precondition of the right to establishment, as the setting up of subsidiaries in other Member States necessarily required capital. At the same time, however, it was believed that unrestrained capital movements could also have significant adverse economic effects. According to the same commentator, "[o]ne reason for caution was the danger of capital moving away from the less developed regions most in need of it in order to take advantage of the skilled workers, better infrastructure, and external economies in industrialized areas. Another reason was the fear of tax avoidance and tax-induced capital movements."[4] The Court acknowledged that the Member States had chosen a more cautious approach towards the movement of capital than with regard to the other Treaty freedoms.[5] It held for example in *Casati* (1981):

[T]he free movement of capital constitutes, alongside that of persons and services, one of the fundamental freedoms of the Community. Furthermore, freedom to move certain types of capital is, in practice, a precondition for the effective exercise of other freedoms guaranteed by the Treaty, in particular the right of establishment. However, capital movements are also closely connected with the economic and monetary policy of the Member States. At present, it cannot be denied that complete freedom of movement of capital may undermine the economic policy of one of the Member States or create an imbalance in its balance of payments, thereby impairing the proper functioning of the Common Market.[6]

The full realization of the free movement of capital was part of the Commission's "1992" agenda. It was implemented by Directive 88/361/EEC, which required Member States to abolish restrictions on movements of capital between persons resident in Member States by 1990. The Treaty of Maastricht introduced Article 63 TFEU in its current form. It established a full liberalization requirement for capital movements not only between the Member States, but also to and from third countries.

As a regulatory tool, the provisions on the free movement of capital and payments were originally directed against capital controls. Such controls could take a wide variety of forms, including restrictions on bank lending to non-residents, authorization requirements, restrictions on the acquisition of real estate by nationals of other countries and rules on importing and exporting foreign currencies. Some early cases, such as *Casati* (1981), deal with capital controls. Since the 1990s, however, the provisions on the free movement of capital have mostly been employed against other types of national measures, such as "golden share" rules and tax measures.

---

3 John Temple Lang, "The Right of Establishment of Companies and Free Movement of Capital in the European Economic Community" (1965) *University of Illinois Law Forum* 684, 710.

4 *Ibid.*, 711.   5 Case C-279/93, *Schumacker* [1995] ECR I-225, para. 10.   6 *Ibid.*, paras. 8–9.

The case for and against international capital controls

From a historical perspective, the free movement of capital is a very recent phenomenon. Even so, by 1990, only thirty countries worldwide had no capital controls (i.e. restrictions on capital movements that did not constitute direct remuneration for trade in goods), of which only one-third were industrialized countries.[7] The postwar system of global economic governance, the Bretton Woods system, was based on capital controls.[8] Capital controls were supposed to reduce short-term capital flows,[9] which were believed to create crises when highly mobile investors collectively rushed in or out of an economy. As currencies were pegged in the Bretton Woods system, capital rushes could also lead to the collapse of the peg.[10] Moreover, capital controls provided a certain degree of autonomy for national governments to enact independent monetary policies (i.e. the ability of states to set the level of money supply in order to steer interest and inflation rates and thereby influence their economy).[11] Generally speaking, capital controls were an integral element of the global post-war economic consensus. It has been argued that the stability of the world economy after the Second World War and the successful development of such countries as Japan, South Korea, Singapore, Taiwan and China[12] would have been impossible without capital controls. The Preamble to Directive 88/361/EEC explained the risk of volatile capital flows as follows: "[L]arge-scale short-term capital movements to or from third countries may seriously disturb the monetary or financial situation of Member States or cause serious stresses on the exchange markets ... Such developments may prove harmful for the cohesion of the European Monetary System, for the smooth operation of the internal market and for the progressive achievement of economic and monetary union."[13]

However, from the 1970s onwards, some economists started to put arguments forward in favor of the free movement of capital. In the 1980s, the liberalization of capital flows became part of the policy prescriptions of the International Monetary Fund and the World Bank for developing countries.[14] The general assumption was that foreign capital could be an important promoter of growth and development. However, on the global level, the free movement of capital was never uncontroversial.

---

7 Alberto Alesina, Vittorio Grilli and Gian Maria Milesi-Ferretti, "The Political Economy of Capital Controls," NBER Working Paper No. 4353 (1993), p. 1.

8 John Goodman and Louis Pauly, "The Obsolescence of Capital Controls?: Economic Management in an Age of Global Markets" (1993) 46 *World Politics* 50, 52.

9 Alesina, Grilli and Milesi-Ferretti, "The Political Economy of Capital Controls," p. 5; see also Council Directive 88/361/EEC for the implementation of Art. 67 of the Treaty, [1988] OJ L178/5, Preamble, recital 6.

10 Alesina, Grilli and Milesi-Ferretti, "The Political Economy of Capital Controls," p. 5.

11 Goodman and Pauly, "The Obsolescence of Capital Controls?," 55.

12 James Crotty and Gerald Epstein, "A Defense of Capital Controls in Light of the Asian Financial Crisis" (1999) 33 *Journal of Economic Issues* 427, 429.

13 Council Directive 88/361/EEC for the implementation of Article 67 of the Treaty, [1988] OJ L178/5, Preamble, recital 13.

14 John Williamson, "A Short History of the Washington Consensus" (2009) 15 *Law and Business Review of the Americas* 7.

Many economists and policymakers blamed global movements of capital for the economic crises since the 1990s, including the crisis of the European Monetary System in 1992 and the Asian crisis of the late 1990s.[15] In the course of these crises, capital controls were sometimes reintroduced temporarily.[16] This also happened for example in Cyprus in 2013, when major banks collapsed and had to be rescued by the public. As larger deposits were obliged to participate in the rescue, the government introduced controls to prevent capital flight. Transfers above a certain amount had to be approved by the central bank.[17]

Today, the debate over capital controls is still ongoing. Harvard economist Dani Rodrik argued, for example, that "there is no evidence in the data that countries without capital controls have grown faster, invested more, or experienced lower inflation."[18] And Nobel Prize laureate Joseph Stiglitz argued that "it has become increasingly clear that there is not only no case for capital market liberalization, but that there is a fairly compelling case against full liberalization."[19] At the same time, some traditional measures of capital control, for example approval requirements, may now appear too bureaucratic and heavy-handed.[20] A measure that makes short-term, speculative capital movements less attractive, while leaving longer-term investments unaffected, is the so-called "Tobin tax" (named after economist James Tobin), a very small tax on capital movements. Such a tax was proposed by the Commission, after long and difficult discussions, in the form of a "Financial Transaction Tax." As a number of Member States strongly opposed such a measure, it was decided that the eleven countries that supported such a tax could pursue the project under the mechanism of enhanced cooperation.[21]

Main Treaty provisions at a glance

Article 63 TFEU prohibits restrictions on the movement of capital and on payments. Unlike the other Treaty freedoms, this also includes movements to and from third countries. Articles 64–66 TFEU allow for various restrictive measures, either by the Member States or by the European legislator. Table 8.1 sets out an overview of the main Treaty provisions with regard to the free movement of capital and payments.

---

15 For an overview, see Crotty and Epstein, "A Defense of Capital Controls," 427.
16 Goodman and Pauly, "The Obsolescence of Capital Controls?," 81.
17 "Cyprus to Keep Capital Controls Through Summer Tourist Season," *Financial Times*, April 26, 2013, www.ft.com/intl/cms/s/0/13e9728e-ae60-11e2-8316-00144feabdc0.html#axzz2duOvgOC5 (accessed September 4, 2013).
18 Dani Rodrik, "Who Needs Capital-Account Convertibility?," in Peter Kenen (ed.), *Essays in International Finance*, No. 207, Princeton University Press, 1998, p. 61.
19 Joseph Stiglitz, "Capital Market Liberalization, Economic Growth, and Instability" (2000) 28 *World Development* 1075, 1076.
20 See e.g. Crotty and Epstein, "A Defense of Capital Controls," 431.
21 As of September 2013, negotiations were still ongoing. See http://ec.europa.eu/taxation_customs/taxation/other_taxes/financial_sector (accessed September 4, 2013).

Table 8.1 Overview of the main Treaty provisions with regard to the free movement of capital and payments	
Provision	**Subject-matter**
Art. 63 TFEU	Prohibition of restrictions on movement of capital and of payments
Art. 64 TFEU	Art. 64(1): Exception for certain restrictions applicable to third countries in existence prior to 1993; Art. 64(2): authorization for EU legislation in regard to third countries
Art. 65 TFEU	Justifications for restrictions imposed by the Member States
Art. 66 TFEU	Authorization for temporary safeguard measures by the Council in regard to third countries in case of serious difficulties for the operation of economic and monetary union

Direct effect

Article 63 TFEU has direct effect. Shortly after the provision was introduced in its current form by the Treaty of Maastricht, the Court held for the first time that "[Article 63 TFEU] of the Treaty lays down a clear and unconditional prohibition for which no implementing measure is needed" (*Sanz de Lera*, 1995).[22] According to the Court, the provision confers "rights on individuals which they may rely on before the courts and which the national courts must uphold."[23]

PERSONAL SCOPE (BENEFICIARIES)

The free movement of capital and payments can be invoked by both natural and legal persons, irrespective of their nationality.

MATERIAL SCOPE

Capital and payments

Article 63 TFEU applies to the movement of capital and of payments. Even though, today, the movement of capital and of payments are both fully liberalized, the distinction retains some relevance, as certain Treaty provisions apply to the movement of capital alone. In particular, Articles 64, 65(1)(a) and 66 TFEU allow for the restriction of capital movements under certain circumstances, but not of payments.

---

22 Case C-163/94, *Sanz de Lera* [1995] ECR I-4821, para. 41. See also *Bordessa*, where the Court found Art. 1 of Directive 88/361/EEC to have direct effect a few months before the decision in *Sanz de Lera*. See Joined Cases C-358/93 and C-416/93, *Bordessa* [1995] ECR I-361, para. 35.

23 *Sanz de Lera*, para. 43.

Payments

"Payments" constitute remuneration for goods, services, labor and capital move-ments.[24] They constitute a necessary complement to the other freedoms, as these would be hindered by restrictions on cross-border payments. The Court defined the distinction between capital and payments in *Luisi and Carbone* (1984) as follows: "[P]ayments are transfers of foreign exchange which constitute the consideration within the context of an underlying transaction, whilst movements of capital are financial operations essentially concerned with the investment of the funds in question rather than remuneration for a service." The Court argued in *Luisi and Carbone* that restrictions on payments render the Treaty freedoms illusory.[25]

Capital

While the Treaty does not provide a definition of the term "capital," the annex to Directive 88/361/EEC provides a list of activities that constitute "capital" within the meaning of the Treaty, termed the "nomenclature." The nomenclature is non-exhaustive and has only indicative value (*Van Putten*, 2012).[26] Table 8.2 sets out the definition of "capital" according to the nomenclature of Directive 88/361/EEC.

The Court has emphasized that the concept of "capital" within the meaning of Article 63 TFEU includes transactions that are granted without consideration, i.e. without a corresponding payment. Inheritances and gifts, for example, are covered by Article 63 TFEU. In *Schröder* (2011), the Court held that "a situation in which natural persons residing in Germany and liable to unlimited taxation in that Member State [who] inherit a house situated in Spain is one that is covered by [Article 63 TFEU]."[27] According to the Court, loans fall under Article 63 TFEU regardless of whether they were given for consideration or free of charge. In *Van Putten* (2012), the Court found that the cross-border lending of a vehicle free of charge constitutes a capital movement within the meaning of Article 63 TFEU.[28]

Delineation between capital movement and other fundamental freedoms

In certain situations, the question arises whether Article 63 TFEU or another Treaty freedom is applicable. A possible overlap of the provisions on the free movement of goods and on the freedom of capital movement exists with regard to objects that serve as legal tender, such as coins or banknotes. The Court held in *Thompson* (1978) that coins which are legal tender in a Member State or are traded on the money markets of the Member States and therefore constitute "means of payment" are covered by Article 63 TFEU, whereas coins that are no longer legal tender fall under Article 34 TFEU.[29]

---

24 Joined Cases 286/82 and 26/83, *Luisi and Carbone* [1984] ECR 377, para. 21.   25 *Ibid.*, para. 34.
26 Joined Cases C-578/10 to C-580/10, *Van Putten* [2012] ECR I-00000, para. 28.
27 Case C-450/09, *Schröder* [2011] ECR I-2497, para. 19.   28 *Van Putten*, para. 36.
29 Case 7/78, *Thompson* [1978] ECR 2247, paras. 28–31; see also *Bordessa*, para. 15.

Table 8.2 The definition of "capital" according to the nomenclature of Directive 88/361/EEC	
Heading	Examples and definitions provided by the Annex
I. Direct investments	Acquisition in full of existing undertakings, participation in new or existing undertaking, long-term loans, reinvestment of profits
II. Investments in real estate	Purchases of buildings and land and the construction of buildings by private persons for gain or personal use
III. Operations in securities normally dealt in on the capital market	Transaction in shares and other securities of a participating nature, bonds; introduction of securities on a stock exchange or placement on a capital market
IV. Operations in units of collective investment undertakings	
V. Operations in securities and other instruments normally dealt in on the money market	Transactions in securities; acquisition of domestic and foreign money market securities and instruments
VI. Operations in current and deposit accounts with financial institutions	
VII. Credits related to commercial transactions or to the provision of services in which a resident is participating	Contractual trade credits (advances or payments by installment in respect of work in progress or on order and extended payment terms, whether or not involving subscription to a commercial bill) and their financing by credits provided by credit institutions
VIII. Financial loans and credits	Includes mortgage loans, consumer credit and financial leasing
IX. Sureties, other guarantees and rights of pledge	
X. Transfers in performance of insurance contracts	Premiums and payments with respect to life insurance, credit insurance or other insurance
XI. Personal capital movements	Loans, gifts, dowries, inheritances
XII. Physical import and export of financial assets	Securities; means of payment of every kind
XIII. Other capital movements	Death duties; damages; authors' royalties

Potential overlaps may also occur with the freedom of establishment. The acquisition of shares of a company may be covered either by Article 63 TFEU or by Article 49 TFEU. The classification does not carry too much importance in many respects, as the provisions grant a similar level of protection. However, two important differences remain: whereas Article 49 TFEU applies only to transactions within the European Union, Article 63 TFEU applies also to transactions to and from third countries. And a second, potentially important, difference concerns what is sometimes called "horizontal direct effect": we have seen that Article 49 TFEU applies not only to state measures, but also to "rules which are not public in nature but which are designed to regulate, collectively, self-employment and the provision of services" (*Wouters*, 2002).[30] In contrast, the Court has not found Article 63 TFEU to apply to non-state actors. We will discuss this issue further in the discussion on "golden shares" below. The Court has developed the following rule to determine whether Article 49 TFEU or Article 63 TFEU is applicable: "[N]ational provisions which apply to holdings by nationals of the Member State concerned in the capital of a company established in another Member State, giving them definite influence on the company's decisions and allowing them to determine its activities come within the substantive scope of the provisions of the Treaty on freedom of establishment."[31] Conversely, investments that do not give definite influence fall under Article 63 TFEU. In some cases, the Court scrutinizes national measures under both Article 49 TFEU and Article 63 TFEU. The Court held that, if "[n]ational legislation not intended to apply only to those shareholdings which enable the holder to exert a definite influence on a company's decisions and to determine its activities but which applies irrespective of the size of the holding which the shareholder has in a company may fall within the scope of both [Article 49 TFEU] and [Article 63 TFEU]" (*Commission* v. *Portugal – Golden Shares*, 2011).[32] A case that concerned the distinction between the provisions on the freedom of establishment and of capital was *A and B* (2007).[33] The case dealt with a Swedish tax rule that put income from branch offices in Russia at a disadvantage in comparison to income from branch offices in Sweden. The applicants held 1.7 percent of the shares of the relevant company and could not therefore control it. The Court took the view that establishing branch offices is a typical element of the freedom of establishment, rendering the capital movement provisions inapplicable in this case. As the freedom of establishment does not extend to branch offices in third countries, the national measure cannot be challenged on the basis of the Treaty. The case of *Scheunemann* (2012) dealt with a German provision according to which shareholdings in capital companies with a registered office in the EU amounting to no more than €225,000 are excluded from inheritance tax.[34] Mrs. Scheunemann was the sole heir to her father; both of them resided in Germany. Inheritance tax was charged to the estate, which included a shareholding, as sole shareholder, in a capital company that had its registered office in Canada. Referring to heading XI of the nomenclature, the Court acknowledged that the tax treatment of inheritances falls, in principle, under Article 63 TFEU. At the same time, a shareholding that enables "the shareholder to exert a definite influence over the company's decisions and to determine its activities" falls under Article 49 TFEU.[35] However, the Court underlined that "[i]n order to determine whether national legislation falls within the scope of one or other of the freedoms of movement, it is clear from now well established

---

30 Case C-309/99, *Wouters* [2002] ECR I-1577, para. 120.
31 Case C-196/04, *Cadbury Schweppes* [2006] ECR I-7995, para. 31.
32 Case C-212/09, *Commission* v. *Portugal – Golden Shares* [2011] ECR I-10889, para. 44.
33 Case C-102/05, *A and B* [2007] ECR I-3871.   34 Case C-31/11, *Scheunemann* [2012] ECR I-00000.
35 *Ibid.*, para. 24.

case law that the aim of the legislation concerned must be taken into consideration."[36] The objective of the measure was to "encourage persons inheriting substantial shareholdings in a company to become involved in its management so as to be
able ultimately to ensure the survival of the undertaking."[37] Accordingly, the Court
found Article 49 TFEU – and not Article 63 TFEU – to be applicable. As the freedom
of establishment does not apply with regard to third countries, an inheritance of a
Canadian company is not covered by Article 49 TFEU.

Cross-border element

Article 63 TFEU applies only in cross-border situations. Unlike the basic Treaty
provisions governing the other fundamental freedoms, Article 63 TFEU applies
not only to all movements both between the Member States, but also between
Member States and third countries. The Court held for example in *Test Claimants in
the FII Group Litigation* (2012) that companies resident in a Member State can
challenge legislation of a Member State relating to the tax treatment of dividends
originating in a third country.[38]

ADDRESSEES

Host and home state

Article 63 TFEU prohibits restrictions on the movement of capital and payments
by both the home and the host state. Examples of restrictive measures by the host
state include cases like *Albore* (2000), where national legislation required prior
authorization by the authorities of the acquisition of real estate by non-nationals.
A case that concerned restrictive measures by the home state was *Sandoz* (1999).[39]
Sandoz GmbH, a company established in Austria, took out a loan of €15 million
from Sandoz Management Services SA, established in Brussels. Sandoz entered
the loan in its accounts books, but no written contract was drawn up. According to
Austrian law, loan agreements are subject to stamp duty at the rate of 0.8 percent of
the value of the loan. If a loan is not set down in a written document, it must be
entered in the accounts books, which entry, however, is not subject to stamp duty.
By contrast, where a person resident in Austria concludes a loan contract outside
Austria that is not set down in a written instrument, but is entered in the borrower's
accounts books, the borrower is liable to pay stamp duty. The Court found that
the provision "discriminates according to the place where the loan is contracted.

---

36 *Ibid.*, para. 20.   37 *Ibid.*, para. 27.
38 Case C-35/11, *Test Claimants in the FII Group Litigation* [2012] ECR I-00000.
39 Case C-439/97, *Sandoz* [1999] ECR I-7041.

Discrimination of that nature is likely to deter residents from contracting loans with persons established in other Member States and therefore constitutes a restriction on the movement of capital."[40]

Non-state actors

The Court has not yet ruled explicitly that Article 63 TFEU applies to non-state actors.[41] Even though the Court has held in a number of the "golden share" cases that articles of association of public limited companies or shareholder agreements can constitute restrictions of the free movement of capital, even though they are private agreements (see e.g. *GALP Energia*, discussed below), the Court found in all these cases that the restrictions were directly attributable to the state. This means that Article 63 TFEU was formally not applied to the actions of non-state actors, but of the state. We will discuss the issue further in the section on "golden shares" below. Like Article 34 TFEU, but unlike Articles 45, 49 and 56 TFEU, the provisions on the free movement of capital currently cannot be assumed to apply to the actions of non-state actors if they cannot be attributed to the state.

APPLYING ARTICLE 63 TFEU: PROHIBITION OF DISCRIMINATION AND OF RESTRICTIONS

Prohibition of discrimination

Like the other Treaty freedoms, Article 63 TFEU embodies the principle of non-discrimination.[42] According to the Court, "the principle of non-discrimination ... requires that comparable situations must not be treated differently and that different situations must not be treated in the same way" (*Van Putten*, 2012). If the situation of, for example, nationals and non-nationals or residents and nonresidents is found to be objectively comparable, differential treatment can only be justified on overriding grounds in the general interest.[43] A Portuguese measure, for example, that prohibited the acquisition by investors from other Member States of more than a given number of shares in certain Portuguese undertakings was found to constitute discrimination on grounds of nationality (*Commission* v. *Portugal – Golden Shares*, 2002).[44]

---

40 *Ibid.*, para. 31.
41 Harm Schepel, "Constitutionalising the Market, Marketising the Constitution, and to Tell the Difference: On the Horizontal Application of the Free Movement Provisions in EU Law" (2012) 18 *European Law Journal* 177, 193.
42 *Van Putten*, para. 43.   43 *Ibid.*, para. 44.
44 Case C/367/98, *Commission* v. *Portugal – Golden Shares* [2002] ECR I-4731, para. 42.

Prohibition of restrictions

According to the Court, national measures may constitute a restriction on the free movement of capital even though they are indistinctly applicable to nationals and non-nationals alike if they are "liable to make . . . cross border capital movements less attractive" (*Van Putten*, 2012). In *Svensson and Gustavsson* (1995), for example, the Court identified the national rules as restrictions because they "are liable to dissuade those concerned from approaching banks established in another Member State and therefore constitute an obstacle to movements of capital such as bank loans."[45] This effect may be caused, for example, if the measures in question create additional costs for cross-border capital movements, as the Court held in *Trummer and Mayer* (1999).[46] In *Busley* (2009), the Court held that not only measures which prevent or limit the acquisition of an immovable property situated in another Member State may constitute a restriction of Article 63 TFEU, but also measures that "are liable to discourage the retention of such a property."[47]

JUSTIFICATIONS

Similar to the other fundamental freedoms, the free movement of capital may be restricted either on grounds explicitly recognized by the Treaty or on overriding grounds of the common interest.

Public policy and public security

Article 65(1)(b)(item 1) provides that Member States have the right to "take measures which are justified on grounds of public policy or public security." In *Albore* (2000), Italian law required foreign citizens to obtain prior authorization for the acquisition of buildings in zones that had been declared to be of "military importance," whereas Italian citizens faced no such obligation. While the Court acknowledged that such a measure could be justified on grounds of public security in principle, it held that the measure needs to be proportionate. According to the Court:

[A] mere reference to the requirements of defence of the national territory . . . cannot suffice to justify discrimination on grounds of nationality against nationals of other Member States regarding access to immovable property on all or part of the national territory of the first State. The position would be different only if it were demonstrated, for each area to which the restriction applies, that non-discriminatory treatment of the nationals of all the Member States would expose the military interests of the Member State concerned to real, specific and serious risks which could not be countered by less restrictive procedures.[48]

45 Case C-484/93, *Svensson and Gustavsson* [1995] ECR I-3955, para. 10.
46 Case C-222/97, *Trummer and Mayer* [1999] ECR I-1661, para. 27.
47 Case C-35/08, *Busley* [2009] ECR I-9807, para. 21.
48 Case C-423/98, *Alfredo Albore* [2000] ECR I-5965, paras. 21–22.

Further derogations in Article 65(1)(b) TFEU

Article 65(1)(b)(item 2) TFEU grants the right to the Member States to "take all requisite measures to prevent infringements of national law and regulations, in particular in the field of taxation and the prudential supervision of financial institutions." The provision grants the right to take measures to prevent infringements of national laws, and gives as (non-exhaustive) examples the supervision of financial institutions and rules in the field of taxation. In particular, the derogation for financial supervision recalls the similar mandatory requirement developed by the Court in *Cassis de Dijon* (1979). In effect, the provision echoes the derogations on overriding grounds in the common interest that the Court has developed with regard to the other freedoms. Article 65(1)(b)(item 3) TFEU allows Member States to "lay down procedures for the declaration of capital movements for purposes of administrative or statistical information."

Differential treatment in tax measures on grounds of residence

Article 65(1)(a) TFEU provides that the Member States retain the right "to apply the relevant provisions of their tax law which distinguish between taxpayers who are not in the same situation with regard to their place of residence or with regard to the place where their capital is invested." Article 65(3) TFEU specifies that the provision "shall not constitute a means of arbitrary discrimination or a disguised restriction on the free movement of capital and payments as defined in Article 63 [TFEU]." The derogation of Article 65(1)(a) TFEU was initially inserted by the Treaty of Maastricht in order to allow the Member States to uphold some forms of differential treatment as long as the tax system is not harmonized.[49] Advocate General Kokott has argued, however, that the "provision does not give the Member States *carte blanche* to apply every form of different treatment of taxpayers according to the place of investment under their national tax law."[50] The Court explained that the provision "is a derogation from the fundamental principle of the free movement of capital, it must be interpreted strictly. It cannot therefore be interpreted as meaning that all tax legislation which draws a distinction between taxpayers on the basis of their place of residence or the State in which they invest their capital is automatically compatible with the Treaty" (*Santander*, 2012).[51] The Court essentially interprets the provision along the lines of the system of justifications it had developed with regard to the other Treaty freedoms. This means that differential treatment must, in any event, conform to the principle of proportionality. According to the Court, "the difference in treatment must concern situations which are not objectively comparable or be justified by an overriding reason in the

49 Case C-319/02, *Petri Manninen* [2004] ECR I-7477, Opinion of Advocate General Kokott, para. 36.
50 *Ibid.*, para. 36.
51 Joined Cases C-338/11 to C-347/11, *Santander Asset Management SGIIC SA* [2013] ECR I-00000, para. 21.

public interest" (*Santander*, 2012).[52] The fact that the Court interprets Article 65(1)(a) TFEU as a specific expression of the general system of justifications is manifest, for example, in the decision in *Blanckaert*.

Case C-512/03, Blanckaert (2005)

According to Dutch law, Dutch residents who receive income in the Netherlands are liable to pay social security contributions. These contributions can be reduced by various deductions. If an individual who was liable to pay social security contributions could claim more reductions than he or she had to pay in contributions, the individual would receive an income tax reduction in the amount of the nondeductible portion. Mr. Blanckaert was a Belgian citizen residing in Belgium. He owned a holiday home in the Netherlands, and received an income from letting it out. However, as a nonresident who received only a small percentage of his income in the Netherlands, he was not obliged to be insured in that Member State. As he did not pay social security contributions in the Netherlands, he also could not apply any deductions related to social security, and no corresponding tax credit was granted to him. Mr. Blanckaert objected to his tax assessment, arguing that the Dutch law created an unjustified difference in treatment between residents and nonresidents.

Can a measure that grants a deduction only to resident taxpayers who are also insured under the social security system of that Member State, but not to nonresident taxpayers who are also not insured under the social security system of that Member State be justified by Article 65(1)(a)?

Yes.

The Court held that, contrary to Mr. Blanckaert's assertion, the Dutch legislation does not differentiate between residents and nonresidents, but between insured and uninsured persons: "Both residents and non-residents who are insured under that system are entitled to those reductions, whereas residents and non-residents who are not insured thereunder are not entitled to them."[53] The Court went on to argue that:

[G]ranting the tax advantage in question in the main proceedings to persons who are not insured under the Netherlands social security system would amount to treating different situations in the same way, since insured persons under that system are entitled only in exceptional circumstances to tax credits in respect of social security. It is only in a situation where an insured person cannot set off reductions in contributions against contributions due that he can seek to obtain such tax credits. On the other hand, non-insured persons, such as the applicant in the main proceedings, would always automatically be entitled to a tax credit by virtue of the grant of reductions in contributions in respect of social security. As there is no obligation to pay contributions, such a person can never offset those reductions against social security contributions due.[54]

---

52 *Ibid.*, para. 23.   53 Case C-512/03, *Blanckaert* [2005] ECR I-7685, para. 45.   54 *Ibid.*

The Court concluded that the rules "can be justified, in the light of [Article 65(1)(a) TFEU], by the objective difference between the situation of a person who is insured under the Netherlands social security system and that of a person who is not so insured."[55]

Restrictions in Article 64(1) TFEU

Article 64(1) TFEU provides that national restrictions on the movement of capital to and from third countries that have been in force prior to December 31, 1993 (or 1999 for Bulgaria, Estonia and Hungary) can remain in place. The provision is what is sometimes called a "grandfather clause" because it allows retaining measures that would not conform to the current system but have been enacted before it came into force. An example can be found in the decision *Fokus Invest* (2010), which we discussed in Chapter 2. The case dealt with a Swiss company that owned an Austrian company called FIAG. FIAG bought a house in Vienna and demanded to be entered in the land register. This was contested by another company, Fokus Invest, who also held a right in the property. A Viennese law held that foreign natural or legal persons or Austrian companies owned by foreign persons must apply for authorization prior to the acquisition of property in Vienna. We have already seen that the agreement between Switzerland and the EU on the free movement of persons does not grant rights to companies comparable to those granted by the TFEU provisions on the freedom of establishment. Accordingly, FIAG could not challenge the Austrian law on the basis of the agreement. However, Article 63 TFEU prohibits restrictions also with regard to third countries such as Switzerland. But, as the authorization requirement was already in place prior to December 31, 1993 the measure was permitted under Article 64(1) TFEU. The Court has pointed out that measures adopted after that date are not automatically excluded from the deroga-tion. It held in *Holböck* (2007) that "[a] provision which is, in substance, identical to the previous legislation, or limited to reducing or eliminating an obstacle to the exercise of [Union] rights and freedoms in the earlier legislation, will be covered by the derogation. By contrast, legislation based on an approach which differs from that of the previous law and establishes new procedures cannot be treated as legislation existing at the date fixed in the [Union] measure in question."[56]

Overriding grounds in the public interest

Similar to the other freedoms, restrictions of the free movement of capital can be justified by derogations explicitly recognized by the Treaty as well as on other overriding grounds in the public interest. National measures must fulfil the proportionality criterion.

55 *Ibid.*, para. 50.   56 Case C-157/05, *Holböck* [2007] ECR I-4051, para. 41.

Requirements of prior authorization of the acquisition of agricultural land could be justified by "social objectives" such as "preserving agricultural communities, maintaining a distribution of land ownership which allows the development of viable farms and sympathetic management of green spaces and the countryside as well as encouraging a reasonable use of the available land by resisting pressure on land, and preventing natural disasters" (*Ospelt*, 2003).[57] Ensuring the pluralistic and noncommercial content of programs may justify restrictions concerning investments in a broadcasting company (*Omroep*, 1993).[58] National rules could also be justified on the ground that they would ensure the transparency of the mortgage system (*Trummer and Mayer*, 1999).[59] Furthermore, the Court recognizes a variety of justifications with regard to taxation.

Justifications relating to taxation

Starting in the 1990s, the Court increasingly focused on national rules on direct taxation, i.e. income and corporate taxes. The Court routinely holds that, "while direct taxation falls within the competence of the Member States, the latter must none the less exercise that competence in a manner consistent with European Union law."[60] At the same time, the Court acknowledged that tax legislation and its enforcement is a highly complex and politically sensitive area that requires a differentiated approach. Justifications so far recognized by the Court with regard to taxation include:

- *Cohesion of the tax system*. This justification concerns tax advantages that are granted only to offset a particular tax levy. Member States are not required to provide equal treatment with regard to the tax advantage if the corresponding tax levy has not been paid. For this justification to apply, the tax levy and the tax advantage must concern the same type of taxation, and must arise with the same individual.[61] In *Commission* v. *Belgium – Purchase of Homes for Primary Residence* (2011), the Court had to deal with a measure by the Flemish Region of Belgium that required the payment of a registration duty in the acquisition of a home for principal residence. This duty could be offset against the duty paid for the previous home, but only if it was located in the Flemish Region as well. The Commission argued that this tax advantage infringed Article 63 TFEU. The Court agreed, but found the measure justified by the need to safeguard the cohesion of the tax system.[62] The system did not grant a tax advantage, but merely ensured that nobody paid the registration duty more than once.

---

57 Case C-452/01, *Ospelt* [2003] ECR I-9743, para. 39.
58 Case C-148/91, *Vereniging Veronica Omroep Organisatie* [1993] ECR I-487, paras. 13–14.
59 *Trummer and Mayer*, para. 30.
60 Case C-250/08, *Commission* v. *Belgium – Purchase of Homes for Primary Residence* [2011] ECR I-00000, para. 33.
61 *Ibid.*, para. 75.   62 *Ibid.*, para. 69.

- *Combatting tax evasion*. This justification can be applied to measures that "target purely artificial contrivances, the aim of which is to circumvent tax law" (*Etablissements Rimbaud*, 2010). In that case, an exemption from property tax was granted only to legal persons established in France as well as in countries that have concluded a convention on administrative assistance to combat tax evasion with France. The claimant in the case was an entity established in Liechtenstein, which had not signed such a convention with France.[63] The Court found the measure to constitute a restriction of Article 40 EEA Agreement, but found it justifiable on the ground of combatting tax evasion. The Court cautioned, however, that "a general presumption of tax avoidance or evasion is insufficient to justify a tax measure which adversely affects the objectives of the Treaty."[64] If an agreement on information exchange is in place with a third country that is as effective as the one in place between EU Member States, restrictions will be unjustifiable (*Veronsaajien oikeudenvalvontayksikkö v. A Oy*, 2012).[65]

- *Safeguarding the effectiveness of fiscal supervision*. This justificatory ground, which first appeared in the decision in *Cassis de Dijon* (1979), allows Member States to "apply measures which enable the amount of both the income taxable in that State and of the losses which can be carried forward there to be ascertained clearly and precisely" (*Futura Singer*, 1997).[66]

- *Maintaining a balanced allocation of the power to impose taxes between the Member States*. International tax law is based on the principle that states have the right to exercise tax jurisdiction in relation to the activities carried out in their territory. The Court has accepted this principle, and routinely holds that measures necessary to ensure that Member States can in fact exercise this right may justify restrictions of the Treaty freedoms (e.g. *Glaxo Wellcome*, 2009).[67]

Proportionality

National measures can be justified only if they are applied in a proportionate manner, as the Court held for example in *Van Putten* (2012). The case dealt with the Dutch tax on motor vehicles. The vehicle tax had to be paid upon registration of the vehicle in the Dutch vehicle register. The tax has to be paid also if a car, which is not registered in the Netherlands, is made available to a natural or legal person residing or established in the Netherlands once it is used on Dutch roads. As the tax amounted to 45.2 percent of the net list price of the vehicle, the costs of the tax could be considerable: Mrs. van Putten, for example, one of the defendants in the case, was required to pay €5,955.[68] The Court acknowledged that Member States

---

63 Case C-72/09, *Etablissements Rimbaud* [2010] ECR I-10659, para. 27.   64 *Etablissements Rimbaud*, para. 34.
65 Case C-48/11, *Veronsaajien oikeudenvalvontayksikkö* v. *A Oy* [2012] ECR I-00000.
66 Case C-250/95, *Futura Participations* [1997] ECR I-2471, para. 31.
67 Case C-182/08, *Glaxo Wellcome* [2009] ECR I-8591, para. 82.   68 *Van Putten*, para. 15.

"may impose a registration tax on a motor vehicle registered in another Member State where that vehicle is intended to be used essentially in the first Member State on a permanent basis or where it is, in fact, used in that manner."[69] However, the national legislation in the case essentially did not take the possibility into account that cars were made available to Dutch citizens for a short period of time: "[T]he defendants in the main proceedings had to pay the full amount of the vehicle tax, as the amount was calculated without any account being taken of the duration of the use of the vehicles concerned and without the users of those vehicles having been able to invoke any right to exemption or reimbursement."[70] The principle of proportionality would require Member States to take this possibility into account, and to grant persons the right to invoke an exemption. Accordingly, the Dutch measure failed to conform to the proportionality requirement.[71]

RIGHTS UNDER ARTICLE 63 TFEU: SECONDARY LAW AND CASE LAW

Prohibition of golden shares for the state

In the first decades after the formation of the EEC, broad segments of the Member States' industries were publicly owned and operated. Utility providers such as postal services, telecommunications, water and electricity providers had either been established as public institutions or nationalized at some point between the late nineteenth century and the early 1980s. Moreover, other industries, in partic-ular heavy industries, were nationalized as well. In the 1980s and in particular in the 1990s, however, the Member States increasingly moved in the opposite direc-tion: they started to privatize, in parts or in full, many of the previously publicly owned companies. Because these companies were believed to play a vital role in the Member States' economies, governments sometimes developed schemes that would allow them continued influence over these companies. Such measures are referred to as "golden shares."

The Commission turned its attention to such provisions in the late 1990s. It laid down its analysis of various "golden share" arrangements in its "Communication of the Commission on certain legal aspects concerning intra-EU investment" (1997).[72] The Communication broadly distinguished between discriminatory and nondis-criminatory measures. The former included such measures as "the prohibition on investors from another EU country acquiring more than a limited amount of voting shares in domestic companies and/or having to seek authorization for the

---

69 *Ibid.*, para. 46.   70 *Ibid.*, para. 48.   71 *Ibid.*, para. 54.
72 Communication of the Commission on certain legal aspects concerning intra-EU investment, [1997] OJ C220/15.

acquisition of shares beyond a certain threshold."[73] The Commission emphasized that such measures were prohibited under the Treaty freedoms, unless they were justified on grounds explicitly mentioned in the Treaty. Indistinctly applicable measures, on the other hand, could also be justified on overriding grounds in the public interest. According to the Commission, these included measures such as "general authorization procedures whereby, for example, any investor (EU and national alike) wanting to acquire a stake in a domestic company above a certain threshold" or "the rights given to national authorities, in derogation of company law, to veto certain major decisions to be taken by the company, as well as the imposition of a requirement for the nomination of some directors as a means of exercising the right of veto, etc."[74] Since the publication of its Communication, the Commission has challenged numerous "golden share" arrangements. Some of these arrangements were established by law, whereas others have been integrated in the company's articles of association (i.e. the company's "constitution"). As Article 63 TFEU has not yet been found to apply to measures enacted by non-state actors ("horizontal direct effect"), "golden share" arrangements must be attributable to the state in order for Article 63 TFEU to be applicable. Table 8.3 sets out some important golden share cases.

The best-known example of a "golden share" arrangement codified in law is the German *Volkswagen* case (*Commission* v. *Germany – Volkswagen*, 2007).[75] Volkswagen had been partly privatized in 1960. The relevant law (the so-called "VW law") also included two measures that were intended to secure the influence of the federal government and of the state government of Niedersachsen (the German *Bundesland* where the company is located), each of which held 20 percent of the shares in Volkswagen.[76] First, the law limited the voting rights of every shareholder to 20 percent of the votes, even if the shareholder held more than 20 percent of the share capital. Second, important decisions such as amendments to the articles of association or a capital increase required the approval of at least 80 percent of the votes, as opposed to the 75 percent required by general law for such decisions. The federal government and the state government of Niedersachsen, therefore, each had a right to veto important decisions. The Court found that "[b]y limiting the possibility for other shareholders to participate in the company with a view to establishing or maintaining lasting and direct economic links with it which would make possible effective participation in the management of that company or in its control, this situation is liable to deter direct investors from other Member States."[77] The Court held that the incriminated provisions of the VW law amounted to a restriction of the free movement of capital. Germany subsequently altered the VW law to conform to the Court's decision. A challenge by the Commission

73 *Ibid.*, para. 7.   74 *Ibid.*, para. 8.
75 Case C-112/05, *Commission* v. *Germany – Volkswagen* [2007] ECR I-8995.   76 *Ibid.*, para. 48.
77 *Ibid.*, para. 52.

Table 8.3 Some important golden share cases

Case	Affected company
C-58/99, *Commission* v. *Italy* (2000)	ENI (oil and gas), Telecom Italia (telecommunications)
C-483/99, *Commission* v. *France* (2002)	Elf-Aquitaine (now Total) (oil)
C-503/99, *Commission* v. *Belgium* (2002)	Société nationale de transport par canalisations (SNTC) and Société de distribution du gaz (Distrigaz) (gas distribution)
C-98/01, *Commission* v. *UK* (2003)	British Airports Authority (BAA) (airport ownership)
C-463/00, *Commission* v. *Spain* (2003)	Repsol (oil and gas), Telefónica de España and Telefónica Servicios Móviles (telecommunications), Corporación Bancaria de España (now BBVA) (banking), Tabacalera (tobacco), Endesa (electricity)
C-282/04, *Commission* v. *Netherlands* (2006)	KPN (telecommunications), TPG (postal services)
C-463/04, *Federconsumatori* (2007)	Azienda Elettrica Milanese (municipal distribution of gas and electricity)
C-112/05, *Commission* v. *Germany* (2007)	Volkswagen (motor vehicle manufacturing)
C-171/08, *Commission* v. *Portugal* (2010)	Portugal Telecom (telecommunications)
C-543/08, *Commission* v. *Portugal* (2010)	Energias de Portugal (electricity)
C-212/09, *Commission* v. *Portugal* (2011)	Galp Energia (oil, gas and energy)
C-105/12, *Essent* (2013)	Essent NV, Eneco Holding NV, Delta NV (electricity, gas)

alleging insufficient implementation of the judgment was dismissed by the Court (*Commission* v. *Germany – Volkswagen II*, 2013).[78]

In other cases, the objectionable "golden share" arrangement was established through the articles of association or shareholder agreements, which are private agreements. The case of *Commission* v. *Portugal – GALP Energia* (2011)[79] dealt with the partial privatization of Portugal's formerly public oil and gas company. Portugal retained ownership of 8 percent of the company's shares, 7 percent through its holding company, Parpública, and 1 percent through the state-owned bank, CGD. Through a shareholders' agreement between CGD and a number of other investors, CGD had the right to appoint a director, who was required to be the chairperson of the board of directors.[80] While the shareholders' agreement is a private agreement to which the Portuguese state is not directly a party, the Court found the measure nonetheless to be attributable to the Portuguese state. The Court held, *inter alia*, that the Portuguese state was factually acting through the CGD, of which it is the sole shareholder. Moreover, GALP Energia's articles of association

78 Case C-95/12, *Commission* v. *Germany – Volkswagen II* [2013] ECR I-00000.
79 Case C-212/09, *Commission* v. *Portugal – GALP Energia* [2011] ECR I-10889.   80 *Ibid.*, paras. 12–13.

were drawn up at a time when the state still held a majority of the company's share capital. Finally, company law generally prohibited attaching a right to appoint a director to certain shares; the law explicitly made an exception for GALP Energia. Consequently, the Court argued, "the right of the State to appoint the chairman of GALP's Board of Directors must be regarded as being attributable to the Portuguese Republic and for that reason comes within the scope of [Article 63(1) TFEU]."[81] The Court subsequently held that such an arrangement constituted a restriction of the free movement of capital.

We have already seen that, if such an arrangement is found in a private agreement such as the articles of association or a shareholders' agreement, Article 63 TFEU applies only if the measure can be attributed to the state, as the Court has not (yet?) found Article 63 TFEU to have horizontal direct effect. If the Court were to extend its adjudication on horizontal direct effect to Article 63 TFEU, this could have potentially significant consequences for companies outside of state control as well.[82] Some argued that "[t]he briefest of glances on the European corporate landscape ... should be enough to realize that the kinds of restriction of shareholders' rights at issue in these cases are lawfully pervasive in 'genuinely' private agreements and articles of associations to the benefit of 'genuinely' private blockholders."[83] A report prepared for the Commission revealed that 44 percent of European companies have so-called "control-enhancing mechanisms" in place.[84] This includes shares with different voting rights or even veto rights, ownership ceilings that prohibit participation over a certain threshold and supermajority provisions that require 50 percent plus 1 vote for important corporate decisions.[85] If the Court applied the same broad definition it uses with regard to the provisions on the free movement of persons ("rules which are not public in nature but which are designed to regulate, collectively, self-employment and the provision of services"[86]), then the articles of association of companies and shareholders' agreements would regularly come under the purview of Article 63 TFEU as well, even if these agreements could not be attributed to the state.

While the Court scrutinized the earlier "golden share" cases on the basis of Article 63 TFEU alone, it has also applied Article 49 TFEU in its more recent case law. In *Commission* v. *Greece – Golden Shares* (2012), the Court argued that an authorization requirement falls under Article 49 TFEU alone if it applies only to "the acquisition of holdings in a strategic public limited company which grant voting rights representing 20 percent or more of the total share capital, with the result that only those shareholders who are able to exert a definite influence

---

81 *Ibid.*, para. 54.
82 See e.g. John Armour and Wolf-Georg Ringe, "European Company Law 1999–2010: Renaissance and Crisis" (2011) 48 *Common Market Law Review* 125, 148.
83 Schepel, "Constitutionalising the Market," 193.
84 ISS Europe, ECGI, Shearman and Sterling, "Report on the Proportionality Principle in the European Union" (2007), http://ec.europa.eu/internal_market/company/docs/shareholders/study/final_report_en.pdf (accessed July 28, 2013), p. 6.
85 "Report on the Proportionality Principle in the European Union," pp. 7–8.   86 *Wouters*, para. 120.

over the management and control of such a company are affected."[87] However, at present, the delineation between those cases where Article 49 TFEU applies and those that fall under Article 63 TFEU is unclear.[88]

"Golden share" arrangements that are indistinctly applicable are justifiable on grounds of overriding reasons in the public interest. In *Commission* v. *Belgium – SNTC* (2002),[89] the Court had to deal with the privatization of two Belgian companies, SNTC and Distrigaz, which were active in the field of distribution of gas. By decree, the Belgian state established the right of the responsible minister to oppose "any transfer, use as security or change in the intended destination of the company's system of lines and conduits which are used or are capable of being used as major infrastructures for the domestic conveyance of energy products," and to appoint two representatives to the board of directors to inform the minister about any such decisions. The Court found the measure to restrict Article 63 TFEU, but justifiable on the grounds of public security. According to the Court, "the objective pursued by the legislation at issue, namely the safeguarding of energy supplies in the event of a crisis, falls undeniably within the ambit of a legitimate public interest."[90] The Court found the measure to be proportionate for three reasons.[91] First, company decisions do not require prior approval by the government; instead, the minister must express opposition to specific decisions, and is also bound by strict time-limits. Second, the regime is limited to certain decisions concerning the energy supply networks. And, third, any intervention by the minister must be accompanied by a formal statement of reasons and is subject to judicial review. In *Essent* (2013), the Court found Dutch measures prohibiting privatization as well as restricting private ownership of electricity and gas transmission system operators in other forms justifiable on overriding grounds in the public interest.[92] Most notably, the transfer of shares held in operators of electricity and gas transmission system operators was subject to authorization by the Dutch government, which would be refused unless the shares were transferred into public ownership. The Court found the measure justifiable because it was aimed at ensuring sufficient investment in the transmission system infrastructure as well as enabling undistorted competition between the private energy providers, which were guaranteed equal access to the transmission system.

In *Commission* v. *Greece – Golden Shares* (2012), the Court reiterated that prior authorization schemes are disproportionate because regulatory objectives could usually be achieved by less restrictive means, namely, by imposing positive obligations on undertakings in the sector concerned instead.[93] Generally speaking, government control mechanisms relating to corporate governance are proportionate

---

87 See e.g. Case C-244/11, *Commission* v. *Greece – Golden Shares* [2012] ECR I-00000, paras. 23–25.
88 Schepel, "Constitutionalising the Market," 194–195.
89 Case C-503/99, *Commission* v. *Belgium – SNTC* [2002] ECR I-4809.   90 *Ibid.*, para. 46.
91 *Ibid.*, paras. 49–51.   92 Joined Cases C-105/12 to C-107/12, *Essent and Others* [2013] ECR I-00000.
93 Case C-244/11, *Commission* v. *Greece – Golden Shares* [2012] ECR I-00000, para. 73.

only if the discretionary power of the government is clearly circumscribed, the factors on the basis of which the government decides are sufficiently transparent, and the decision is subject to independent review. By contrast, the Court has found authorization schemes to infringe the Treaty freedoms that "[confer] a discretionary power on the administration which is difficult for the courts to control and which includes a risk of discrimination" (*Commission* v. *Greece – Golden Shares*, 2012).[94]

Restrictions, authorization and notification requirements on the acquisition of immovable property

Some Member States maintained provisions which restricted in some form or another the acquisition of immovable property, either by restricting some forms of ownership or by making the acquisition subject to authorization or notification requirements. In *Konle* (1999), a law of the Austrian state of Tyrol subjected the acquisition of real estate there to prior authorization. Applicants had to prove that they would not use the property as a secondary establishment. The asserted objective of the measure was to prevent the sprawl of residences solely used as vacation homes. The Court found the measure to restrict Article 63 TFEU and held that less restrictive measures could similarly serve this purpose, such as fines for buyers who did not establish primary residence on the real estate they had acquired.[95] In *Reisch* (2006), the Court ruled that a system of prior authorization of the acquisition of real estate would infringe Article 63 TFEU, but a system merely demanding notification to the authorities without a need to await authorization would not.[96] In *Festersen* (2007),[97] the Court ruled that Article 63 TFEU prohibits a law that lays down as a condition for acquiring an agricultural property the requirement that the buyer takes up permanent residence on that property. In *Eric Libert* (2013), a number of rules imposed by the Flemish region in Belgium on social housing and the transfer of real estate were challenged.[98] According to one challenged measure, transfers of immovable property in certain designated municipalities were subject to the requirement that a "sufficient connection" between the prospective buyer or tenant and those municipalities existed. Whether this condition was satisfied was verified by a provincial assessment committee. The Court found the requirement to restrict Article 63 TFEU as well as the other Treaty freedoms.[99] According to the Flemish government, the objective of the measure was to guarantee sufficient housing for the low-income or otherwise disadvantaged sections of the local population. The Court held, however, that the measure was not specifically targeted at low-income persons: the criteria that defined whether a "sufficient connection" to the municipality existed merely related to questions such as prior residence in the municipality or the existence of professional, social or

---

94 *Ibid.*, para. 79.   95 Case C-302/97, *Konle* [1999] ECR I-3099, para. 47.
96 Case C-103/05, *Reisch Montage* [2006] ECR I-6827.   97 Case C-370/05, *Festersen* [2007] ECR I-1129.
98 Joined Cases C-197/11 and C-203/11, *Libert* [2013] ECR I-00000.   99 *Ibid.*, para. 48.

family relations with the commune. The Court concluded that "[s]uch conditions may be met not only by the less affluent local population but also by other persons with sufficient resources who, consequently, have no specific need for social protection on the property market. Those conditions thus go beyond what is necessary to attain the objective pursued."[100]

Restrictive investment requirements for public institutions

Sometimes national measures require public institutions or their contractors to choose domestic over non-domestic investments, or they subject non-domestic investments to additional conditions. In *VBV* (2012), the Court dealt with a national measure in the field of social insurance.[101] Austrian employers are required to pay an ongoing contribution of a certain percentage of the monthly remuneration to the employee's severance fund.[102] When the employment relationship ends, the employee may claim payment from the severance fund by which he or she is covered. According to the national measure, the severance fund may only invest its assets in units of an investment fund established in another Member State if that fund has been authorized to market its units within Austria. This means that the severance funds could not invest in funds located in other Member States whose financial products had not been approved by the Austrian authorities. The Court found that the measure "has a restrictive effect with regard to investment funds established in other Member States in so far as it obliges them, if they wish to sell their units, to undergo the procedure for authorization within the national territory provided for by that legislation."[103] The measure therefore constituted an impediment to cross-border movements of capital.

In *Commission* v. *Poland – Pension Funds* (2011),[104] the Court dealt with rules that governed the Polish pension system. Among other rules, the Commission criticized a provision according to which only up to 5 percent of the assets of a pension fund could be foreign investments. Moreover, the Polish law provided a list of permitted investment products, which was more limited with regard to foreign investments than for investment in Poland. The Court found that the Polish law "imposes both quantitative and qualitative restrictions on [pension funds] with regard to investments made outside national territory, and in particular in other Member States."[105]

In *Woningstichting Sint Servatius* (2009),[106] the Court had to deal with a Dutch measure concerning the funding of public housing projects. In the Netherlands, public housing is operated by public-interest organizations, which have as their task to operate public housing in an assigned geographical area. Projects that do not conform to the criteria must be authorized by the competent minister.

100 *Ibid.*, para. 55.   101 Case C-39/11, *VBV* [2012] ECR I-00000.   102 *Ibid.*, para. 5.   103 *Ibid.*, para. 26.
104 Case C-271/09, *Commission* v. *Poland – Pension Funds* [2011] ECR I-00000.   105 *Ibid.*, para. 51.
106 Case C-567/07, *Woningstichting Sint Servatius* [2009] ECR I-9021.

Servatius, which is assigned to operate in the Maastricht area, planned to construct housing in Liège, a Belgian municipality located around 30 km from Maastricht, and applied for authorization of the project to the Dutch authorities. The application was refused, however, on the ground of the project's location in Belgium. The Dutch authorities held that Servatius had failed to show how the project would be of benefit to the Dutch housing market and for persons seeking accommodation in the Maastricht region. According to the Court, the measure restricted the movement of capital, as the authorization requirement is likely to discourage persons from making investments in immovable property in other Member States.[107] The Court accepted in principle that "requirements related to public housing policy in a Member State and to the financing of that policy can also constitute overriding reasons in the public interest and therefore justify restrictions such as that established by the national legislation at issue in the main proceedings."[108] Furthermore, the Court was of the view that the procedure requiring prior authorization may be justifiable if the policy goals cannot be achieved by less restrictive measures. However, the Court found that the national measure did not fulfill the proportionality requirement, as it did not provide "specific and objective criteria from which the institutions concerned can ascertain in advance the circumstances in which their application for authorization will be granted and on the basis of which the courts, if an action is brought before them in respect of a refusal of authorization, may exercise their powers of review to the full."[109]

Direct tax cases

Since the 1990s, the Court has assessed national direct taxation rules with regard to their effect on the free movement of persons and of capital. Today, direct taxation cases make up a significant part of the case law on the free movement of capital.

Taxation of dividends

Dividend payments constitute a part of a person's income, and are therefore subject to income tax. Many Member States allow shareholders to deduct the corporation tax paid by the company from the shareholder's income tax. This is based on the view that the profit of companies is already being taxed through the corporation tax: if the dividend is taxed again as part of the shareholder's income, this would constitute economic double taxation, which many Member States wish to avoid. However, national tax law has often restricted this possibility to dividends paid by domestic companies, as otherwise they would grant a tax break for a tax that the country itself has not levied.[110] The Court has found such restrictions to conflict with Article 63 TFEU, for example in the decision in *Manninen*.

---

107 *Ibid.*, paras. 21–24.   108 *Ibid.*, para. 30.   109 *Ibid.*, para. 37.   110 *Manninen*, para. 41.

Case C-319/02, Manninen (2004)

A Finnish law allowed shareholders to deduct the corporation tax paid by a company from the income tax they pay on dividends they receive. However, this tax break was only available with regard to dividends distributed by Finnish companies. For dividends distributed by non-Finnish companies, on the other hand, no tax break was available. Petri Manninen, a Finnish national subject to income tax in Finland, received dividends from a Swedish company. He paid income tax, but did not receive the tax break that a shareholder of a Finnish company would have received.

Does a rule conflict with Article 63 TFEU that grants a tax break only for dividends distributed by domestic companies, but not by foreign companies?

Yes.

According to the Court, "the Finnish tax legislation has the effect of deterring fully taxable persons in Finland from investing their capital in companies established in another Member State."[111] The Finnish government contended that, "if a tax credit were to be granted to the recipients of dividends paid by a Swedish company to shareholders who were fully taxable in Finland, the authorities of that Member State would be obliged to grant a tax advantage in relation to corporation tax that was not levied by that State, thereby threatening the cohesion of the national tax system."[112] The Court responded that a mere reduction of tax revenue could not justify a restrictive measure.[113] The justificatory ground of protecting the "cohesion of the tax system" has been developed in *Bachmann* (1992) with regard to a tax break that was granted solely to prevent double taxation of the same economic transaction. The Finnish measure aimed at preventing double taxation (i.e. taxation of the same profit through corporation and income tax) with regard to dividends paid by Finnish companies, while upholding double taxation with regard to dividends received from non-Finnish companies. This means that, with regard to dividends from non-Finnish companies, the measure aimed at the very opposite objective than the measure scrutinized in *Bachmann*. Accordingly, it could not be justified on the ground of the cohesion of the tax system.

In *Commission* v. *Spain – Dividends* (2010), the Court had to deal with legislation according to which the dividends distributed by a company resident in Spain to another company resident in Spain which has held, for a continuous period of at least one year, a direct or indirect shareholding of 5 percent or more in the distributing company may be deducted in full from the taxable income of the recipient company.[114] By contrast, dividends distributed to companies resident in

---

111 *Ibid.*, para. 22.   112 *Ibid.*, para. 41.   113 *Ibid.*, para. 49.
114 Case C-487/08, *Commission* v. *Spain – Dividends* [2010] ECR I-4843, para. 41.

another Member State are exempt from the income tax on nonresidents only where the recipient company had a direct shareholding in the distributing company of at least 20 percent. The Court found this differential treatment to constitute a breach of Article 63 TFEU.

In *Commission* v. *Portugal – Dividend Payments to Pension Funds* (2011), the Commission challenged the Portuguese tax system applicable to pension funds because it established a difference in treatment with regard to the place of residence of these funds. According to Portuguese tax law, pension funds established in Portugal are exempt from corporation tax. Entities that are not established in Portugal, on the other hand, are subject to corporation tax in respect of income obtained in Portuguese territory. According to the Commission, this created differential treatment: dividends paid to pension funds established in Portugal are exempt from corporation tax, whereas dividends paid to nonresident pension funds are subject to it. According to the Court, "[t]hat difference in treatment has the effect of dissuading non-resident pension funds from investing in Portuguese companies and savers resident in Portugal from investing in such pension funds."[115]

Preferential tax treatment of income from domestic sources other than dividends

The Treaty freedoms also prohibit a disadvantageous tax treatment of income from non-domestic sources other than dividends, though often these cases fall under the other Treaty freedoms, and not under Article 63 TFEU. In *Commission* v. *Belgium – Taxation of Pension Contributions* (2007),[116] the Commission challenged a Belgian measure that allows contributions and premiums due in respect of supplementary pension and life assurance to be deducted from income tax as business expenses only if it is paid to insurers established in Belgium. However, income resulting from such schemes is fully taxable in Belgium if the individual resides within that Member State, regardless of whether the insurer is established in Belgium or not. According to the Court, "the national legislation has the effect of granting a tax advantage which varies depending on the place in which those contributions and premiums are collected and is accordingly likely to dissuade employed and self-employed persons from exercising their right to move freely in another Member State."[117] The Belgian tax measure therefore restricts Articles 45 and 49 TFEU.

Taxation of income from immovable property

A number of cases concern tax benefits granted in connection with immovable property. The case of *Busley* (2009) dealt with Spanish nationals resident in Germany who owned a house in Spain, for which they received a rental income.[118] The German tax system provided disadvantageous treatment to immovable property located

---

115 Case C-493/09, *Commission* v. *Portugal – Dividends* [2011] ECR I-9247, para. 30.
116 Case C-522/04, *Commission* v. *Belgium – Taxation of Pension Contributions* [2007] ECR I-5701.
117 *Ibid.*, para. 66.   118 Case C-35/08, *Busley* [2009] ECR I-9807.

outside Germany in two ways. First, losses incurred with regard to income from the letting of immovable property situated in Germany could be taken into account in full in the year in which they arose, whereas rental losses from an immovable property situated outside Germany are deductible only from the subsequent positive income derived from letting that property.[119] And, second, for property situated in Germany, the decreasing-balance method of depreciation can be applied, which results in higher rental loss figures in the earlier years. For property located in other countries, only the straight-line method of depreciation can be employed, which results in the same losses for each year. While persons holding a property located outside Germany for a sufficient period of time will have a similar opportunity of offsetting all losses as persons holding property located inside Germany, the Court held that the former is deprived of a cash-flow advantage in the shorter term.[120] The tax position of a person owning immovable property in another Member State is less favorable than it would be if that property were situated in Germany.[121] This constitutes a restriction of Article 63 TFEU.

In *Schröder* (2011), the Court had to deal with a German measure on the deductibility of an annuity paid for immovable property from income tax.[122] Mr. Schröder had acquired immovable property situated in Germany from his parents, and paid an annuity in the form of a monthly sum of €1,000 to them in return. He received a monthly income from the letting of the property. Mr. Schröder was a German national resident in Belgium, which means that he was subject only to limited income tax liability in Germany. Accordingly, he was subject to income tax only with regard to the income made in Germany, i.e. the rental income. He was not permitted to deduct the annuity paid to his parents from the rental income, as German tax law allows this possibility only to residents. The Court acknowledged that Member States have the right to distinguish between residents and nonresidents if their situations are not objectively comparable (as also expressed in Article 65(1)(a) TFEU) or if such distinction is justified by an overriding reason in the public interest, and fulfill the proportionality requirement.[123] However, the Court held that, "in relation to expenses, such as business expenses which are directly linked to an activity which has generated taxable income in a Member State, that residents and non-residents of that State are in a comparable situation."[124] Accordingly, the German measure was found to be an unjustifiable restriction of Article 63 TFEU.

Tax breaks for inheritances and charitable donations

In recent years, individuals have increasingly challenged national tax rules that granted tax benefits solely with regard to capital located within the Member State. One of these cases is *Jäger* (2008).[125] The case dealt with the situation of Mr. Jäger,

---

119 *Ibid.*, para. 22.   120 *Ibid.*, para. 25.   121 *Ibid.*, para. 26.
122 Case C-450/09, *Schröder* [2011] ECR I-2497.   123 *Ibid.*, para. 35.   124 *Ibid.*, para. 40.
125 Case C-256/06, *Jäger* [2008] ECR I-123.

a resident of France, who was the sole heir of his mother, who was last living in Germany. He inherited land in France used for agriculture and forestry. According to the German inheritance tax law, agricultural land situated in Germany is assessed at 10 percent of its fair market value, whereas agricultural land situated in other states is assessed at its full market value. The Court found the measure to infringe Article 63 TFEU. The German government claimed that such differential treatment could be justified on the basis of Article 65(1)(a) TFEU. However, the Court rejected the assertion that the situation of assets located inside and outside Germany were not objectively comparable. The Court found it conceivable that objectives connected with the carrying on of the activities of agricultural and forestry holdings and preservation of jobs in cases of inheritance may be in the public interest and capable of justifying restrictions on the free movement of capital. However, it held that "there is no evidence in the present case to support a finding that the holdings established in other Member States are not in a comparable situation to that of holdings established in Germany."[126]

A number of cases concern tax breaks for charitable donations. An Austrian tax law granted tax deductions for gifts to research and teaching institutions exclusively where those institutions were established in Austria (*Commission* v. *Austria – Deductibility of Gifts*, 2011).[127] The Court found this measure to be in breach of Article 63 TFEU: "[W]hile a Member State can lawfully reserve the grant of tax advantages to bodies pursuing certain objectives in the public interest, it cannot, however, reserve the benefit of those advantages solely to bodies established in its territory."[128]

SECONDARY LAW

The chapter of the Treaty dealing with the free movement of capital and payments authorizes a number of secondary law measures, all of them relating to the movement of capital to and from third countries. Additionally, measures that touch on the free movement of capital may also be based on other Treaty provisions. Regulation 1889/2005, for example, which authorizes controls of cash entering or leaving the Union for the purpose of combatting money laundering, is based on Article 114 TFEU, the general harmonization provision.[129] Regulation 881/2002, which allows the freezing of the financial assets of individuals and organizations suspected of terrorism (and which was the subject of the famous *Kadi I* and *Kadi II* cases), has Article 75 TFEU as its legal basis, which

---

126 *Ibid.*, para. 52.   127 Case C-10/10, *Commission* v. *Austria – Deductibility of Gifts* [2011] ECR I-5389.
128 *Ibid.*, para. 33.
129 Regulation 1889/2005 of the European Parliament and of the Council on controls of cash entering or leaving the Community, [2005] OJ L309/9.

is part of the Treaty chapter on the Area of Freedom, Security and Justice.[130] Table 8.4 sets out an overview of the legal bases for secondary law measures concerning the free movement of capital.

Table 8.4 Overview: legal bases for secondary law measures concerning the free movement of capital	
Treaty provision	**Subject-matter**
Art. 64(2) TFEU	Measures on the movement of capital to or from third countries (ordinary legislative procedure)
Art. 64(3) TFEU	Measures which constitute a step backwards in Union law as regards the liberalization of the movement of capital to or from third countries (Council deciding unanimously)
Art. 65(4) TFEU	Commission decision stating that restrictive tax measures adopted by a Member State concerning third countries are to be considered compatible with the Treaties in so far as they are justified by one of the objectives of the Union and compatible with the proper functioning of the internal market
Art. 66 TFEU	Safeguard measures with regard to capital movements to and from third countries when they cause or threaten to cause serious difficulties for the operation of economic and monetary union

Further reading

CONNOR, TIM, "'Market Access' or Bust? Positioning the Principle Within the Jurisprudence of Goods, Persons, Services, and Capital" (2012) 13 *German Law Journal* 679

CORDEWENER, AXEL, "Free Movement of Capital Between EU Member States and Third Countries: How Far Has the Door Been Closed?" (2009) 18 *EC Tax Review* 260

CORDEWENER, AXEL, KOFLER, GEORG, and VAN THIEL, SERVAAS, "The Clash Between European Freedoms and National Direct Tax Law: Public Interest Defences Available to the Member States" (2009) 46 *Common Market Law Review* 1951

GERNER-BEUERLE, CARSTEN, "Shareholders Between the Market and the State. The VW Law and Other Interventions in the Market Economy" (2012) 49 *Common Market Law Review* 97

HINDELANG, STEFFEN, "The Free Movement of Capital and Foreign Direct Investment: The Scope of Protection in EU Law" (2010) 21 *European Journal of International Law* 496

KENEN, PETER, "Capital Controls, the EMS and the EMU" (1995) 105 *Economic Journal* 181

O'BRIEN, MARTHA, "Taxation and the Third Country Dimension of Free Movement of Capital in EU Law: The ECJ's Rulings and Unresolved Issues" (2008) 6 *British Tax Review* 628

RINGE, WOLF-GEORG, "Company Law and Free Movement of Capital" (2010) 69 *Cambridge Law Journal* 378

SCHEPEL, HARM, "Constitutionalising the Market, Marketising the Constitution, and to Tell the Difference: On the Horizontal Application of the Free Movement Provisions in EU Law" (2012) 18 *European Law Journal* 177

USHER, JOHN, "The Evolution of the Free Movement of Capital" (2007) 31 *Fordham International Law Journal* 1533

ZUMBANSEN, PEER, and SAAM, DANIEL, "The ECJ, Volkswagen and European Corporate Law: Reshaping the European Varieties of Capitalism" (2007) 8 *German Law Journal* 1027

---

130 Council Regulation 881/2002 imposing certain specific restrictive measures directed against certain persons and entities associated with Usama bin Laden, the Al-Qaida network and the Taliban, and repealing Council Regulation 467/2001 prohibiting the export of certain goods and services to Afghanistan, strengthening the flight ban and extending the freeze of funds and other financial resources in respect of the Taliban of Afghanistan, [2002] OJ L139/9.

Index

Page numbers in italics refer to tables.

317